economic development, peace, and international law

POLEMOLOGICAL STUDIES

edited by Prof. Dr. B. V. A. Röling

1 DE OORLOG IN HET LICHT DER WETENSCHAPPEN

2 APPROACHES TO THE STUDY OF INTERNATIONAL RELATIONS, 2nd edition by Dr. Ch. Boasson

3 DE OORLOG IN HET LICHT DER WETENSCHAPPEN
tweede serie

4 ASPECTEN VAN DE KOUDE OORLOG

5 OPSTAND EN REVOLUTIE
onder redactie van prof. mr. B. V. A. Röling.

6 ECONOMISCHE GEVOLGEN VAN ONTWAPENING
door dr. W. F. Duisenberg; met een woord vooraf van prof. mr. B. V. A. Röling.

7 WORLD PEACE THROUGH WORLD ECONOMY
Selected studies in the problems of creating a world economic order.
Introduced by professor Jan Tinbergen.

8 INLEIDING TOT DE WETENSCHAP VAN OORLOG EN VREDE
Teleac-cursus Polemologie door prof. mr. B. V. A. Röling.

9 NIEUW-GUINEA EN DE VOLKSKRANT
door dr. C. V. Lafeber; met een woord vooraf van prof. mr. B. V. A. Röling.

10 REVOLUTIE IN LATIJNS-AMERIKA
prof. dr. W. J. Wieringa, dr. H. Riemens, drs. R. de Jong, dr. R. A. M. van Zantwijk, dr. A. L. Constandse, drs. A. E. van Niekerk.

11 NATIONALISME IN DE 3E WERELD
OSGN-congres 1970

12 KONVERGENTIE EN EVOLUTIE
De Konvergentietheorie van Tinbergen en de evolutie van ekonomische ordes in Oost en West, door dr. J. van den Doel.

13 DE METAMORFOSE VAN DE OORLOG IN DE 18E EN 19E EEUW
Tien historische studies over oorlog, strategie en legervorming, door dr. F. C. Spits.

14 Prof. Dr. F. A. M. Alting von Geusau, DENKEN OVER WERELDVREDE

15 KRITISCHE POLEMOLOGIE, studies over politiek, vrede en geweld onder redactie van Hylke Tromp

16 Dr. Wil D. Verwey, ECONOMIC DEVELOPMENT, PEACE AND INTERNATIONAL LAW

Dr. Wil D. Verwey

ECONOMIC DEVELOPMENT
PEACE
AND INTERNATIONAL LAW

ASSEN 1972

VAN GORCUM & COMP. N.V., DR. H. J. PRAKKE & H. M. G. PRAKKE

© 1972, by Royal VanGorcum Ltd., Assen, The Netherlands

No parts of this book may be reproduced in any form by print, photoprint, microfilm or any other means without written permission from the publisher

The publication of this book was made possible through a grant from the Netherlands Organization for the Advancement of Pure Research (Z.W.O.)

ISBN   90 232 0992 3

Printed in the Netherlands by Royal VanGorcum Ltd.

Preface

There is no doubt that international law in its present form is based on the law as it evolved since the 16th century in Europe, though in many aspects the roots of international law reach much farther back, deep into antiquity. But the system of present international law is of European origin. There in Europe, as a reaction to the hierarchical structure under Pope and Emperor, developed the concept of international law as law between souvereign states.

As the starting point Francisco di Vitoria may be mentioned, who protested against Spanish aggression and cruelty in the Americas. He based his protest on international law, as a natural law of equality, applicable in the whole world, formulating rights and duties of states and peoples wherever living.

During the 17th and 18th centuries, Europe witnessed the change from natural law to positive law. One might say that the line goes from Vitoria via Grotius to Vattel. The supremacy of positive law was furthered to a great extent because this positive law expressed the power position. Natural law was pushed into the background by the attractiveness of the new positive law which, in 'unequal treaties', legalized the positions of privilege.

Emeric de Vattel witnessed in his own day positive law becoming the valid international law, formulated in treaties and custom. But this change accompanied another: what had been worldwide international law became European international law, determined by European treaties and customs. It was international law valid among the European states. Through the gradual expansion of this group of states during the last centuries did international law again become worldwide, but now as positive law.

The gradual expansion of the group of states who created international law, and among whom it was accepted as valid, can best be indicated by phases. In the beginning, European international law applied only to the Christian States. In that period, Christianity was the central official value. We may call this period the phase of the

Christian Nations. With the admission of Turkey in 1856 'to participate in the public law and concert of Europe,' this terminology could no longer be maintained. Meanwhile, another criterion had arisen: that of civilisation. In the second half of the 19th century, civilisation became the common starting-point. The states also named themselves after this criterion. The phase of the *Civilised Nations* meant an expansion of the family of nations to include several American and Asian states. The third phase commenced in the second half of the 20th century. The nations, united in the UN, no longer recognize civilisation as the common starting-point. After two world wars which severely undermined the authority of European civilisation, peace was regarded as the generally shared value. The members of the UN call themselves '*Peace-loving Nations*' (art. 4). They recognize all existing civilisations and religions as equally endowed with rights, and they accept peace as the binding common starting-point. With this, the international law community again became universal in principle, since peace generally came to be recognized as the official value.[1]

The common starting-points – Christianity, Civilisation, Peace – were not limited in their importance to only the territorial applicability of international law. As values common to the members of the respective international law communities, the aforementioned criteria of the three phases formed the source of new legal development. In the decision-making process which preceded legal formulation, these nuclei served as sources of inspiration and as reasons for consensus. Proposals toward legal development were made as 'demands of Christianity,' 'consequences of Civilisation,' or as 'conditions of Peace.' In our phase of peace-loving nations it is therefore understandable that the motivation of fundamental legal change (de-colonization, recognition of universal human rights, non-discrimination, responsibility of the collectivity for its members in the economic and social areas – and, of course, the limitation of national souvereignty with regard to arms) is to be found and to be given in the demands of Peace.

There is yet a third function of the commonly accepted central value: the legitimation of discrimination and inequality. Thus did Christianity, and later Civilisation, legitimize the colonial system.

---

[1] A more detailed description of this development in 'International Law in an Expanded World,' Amsterdam 1960, an elaboration of a paper published in Dutch under the name of 'Europees volkenrecht of wereldvolkenrecht?' (International Law: European Law or World Law?'), den Haag 1958.

Portugese and Spanish conquests were at the time officially justified by the papal trust to spread the Christian faith. At the Congo Conference of Berlin (1885) the partition of Central Africa was justified with the sacred trust 'to bring the blessings of civilisation.' Also the Covenant of the League of Nations mentioned the 'sacred trust of civilisation.' The Charter of the UN still harbors the thought of the 'sacred trust' (art. 73), among many other reminiscences of times past.

In the present time the concept of peace also fullfills a function of legitimizing structural inequality. The special position of the Permanent Members of the Security Council – in spite of the recognized principle of souvereign equality of UN members – is an example of this. Another is the Non-Proliferation Treaty, in which the nuclear have-nots are made to be nuclear have-nevers.

The point of this short history of international law, as relevant to the subject 'Economic Development, Peace, and International Law,' is that the commonly accepted value of our time is Peace, and that this criterion coincides with the quantitative expansion of the international law community to a world community.

This quantitative expansion at the same time indicated a qualitative change. Formerly, international law fullfilled its functions among the self-supporting, developed states. This function was especially to harmonize the freedom of one state with the freedom of others, while the economic life was left to the economic laws of the market (besides the measures of national protection against external influences). In our time, the majority of the family of nations consists of poor, vulnerable states, late-comers in an industrialized world. They have different needs, and impose different demands on international law. They want to see the legal principle of freedom filled in with the legal principle of protection of the economically weak against the economically strong, and with the legal principle of assistance which must be made available and promoted by the rich countries.

This endeavour of the young, poor countries coincides and is related with the internal development in the old, rich countries, who evolved from the liberal 'Rechtsstaat' to the social welfare state: the state which concerns itself with the fate of all its members as expressed in its attempt to reach full employment and to attain a decent standard of living for all members of its community. This promoted the idea that also the international community ought to be developed into a welfare community. The UN is, according to its Charter, primarily a peace preserving organization. In practice, the UN already moves in the direction of an organization whose purpose is to promote the well-being of her members – see the resolutions of the General

Assembly, and especially the functions of specialized and special agencies, such as UNESCO, FAO, WHO, UNCTAD, and UNOID.

In connection with their particular situation, the developing countries demand a particular place in such a welfare community. They ask for a new inequality – now an inequality in their own favor. Here and there such a special position is already recognized in law, such as in part IV of GATT, but generally things are kept to a formulation of rules which should be accepted as legal rules, such as the principles of UNCTAD: lex ferenda.

But the claim is strong. As ever, the weak and destitute appeal to natural law in order to breach the authority of the recognized positive law. This natural law is vaguely and insufficiently formulated in the principles of the UN Charter (about souvereign equality, self-determination, and collective responsibility). Just as in the Covenant of the League of Nations war was 'a matter of concern ... to the whole League' (art. 11), so has world-poverty become 'a matter of concern' to the UN community. But the consequences have not yet been drawn, neither in the UN Charter, nor in the UN practice. The world community has not yet recognized nor realized an international law that is attuned to this new task, and which would lead to a legal arrangement in the economic field contributing to the abolishment of world poverty.

This new law also might find expression via the recognized source of the 'general principles of law' (art. 38, Statute of the Court). Practically all states now officially accept the promotion of the welfare of their citizens as one of the legal duties of the state. Thus the legal concept of collective responsibility of the community for the social and economic well-being of its parts has become a general principle of law recognized by the nations. Hence the properly founded demand to recognize this principle also in international law.

It is occasionally asked, whether present international law still rests on universally recognized, general foundations. Thoughts go out especially to the ideological cleavage between West and East, and to the deep-seated factual differences (and the concomitant differences in needs and conceptions) between North and South. This question can be answered in the affirmative. The point is whether the North is prepared to assign world-wide applicability to the nationally accepted principles of the welfare state. Compared with the socialist countries, the Western countries have the advantage in this. They are able to satisfy the demands of a universal international law by giving world-wide application to their nationally recognized law principles. The principles concern community action for the benefit of those members who require protection and assistance. This aims at correcting, by legal measures, the effects of economic laws in the open market. It means that the market mechanism remains recognized, but that it becomes regulated in those instances where this is necessary for the interests of the community. On the other hand, *national* economic planning in the socialist countries is, as dogma, so highly elevated (it appears to me, that this has less to do with Communist doctrine than with their minority position in the world), that they have more difficulty with the acceptance of economic world planning by a world organ, when such an arrangement turns out to be necessary for the common good.

The basic principles of social-economic world-justice are proposed and defended by statesmen and international civil servants with the thesis that the realisation of these principles is a prerequisite for peace – understandably so in the era of 'Peace-loving Nations.' Wil Verwey gives numerous examples of this in his book. Also in the world of aid-practitioners we hear from most highly placed persons, such as presidents of the World Bank, the repeated warnings that it will not be possible to maintain peace without development of the poor countries.

This is a problem which falls outside the competence of the jurist, but lies rather in the field of the polemologist, the student of the science of war and peace. Peace science has concerned itself with this problem. It has led to a differentiation between the concept 'peace' in a negative sense (marked by the absence of war), 'negative peace,' and the concept of 'positive peace,' which refers to a commonly accepted order of justice. Jurists have had the tendency to concern themselves especially with negative peace, hence their interest in the prohibition of war, and the maintenance of this prohibition. One may wonder, however, whether peace can be guaranteed in this way. There is also the question whether this is not paying too much attention to one type of war – war as an instrument of national policy – while ignoring the concept of unintentional, accidental war. Finally, it is still a matter of conjecture whether the prohibition of war can be effected as long as the reasons for violent conflict are not eliminated.[2]

The UN Charter assumes the peace concept in its negative sense. The organisation was set up to save succeeding generations from the scourge of war, according to the Preamble.

---

[2] More about this in my: Hat das Kriegsverbot noch einen Sinn? in Jahrbuch für Internationales Recht, 1969, p. 174-187.

But the Charter mentions as its first purpose 'to maintain international peace and security.' Next to peace – the absence of war – security is mentioned, that is, the absence of the danger of war. Security is related with the future. Some people connect the concept of security before everything else with 'deterrence' through weapons; that is the reason why this concept of security in the theory of international relations is connected with the constant urge for more military power.

But a more important aspect of security is stressed in the argument that unbearable injustice is incompatible with security. If structural violence has reached a certain intensity, and is felt by the under-dog as intolerable injustice, it will lead to violent action. Such violent action, to change the conflict situation by internal or external war, cannot be prevented by whatever forms of deterrence.

In view of this the practice of the UN – on the basis of a rather extensive interpretation of the Charter provisions – has been based on the conviction that negative peace cannot be maintained in the long run, if vital needs of peoples or of states remain unfullfilled – hence the UN activity in the fields of human rights, social-economic relations, and development of poor countries.

Understandably, peace research arrived at similar conclusions. Negative peace can be maintained in the long run only if a certain minimum level of justice is satisfied. There are needs and values for which a people or a state will fight, regardless of legal prohibitions or however strong the forces of 'law and order' may be. Vietnam is a clear example of this. This is the primary reason why the science of war and peace concerns itself with the concept of positive peace. There is yet another: if peace science were to concern itself with studying the means of keeping the negative peace 'at any price,' it would become an instrument of despotism and exploitation; it might give reprehensible powers in the world the necessary means to maintain an intolerable status quo. Here is again the train of thought which found expression in the words of the Mexican delegate at the inception of the UN, when he demanded that the Charter be 'an instrument of well-being and happiness against the horrors of a peace without hope, in which men would be subjected to humiliating privations and injustices.'

To us the first viewpoint is especially important, namely whether it is true or not that the abolishment of poverty is, in fact, a 'condition of peace.' Where abolishment of poverty is possible only through development, the corollary of development as a factor of peace becomes part of the question.

Wil Verwey, jurist and staff member of the Polemological

Institute at the University of Groningen, has attempted to answer this question. Part of his studies on the relation of 'Economic Development, Peace, and International Law' is devoted to investigation of the thesis that the poverty problem requires a solution for the sake of the prevention of war (while humanitarian aspects play herein a role, namely insofar as they are of polemological relevance).

The investigation presents some great difficulties to the polemologist. It is easy to echo Mr. McNamara's proposition that the turbulence in the young countries can be attributed to desperation, and that to give hope by making development possible would remove the cause for turbulence, and thus also remove the turbulence. The relations are more complex, and one can only arrive at the conclusion that – once the expectations of the better life have been aroused – poverty as well as development will be accompanied by violent processes. Violent social turbulence can be the result of too little development as well as of too fast development. There are coups and revolutions from the left and from the right in the Third World. That development offers the guarantee for an evolutionary and non-violent change, appears simply to be not true. Also, internal turbulence and violence leads easily to intervention by the Super Powers, who are out to keep friendly regimes in the saddle, or to give them the needed boost.

Must the polemologist than conclude that the relations between poverty and war, development and peace, do not exist, and that from a polemological viewpoint there just are no arguments in favor of world development? Dr. Verwey, rightly, does not conclude this. The world may not – and that is one of his conclusions – permit 'the widening of the gap' between rich and poor countries to go unchecked. On the contrary – the poverty problem must be solved. Development must be brought about, even if this process will occasionally be accompanied by internal unrest and violence.

The polemological reasons are clear. Neglect of the poverty problem by the rich world, if it continues on the road now being followed – a road that shares with the 19th century domestic 'care of the poor and charity' a lack of results – shall lead to a Cold War between North and South. Because poverty – through the expectation of 'the better life' – turned from static, apathetic poverty into dynamic, insurgent poverty, unending poverty will foster enmity towards the rich world. Because of the part it played in colonialism and neo-colonial economic exploitation, the rich world is easily perceived as the cause of all misery.

Tremendous tensions will emanate from this, the more so since the increasing desperation will lead, in some countries, to 'extreme solutions' from left and from right, from communism to fascism, with all the consequences of possible intervention by the Cold War Powers.³

Conceivable is the gathering around China by poor states at the point of despair. Such a development can be expected if it turns out that China's way – i.e. without outside help, working under iron discipline on a centrally led economy – leads to better results than the course followed by India and Pakistan.

For this development China has ready the doctrine of Lin Piao: just as the Chinese countryside gained control over its cities, so will the world countryside (the developing countries) gain control over the world cities (the rich countries).

At times the prospect of war between North and South is even mentioned. Generally this is thought to be unrealistic, since the poor world is simply too poor to do battle with the rich world. But if the poor world were to be gathered under the leadership of China, a nuclear Power soon to be reckoned with, this prospect of war is not so inconceivable.

Meanwhile, a different development is more likely. Rather than wars between states in the traditional sense, in the future one will have to think of irregular violence by extremist groups. When desperation has risen to the level as is the case, for other reasons, with the Palestinians, it is likely that extremist groups will employ violent activity in order to demand attention for their position. They create dismay in the rich world through deeds of terror against it such as destruction of factories, of mines, pipe-lines or banks, or the taking as hostage or killing important people. They hope, by these deeds, to move the rich world finally into taking those measures which she – from clear self-interest – should have taken long ago. Irregular warfare – in Latin America, in Asia, in Africa – is the picture for the future, if the rich world shortsightedly were to continue to withhold its share in the solution of the poverty problem.

There exists still another compelling reason for the solution of the poverty problem through concerted development measures. That reason is the growing need of a functional world unity, one world. In many regards the problems of our time – the atomic age, which at present can also be called the ecological era – cannot be solved any longer on the basis of the existing international state anarchy – that is the world system of national sovereign states. The decisions necessary in our time to prevent effectively nuclear holocaust – at present the sovereign political units try to prevent nuclear war by the

---

³ Appropriate here is Gunnar Myrdal's allusion to 'the Latin American Powder Keg' (The Challenge of World Poverty, New York, 1970, p. 452).

insufficient and inadequate means of nuclear deterrence – demand some form of world unity.

The ecological problems too compel to adopt another system of decision-making than the now prevailing system on the basis of national sovereignty. The problems of pollution and of depletion confronting our world today cannot be solved adequately by international decision-making. A regime for the river Rhine demands a regional solution, a High Authority for the Rhine. Effective regulation for the purpose to prevent that our oceans become dead water demands a High Authority for the Seas. Ecological problems force upon mankind a system of trans-national decision-making.

The same applies to the depletion problems. One can easily imagine that the national states will try to safeguard their vital interests in scarce materials by political and military power. To such a disquieting development points the publication by the American Secretary of the Interior, Walter J. Hickel:

'Indeed, the extent to which a nation possesses or controls natural resources is probably the most important determinant of its world position. We will disregard this principle at our peril.' 'At stake is not simply our ability to feed our own people. Of this I have little doubt. The real stake is leadership in a protein-hungry world'.[4]

If ecological problems, in this case the depletion problems are to be solved on the basis of the competition between heavily armed sovereign states, then it will lead to tensions which can only end in war. These problems cannot be solved on the basis of a decision-making process stemming from the past, and which is no longer adequate to the present challenges. The kind of decision-making was already insufficient with the coming of the atomic age. Now it is confronted, too, with the challenges of the ecological age. Changes of this magnitude have never presented themselves before in such a short period of time. As such it is 'unprecedented that the transition from the nuclear age to the ecological age has come about in a matter of decades, in such a short interval of time; the political leadership of the world acts largely in accordance with precepts, values, and institutions that are two major historical transformations behind the actualities of the present situation.'[5]

To solve these problems, to find the answers to these challenges – and this is a condition of peace – some form of federal world unity is necessary. This seems to me one fundamental finding of peace research. The other fundamental finding is that in our present world

---

[4] Introduction to 'Marine Resources Development. A National Opportunity,' quoted in Richard A. Falk: This Endangered Planet, Prospects and Proposals for Human Survival. New York 1971, p. 167.
[5] R. A. Falk, op. cit. p. 260.

such a world unity is impossible. A political world unity formed on the basis of free decisions – and that is what we discuss here, because the possibility of world domination by one Super Power is impossible without nuclear war – is only feasible in case of a rather deep going consensus as to values and interests, and of a universal feeling of solidarity. As long as the world is divided in ideological blocs (East-West), such a unity is not feasible. In the same way such a unity is not possible as long as the clash of interests exists as nowadays between the rich and the poor countries (North-South). The gap between the rich and the poor world – and this gap is widening – prevents the world unity necessary for survival in the atomic and ecological era.

Hence the necessity that from our side everything is done necessary to further the development of the poor parts of the world. And this, notwithstanding the fact that development will be accompanied by occasional violence, and notwithstanding the insight that development there, inevitably, will have bearing upon the possible level of our material well-being here.

Doing from our part everything to further the solution of the poverty problem does not mean only a more adequate transfer of capital and know-how. It means also for the rich countries a fundamental revision of the national protection of their agriculture and industry, in favour of the developing countries. It means also a fundamental interference in the free-market mechanism and the present international trade system. Inevitable for survival is world economic planning. The organisation of the world must become a world welfare organisation, will it ever be an effective peace organisation.

In the book of Dr. Verwey the problems of poverty and development are dealt with from a specific angle: The furtherance of world peace. This polemological viewpoint concerns the removal of the causes of war and the realisation of the conditions for peace.

The plea for the envisaged changes in the international economic policy towards developing countries can also be given from another viewpoint. The arguments then are humanitarian, legal, and even economic. The polemologist as such is concerned only with the question of peace maintenance. Reasonable insight into the problems of war and peace leads to that which Inis Claude (in the field of arms policy) calls 'prudential pacifism'[6] and Gunnar Myrdal, in the economic field, refers to as 'rational generosity.'[7]

Prof. Dr. B. V. A. Röling

[6] Inis Claude: The Changing United Nations, New York, 1967, p. 9.
[7] Gunnar Myrdal: The Challenge of World Poverty, New York, 1970, p. 298.

Acknowledgements

I would like to express my gratitude to Professor Bert Röling, director of the Polemological Institute at the State-University of Groningen. During the six years that I have spent as his assistant in International Law, and as a research fellow at the Institute, I have had the privilege of learning a great deal from this eminent scholar. His personality and his devotion to the cause of justice have inspired me to choose the topic of this book. Röling belongs to the select group of international lawyers whose writings have strongly contributed to a new approach, in the sense of what Jenks has called 'the international law of mankind.' In addition to demonstrating the shortcomings of traditional – Europe centred – international law, Röling has contributed to the plea for a universal law of co-operation which would serve all members of the human family equally. His book 'International Law in an Expanded World,' published in 1960, has for years been withheld the recognition it deserves. I can only hope that my book may help to promote the ideas he introduced.

I would also like to thank Professor Laurens Jan Brinkhorst for his valuable advice and comments on the manuscript.

Furthermore, I would like to thank Mr. Willem and Mrs. Gwen Bergman for the linguistic assistance they gave, and Miss Hannie Jippes and Mrs. Jelly Waskowsky for their typing assistance.

Finally, I am much obliged to the Netherlands Organization for the Advancement of Pure Science (ZWO) for its generous grant which made the publication of this book possible.

Groningen, February 22, 1972

CORRIGENDA

W. D. Verwey: Economic Development, Peace and International Law

Page 34, replace the fourteenth line from top by:
This phrase may be understood to incorporate etc.

page 265, second line from top, read:
ments. On the other hand some authors attribute great significance to these developments. Lauterpacht etc.

Contents

Introduction 1

CHAPTER I:
POLEMOLOGICAL ASPECTS OF POVERTY AND DEVELOPMENT:
THE INTERNAL CONTEXT 7

A. *Poverty* 7
  1. Perception of injury, hope, and frustration 7
    1.1. Perception of injury 7
    1.2. Hope 10
      1.2.1. Apathy 11
    1.3. Frustration 18
      1.3.1. Level of prosperity 22
      1.3.2. Some examples 25
    1.4. Some prospects 29
  2. Population increase, and surplus-population 37

B. *Economic Development.* 39
  3. Literacy, education, and communication 41
  4. Improvement of diet 47
    5.1. Positive material experience 47
    5.2. Rate of growth: too slow 51
    5.3. Rate of growth: too rapid and uneven 54
  6. Modernization: social disruption, alienation, and urbanization 57
  7. Modernization: industrialization, social mobilization, and political participation 62
  8. Group-centrism 74
  9. Deterioration during initial period 86
  10. Sudden deterioration after a period of progress 89
  11. Opposition: against certain aspects of development 92
  12. Opposition: by status quo groups, and the consequences of negative experience 94
  13. Military government 97
  14. Internal prospects 101

CHAPTER II:
POLEMOLOGICAL ASPECTS OF POVERTY AND DEVELOPMENT:
THE INTERNATIONAL CONTEXT 104

A. *Relations Among the Super Powers:*
   Intervention and the Welfare Gap 104
1. Intervention and civil strife 105
   1.1. The United States 106
   1.2. The Soviet Union 109
   1.3. China. 112
   1.4. The new arena of the Cold War struggle 115
2. Intervention by aid 118
   2.1. Economic relations with the Third World 119
       2.1.1. The United States 119
       2.1.2. The Soviet Union 130
       2.1.3. China 145
       2.1.4. Other donors 157
       2.1.5. Cold War confrontation 158
   2.2. Consequences for the internal stability in recipient countries 166
       2.2.1. Discontinuity 166
       2.2.2. Waste 173
   2.3. Military aid and the Cold War 181
       2.3.1. The United States 183
       2.3.2. The Soviet Union 187
       2.3.3. China 192
       2.3.4. Consequences for the developing countries. 193
       2.3.5. Consequences for international peace in the Third World 195
       2.3.6. Consequences for world peace 196
   2.4. Bilateral aid: does it pay? 200

B. *Relations Among the Developing Countries Inter Se* 216

C. *Relations Between Poor and Rich Countries.* 224

CHAPTER III:
THE ROLE OF INTERNATIONAL LAW: AN OUTLINE 230

Peace Through Welfare: Towards a Development Strategy on the Basis of Law 230
1. International law as a peace-promoting factor: from negative peace to positive peace 230
2. Present rules and principles: effects and challenge 236
3. Towards a strategy of peace through an international law of global welfare 249
   3.1. Historical preamble: developments on the national scene 249
   3.2. The legal roots of the strategy 255
       3.2.1. The emergence of transnational social and economic human rights . 255
       3.2.2. The recognition of 'the developing countries' as special subjects of international law 265
       3.2.3. The recognition of 'mankind' as a supreme legal value, and the duty to co-operate for global welfare. 273
       3.2.4. The relevance of these legal roots in their polemological context. . . 281
   3.3. A strategy for global welfare 283
       3.3.1. Measures to be taken by developing countries 287
       3.3.2. Employment, agricultural rationalization, and industrial development . 293
       3.3.3. International division of labour, endorsed by new patterns of international trade 296

3.3.4. The acquirement by the developing countries of specific natural resources	315
3.3.5. Trade in and prices of primary commodities	318
3.3.6. Nutrition	320
3.3.7. Economic growth	326
3.3.8. Financial assistance	329
3.3.9. The necessity of a global center of co-operation	334
3.3.10. The emerging law of the world community	339
Appendix : *Non-Intervention*	343
Selected Bibliography	350

List of abbreviations of periodicals

A.J.I.L.	—	American Journal of International Law
A. P. Sc. Rev.	—	American Political Science Review
A. Soc. Rev.	—	American Sociological Review
Ann. Fr. D.I.	—	Annuaire Français de Droit International
B.Y.I.L.	—	British Yearbook of International Law
Bull. At. Sc.	—	Bulletin of the Atomic Scientists
Can. Y.I.L.	—	Canadian Yearbook of International Law
Chin. Q.	—	China Quarterly
Conf. St.	—	Conflict Studies
Dept. State Bull.	—	Department of State Bulletin
Eur. Arch.	—	Europa Archiv
For. Aff.	—	Foreign Affairs
Ind. J.I.L.	—	Indian Journal of International Law
Int. Aff.	—	International Affairs (London and Moscow)
Int. Comp. L. Q.	—	International and Comparative Law Quarterly
Int. Conc.	—	International Conciliation
Int. Enc. Soc. Sc.	—	International Encyclopedia of the Social Sciences
Int. Her. Trib.	—	International Herald Tribune
Int. J.	—	International Journal
Int. Org.	—	International Organization
J. Confl. Res.	—	Journal of Conflict Resolution
J. Econ. Hist.	—	Journal of Economic History
J. Int. Comm. Jur.	—	Journal of the International Commission of Jurists
J. Mod. Afr. St.	—	Journal of Modern African Studies
J. Peace Res.	—	Journal of Peace Research
Kees. Hist. Arch.	—	Keesing's Historisch Archief (in Dutch)
Kron. Afr.	—	Kroniek van Afrika (in Dutch)
Ned. T.I.T.	—	Nederlands Tijdschrift voor Internationaal Recht
N.Y.R. Books	—	New York Review of Books
N.Y.T.	—	New York Times
Pac. Aff.	—	Pacific Affairs
Peace Res. Rev.	—	Peace Research Review
Proc. Ac. Pol. Sc.	—	Proceedings of the Academy of Political Science
Proc. A. Soc. I.L.	—	Proceedings of the American Society of International Law
Proc. IPRA	—	Proceedings of the 2nd Conference of the International Peace Research Association
Rec. Cours	—	Recueil des Cours (Hague Academy of Int. Law)
Rev. B.D.I.	—	Revue Belge de Droit International
Rev. D.I. Lég. Comp.	—	Revue de Droit International et de Législation Comparé
Rev. F. Sc. P.	—	Revue Française de Science Politique

Rev. Gen. D.I.P.	—	Revue Générale de Droit International Publique
Rev. Int. Aff.	—	Review of International Affairs
USNWR	—	US News & World Report
W.P. Rep.	—	War/Peace Report
W. Pol. Q.	—	Western Political Quarterly

Introduction

Much has been said but less analytical investigation has been made concerning the alleged relation between poverty and peace. Discussion on this topic has been filled with phrases and unchecked assumptions, often lacking valuable information and verified data; to such extent that it may not even be superfluous to start this study anno 1972 with the (often evaded) question:
does a relation between poverty and peace exist?

It might seem rather disrespectful for a lawyer to put the question as boldly as this in view of the fact that organizational instruments like the UN Charter, solemn declarations like the Universal Declaration of Human Rights, important treaties like the Covenant on Economic, Social and Cultural Rights, and influential resolutions like those of the Final Act of the Teheran Conference on Human Rights, all take the existence of such a relation explicitly or implicitly for granted.
Thus we read in article 55 of the UN-Charter:

'With a view to the creation of conditions of stability and well-being which are necessary for peaceful and friendly relations among nations ..... the UN shall promote:
a. higher standards of living, full employment, and conditions of economic and social progress and development;
b. solutions of international economic, social, health and related problems; and international cultural and educational cooperation; and
c. universal respect for, and observance of, human rights and fundamental freedoms for all without distinction as to race, sex, language, or religion'.

The Preamble of the Universal Declaration of Human Rights says:[1]

'Whereas the recognition of the inherent dignity and of the equal and inalienable rights of all members of the human family is the foundation of freedom, justice and peace in the world ...'; and
'Whereas it is essential, if man is not to be compelled to have recourse, as a last resort,

---

[1] G.A. Res. 217 (III), 10 Dec. 1948.

to rebellion against tyranny and oppression, that human rights should be protected by the rule of law ...'.

Equally the Preamble of the International Covenant on Economic, Social and Cultural Rights states:[2]

'Considering that .... recognition of the inherent dignity and of the equal and inalienable rights of all members of the human family is the foundation of freedom, justice and peace in the world, ...'.

Resolution XVII of the Final Act of the Teheran-Conference on Human Rights[3]

'calls urgently for the preparation of a global strategy of development by the UN', after it has been ascertained that the ongoing widening of the gap between rich and poor 'is not conducive to international peace and understanding'.

Notwithstanding these important statements, lawyers should still go into that fundamental question, if only to find out how and where exactly the relationship between poverty and peace is critical, after its existence has been determined.

As a starting point for this complex problem, it may be appropriate to recall the speech made by Robert MacNamara, in Montreal on May 18, 1966.[4] In that important speech the then U.S. Secretary of Defence reached the conclusion that the great amount of violence in the Third World today is a direct consequence of bad economic conditions. He stated that 'without internal development of at least a minimum degree, order and stability are simply not possible.' To bear out his statement, the Defence Secretary brought to light some illuminating data. According to the data, during the period 1958-1966 there have been '164 internationally significant outbreaks of violence – each of them specifically designed as a serious challenge to the authority, or the very existence, of the government in question,' whereas 'only 15 of these 164 significant resorts to violence have been conflicts between two states' (which means that almost all conflicts of international significance were originally internal conflicts, a conclusion of outstanding importance for the present discussion).

---

[2] Annex to G.A. Res. 2200 (XXI), 16 Dec. 1966.
[3] UN Publ. A. Conf. 32/41 (1968) p. 14.
[4] For the text see Survival (July 1966) pp. 210-216. See also B. M. Russett, et al. – 'World Handbook of political and social indicators' ('64), pp. 99-100, in which he gives figures on the number of deaths per million of inhabitants caused by internal violence, and concludes that from the industrialized countries only Hungary, Poland and Bulgaria belonged to the 50% most violent countries in the world during the period 1950-1964.

During this period there had been only 1 major upheaval in the 27 rich countries of the world (rich according to the criteria of the World Bank), but at the same time of the 38 very poor nations no less than 32 suffered from significant conflict, in most cases of a prolonged nature. Because the speech is well-known, it is not necessary to quote further statistics from it.

Even though MacNamara expressed some very important points, his address left the basic questions unanswered. It is one of the purposes of this study to go deeper into these questions.

For instance, he did not answer the question why precisely *in our days* poor people plunge into acts of violence, although gaps between the rich and poor sections of societies have existed unchallenged for long periods, and although the present division between the rich North and the poor South has existed for generations. History has proven that the Marxist hypothesis, which states that revolutions occur when people are economically depressed, to be much too general and in itself even incorrect. The question remains, what processes and mechanisms lead poor people to aggressive behaviour, and under what circumstances?

Furthermore, MacNamara left us with the question whether the violence noticed was a consequence of the *state of poverty as such* or of *the process of economic development*, i.e. the fact that people in the Third World have begun to walk the road leading to a higher level of welfare.

Finally, one could even say that his statistics in themselves do not provide conclusive evidence, that indeed economic factors should be considered causative to those riots and wars: most of the poor countries are also young countries, in which many political, ethnic, racial, religious and other social problems act in themselves as disturbing factors, undermining national and international understanding. Yet, it must be said that here are obvious reasons to suppose that poverty and development are indeed factors to be taken into account while searching for an explanation to the almost endemic violence in the Third World. Latin America is a clear case in point. The Latino countries can not be numbered among the group of 'young countries' struggling for their identity, but as part of the Third World they rank high among the group of countries with a large measure of instability; instability which is ever increasing. Furthermore, it seems difficult to deny any relationship between the relatively high level of welfare and the remarkably low degree of social violence in the rich countries as a whole, since 'a developed economic system manages to satisfy the material demands of the population, thereby lessening the number and intensity of demands directed against the political system,' as Duff and McCamant have concluded.[5] If social disturbances occur in the rich countries, moreover, close analysis nearly always reveals that more or less important economic contradictions are also part of the conflict.

The first part of this book tries to analyze the polemological aspects of economic inequality in the present world. It was considered appropriate for analytical reasons to distinguish between intra-national (or internal) and inter-national (or external) aspects of the problem, although in many points there is a connection between the two, as will be seen.

Chapter I deals with factors relevant to the internal scene of Third World countries; first, those relating to poverty (A), second, those connected with economic development (B).

An endeavour has been made to collect both relevant theoretical material and analytical field studies, and to check these, if possible, against the background of actual situations and conflicts. The reader will find 14 sets of factors which played or may play a role in socio-economic conflict in the Third World. Such a list is certainly not exhaustive, it might even be infinite. It seemed useful nevertheless to investigate whatever relevant factors and processes we could find, in order to determine whether the relation between poverty and peace exists. It should be remembered in this connection that we have (as yet) no typology relating types of violence to stages or patterns of economic or social development. We know in fact too little of the conditions, incidence, or functions of different forms of violence. Moreover, the worth of theoretical studies which give us information on, for instance, revolutions of the past may be questionable in view of present-day situations.

As for the examples and case-studies, which have been chosen to illustrate the relevance of the theoretical concepts described here, it should be added that these are not to be considered on their own but only in connection with the theories presented; such examples certainly do not pretend to constitute exhaustive analyses of the situations they describe, since they have only been used and analysed as far as they were supposed to function within the context of the topic of this book.

The distinctions made between the several categories of factors is a rather arbitrary one. In many cases, factors mentioned in different sections are closely related. Yet, for the sake of analytical clearness, it

---

[5] E. A. Duff & J. F. McCamant – 'Measuring Social and Political Requirements for System Stability in Latin America', LXII Am. Pol. Sc. Rev. ('68) p. 1127.

proved sometimes inevitable to put closely interwoven variables in different sections.

Chapter II deals with factors relating to the international scene, on three different levels. The relations among the Super Powers within the context of the present topic and within the framework of the Cold War are first examined (A). Thereafter the relations among the poor countries *inter se* (B), and the relations between the rich countries and the poor countries as opposing groups (C) are discussed.

Chapter III proceeds on the basis of the conclusions reached in the previous Chapters, in order to outline a polemologically justified development strategy. Questions of economic capacities, in particular in connection with the world's growth capacity in view of recent data concerning scarcity of resources and environmental pollution, are taken into account. Furthermore, present international law on all these questions is analyzed and criticized. An effort is also made to outline the ways along which international law could be developed in order to support the realization of such a peace-promoting economic strategy.

The meaning of a few terms and expressions often used in this book should be explained beforehand.

The term 'Third World' refers to all the Asian, African, and Latin American countries, with the exception of Japan, China, and the Union of South Africa.

'Foreign aid' refers exclusively to official governmental assistance, unless indicated otherwise.

The term 'violence' refers to 'personal' or 'direct' violence, and does not include 'structural' violence, by which one means a specific social system as being oppressive.[6] As far as 'structural' violence is concerned, one can distinguish between 'conscious structural violence' (of which people are aware) and 'unconscious structural violence' (of which people are not aware); a situation of conscious structural violence will be indicated here by a combination of the terms 'systemic (or structural) deprivation' and 'systemic (or structural) frustration.' 'Social violence' refers to those violent expressions of a conflict situation which are goal-directed, in the sense that the status quo is at stake; in contrast to aggressive social behaviour resulting from other motives.

The expression 'polemological aspects' indicates those aspects of a situation which tend to increase or to decrease the risk of conflict or

---

[6] See the excellent article by Johan Galtung – 'Violence, Peace, and Peace Research', 6 J. Peace Res. ('69).

violence, or tend to create or to remove obstacles in the achievement of peace once violence has broken out.

It can be said that this study has a twofold purpose, a theoretical and a practical one.
The theoretical purpose is to link polemological and legal thinking, enabling lawyers to search for a more realistic and more policy-oriented basis underlying legal constructions, which is often neglected by members of the legal profession when dealing with the problems of war and peace.
The practical purpose is again twofold. On the one hand, it is to analyze the polemological aspects of the phenomena of poverty and economic development. On the basis of what was reached, a peace-promoting welfare strategy was outlined. On the other hand, the practical purpose is to conclude from this analysis, what contributions international law has made in the past and what contributions it could make in the future.
In both connections this book should be considered – and it is hoped it will serve – as a general framework for further detailed studies. The comprehensive and multi-disciplinary approach of this study and the large number of topics which had to be dealt with, prevented analysis of all its segments in depth, and several detailed problems could only be touched upon.

Chapter I

Polemological Aspects of Poverty and Development: The Internal Context

Chapter I has been divided into two parts (A and B). As the reader may have noticed from the introductory remarks, it was considered of great importance to distinguish between the polemological consequences of poverty and those of the process of economic development. It is one thing to investigate if and why poverty might constitute a source of conflict in the present era; it is no less important, however, to know if and how a development process may create instability. Only on the basis of such knowledge it becomes possible, from the polemological point of view, to determine not only *whether*, but also *how* development is to take place.

A. POVERTY

1. *Perception of injury, hope, and frustration*

1.1. *Perception of injury*

Throughout human history there have been haves and have-nots. Many periods are known during which the last mentioned revolted as anti-status quo forces; there were also many periods, however, when they did not. This observation implies that a very unequal society can be a very stable one. A major characteristic of a stable unequal society is the passive acceptance by the underdog of his low position. In many cases this kind of acceptance has been based upon religious conviction, in the sense that the actual position is perceived as natural, God-given, perhaps even as a punishment for former sins. Many experts today think that this religious subjugation which often results from the need to make actual life bearable, is the outcome of psychological defense mechanisms rather than absolute religious axioms. This opinion is supported by the observation that many

periods and cultures have been characterized by stable rigid hierarchic structures which were not acceptable to religious principles, and yet remained unchallenged for a long time (see below, section 1.2.1.).
Before an underdog-section of a given society can think of challenging the prevailing system, a basic condition must be fulfilled: one must *perceive the situation as unequal and injurious*, and *not* – by religion or other cultural value – *necessary and unchangeable*.

Recent history has witnessed two processes of high importance to the present context.
In the first place, technical developments in the field of mass communication and increased levels of education throughout the world have made it commonplace to say that our globe becomes ever smaller. People in the rich part of the world know of the living conditions of their fellows in the poor countries, and, the poor become increasingly conscious of the rich, their living conditions, and their society. Their frames of reference have been enlarged.
In the second place, the unprecedented process of de-colonization paved the way for entirely new human relations both on the international and on the national level. Within their own communities most people in the Third World had been accustomed to rigid hierarchic social patterns and large inequalities, these often being accepted in former times as God-given and unchangeable. The subjugation resulting from their colonization was for a long time considered unchangeable not in principle, but in practice.
Having reached political independence, however, these people were confronted with a new kind of inequality on the international level, which they would not tolerate as they did those inequalities resulting from the power politics during the colonial period. The achievement of legal equality where national entity was concerned, combined with important developments such as the recognition of universal Human Rights, stimulated the demand for equality in other dimensions as well.
The entire process, i.e. of understanding that a better life does exist, had it's roots in the colonial era. The people of the South gathered their first experience of this process when they became part of the Western imperial pattern. At that time Western merchants, educators, administrators and others brought the ferment of new ideas and a new sense of the need for, and the right to, a better life, an equal life. In the beginning this was a slow process, since most people in the colonial world did not even think of the right to or the possibility of equality. It was after the Napoleonic wars that the idea of national liberation became important to the Third World. It is

said that the Japanese victory over Russia in 1905 was celebrated even in Africa, the reason being that a European Power had been defeated by a non-European one. Yet is was probably after the Second World War that for the first time the majority of these peoples became really concerned with their relative deprivation and began to listen to those leaders who asked them: 'why do you accept this?.' The second World War brought about resistance-movements and political consciousness in the colonial world, and the resulting anti-colonial struggles brought national independence and self-determination. This process in turn brought about with it the *demand for equality* – equality on the human, the political and the economic level.

This demand was intensified by several other developments. In the first place, new national leaders stimulated their peoples into believing in the fight for a better life, equal to that of the peoples in the rich part of the world, the meaning of which was shown to them through the increasing stream of information and communication. In the second place, they were told and convinced that their bad conditions were the result of the policies of the former colonial Powers, who had exploited them, stolen their natural resources and oppressed their just wishes. In the third place, they were convinced of their equal rights as human beings, this conviction being strengthened by the presence and work of the United Nations. The principles embodied in the UN-Charter implied a dramatic change of thinking. Formerly, the Members of the League of Nations had refused to accept the principle of racial equality (notwithstanding Japan's urgent plea), but racial equality together with other equalities were finally accepted and put into the Charter with capital letters. Moreover, when plans were proposed for bringing economic welfare to the deprived parts of the world and when the magic phrase of 'economic aid to developing countries' was conquering the minds of poor peoples, silence and apathy, as characteristic features of the 'culture of the poor' were challenged.

At the same time, the new kinds of human relationships and the new demands on the international level, and the modernizing processes pursued at home by the effort to build up the newly independent states, stimulated the demand for change on the *intra-national* social scene as well. Once formerly rigid patterns on a global scale were successfully challenged, the inevitability of such patterns at home was called in question: the demand for change on the international level was transplanted to the national scene. Even centuries old, deep rooted, religiously-based social structures were questioned. In the era when the demand for economic development and welfare for all without distinction is prevalent it seems merely logical that the large gaps in prosperity existing between the privileged few and the poor masses, which characterize social relations in many developing countries, will become a major object of attack.

Objective (or absolute) poverty became subjective (or relative) poverty by the process of comparing. People began to reject, as Behrendt put it,

> 'nicht sosehr das Elend als solches als vielmehr die nunmehr erlebte Ungleichheit, die man jetzt als menschlich verursachtes Unrecht – anstatt, wie bisher als schicksalhaftes Unglück – empfindet'.[1]

In other words, 'Wants' have always been with the people of the Third World, but 'Demands' are new.

The importance of consciousness and rejection of inequality to social unrest was already recognized by Alexis de Tocqueville, when he wrote:

> 'Presque toutes les révolutions qui ont changé la face des peuples ont été faites pour consacrer ou pour détruire l'inégalité. Ecartez les causes secondaires qui ont produit les grandes agitations des hommes, vous en arriverez presque toujours â l'inégalité'.[2]

In this light the term *'conscious structural violence'* may be appropriately introduced, indicating an oppressive social structure of which people are aware.[2a] Awareness of structural violence entails the demand for change. The recognition of *un*conscious structural violence is important, since this makes it possible to indicate situations which may eventually give rise to anti-status quo movements, once people come to perceive such a situation as violating their rights.

But even then the situation becomes only *potentially* unstable, since the emergence of consciousness may not be enough in itself to arouse people. Before they will participate in any process of social change, a second condition must have been fulfilled.

1.2. *Hope*

Somehow people must believe that they *can* change existing conditions. If they do not believe in their chances, if they have no hope,

---

[1] R. F. Behrendt – 'Soziale Strategie für Entwicklungsländer' ('65) pp. 167-168: 'not so much the situation of misery as such, as the by now realized inequality, which is experienced now as injustice caused by man – instead of, as before, as natural misfortune.'

[2] A. de Tocqueville – 'De la Démocratie en Amérique' II (éditions M-Th. Génin, '51) p. 344; an English translation, called 'Democracy in America' has been published as a Vintage Book in 1954; vol. II p. 266 reads: 'Remove the secondary causes that have produced the great convulsions of the world and you will almost always find the principle of inequality at the bottom.'

[2a] on the concept of structural violence, see J. Galtung – 'Violence, Peace, and Peace Research,' 6 J. Peace Res. ('69) pp. 167ff.

they remain apathetic. This fundamental consideration explains much of the apathy still prevailing in the Third World (see below), which often is misunderstood. The late President Kennedy once said to Congress, when talking about the US aid program:

'Freedom, all freedom, is threatened by the subtle, varied and unceasing Communist efforts at subversion in Latin America, Africa, the Middle East, and Asia. And the prospect of freedom is also endangered or eroded in countries *which see no hope* – no hope for a better life based on economic progress, education, social justice, and the development of stable institutions.'[3]

It is hope itself, however, which stimulates people to act, and which stimulates them to revolt violently.
When people organize a social revolt (even as a last dramatic resort), it is because they hope to reach by means of violent action some of their goals. People who have no hope at all, remain apathetic. This is what Kropotkin meant with his aphorism 'the hopeless do not revolt.' The hope to get or the hope to take; that doesn't matter. Hope means the end of apathy. Behrendt says that the fact whether 'die subjektieve Entwicklungsbedürftigkeit' leads to action, or not, depends entirely on being able to trust that the possibility of change will occur.[4] In the same sense Millikan and Rostow write about the enormous developments which took place during this century:

'This revolution is rapidly exposing previously apathetic peoples to the possibility of change. It is creating in them new aspirations for education, social improvement, and economic development, ... the spirit of revolt does not bread easily among people who are chronically destitute. In rigid feudal societies which still characterize some parts of the world the poor have for generations accepted a fatalistic view; and poor people do not revolt when they believe change to be inherently impossible.'[5]

1.2.1. *Apathy*

The insight gained concerning the significance of the factor hope will help us to explain also the rather high degree of apathy still prevailing in many poor countries. A popular argument often used against economic aid to developing countries is the phrase of the 'leak bucket': you can put in as much money as you want, but you better not, since those lazy people do not want to work for themselves; they are disinterested and apathetic, and nothing would help such people.

[3] Dept. State Bull. (April 22, '63) p. 592; my italics.
[4] R. F. Behrendt, p. 180.
[5] M. F. Millikan & W. W. Rostow – 'A Proposal; Key to an Effective Foreign Policy' ('57) pp. 5, 20.

It appears that we are confronted here with a very important problem. Some scientific observers have indeed reached the conclusion that, in view of the apathy which characterizes the attitude of poor people in several parts of the world, the endeavour to increase prosperity in such regions might be a rather useless one. Three examples of this apathetic attitude will be discussed here; it was found to exist among certain 'Indian' groups of the Andes by Osborne and Mangin, among Thai peasants by Young, and among peasants in India by Kusum Nair.[6]

In the first place, it is a well-known fact that a bad physical condition, as a result of inadequate nutrition, also contributes to a passive mind (we come back to this in section 4). This, however, is not the only circumstance to be taken into account when considering the phenomenon of apathy. Various political, social, and historical variables are important in determining people's attitude.

Concerning the 'Indians' in Latin America it is important to note first that, in contrast to the 'mestizo', the 'mulatto', and the 'European' countries on that continent, the basic sociopolitical feature of the traditional 'Indian' societies is the drastic subordination of a large segment of the population which is separated by a considerable social distance from the dominant class. The rigid character of social (or racial) distinctions is very old, and has acquired a sense of permanency, because the Indian has become accustomed to the dictum that it would be impossible to change it. The Indian's stolid acceptance of his weakness and suffering has been observed by several psychological anthropologists such as Mangin. In connection with Peru he states:

> 'The humble, passive, tranquil, modest individual described by many informants as the ideal personality type is not strong and forbearing but rather frightened and ineffective.'[7]

In the same sense Hagen describes the way in which these attitudes are perpetuated by the dynamics of home life and are related to the authoritarian behaviour of the father, formed by early training and reinforced by cultural norms.[8]

---

[6] H. Osborne – 'Indians of the Andes: Aymaras and Quechuas' ('52) pp. 210-211; W. T. Mangin – 'Mental Health and Migration in Cities: A Peruvian Case,' in Heath and Adams (eds.) – 'Contemporary Cultures and Societies of Latin America' ('65); K. Young – 'Thailand's Role in Southeast Asia,' 56 Curr. Hist. ('69); Kusum Nair – 'Blossoms in the Dust: The Human Factor in Indian Development' ('62) p. 193; F. G. Baily – 'Politics and Social Change; Orissa in 1959' ('63) p. 88.
[7] W. T. Mangin, p. 551.
[8] E. Hagen – 'On the Theory of Social Change' ('62) pp. 204-205.

On the other side of the globe a similar explanation is given by Young in connection with the ineffectiveness of the guerilla movement in Thailand. According to him the Thai farmer and his family, as individuals and as a part of the large rural majority of Thailand's population, are not susceptible to revolutionary ideas. They are too individualistic and too traditional, and remain rooted in their religious customs; they do not subscribe for example to the materialistic appeal of Communist doctrine.[9]

Yet the question remains in relation to the Latin Indians and with the Thai, to what extent is the observed docility and apathy the consequence of an unconscious but rational mode of adaption to the realities of the social structure, and to what extent is it strengthened by rational religious convictions? It would seem obvious that the influence of impeding cultural and religious customs is the strongest in those countries where social distinctions are particularly rigid and social mobility is particularly difficult. Under such circumstances people tend to become hopeless, and they develop psychological defense-mechanisms, enabling them to survive. This is what Mason means when he writes:

> 'The apparent permanence of a situation may make tolerable what may otherwise be utterly intolerable.'[10]

People's way of life may become dominated by such mechanisms, when the situation remains unchanged for a very long time, and then they may react rather passively and seemingly disinterested to new stimuli: they need time to develop an active mind out of the 'there is nothing we can do'-attitude.

This, for instance, is the case in the 'Indian' countries. In comparing the 'Indian' countries, with 'mestizo', 'mulatto', and 'European' countries on the Latin American continent, we can observe in the latter cases large inequalities and even strong class divisions, but they are no more than that. They are not yawning gulfs between different linguistic, cultural, and – above all – racial groups. In the 'mestizo,' 'mulatto' and European countries we find to a much larger extent, social mobility for all groups, even if some of them may never reach the upper class. A Brazilian folk saying sums it up as follows: 'a poor white is a negro and a rich negro is a white'; an expression like this could not be heard in relation to traditional Indian countries, because there are no rich Indians.

---

[9] K. Young, p. 99.
[10] Ph. Mason – 'Race Relations' ('70) p. 164.

Within the framework of this book it is very important to note that the relative weakness of social restraints in non-Indian countries seems to result in greater brutality and violence in politics,[11] a plausible explanation being, that the social gaps in Indian countries are so wide, that the underdogs have lost all hope for substantial improvement. *In non-Indian countries social restraints are not strong enough to withhold the underdogs from (violent) social action.*
It would seem, therefore, that the prevailing apathy among Indians might not (only) be explained by reference to cultural and religious patterns, but rather by the fact that *they simply do not yet believe in the potential success of any endeavour to change the status quo*. Whatever the relevance of religious or cultural inhibitions may be, it seems that an attitude of clinging to old beliefs and customs is a typical feature of people who feel the beginnings of a disturbing social process, but still too afraid and too uncertain to take part in it; even if they have nothing to gain from the status quo. This is particularly true when the process of change comes as a sudden shock instead of a gradual development (see below on the Colombian Violencia). In view, however, of what happens in many traditional developing societies today, in particular among the younger generation, the permanency and independent character of such inhibitory cultural and religious customs seems rather doubtful: their strength seems to depend largely on other social phenomena and developments, and people's realization that such developments are possible and good.

This is illustrated not only by the varied behaviour of 'underdogs' in other Latino societies, where social structures are less rigid, and where consequently the endeavour to improve one's situation is potentially more successful; it is also illustrated by the brutal fury of the occasional revolts of groups of Indians in Peru, Equador, and Chile, which from time to time reminds the upper class of the fragility of the political order. Governments realize that the probability of Indian revolt is great because of the increasing political participation on the side of the Indian population. They also know that these revolts may bring with them possibilities of political changes in unknown directions and fear that they will get out of hand – resulting in unforseeable violence.[12] Recent developments in Chile (see p. 32) are a clear case in question.

Concerning the situation among poor peasants in India, Kusum Nair follows the same line of thinking; she argues that in India one of

---

[11] M. C. Needler – 'Political Development in Latin America: Instability, Violence and Evolutionary Change' ('68) pp. 114ff.
[12] idem, p. 106.

the principal assumptions on which present planning for the development of the rural sector is based – i.e. that the desire for higher levels of material wealth is prevailing among the poor masses – is not valid. There exists, in her opinion, a ceiling rather than a floor.[13]

Here again one must not overlook, however, the extremely rigid traditional social system of rural India. Recent studies have shown that the benefits of community development programs have gone, by and large, to the traditional élite, at the expense of the poor.[14] The upper class is so strong and well-organized, and the masses of underdogs are so afraid and unorganized, that in most cases where it was tried it proved *impossible at the time* to break through the existing structure. This is so, partly, because the larger landowners and private traders supply much of the leadership and financial support of district- and state-Congress party organizations. Understandably therefore, the Congress leadership in the states thought it most expedient on the one hand to give loud public support to the ideologically determined development policies of the five-year plans, but on the other hand co-operated privately with the landed interests in order to prevent any effective implementation.[15] The problem in India is that the direct power to enact and implement land-reform legislation is vested in the states.

Mindful of this situation most people *do not yet believe* in the potential success of endeavours to change it; that is, they have not trust, no hope, and thus they remain in or return to their apathetic attitude. The task of bringing about change is perceived to be too difficult, be it by five-year plans or by some process of democratization.[16] An illustrating example of the impeding influence of traditional structures has been described by Magdoff in relation to the seeming indifference of small Indian farmers to undertake simple work needed to irrigate the land they cultivate. The Indian government spent large sums of money to dig broad canals in order to make more water available for farming, but in some regions the farmers failed to take advantage of

---

[13] Kusum Nair, p. 193.
[14] G. D. Berreman – 'Caste and Community Development,' XXII Human Organisation (Spring '63); J. S. Uppal – 'Implementation of Land Reform Legislation in India; A Study of Two Villages in Punjab,' IX Asian Survey ('69) pp. 359-372; also C. N. Bhalerao – 'Some Social, Political and Administrative Consequences of Panchayati Ray,' IV Asian Survey ('64) pp. 805-806.
[15] Francine R. Frankel – 'Ideology and Politics in Economic Planning; the Problem of Indian Agricultural Development Strategy,' XIX World Politics ('66-'67) p. 640.
[16] How difficult it proved to be, for instance, to try to democraticize traditional structures by decentralized administration and direct elections, becomes clear from J. Narain – 'Democratic Decentralization and Rural Leadership in India: The Rayasthan Experiment,' IV Asian Survey ('64) pp. 1013-1022.

this potential boost for their output; they did not dig the ditches needed to bring the water from the rivers and canals to their small plots. When Magdoff asked a U.S. agricultural specialist whether the reason for this was laziness, stupidity, or ignorance, he was answered: none of these. The simplest and most ignorant farmer knows the importance of water, but the irrigation ditches had to pass over land owned by big land-owners who exacted a tax for the use of the ditches – a tax the farmers could not possibly pay....[17]

To this must, of course, be added the inhibitory influence of deep-rooted cultural patterns and religious beliefs. But in this connection one might put the same question as before: Is such apathy, fed by such customs, really a feature of the poor Indian peasant, or is it, like these customs, determined by the absence of hope of improvement?

Herskovitz belongs to the group of authors who think that all human beings strive for the general goal of improving conditions. This endeavour is partially reflected in the general refusal to accept any lowered level of welfare. He says: 'The development of wants of a people is irreversible... there is no study of cultural change in process, or of contact between peoples having different cultures, which does not document the proposition that people give over an item in their cultural store, only when it becomes apparent that a more desirable substitute, iron implements for stone tools, for example, is at hand... There is nothing more difficult to accept than a lowered level of living.'[18]

One author rejects the theory of 'characteristic apathy' in very radical terms. He denies the validity of any distinction between spiritually oriented and materialistically oriented people. He states that no ethnic entities exist which are indifferent to material factors; people do not fail to differentiate in some fashion between being relatively better off and relatively worse off materially, and some preference for the first is always shown. The failure to envisage possibilities of improvement explains the alleged spiritual qualities rather than spiritual criteria themselves.[19]

This might be a rather radical view to some readers – longstanding religious and spiritual customs may act, for some time, as an independent influence on the behaviour of people –, but probably this author is right to a large extent. There are clear examples of formerly

---

[17] H. Magdoff – 'The Impact of U.S. Foreign Policy on Underdeveloped Countries,' XXII Monthly Review 10 ('71) p. 6.
[18] M. Herskovitz – 'Economic Anthropology' ('62) p. 4.
[19] M. J. Levy, jr. – 'Social Patterns (Structures) and Problems of Modernization,' in Moore and Cook (eds.) – 'Readings in Social Change' ('67) p. 194.

apathetic and disinterested people who became stimulated to work for a materially better future, *as soon as they gained real hope in reaching it.* Characteristic of this attitude is Bourguiba's endeavour to break through the impeding custom of Ramadan. The President once said to his people:

> 'I can better serve my country by not hanging around in a corner yawning and hungry because it is Ramadan... I hope to the contrary to make Ramadan to the most productive month of the year. To those who want to practice ascetism, I propose to work an hour extra!'[20]

Staley too thinks that the days of apathy are counted. In the East, he says, there was a time when happiness was thought to be increased by diminishing the level of necessities; but now the time is coming when people refuse to level down their needs, and instead demand an increase of material possessions.[21]

In this light it is not very surprising that Russett concludes that 'inequality of land distribution does bear a relation to political instability, but that relationship is not a strong one,'[22] for Russett's data were collected in 1964. Many hold that we are only now on the eve of an enormous social earthquake throughout the Third World. *At this moment* in history many people are still apathetic, being caught between utopianism and fatalism, as they see no real hope yet. Russett's data can tell us little about the situation in, let us say, twenty years from now. By then the possibility of change, be it peacefully or otherwise, may have become acute and may very well dictate the course of events. Therefore, the important outcome of Russett's data might be not so much that the studied relation is 'not a strong one,' but that in our days there is '*a* relation.'

In this light the rural situation in South Vietnam illustrates the point. Some of the provinces, where inequality among the population is the greatest, happen to be at the same time the most 'secure' ones. Some authors think this very strange, but one explanation seems plausible:

---

[20] N.Y.T. (March 6, '62).

[21] E. Staley – 'The Future of Underdeveloped Countries' ('54) pp. 20-21; in the same sense Edward Shils begins his booklet on 'Political Development in the New States' ('62) as follows:

'There are very few states today which do not aspire to modernity. The day of rulers who were indifferent to the archaism of the society which they governed has almost disappeared. The leaders of nearly every state – both the old established as well as the new states of Asia and Africa – feel a pressing necessity of espousing policies which will bring them within the circle of modernity.'

[22] B. M. Russett – 'Inequality and Instability; the Relation of Land Tenure to Politics,' XVI World Politics ('63-'64) pp. 442-454, 449.

These provinces still know the land-lord pattern, reestablished in 1955 by Ngo Dinh Diem, and the fact that this situation still exists can only be explained by the circumstance that they are still more or less under the rule of Saigon and the overwhelming presence of US and ARVN soldiers. Under these circumstances no poor peasant believes yet in any possibility to see his position, as it had been improved before 1954 by the Viet Minh, restored – so he keeps silent.
The case is quite contrary in those provinces where Saigon's rule is doubtful, and where the promises of the NLF have a concrete value.

In order to understand the polemological relevance of the factors discussed hitherto, a third one must be added, namely frustration.

4. *Frustration*

'Frustration,' according to Berkowicz, refers to an interference with ongoing goal-directed activity. Such interference implies a break-effect, which arouses anger. Aggressive responses tend to occur when they are evoked by an external cue, that is, when the angered person sees an attackable object or person that he associates with the source of frustration.[23]
In 1939 Dollard c.s. formulated the 'frustration-aggression theory' as the basic postulate

> 'that the occurrence of aggressive behavior always presupposes the existence of frustration and, contrarywise, that the existence of frustration always leads to some form of aggression.'[24]

Although they made this categorical statement, the study shows that Dollard and his colleagues did not intend to suggest that aggression was considered the only possible response to frustration. Many later studies have clarified this point, suggesting that a range of reactions may occur, the quality of which depends on various social, psychological, economic and other variables, which have as yet not been sufficiently analyzed. They may consist of an extra effort to reach the goal set, the occurrence of an idée-fixe, resignation and indifference by way of psychological escape-mechanisms, and aggression, the last alternative being the most common reaction.[25]

[23] L. Berkowicz – 'Aggression' ('62) pp. 58-59.
[24] J. Dollard et al. – 'Frustration and Aggression' ('39) p. 3.
[25] N. E. Miller et al. – 'The Frustration-Aggression Hypothesis,' XLVIII Psychological Review (July, '41) p. 339;
R. Lawson – 'Frustration, the Development of a Scientific Concept' ('65) pp. 14, 19, 22, 27, 48, 50;
J. C. Davies – 'Toward a Theory of Revolution,' 27 Am. Soc. Rev. 1 ('62) pp. 5 ff.

In transplanting this crucial thesis from psychology to the field of sociology, it could be said that breaking off a firm belief (the interference) in the fulfilment of roused communal expectations (the goal-directed activity or process) will often create an aggressive attitude among the frustrated group. To put it within the framework of the present study: When people have come to perceive an existing situation as unjust and not necessary (1), and have been promised or otherwise count upon a better future (2), and this hope is then destroyed (3), they may be expected to develop an aggressive mind.

Taking Lerner's equation that Frustration $= \dfrac{\text{Want}}{\text{Get}}$ – perhaps better 'Demand,' which people believe to have a right to and expect to get –, then an increase in Want without an increase in Get leads to Frustration.[26] I did not come across any author doubting the validity of applying this psychological axiom to social processes. On the contrary, like so many, Lerner states that people will not continue to participate in institutions that constantly frustrate their wants, and Gurr says even categorically: 'relative deprivation is the basic precondition for civil strife of any kind.' In connection to his concept of 'relative deprivation,' by which he means 'actors' perception of discrepancy between their value expectations and their value capabilities,' he adds in his recent book 'Why Men Rebel':

> 'The frustration-aggression and the related threat-aggression mechanisms provide the basic motivational link between RD (relative deprivation) and the potential for collective violence... the primary source of the human capacity for violence appears to be the frustration-aggression mechanism. Frustration does not necessarily lead to violence, and violence for some men is motivated by expectations of gain. The anger induced by frustration, however, is a motivating force that disposes men to aggression ...'[26a]

The role of the factor 'hope' is not always made explicit in such studies. In many cases, however, it seems to be recognized implicitly; e.g. Hoselitz and Willner make a distinction between 'aspirations' and 'expectations,' explaining: 'unrealized aspirations produce feelings of disappointment, but unrealized expectations result in feelings of deprivation. Disappointment is generally tolerable; deprivation is often intolerable. The deprived individual feels impelled to remedy, by whatever means are available, the material and psychic frustrations

---

[26] D. Lerner – 'Social Aspects of Modernization,' Int. Enc. Soc. Sc. ('68) p. 392.
[26a] T. Gurr – 'A Causal Model of Civic Strife: A Comparative Analysis Using New Indices,' LXII Am. Pol. Sc. Rev. ('68);
idem – 'Why Men Rebel' ('70) pp. 24, 36-37; in his book Gurr gives a summary of many other studies indicating the validity of applying this psychological theory to social processes.

produced in him. Whereas disappointment may breed the seeds of incipient revolution, deprivation serves as a catalyst for revolutionary action.'[26b]

Of particular importance is the notion of *'systemic frustration,'* defined by the Feierabends as a situation

> *'in which levels of social expectations, aspirations and needs are raised for many people during significant periods of time, and yet remain unmatched by equivalent levels of satisfaction.'*[27]

Systemic frustration is bound to become very intense eventually, and it is important to note here that several authors have reached the conclusion that high levels of frustration correspond with a high risk of violence. This mechanism was found to be at work among American soldiers during the second World War by Stouffer. He recognized that in those units in which the chance of promotions was believed to be higher than in others, the men reacted more discontented, if promotions did not occur, than in units where the chance was considered to be lower. His conclusion was that discontent increases among people according to the existence of higher, but unsatisfied, expectations.[28]

Within the present context Huntington seems to have affirmed this thesis, when he found that instability in Latin America was less frequent early in the twentieth century than it was in the middle of this century;[29] an obvious explanation being that mass-support to development plans, and consequently the degree of mass-frustration, is a relatively recent phenomenon, while demands and hope scarcely prevailed in previous periods.

Gurr has reached a similar conclusion, where he states in general that 'strife varies directly in magnitude with the intensity of relative deprivation.'[30] In this opinion he is supported by the Feierabends, who found that the level of political instability increases with the level of frustration.[31]

[26b] B. Hoselitz & Ann Willner – 'Economic Development, Political Strategies, and American Aid,' in M. A. Kaplan (ed.) – 'The Revolution in World Politics' ('62) p. 363.
[27] J. K. Feierabend & Rosalind L. Feierabend – 'Aggressive Behaviours Within Polities, 1948-1962: a cross-national study,' X J. Confl. Res. ('66) p. 250.
[28] S. A. Stouffer et al. – 'The American Soldier: Adjustment during Army Life' I ('49) pp. 250ff.
[29] S. P. Huntington – 'Political Development and Political Decay,' XVII World Politics ('64-'65) pp. 407-408.
[30] T. Gurr – 'A Causal Model of Civic Strife: A Comparative Analysis Using New Indices,' LXII Am. Pol. Sc. Rev. ('68) p. 1104.
[31] Feierabend & Feierabend, p. 261.

Yet, it seems doubtful whether such a general conclusion is justified. To explain this, another concept must be introduced, *'frustration threshold.'* By this term that level of frustration is meant beyond which frustration becomes unbearable. It is not at all certain that people who have reached this level will react in an aggressive way. At this point, two entirely different modes of reaction are possible: people will *either loose all resistance and fall back into a state of apathy, resignation, and ritualism*; or they will turn to aggressive behaviour. Which kind of reaction occurs would seem to be determined mainly by the prevailing belief in the *possibility of violent action.*

This is in line with the previous discussion on the phenomenon of apathy: People having no trust, no hope in the possibility of change tend to develop psychological escape mechanisms enabling them to survive, to live with their circumstances. People having hope for success of action will rather turn to violence once their frustration threshold is reached. Which kind of reaction will occur, would seem to depend mainly on the following three variables:

1^0. *previous experience*

People learn from and are influenced by history. If they have formerly tried to use force against status quo factions of their society without achieving any success, they may be less inclined to try this another time, unless the circumstances have substantially changed. The tinminers of Bolivia tried it several times, and there were periods when all of them had weapons in their homes. Every time their endeavour ended, however, in a bloodbath, without reaching any of their goals. Today, the tinminers are more depressed, more passive, and would not easily turn to violence again if their chance of success would not substantially improve.

2^0. *perceived strength of status quo-forces.*

If those sections of the population which feel deprived perceive the status quo sections as very powerful, they will rather be impressed than try to fight them. It is not very strange that several experts have found that the least developed among the poor nations are also the most stable dictatorships. As soon as some development process gets under way, and the underdog's living conditions have improved – contributing to fresh hope and belief that the privileges of the higher circles are no longer untouchable – instability increases. This has been determined e.g. by the Feierabends and by Lipset. The author last mentioned found that according to his indices of wealth – income, number of radios, telephones, newspapers, motor vehicles, and physicians per capita – the countries he classified as 'stable dictatorships' rank lowest on the scale.[32]

[32] idem; S. M. Lipset – 'Political Man: The Social Basis of Politics' ('63) pp. 27ff.

3°. *level of social consciousness and organization of deprived groups.*
The step from resistance to resignation presupposes the absence of perceived power of the anti-status quo groups. If only small sections of deprived people have been aroused, they may easily fall back into apathy if their hopes are destroyed. The situation is quite different if large segments of the population have been mobilized, have reached a certain level of political participation, have become conscious of their common aims, and have become organized. If that happens, perceptions of the prevailing power relations may become entirely different, and it seems justified to suppose that if deprived people reach their frustration threshold 'en masse,' being conscious of their common interests and able to organize and combine their potential power, the risk is high that they will turn to violence. As we shall see below and in following sections of this Chapter, the level of social consciousness and organization is a very important factor, and can very well help to explain whether violence will occur; e.g. the situation in Latin America can be very well understood in connection to this variable.

The hypotheses discussed here can be put together in a very simple model, presented at p. 23.

1.3.1. *Level of prosperity.*

It should be clearly understood that this model only applies to poor countries. In the first place, the lower sections of people in countries with a high level of common welfare are not confronted so much with the 'choice' between apathy or violence; if they do not succeed in reaching new goals, they may resign but this is quite another thing than the total passivity which characterizes the attitude of the apathetic people meant above. In the second place, economic development is bound to entail higher levels of social consciousness and political participation, implying that there is no need to despair, because there is much more hope that improvement will eventually be achieved in peaceful ways. Even if people may become frustrated, their position is mostly not so bad, and goods and conditions to be preserved are mostly of that order, that they will not easily turn to violence if they can not fulfil their expectations. Where such minimum level of welfare lies, constitutes a question without an absolute answer; it might well depend on regional circumstances (the level of welfare in neighbouring countries), history (previous levels of welfare), degree of new expectations roused, etc.

In any case, it is not very surprising to find that the rich countries are on the whole much more stable societies than the developing countries

RELATIONSHIP BETWEEN DEPRIVATION AND DIRECT SOCIAL VIOLENCE IN POOR COUNTRIES

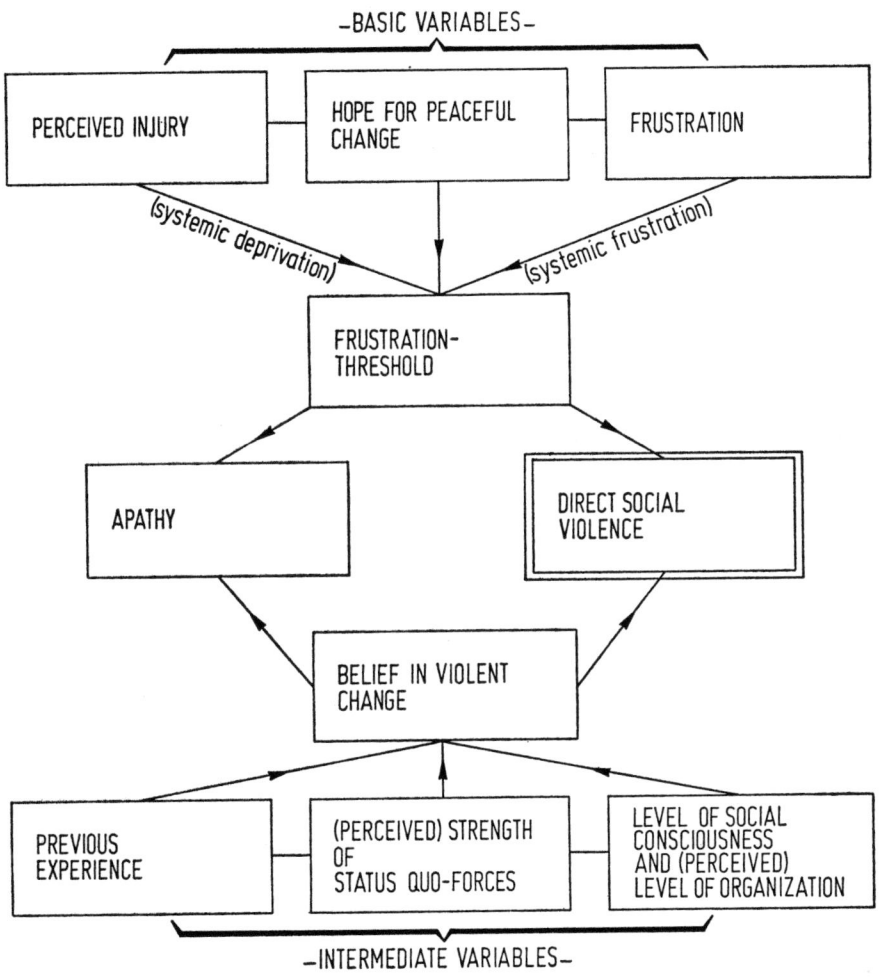

as has been indicated in the introduction. Duff and Mc. Camant, who found such a correlation, have been mentioned there. Likewise the study by the Feierabends reveals that modern industrialized countries are far more stable than transitional (developing) countries, and more stable than traditional (underdeveloped) countries, although also the rich countries often witness a high degree of economic inequality.

To some degree authors like Lipset, Almond and Coleman, seem to allege that the same consideration would hold for the Third World today already. Lipset found that the countries he classifies as 'democracies' (implying, which is relevant here, a certain degree of peaceful change capacity) rank relatively high on his scale of indices of wealth.[33] Almond and Coleman show a similar correlation, the democratic process being defined in terms of degree of political competitiveness. The countries coded as 'competitive' were more likely to be found at the upper end of economic ranking.[34]

One might doubt, however, the validity of these findings, as Needler does. Both the indices used and their qualification of being 'democratic' seems to be debatable. By introducing the wealth-index of 'life expectancy,' and by claiming the existence of both constitutional observance *and* popular political participation in order to be recognized as 'democratic,' he has added probably valuable variables. On this basis he was nevertheless convinced of the essential correctness of the point made by the aforementioned authors, concluding:

> 'it can be stated with a considerable degree of assurance that political development, conceived of as the heightening of both observance of constitutional norms and popular participation in politics, is indeed commensurate with economic development.'[35]

The pressure for violence decreases along with the improvement of living conditions, and above a certain level of common welfare nobody would risk loosing (by means of civil wars) what he already has in order to gain more. Advancing what follows in section B of this Chapter, one remark of caution must be made here: the considerations presented here show the *level*, not the process of development. And even so, the conclusions reached by the authors mentioned here seem doubtful if they are taken as absolute conclusions as far as the developing countries are concerned. As will be shown below, the achievement of higher levels of welfare can result in a high level of *instability*, when people have not reached what they perceive as the minimum of their goals. They may become impatient or find themselves in a state of impetuosity, which contributes to intensified

---

[33] idem.
[34] G. Almond & J. S. Coleman – 'The Politics of Developing Areas' ('60) p. 541.
[35] M. C. Needler, p. 91.

frustration if their increasing expectations are not fulfilled. If the indices used by the authors are relevant, it might well be that for some reason the more advanced countries of Latin America – to which their studies relate – are in a relatively favourable position, since elsewhere in the Third World the achievement of higher levels of welfare would seem to contribute rather to more instability than to democratically functioning systems. Much research is still needed in this field. It is certain, however, that there are levels of welfare above which frustrations usually do not become intense enough to provoke either apathy or violent behaviour.

1.3.2. *Some examples.*

A few examples may illustrate the relevance of our hypothetic model. It should be recognized that only a few important variables have been selected, and that many sub-variables may have to be taken into account, the occurrence and importance of which must as yet be studied in more detail. Lots of examples could be presented at this point, but it appears that people's perception of deprivation, their hopes, and their social mobilization are often stimulated in particular under circumstances of economic development in their direct environment, even if they are not immediately involved themselves. In many cases it will be extremely difficult to determine whether people's actions were influenced more by conscious poverty or by any process of development, but in view of the consideration just mentioned, it seemed more appropriate to discuss such cases in which economic development may be involved in part B. The examples presented at this point may well be considered to have little direct connection with any development process.

1[0]. The first example, relating to Latin America, has been mentioned in part before, where we dealt with the phenomenon of present day – apathy, and where the hypotheses illustrated in the present model were introduced. Nevertheless, its importance for the near future may be considered outstanding, which justifies the need to reiterate some points. Huntington, who found that the level of political instability in Latin America was much higher in the middle of the twentieth century than at its beginning, has been mentioned; the explanation suggested here was that some poor sections of Latin American societies have only recently begun to reject the status quo and to develop new expectations, leading hitherto in most cases to increased levels of frustration. This is in line with Needler's conclusions concerning the different levels of stability in the traditional 'Indian' countries on the one hand and the 'mestizo', 'mulatto', and

'white' countries of this continent on the other hand. The poor masses in the 'Indian' countries are only very slowly beginning to question the inevitability of their position, they scarcely have any expectations or hopes, their level of social consciousness and organization is particularly low, and they perceive the vested interests as practically untouchable. Thus, if small groups of these people develop expectations and are frustrated, they will easily loose resistance and fall back into ritualism and apathy. While this pattern of social conditions and reactions may be true at present for large sections of deprived people in non-Indian countries as well, social structures are not entirely rigid and untouchable, and allow certain groups to develop higher expectations and higher levels of underdog-solidarity, which explains the occurrence of some hope for success by violent action resulting in a somewhat higher level of political instability. An illustrating case in point are the Bolivian tinminers. They traditionally constitute one of the most centralized groups of underdogs on the continent. Living in great misery, feeling very deprived, conscious of their common interests, relatively well organized, thus perceiving the gap between their own potential power and the strength of the upper circles exploiting them as not so tremendous as it looks to other poor sections, they often tended to react in a violent way to the systemic frustration of their hopes for a better future. Yet, after several failures and many deaths, their belief in the possibility of violent action has decreased to a large extent on the basis of this negative experience. It is not surprising, then, to see that this formerly very active section of the Bolivian masses today makes a very depressed and passive impression. Che Guevara had hoped that he could arouse the campesinos against the landlords, but he did not realize enough how difficult it is to arouse people who have learned to accept the facts of a most miserable life, who are so passive and apathetic, and who have lost all hope. Before such people can be brought to fight for a better life, for which men like Camillo Torres and Guevara hoped to stimulate them, their outlook and organization must have changed fundamentally. Whether such change may be expected to take place, will be discussed below and in section B.
At this point we would like to remind the reader of the Colombian 'Violencia' from 1948 to 1965. Colombia, the Latino country with the oldest 'democratic' political tradition, and accordingly with the highest level of social organization capability, lost 200.000 people in a massive internecine slaughter during the period mentioned. Although people did not at that time organize along existing social patterns – the reasons for this are discussed in sections 6 and 12 below –, but rather along existing political patterns, the direct cause is

considered by many experts to be found in the combination of systemic economic frustration and the sudden hope roused by the success of the Liberal Party which promised to realize radical improvement at the cost of the traditional élites. Today, 90 per cent of Columbia's students are in favour of a drastic and radical change.[36]

2⁰. A second example is the Philippines. During the second World War a new political élite was formed by the resistance movement in the countryside. After the War, American dollars flew into the country, and the peasants were promised a better life. As it became clear that the Government would not stick to its promises of land-reform, the backwardness in comparison to other regions, the exploitation by now rejected, and the frustration resulting from the broken promises, created an aggressive attitude in the Central Luzon province. On the one hand, the former resistance people, feeling confident that their experience and strength would be assets when faced with a violent confrontation, reorganized and started the Hukbalahab revolt. On the other hand, although they succeeded in mobilizing substantial sections of the peasantry within their own region, many others were too afraid and could not be convinced of the potential success of violence, in particular the peasantry in other regions of the country. This situation explains why the revolt for the Government was difficult to be overwon in Luzon, but could finally be separated and encircled. At the time there was still no broad basis to ensure large-scale support for the Hukbalahab movement.[37]

3⁰. This situation was different from that which occured in Vietnam. In this country not only a strong resistance movement was born during the second World War, but a broad popular basis of support throughout the countryside was built up during the successful liberation war against the French colonial administration.
A basic political act, realized by the Viet Minh at the time of the victory of Dien Bien Phu, was the destruction of large-ownership resulting in the distribution of land among the small former tenants. For the first time in their life innumerable poor peasants were the proud owners of their own land. After the Geneva Conference, however, at which Vietnam was provisionally partitioned along the 17th parallel, the newly installed leader of the South, Ngo Dinh Diem, restored large ownership and thus frustrated the high expectations roused among the peasants by the Viet Minh. In the case

[36] R. C. Williamson – 'Toward a Theory of Political Violence: the case of rural Colombia,' XVIII W. Pol. Q. (March '65) pp. 35-42.
[37] e.g. R. L. Hough – 'Development and Security in Thailand: Lessons from Other Asian Countries,' IX Asian Survey ('69) p. 184.

of this country, however, there was a broad base for resistance, there was trust in their own strength, and there was not such great fear of an unknown government. Thus it is not surprising that from 1958 on the violent revolt in South Vietnam began, leading in 1960 to the creation of the National Liberation Front and eventually to what is today the Vietnam war. This is not the place to discuss the relevance of the alleged 'North Vietnamese aggression' as put foreward by the American Government; from all the information that is available today it is clear that the war in South Vietnam began and still mainly is a war of the South Vietnamese peasantry against a Saigon régime that it never chose. The question whether this revolt would have collapsed without the support from their North Vietnamese compatriots, is entirely irrelevant (In any case the answer to that question is more difficult than the answer to the question whether the Saigon régime would have suvived without the massive American intervention). It can be said with certainty that the hope of change by violence has never diminished. Whatever political or ideological motives may later have been added to the reasons behind this struggle, it is certainly true that the frustration resulting from Diem's repressive economic measures has played an important role.

4^0. Mexico is the last example I should like to mention here, because developments there are considered by many experts to be a warning signal to our present world. By the beginning of this century large sections of the Mexican population became involved in the political struggle between progressive and conservative forces. Mexico is also traditionally one of the politically better organized countries of Latin America, and the level of social consciousness, perceptions of injury, and hope for the success of violent action were high enough among substantial groups to sustain the revolution from 1910 to 1916. Since then, Mexico belongs to the group of Latin countries which have a relatively progressive administration, although the words are increasingly alienated from the deeds. Large sections of the Mexican population have not yet been mobilized, others have lost all hope. Yet, it seems that this is one of the countries in which social consciousness has developed to such an extent, that it can hardly be expected that large numbers of people will eventually fall back into a state of apathy and desperation. On the contrary, the hopes roused at the time of the revolution have never vanished entirely, and many think that Mexico is again becoming a very explosive society. In due course the belief in the strength of deprived sections of the population may become high enough to provoke large-scale violence as a consequence of what has been described here as systemic frustration. The Mexican policy of aspiration can continue in a peaceful way only as long as the Mexicans believe that their government and this policy can succeed, in the end, in carrying out their promises of putting into action the values of a modern, secular, industrial world.

This might in the long run hold true for all developing countries alike. They all are, or will become, 'political systems based upon hope, and they will survive as long as hope (of peaceful change) remains alive,' as Almond and Verba have put it.[38] Anticipating what follows in Chapter II on the internationally polemological aspects of poverty, it is this insight which underlines the importance of Fullbright's remark:

'the security of the rich is best assured by providing hope *and opportunity* for the poor.'[39]

The relevance of these quotations is based upon the assumption that we are just entering a new human era, an era in which apathy is eroded and in which social consciousness is bound to increase.

1.4. *Some prospects.*

In view of the changes that have taken place in the Third World during the last few decennia, in comparison to the virtually static situation that characterized a very long period before, the conclusion seems inevitable that a huge social process has started which can not be turned back anymore. Taking into account the ever increasing influence of mass communication, the appearance of signs of modernization nearly everywhere, the ever increasing migration to towns in all developing countries, and the ever increasing amount of violence and instability, it seems justified to say that we are only at the beginning of a process that might be depicted as an enormous social earthquake.
Enlarged frames of reference, in particular among the younger people, will cause feelings of deprivation to occur even in the most remote regions of the poor countries. It is noteworthy, that the most static and traditional societies on this globe are no longer the most quiet ones. Like many others, the Feierabends have found that today the most traditional and hitherto most static societies – the very poor nations – are no longer the most quiet ones. Everywhere the signs of discontent, of anger, and of revolt appear. Professor Dasgupta may be right when he says that today it is fundamentally incorrect to

---

[38] S. Verba & G. A. Almond – 'National Revolution and Political Commitment,' in H. Eckstein (ed.) – 'Internal War. Problems and Approaches' ('64) p. 231.
[39] J. W. Fullbright – 'The Arrogance of Power' ('66) p. 224.

speak of 'peace' in connection to the situation in a poor country; I think he found the exact term to describe the present situation: he calls it 'peacelessness,' expressing that there is (still) no war, but neither peace anymore.[40]
An interesting enquiry has been made by Davies, the results of which may be called significant since they throw light upon the prevailing mood among the poor in one of the most important developing countries, Brazil. He asked similar questions to rich and poor Americans, and to rich and poor Brazilians. The statement 'all those big people who drive around in fancy cars and look down on ordinary people are all going to suffer for it some day' was thought correct by only 1 out of 37 rich Americans and 1 out of 3 poor Americans, while it was thought correct by 2 out of 3 rich Brazilians and 3 out of 4 poor Brazilians. To the statement that a few strong leaders will improve the country's condition (a question concerning preference to some dictatorial system) 'yes' was replied by 1 out of 6 rich Americans and 2 out of 5 poor Americans, and by no less than 20 out of 31 poor Brazilians. The answer to the question 'do you think of yourself as being as good as everybody else' is very instructive; while 79% of the poor Americans replied with 'yes,' only 56% of the poor Brazilians reacted that way. This reaction clearly indicates the lack of consciousness *still* characterizing a large section of the poor in Brazil.[41]

Yet, it seems inevitable that such poor sections become increasingly aware of their rights as human beings. They will increasingly reject the prevailing circumstances, and become increasingly conscious of their common interests. The increasing amount of riots, of civil wars, and in general of underdog participation in social and political affairs, suggests that the ideas of the 'avant-garde' are slowly winning over large sections of the population. Consequently, social consciousness and underdog solidarity will increase, and so will their level of *organization*. And this is of crucial importance in view of the near future:
It has been discussed before that the step from resistance and hope via frustration to apathy presupposes the absence of power; *if substantial segments of an organized population are involved, however, systemic frustration must be feared to result in large-scale violence.*
Social consciousness and organization create the possibility of challenging a hitherto untouchable status quo, which by itself rouses

---

[40] S. Dasgupta – 'Peacelessness and Maldevelopment,' Proc. IPRA ('68) II, pp. 19ff.
[41] J. C. Davies – 'Political Stability and Instability: Some Manifestations and Causes,' XIII J. Confl. Res. ('68) pp. 1-17.

hope for peaceful change, and will – in case peaceful change proves impossible – contribute to violent polarization.

Whereas one present feature of many young countries is the stress layed on the building of 'mass-parties,' another common feature has been the failure to realize them. Many 'populist' leaders like U Nu, Sukarno, Nkrumah, and Kenyatta, men who presented themselves as 'solidaritymakers' (to use the expression of the Australian politicologist Feith), as leaders from and for the people, promised that all should equally participate in and profit by the building of a new prosperous state. But sooner or later – perhaps with the exception of Nyerere's Tanzania to some extent – this mass participation became a hollow shell. The failure of governments to live up to the promises made at independence, the marked difference between the standard of living of the people at the top and the others, the inability to solve internal problems and to unite the people behind their government, and gradually the alienation between the people and the (often military) government, all this led to a steady decline in popular participation, where it had been substantial. Popular rejection of the regime in power resulted consequently in a more totalitarian state.[42]

In other words, real political mass-participation in the young countries has hardly been realized. And it would be a mistake to underestimate the significance of this state of affairs. The Chinese peasants in 1926-'27, the Philippinese peasants after the second World War, the South Vietnamese peasants after the Presidency of Ngo Dinh Diem, the tin-miners of Bolivia during the 1960's, have all shown how important organization and the belief in common action is.

Whereas until now the successful organization of deprived sections of Third World societies had usually grown out of war (be it the second World War or a struggle for national independence), there is at present a more general trend towards mass organization.

The situation in Latin America is an illustrating example in this respect:

It seems correct, on the one hand, to mention as one of Latin America's features the fact that its enormous masses of poor and hungry people as entities have shown until now little revolutionary spirit; but it would seem no less correct to determine that this enormous proletariat is characterized also by a fundamental lack of class-consciousness, co-operation and organization (we come back to this in section 7). In recent years, however, Latin American countries, which, unlike the young countries of Africa and Asia, are not torn by tribal or religious struggle during the disturbing process of neo-

---

[42] e.g. L. Gray Cowan – 'The Military and African Politics,' XXI Int. J. ('66) pp. 289 ff.

colonial nation-building, witness nevertheless the same increasing degree of political instability and social violence; a development which in the case of this continent cannot be conclusively explained except *by reference to the economic situation*. During the period 1954-1964, 17 out of 20 Latin American countries experienced coups or coup attempts (the exceptions being Chile, Mexico and Uruguay), while now the traditional internecine military coup in this hemisphere seems to be in a process of transition to more violent forms of social change,[43] which is of utmost importance. Moreover, according to Gurr, during the period 1961-1963 only, 7 Latin American countries suffered from civil wars and no less than 19 witnessed violent turmoil.[44] And it should not be overlooked that political instability is not always evidenced by violence, but may be present silently for a long time before emerging in the form of violent dissidence. Within this picture the fact that the Chilenian 'Lumpenproletariat' was among the main deserters of Frei during the municipal election of 1967 and constituted an important factor in the election of Allende to the Presidency, and the challenging policies of some nationalist regimes like the Peruvian and the former Bolivian governments, are signs as well as consequences of the same sociological process: people are beginning to realize that they have to organize in order to play a role and have a say in what goes on.

This process might soon become a snowball, not only intra- but also transnational. Successful organization in one country may stimulate poor people in other countries, and the longer they have to wait for improvement, and the more impatient they become, the higher the risk is *that such mass organization might be used not for peaceful pressure, but for violent change*. It would be a grave mistake not to consider 'systemic apathy' as a very temporary phenomenon. In this sense Myrdal might be right when he speaks of 'The Latin American powder keg.'

A second important trend which can be noted in our days is the tendency *to seize new promises as a pretext for violent action*.
This appears to be the case in particular if new expectations are roused by reforms or promises after a preceding period of frustration. This trend, which points to increasing impatience, can be explained as

---

[43] S. P. Huntington – 'Political Development and Political Decay,' pp. 407-408; M. Midlarsky & R. Tanter – 'Toward a Theory of Political Instability in Latin America,' J. Peace Res. 3 ('67) p. 215.
[44] T. Gurr & Ch. Ruttenberg – 'The Conditions of Civil Violence: first test of a causal model' ('67) pp. 40-43.

follows: people become increasingly conscious of belonging to a group with common interests on the one hand, while on the other hand they find themselves in a state of hurry and anger; they refuse to accept any further frustration, and are anxious to get what they have been promised for so long, *they want to speed up reforms*, and use their own pressure to prevent another failure. *Thus, whereas in former times new promises would soothe angry people, they might at a certain moment rather act as a factor stimulating violent behaviour, caused by now not by present, but by previous frustration.*

One might here think of the rural disturbances in Java from 1960 onwards, when Sukarno's proclamation of agrarian reforms went hand-in-hand with popular uprising among the innumerable starving peasants, eventually leading to large-scale violence, and a sudden increase in power of the PKI (the communist party) and the BTI (the leftist peasant's association), ending in a terrible massacre of the communists.

Another good example is constituted by recent events in Chile, after the election of Allende to the Presidency. Since the time of the Spanish conqueror Pedro de Valdivia, the Arauca-Indians have been victims of colonization, oppression, and exploitation. The conquerors, and later immigrants, mainly from Germany, Switzerland and the Balkan countries, occupied the best parts of their territory, leaving them in hunger and misery. For years now, and in particular since Eduardo Frei came to the Presidency, their descendants, some 500.000 Mapuche-Indians, have been promised good land, governmental assistance, and better living conditions. But even Frei could do little to live up to his government's promises. Consequently, during the last years, unrest among the Indians increased, while they waited in vain for the fulfilment of these promises. And then suddenly Allende appeared on the scene with his reform plans for the sake of all deprived sections of Chilenian society, the first Marxist President after Castro on the American continent. All of a sudden a better future seemed to be within reach: Mindful of their neglect, their hunger, and their misery (60% of their children die before they are one year old), and frustrated by many unfulfilled promises, Allende's proclamation of fundamental reforms was a signal for the Mapuches to take the future into their own hands. Stimulated by, but by now too impatient to wait for the new reforms, they began to revolt against the landowners in their territory, expelled them by force, and occupied their haciendas. In the meantime committees have been set up to defend their regained possessions, while on the other side the rightist Agricultural Union is organizing for a counter-offensive. Similar events have occurred recently in Peru. Such examples show that new expectations preceded by a period of frustration may act as accelerators in provoking violence.

A third, perhaps the most important, trend should be noticed. While dealing with the relation between deprivation and violence, Gurr seems to consider 'roused hope' as a non-crucial intervening variable, since he links deprivation directly to aggressive behaviour. He speaks of 'relative deprivation' which he defines as

> 'actor's perceptions of discrepancy between their value expectations (the goods and conditions of the life to which they believe they are justifiably entitled) and their value capabilities (the amounts of goods and conditions that they think they are able to get and keep) ... one innate (psychological) response to perceived deprivation is discontent or anger, and anger is a motivating state for which aggression is an inherently satisfying response.'[45]

Gurr seems to consider 'roused hope' as a non-crucial intervening incorporate the factor 'roused hope,' but it does not have to be understood that way; and it probably should not, since he considers an increase of value expectations ('aspirational deprivation') primarily as a function of the demonstration-effect of improvements elsewhere – which might rather increase discontent than hope (see below, section 3). In connection to the future he might be correct to some extent by neglecting the intervening variable of hope for peaceful change, hitherto obviously of great importance: today one can notice in many parts of the developing world that people are against their governments or their wealthy compatriots, *without having suffered from frustrated hope of peaceful reforms*. Even in those parts of the world where the poor never saw the slightest chance of peaceful improvement, events suggest that the situation may become unstable.

It seems questionable whether the frustration-aggression theory in a strict sense provides a sufficient explanation to understand this new trend. One could perhaps argue that the unprecedented process of becoming conscious of position and rights confronts these people with a kind of historical shock: whereas anger is normally the result of preceding frustration, for these people anger and the realization of being frustrated come at the same time. Their fury is roused against the situation they have passively accepted for so long.

Another argument could be that consciousness of social position becomes increasingly accompanied by consciousness of class, i.e. through mass media and demonstration-effects at home and abroad people become able to look beyond previous narrow individual and

---

[45] T. Gurr, note 30 supra; and see his recent book 'Why Men Rebel' ('70) pp. 24ff., where he elaborates his theory.

social frames of reference, to develop feelings of macro-social solidarity and to understand the potential power of combined masses. What they learn about experiences with peaceful change will be enough to make them 'violence-minded.' Now that impatience and non-acceptance become crucial determining factors, moreover, it seems reasonable to expect that the longer they have to wait in vain, the more open they become to the ideas of social leaders who believe that *the only chance lies in violent change.*

The success of the hard-wing communists in Bengalen, recent violent developments in Kerala, the violence in Southern Sudan, the regular protests of starving people against food prices, and the increasing number of bloody incidents throughout the Third World in general, are signs of the same trend: people are becoming both more awake and more impatient; their actions may become less dependent on the previous frustration of hope for peaceful reforms as they become determined by the expected negation of *their plain rights and demands.* These demands are the 'expectations' meant by Gurr.

Finally, a trend of a different kind may be noticed. Apart from social violence resulting from goal-directed action as described above, another – though related – source of violence may increasingly contribute to turning Third World societies into the scene of turmoil.
This concerns the rather blind expression of aggressiveness – some speak of a 'need aggression' – resulting from the feeling to live in unbearable circumstances. Like the youthly criminal who may commit a murder without pursuing any conscious goal, driven by anger on society and his own place therein, entire groups of people may turn to aggressive behaviour towards others without expecting or even pursuing any profit.
Berkowicz suggests that an angered person is not likely to strike out at any object in his environment, but only at the targets he thinks are responsible. Although aggressive behaviour resulting from frustration will often be goal-directed, this does not have to be the case, however. Maier has undertaken several studies which support the thesis that innate frustration-induced behaviours may become ends in themselves for the actors, unrelated to further goals, and are qualitatively different from goal-directed behaviour:

'Aggression then becomes a function of the frustration, the previously existing goal response having been replaced by behavior which is controlled by an entirely different process.'[45a]

[45a] N. R. F. Maier – 'The Role of Frustration in Soci al Movements,' LXIX Psychological Review ('42) p. 587; see also idem – 'Frustration: The Study of Behavior Without a Goal' ('49) pp. 92 ff.

The important social phenomena of group-centrism and xenophobia will be discussed in section 8, because they appear to be of particular importance during a period of economic progress; yet, they should be mentioned here in connection to the question whether or not hunger, scarcity and perceived deprivation may be considered to be importantly contributing to the outbreak of violent conflicts which one is used to describe in terms of political, racial, ethnic or religious terms merely Thus, in connection to India and Pakistan one might ponder the question: Would as much violence occur there as it presently does, if those people lived in prosperity? Dasgupta's findings suggest a negative answer to this question. He revealed important economic interests underlying the religious riots at Rourkela. Another study, by Feldman, adds substantial data to Dasgupta's conclusions; he found that in India 300 Hindu's died during 730 riots which had nothing to do with Hindu-Muslim antagonism. Similarly, 500 Muslims in Pakistan lost their lives at the hands of fellow Muslims (more than at the hands of Hindu's). People in this part of the world show an increasing readiness to resort to violence (in India 22 communal riots occurred in 1966, 42 in 1967, and 49 in the first eleven months of 1968, as revealed by Minister of State Shukla to the Indian Parliament), and certain of these riots have clear economic aspects.[46]

Such findings at least suggest that a lot of violence would probably occur there even if the religious animosities were not prevailing, and the question is: is this violence indeed the result of religious animosity or is this fervent religious animosity rather the result of some need of violence? Probably both factors, the religious and the economic one, are interrelated and tend to intensify each other: deprivation and scarcity contribute to group-centrism and xenophobia, which in this case is directed at a rival religious group; and the existence of religious anomosity prevents co-operation and contributes to concentration on the own group in matters like distributing jobs or food. The situation in Northern Ireland also shows a clear relationship between economic and religious affairs.

If this suggestion is correct, the aforementioned data strongly demonstrate that hunger and scarcity are important factors in contributing

---

[46] S. Dasgupta, note 40 supra;
H. Feldman – 'The Communal Problem in the Indo-Pakistan Subcontinent: Some Current Implications,' XLIII Pac. Aff. 2 ('69) pp. 145 ff. (He mentions food riots in Ahmedabad (5 deads); Bellary (2 deads); Guntakal (3 deads) all of them in 1964. In 1966 a riot in Andhra cost 17 lifes; it was caused by agitation to support the demand that the fifth steel plant, bringing new employment prospects, be set up at Visakhapatnam); The Times, (Nov. 1 and 3, '66).

to a violence which at first sight seemed to have exclusively other causes.

The variety of bases for political stability suggested in the literature can be summarized as follows:
1. it does for some reason not occur to people to do anything else but obey;
2. people have no power to challenge the status quo;
3. the system gratifies the needs they feel;
4. people believe it right to obey, even if they receive no palpable benefits from their obedience (e.g. in case of democratic majority rule, or a rule accepted as the expression of divine command).

Whereas alternative three explains much of the relative peacefulness in industrialized countries, number two would explain the same for many poor countries – at present. For all reasons given above it seems justified to expect that this basis of obedience will disappear in the near future, and that the only hope of peace lies in the realization of alternative three throughout the world, which implies peace based on global welfare. Poverty in our days is becoming a polemological problem of tremendous importance.

2. Population increase, and surplus population.

A particular factor to be taken into account in this context is the rather explosive population increase in most of the poor countries, which is due to better medical care, understanding of hygienics and better (knowledge of) nutrition.
It is a well-known psychological postulate that people tend to resist when the standards are lowered, be they the social standards or the material standard of living (see item 9). This axiom is generally understood to mean that people will react against an *absolute* decrease in matters like rank (degradation) or status, or against an *absolute* deterioration of the standard of living. However, it may also be understood to mean that people tend not to accept a *relative* deterioration, which is the case for instance when a salary remains the same, but more mouths have to be fed from it.
Although wages and salaries in an absolute sense may have increased to some extent, the sharp increase of the population in the Third World (2.1% per year on an average, compared to 1.3% in the rich countries), if not accompanied by equivalent increases of food production and employment, will cause a factual or relative shrinking of at least the rate of growth in per capita income and in many cases

even a shrinking of the per capita income itself – which implies a deterioration of living conditions.

If economic development continues to remain a dream rather than a reality, and the population explosion rather a reality than a nightmare, many people may be expected to react against such a relative deterioration of their living conditions. Increasing protests against scarcity-prices for food are symptomatic.

Under circumstances of scarcity, population growth results soon in surplus-population, and at present this is indeed what prevails already in most poor countries (see further Chapter III, section 3.3. ff., where the population problem and its consequences are discussed in the light of the report of the Club of Rome and similar studies).

Surplus population has never been a benefit to any society, and it may become a serious danger to peace in itself. Bouthoul even describes it as a fundamental cause of violent conflict and he states that his enquiry showed that 'la cruauté des événements politiques tend a être proportionelle au croît démographique des pays dans lesquelles ils se produissent.'[47]

Many may have objections to such rather cataclysmic theories, but few will negate that surplus population is a danger to the stability of any society, especially to a society characterized by poverty, hunger and unemployment (We will come back to the last factor under heading 7).

Having reached the point of transition to section B (Economic Development), the following closing remark might be appropriate:
According to Martin, chairman of the DAC (Development Assistance Committee of the OECD), at this moment at least one billion people have to live on less than $ 100 a year. Endeavours to improve the situation by initiating programmes for birth control have been of little consequence, so far. This is not very surprising; if people should be induced to change their longstanding behaviour it must first be recognized as useful and profitable by them. In this age many experience their conditions of living as so bad and hopeless, that they are hardly susceptible to constructive programs like birth control. They must be made to understand what they will gain from this, and therefore, in my opinion, the only chance for promoting birth control – i.e. to stop the population-explosion – would lie in a preceding or at least a simultaneous substantial improvement of people's conditions of

---

[47] G. Bouthoul – 'La Surpopulation. L'inflation démographique' ('64) p. 18: 'the cruelty of political events tends to be proportional to the growth of the population in the countries where they occur'; see also P. Ehrlich in The New Scientist (Oct. 2, '69).

living. This has been recognized in several important reports on development assistance, among which the report of President Nixon's Task Force states:

'Family planning assistance is an integral and necessary part of total development assistance and not a substitute for other development assistance...'[47a]

B. *Economic Development*

The relation between peace and economic development has not been emphasized in the discussion of the last few years as much as the relation between peace and poverty; partly perhaps because the growing gap between rich and poor was generally considered the chief danger; partly also perhaps out of fear that too much emphasis on the disturbing corollaries of the development process would strengthen the arguments of those who oppose foreign aid programs.
Whatever the main reason, the result has been a general neglect of the polemological aspects of economic development. This is a pity, because those who fear a negative impact from this discussion on aid programs, seem to realize insufficiently that by neglecting this aspect they might in the long run create more obstacles than they would have by facing the realities: it is one way for the ostrich to bury its head in the sand in order not to see the approaching tornado but it is a far better way to keep its eyes open and try to evade it.

The mistake of exclusively paying attention to the dangers of poverty has not only been made in popular or scientific discussion; it has also been made by governments defending their aid programs, as it has been made in the Charter of the United Nations. There it is said in article 55:

'With a view to *the creation of conditions of stability* and well-being which are necessary for peaceful and friendly relations among nations...... the UN shall promote: higher standards of living, full employment, *and conditions of economic and social progress and development.*'

The reason for being silent about any peace-disturbing effect of the development process itself is obvious in this case: i.e. that one of the supreme goals of the UN, namely economic welfare for all, is not thwarted.
Similar neglect has been and is prevalent in the defence of national

---

[47a] see Ch. II, note 293.

aid programs, in particular of those at the time when the Cold War was at its height. Taking the United States as the most important donor, it would be possible to fill books with statements indicating this point. Generally, it can be said that these programs were (and are) based on two political presuppositions:

1. Poverty is fertile soil for communism;
2. Economic aid will make possible peaceful evolution instead of violent revolution.

President Kennedy stated in his foreign aid message to Congress in 1961:

'The 1960's can be – and must be – the crucial 'decade of *development*' – the period in which an enlarged community of *free*, *stable* and self-relient nations can reduce world tensions and insecurity.'[48]

The same kind of thinking is again in fact expressed in those famous words of the late President:

'Those who make peaceful revolution impossible will make violent revolution inevitable.'

Equally former Foreign Secretary Rusk can be quoted, speaking to the House Committee on Foreign Affairs in 1963:

'The economic aid provided by the US and its allies makes it possible to prevent conditions of stagnation and hopeless poverty from leading to political unrest and the growth of communism'; on the other hand 'as each new or newly awakened independent nation emerges into the modern world – *as it moves forward economically and socially and achieves political stability* – it adds to the strength of the community of free nations.'[49]

Finally, we have Defence Secretary MacNamara stating:

'as development progresses, security progresses' and 'our economic assistance is designed to offer a reasonable alternative to (that) violence.'[50]

From such statements it becomes clear that *economic development is considered the medium which substitutes stability for instability, peace for violence, evolution for revolution.* None of them contains any reference to the fact that development itself may lead to social unrest, if not to violence.

This kind of 'either-or'-thinking appears also in Resolutions of the OAS and statements on the Alliance for Progress. For instance, Resolution 1 of the OAS Punta del Este-Conference (1962) states that the struggle against communism and violent revolution can be fought

[48] H. Doc. 117, 87th Comp., 1st Sess., p. 20 (my italics).
[49] Dept. State Bull. (April 29, '63) p. 666.
[50] see Survival (July '66) p. 214.

by stimulating socio-economic development;[51] and the Alliance for Progress is based on the idea that improvement of education and welfare will lead to social content and thus to political stability. It may be characteristic of this way of thinking that on separate occasions both the President and the Secretary of State have compared the Alliance for Progress to the New Deal, obviously overlooking the crucial difference that the New Deal pursued social and economic reforms within the context of existing political institutions, and in a society already highly integrated and fully industrialized.[52]

When it can be concluded that aid leads to stability and peace, without making an enquiry into the correctness of such a bold assumption, the reaction to any adverse development is (and I think we can witness that today) frustration on the side of the donor, contributing to an aversion to any aid at all. Therefore, before starting any aid program one should try to understand and be conscious of the potential negative developments, enabling one to prevent or correct them as much as possible.

In this sense the late Senator Robert Kennedy was somewhat closer to the problem – although he also remained very optimistic – when he said after a visit to Latin America:

'The Latin American peoples do not accept any more poverty, illiteracy and injustice. Revolution is inevitable, but intelligent US policy can keep it in peaceful channels.'[53]

Now we shall turn to polemological aspects of the development process.

3. *Literacy, education and communication*

Under item 1 consciousness was discussed as being one of the factors to be kept in mind. In that item it was emphasized that consciousness of relative deprivation could be enhanced by literacy and communication. Under this heading we go further into the subject of literacy, education and communication, as some of the first goals and results of development to be expected.

There can hardly be a process of development without communication between those who want to develop and those who show how

---

[51] Resolution 1 ('Communist Offense In America'), Punta del Este, Jan. 13, 1962; for the text see 56 A.J.I.L. ('62) pp. 604-605.
[52] see E. Kenworthy – 'Argentina: The Politics of Industrialization,' 45 For. Aff. (Oct. '66) p. 465.
[53] N.Y.T. (May 10, '66) p. 3.

to do it. Written material is one of the means of communication: newspapers, instruction books, information pamphlets etc. It has often been stated that development is impossible without reducing illiteracy in the Third World. Literacy indeed is one of the crucial conditions of development. This insight makes UNESCO one of the basic organizations contributing in the early stages of economic development. The same holds true, of course, for general and specialized education.

In this field it can be stated that the relation between literacy/education and peace has often been stressed, whereas the eventual relation between these factors and unrest has just as often been neglected. Resolution XII of Teheran calls on 'the United Nations and its specialized agencies, especially UNESCO, to do their utmost to stimulate efforts for enhancing the contribution which literacy can make in the contemporary world to the safeguarding of peace.'[54]
The same positive relation is suggested in the literature by authors like Duff and McCamant, where they conclude:

> 'A government that spends a large proportion of its budget on education for the general population, develops long-range support of the society, while investing in human resources, which is probably the best way to promote sustained economic development.'[55]

There is reason to doubt, especially during the initial stages of development, whether literacy and education will have this positive influence. One might even wonder whether it will at all have a positive influence as its principal effect. Lerner compares the relative instability of Egypt with that of Turkey by stating that Egypt is only half as literate as Turkey. He then places this conclusion in the context of over-all development, according to which Egypt is twice as urbanized but only half as literate as Turkey. 'Imbalances' are created which 'tend to become circular and to accelerate social disorganization,' including political as well as economic disorganization.[56] This illuminates an obviously crucial deliberation: if literacy and education are accompanied by developments on other levels there is bound to be a positive change; if they *precede* economic and social development, however, the situation is quite different. Literacy not only enables former illiterates to read what a certain government or organization wants them to read, and it not only makes it possible for them to read about technical or agricultural things; literacy and education, and conse-

---

[54] UN Publ. A/Conf. 32/41 ('69) p. 13.
[55] E. A. Duff & J. F. Mc. Camant – 'Measuring Social and Political Requirements for System Stability in Latin America,' LXII Am. Pol. Sc. Rev. ('68) p. 1128.
[56] D. Lerner – 'The Passing of Traditional Society' ('58) pp. 87-89.

quently communication, also enable people to escape from thinking in local terms, change traditional behavioral patterns, and broaden the general horizon. These three, education, literacy, and communication, also stimulate people to think more about society, the world, and their own place therein. Therefore these factors, as first results of the development process, may very well become destabilizing factors of the first degree.

Since World War II the process of 'empathy' – the psychic mechanism that enables a person to put himself in another's situation and thus nourish the hope of upward mobility – has been accelerated in the young countries by mass media and the ability to read. The unprecedented spread of communication, made possible by literacy and different forms of education, has created and strengthened new images. Thus, literacy and education by themselves may set into motion the process of change now irreversibly under way, and arouse unprecedented expectations. Such expectations are continuously further fuelled by newspapers, radio, television. Because of these media the knowledge of UNCTAD Conferences, Technical Assistance operations and the increasing awareness of Human Rights is awakened. In general, this is what psychologists mean when they speak of 'the extension of the frame of reference.' The aspirations awakened by education and communication tend to set, indeed, impossible standards of performance for the leaders of the developing countries, as these standards become too soon based upon the achievements of the technologically advanced countries. Moreover, the increasing gap between the rich and the poor nations in a world which has become 'like a fishbowl' (O'Connell), or a 'global village' (McLuhan), tends to exacerbate impatience even further. The result is bound to end in a large-scale frustration.

It is not very surprising, then, to notice that several authors consider education not so much a stabilizing as a potentially *destabilizing* factor under present circumstances. Among these are Millikan, Rostow, Bloomfield,[57] and Lerner. The writer last mentioned explicitly denies the necessity of any attendant material improvement for people to become mobilized:

> 'Political mobilization does not necessarily require movement to the cities. Increases in communications, which can stimulate increases in aspirations, may be sufficient for the revolution of rising frustrations.'[58]

---

[57] compare Millikan & Rostow, p. 24; L. P. Bloomfield in XII Orbis 3 (Fall '68) p. 671.
[58] D. Lerner – 'Toward a Communication Theory of Modernization,' in L. Pye (ed.) – 'Communications and Political Development' ('63).

In relation to communication in general de Schweinitz speaks of the 'demonstration-effect': people's aspirations are roused in particular when they see the results of development in their direct environment. This way of communication has a very strong effect, even if people would have no share at all in the progress they see.[59]

In this connection Goodsell's study of Mexico is very interesting and illuminating. He places recent riots, and in particular the students' revolt, in the framework of Mexico's economic development. Despite the good record that successive Mexican governments have racked up in terms of economic growth and social justice in the past 25 years, the stern fact remains that probably half of Mexico's 45 million people have shared little or not at all in this process. They are the farmers of the countryside – all of whom eke out a rather miserable existence and provide a sharp contrast to the growing middle class in the towns and cities. While these poverty-stricken groups have shown only limited indications of restlessness in former times, occasional and increasing incidents have occurred during the past several years. The students' unrest in 1968 is being taken by some observers as a warning of what may be in store for Mexico. It seems important to note that Mexico has witnessed an impressive social revolution, and is one of the most 'democratic' countries in the American hemisphere. People there are more conscious than in many other developing countries, and the 'demonstration-effect' of development may have particularly strong consequences in this country. Therefore, many warn that if Mexico cannot keep up the revolution begun in 1910, and, above all, if it cannot carry progress into areas hitherto untouched by this revolution, the break-up of a longstanding political consensus lies in store.[60]

In this sense Lewis, one of the recognized experts, concludes:

'Indeed, the political stability of Mexico is grim testimony to the great capacity for misery and suffering of the ordinary Mexican. But even the Mexican capacity for suffering has its limits, and unless ways are found to achieve a more equitable distribution of the growing national wealth, and a greater equality of sacrifice during the difficult period of industrialization, we may expect political upheavals sooner or later.'[61]

Althoff too thinks that the demonstration-effect has severe consequences. Through literacy and mass communications it becomes gradually more and more impossible, he says, 'to keep any socially, economically and politically suppressed group, no matter how conservative culturally and unaware politically, in a state of ignorance very long.' Althoff

---

[59] K. de Schweinitz, jr. – 'Industrialization and Democracy' ('64) p. 68.
[60] J. N. Goodsell – 'Mexico: Why the Students Rioted,' 56 Curr. Hist. (Jan. '69) pp. 31 ff.
[61] O. Lewis – 'The Children of Sanchez' ('60) pp. XXX-XXXI.

introduces a 'political demonstration-effect' of events elsewhere in the world, and says:

> 'The political élite of Latin America cannot keep the workers and peasants they suppress ignorant of events in, for example, Canada, the USSR, China, or Cuba; and with this knowledge eventually comes awareness, albeit a very limited one, of what state power can do and the methods by which state power can be influenced or perhaps even gained. Proper leadership can turn this limited awareness into discontent with the established political system and build a new awareness of the potential political power of the masses upon this discontent.'[62]

It might be considered a proof of the potential correctness of Althoff's view to note that Kerala, one of India's states with the highest literacy rates, was the first one to elect a communist government.[63]

On another level there is the serious problem of the so-called 'newly educated.'

The importance of discussing this group in this connection may become clear from recent history: the Colonial Powers gave a Western education to many intelligent natives. They used them in the administration, but later on refused them a fully equal position. The newly educated élite who were promised everything, and aspired to much, got little in return. This frustrating process is seen by Malinowski as causal to the growing fervent nationalism and racial sentiments of the later national élite in former colonies.[64]

Today the same process can be witnessed again in a different context. The modern intellectual and in general the newly educated groups of the young states are unanimously in favour of economic progress. They are ambitious in a dual sense – on the one hand they are eager to to see dramatic accomplishments and want to see their country highly developed as soon as possible; on the other hand they are personally ambitious to see that energy which was put into their studies honoured by better jobs and a higher standard of living. When they finish their studies they have developed strong hopes of being succesful and reaching the first as well as the second goal. They have learned to hope for an ever rising sun, and then suddenly they find themselves standing in the rain: they find a population unable or unwilling to work towards their goals with the same spirit; they find enormous obstacles created by social and cultural traditions; they come to

---

[62] Ph. Althoff – 'The Latin American Common Man: Political Integration or Civil War,' XXIV Int. J. 3 ('69) pp. 489-490.
[63] compare K. Deutsch – 'Social Mobilization and Political Development,' LV Am. Pol. Sc. Rev. ('61) p. 496; Millikan & Rostow, p. 20.
[64] B. Malinowski – 'Die Dynamik des Kulturwandels' ('51) pp. 301 ff.

realize that the resources are too limited and the problems too complex. In addition there is the pressure from their own circle, from public opinion, from intellectuals and students, all of which increases their resentment and impatience. Finally frustration kills their hopes.

The same happens to many on the micro-level. Having finished their study, the newly educated feel that they have a right to an adequate job. Their hopes have risen during their study, when they came to realize that they could do something, that they knew something, that they were somebody. But then, the job is not there – either because there are not enough places, or because their field of study proves to be irrelevant to the most pressing needs of their country. This happens to be the case because, on the one hand, it is practically impossible to synchronize educational expansion with economic growth – skills being ideally taught within a system that keeps a little ahead of the needs of the economy so as to stimulate growth and meet its advance – and because, on the other hand, too many young persons are sent into the labour market with irrelevant skills, often leaving the market short of badly needed technicians in many specific fields.

Education is the largest industry in many African countries, and it is also the most important cause of rural depopulation and urban unemployment.[65] The seriousness of the situation becomes clear from the figure that in one Asian country alone, half a million high school and college graduates – fully 10% of the total – are out of work, whereas many others who did find a job are underemployed.[66] In South Korea or Burma the number of educated people rapidly exceeds the number of adequate jobs and one speaks of the 'reserve army of educated unemployed'.[67]

Similarly, many young people from North East Thailand who left their countryside with high aspirations saw that their roads were blocked.[68]

There is a growing number of young ambitious people who were encouraged by their studies to hope for better standards for their country and themselves, only to find out later that much remained the same. But these people are generally well-educated and militant, and may have the capacities of political leaders. Once they realize the danger

[65] J. O'Connell – 'The Inevitability of Instability,' 5 J. Mod. Afr. St. 2 ('67) p. 185.
[66] see Mac. Namara's address as the President of the World Bank (Sept. 29, '69) p. 8. It is not revealed to which countries the figures relate.
[67] Mya Maung – 'Cultural Value and Economic Change in Burma,' IV Asian Survey ('64) p. 761.
[68] A. Th. Kirsch – 'Development and Mobility among the Phu Thai of Northeast Thailand,' VI Asian Survey ('66) pp. 370-378.

of falling back into the misery of the masses of under- and unemployed, they may become the organizers of revolt. Such considerations make Huntington's remark valid, when he says:

> 'political participation by illiterates is more likely to remain limited, whereas participation by literates is much more likely to snowball with potentially disastrous effects on political stability.[69]

4. *Improvement of diet*

On this point we can be short, since it is very obvious.
Inquiries made into the relation between nutrition and productivity have shown a positive correlation. F.A.O.-reports ascertain that lack of sufficient protein is a better explanation of the often low productivity of workers in poor countries than their supposed laziness.
Better nutrition as being one of the primary goals of economic development results in a more active human environment. It is one of the factors which helps to diminish apathy. For this reason it is a factor worth mentioning in this connection, as it has been done by Millikan and Rostow, when they write:

> 'awareness combined with the stimulating effects of better nutrition (are) likely to release psychological and political pressures for change which may find expression in revolt.'

MacNamara, in his new capacity of President of the World Bank, spoke to the Board of Governors on Sept. 29, 1968, on this subject. He called protein deficiency a hidden hunger which draws away alertness and energy and leads to lethargy and ineffectiveness.

'Underdeveloped areas of the world,' he said, 'have often been unfairly accused of being peopled with indolent, ambitionless citizens who fail to respond to challenges of improving their own and their nation's lot. But it is becoming clear that caloric and protein deficiencies result in masses of undernourished people who cannot physically and mentally function as alert, energetic and productive citizens.'
It seems quite clear that diet improvement is one of the factors which can activate hitherto passive people.

5.1. *Positive material experience*

Under heading 1 the argument was discussed that social consciousness in itself may be enough to arouse people.

[69] S. P. Huntington, p. 420.

In section 3 the hypothesis was discussed, according to which education and communication – greater knowledge in general – may be considered to intensify people's aspirations. In particular the 'demonstration-effect' was considered of great importance: more and more people see the obvious manifestations of economic development in their direct environment – new factories, roads, fancy cars, hotels, municipal institutions – without directly benefiting from these themselves. Such manifestations of growth may be expected to aggravate an already existent sense of deprivation.
This demonstration effect could be called 'positive psychological experience,' – which, if it results in unfulfilled expectations, may have negative consequences of course – in contrast to the situation in which people themselves profit directly from some development process, in which case we could speak of 'positive material experience.'

Some theories have been presented, according to which consciousness and communication are not considered the crucial factors in activating deprived people. It is necessary for people to directly experience material improvement in order for them to understand the better life they seek and long for. Sometimes this claim is softened by the fact that consciousness and knowledge may be enough to arouse people, but that some practical experience usually functions as an important accelerator.
Stone, for instance, states that the psychological factor (expectation) is crucial and more important than the material factor (economic growth or not), but he recognizes the importance of the last one.[70] Whichever factor may be the most important one, the relevance of both of them seems beyond doubt; in any case the correctness of the one would not exclude the correctness of the other.

Having discussed the relevance of the psychological factor before, we can go into the material one now. The argument here is as follows:
When people have come to believe in a better future because they have got the real taste of it, they may feel shocked, since at that moment they experience the reality of their position in the full sense. As Heilbroner says, 'As change begins to manifest itself, as the ideas of development trickle down from leaders to followers, a terrible change begins to take place: the underdog awakes to his lowly position.'[71]
Once the underdog has tasted a better way of living, he suddenly

---

[70] L. Stone – 'Theories of Revolution,' XVIII World Politics' ('65-'66) p. 173.
[71] R. L. Heilbroner – 'The Great Ascent' ('63) p. 130.

wants to shake off all remnants of his former status and this brings about the real revolution of *rising* expectations. That is why the most likely protagonists of revolution, according to Morgenthau, are 'those groups that have begun to rise in the social and economic scale and have not enough to satisfy their aroused expectations.'[72]

Therefore, in the words of Bloomfield, 'the inherently hopeful situations characterized by national independence, aid programs, growing school populations and concerned citizens, may well be the ones likely to generate violence in the period ahead.'[73]

The theory is supported by several analytical studies among which a prominent place is taken by Crane Brinton. He studied the four important revolutions against the old regimes in the United States, England, France and Russia, and found that one of the most important uniformities was that these were all societies on the whole on the upgrade economically before the revolution came, and the revolutionary movements seem to originate in the discontents of not unprosperous people who feel restraint, cramp, emergence, rather than downright crushing oppression.[74] His findings led him to say:

'There is some indication that by the twentieth century one can risk the generalization: the more prosperous the peasants, the more discontented'.

Likewise Horowitz can be mentioned here, writing:

'It is after an initial economic spurt that revolutionary sentiments are crystallized and mobilized. The condition of the factory proletariat in Russia was worse in the opening years of World War I; by 1917 it was improving. The condition of the American tradesmen was superior in 1775 to that of 1773 or 1774. King George had agreed to rescind much of the oppressive taxation legislation when the colonists assumed insurrectionary measures. What this means is that if development is encouraged successfully, a revolution may not be avoided or even delayed! Quite the contrary, development often makes the chances of revolution higher.'[75]

The same opinion is also held by Gerschenkron,[76] and Benham, in connection with India, writes:

---

[72] H. Morgenthau – 'A Political Theory of Foreign Aid,' LVI Am. Pol. Sc. Rev. ('62) p. 306.
[73] L. P. Bloomfield – 'Future Small Wars: Must the US intervene?,' XII Orbis 3 (Fall '68) p. 671.
[74] C. Brinton – 'The Anatomy of Revolution' (Vintage Books, '56) p. 264.
[75] J. L. Horowitz – 'Three Worlds of Development' ('66) p. 309.
[76] A. Gerschenkron – 'Reflections on Economic Aspects of Revolution,' in H. Eckstein (ed) – 'Internal War. Problems and Approaches' ('64) pp. 196-197.
[77] F. Benham – 'Economic Aid to Underdeveloped Countries' ('62) pp. 89-90.

'It is not true that poverty breeds Communism ... India made some economic progress from 1952 to 1957, and the Communist vote grew from 4 million to 12 million. If any generalization on this subject is valid, it is that in a poor country the growth of education and industrialization is likely to lead to discontent and a search for ways of speeding up economic growth.'[77]

Midlarsky and Tanter point to Latin America, where they conclude that 'Cuba and Venezuela were enjoying a relatively high level of prosperity before the rise of Castro in Cuba and the outbreak of guerilla warfare in Venezuela.'[78]
More examples supporting the correctness of this theory could of course be given. Thus one could think of the rural violence in Columbia, which became very serious at a moment when the main source of income, the coffee price, had become higher: in 1945 it was 15.9 cents per pound, in 1947 30.1 cents; in 1949 37.4 and in 1951 even 58.7 cents a pound. Equally one might think of the negroes in the United States who started to fight against their unequal position, after a middle class had formed among them, which saw the road to *further* emancipation blocked.[79]

On the political level an analogous mechanism has been found, for instance by de Tocqueville, who observed already in his days:

'... l'experience apprend que le moment le plus dangereux pour un mauvais gouvernement est d'ordinaire celui òu il commence à se reformer,' because '... le mal est devenu moindre, il est vrai, mais la sensibilité est plus vive.'[80]

The same conclusion is reached by Coleman, who mentions as examples the great French Revolution, the Revolution of 1848 (after the impopular Guizot-government had fallen) and the Hungarian revolt of 1956 (after the surviving victims of extreme tyranny had been released). Generalizing on despotism he states that (despotic) governments are often overthrown, not when they are being most tyrannical, but rather when the established élite loses its self-confidence and starts making halfhearted attempts to become more liberal (which clearly illustrates the same kind of argument).[81]

Yet, with all that follows under later headings in mind, the present author is inclined to add a condition to the validity of this theory: many examples prove that deprived people may react very peacefully

---

[78] M. Midlarsky & R. Tanter, p. 211.
[79] Fenna v. d. Burg – 'Armoede en Geweld,' Nesbic Bull. (Dec. '67) p. 260.
[80] A. de Tocqueville – 'L'Ancien Régime et la Revolution,' oeuvres complètes (ed. I. P. Mayer) II, Gallimard, 7e ed., vol. I ('52) p. 223.
[81] J. S. Coleman – 'Political Aspects of Modernization,' Int. Enc. Soc. Sc. 10 ('68) pp. 501-502.

to positive experience; namely, when the improvement is perceived as substantial (a), and when it holds the promise of continuity (b). On the other hand, if people experience improvement without feeling trust that these conditions are satisfied, they tend to seize such insufficient improvement as a factor intensifying their aspirations.

Once there is a small hole in the dam, the pressure of the running water will make it bigger, until the dam breaks. Once a small hole is made, one should build at the same time the channels through which the water can be led; if this is not done, the water will ruin the country. Once the changing process has started, it must go on continuously and uninterruptedly – and not (as is the case at present) by leaps and bounds.

Latin America, at the time of the World Wars, is a clear example in this connection: these were the most peaceful periods that continent witnessed during this century. The explanation is clear – the economies in that part of the world experienced such a boom, that for a short period people's rising aspirations were met by equivalent material improvement. As soon as political and war developments brought this expansive market to an end, Latin America returned to a period of high instability.

All that has been said under this heading suggests that only those developing systems that derive their stability from their intrinsic capacity to generate and absorb *both* substantial *and* continuing improvement, will have a chance.

5.2. *Rate of growth: too slow*

The present section is closely related to the previous one. Under the former heading it was suggested that some shock effects may occur resulting from an initial improvement of conditions. This indicates the importance of the *continuation* of the improving process. Here it is added that even if development is continuous and uninterrupted, people may become intolerant when the process is too slow – then, the *rising expectations* far exceed the rising satisfactions. For 'if the pace of economic development fails to match the aspirations of the increasing population of the underdeveloped, social and political unrest will grow.'[82] This is exactly what may be expected to happen because of several reasons, of which a few important ones are mentioned here:

In the first place, most developing countries lack many badly needed resources, they equally lack skilled labour, and are in want of many

[82] J. S. Berliner – 'Soviet Economic Aid' ('58) p. 26.

other assets in practically every sector of the economy. There is, moreover, a natural limit in all the resources from the country itself and from abroad. For this reason it seems only logical to expect, during the first phase of development, some slowness.

In the second place, during the early phase one has to take into account the great deal of apathy amoung those groups which are not yet conscious and convinced of their possibilities.[83] This apathy acts as a brake on the programs of those who urge and work for substantial change. The resulting stagnation may lead to frustration among the roused in the beginning stages.

An illuminating example – be it a contrario – in this connection, is Mali. This country is one of the few developing societies, where most of the inhabitants were accustomed to political organization (on the local level) before independence. This enabled the government, by using and transforming existing organizational patterns, to introduce agricultural reform programs to people who were used to accepting and applying directives aimed at improvement of the common welfare.[84] A situation like this, however, is absent in many other developing countries.

In the third place, there is the problem of incompetent governments (see section 13). The initial phase of development, in particular, is usually marked by large scale corruption, which is clearly detrimental. The study made by Wraith and Simpkins reveals a causal connection between the level of economic development and corruption. They present a long list of examples, of the most incredible corruption in former British colonies in W. Africa, which they believe to be applicable to any other region. They also compare this list with pre-industrial Britain itself – today known for its high standard of probity in government! They conclude that 'the first thing that emerges from examination of bribary and corruption in eighteenth and nineteenth century Britain is that little that happens today in Asia or Africa could be worse.'[85]

So, again, it would seem that – like laziness – it may not be so much an ethnical feature that causes corruption, as it is a socio-economic situation found in a certain phase of development. This finding is supported by Leys who found that corruption correlated to a high inequality in the distribution of wealth. The existence of considerable absolute poverty, the function of political office as the primary means

---

[83] see pp. 57ff.
[84] N. S. Hopkins – 'Socialism and Social Change in Rural Mali,' 7 J. Mod. Afr. St. 3 ('69) pp. 457ff.
[85] R. Wraith & E. Simpkins – 'Corruption in Developing Countries' ('64) p. 173.

of gaining access to wealth, conflict between changing moral codes, weakness of social and governmental enforcement mechanisms and the absence of a strong sense of national unity[86] – these are alle circumstances which prevail during the initial phase of economic development.

Such factors – among many others – limit the needed rapidity with which economic development can increase national wealth and well-being, and justify some fear that under present conditions the process of rising expectations is likely to transcend into a process of rising frustrations.

It is important to remember in this connection that the beginning of a development process tends to activate the hitherto deprived, and to stimulate their organization. Under such conditions an increased feeling of some class consciousness and power will intensify aspirations; and, if stagnation occurs, will intensify feelings of frustration. This is the crucial political problem in the very beginning of economic development: the hitherto underdogs have reached a state when they can organize an opposition against the hitherto well-to-do.

A sustained and substantial economic growth is necessary in order to keep public welfare ahead of social mobilization. In view of this dictum Fenwick has written that the task for the US in Latin America is 'to make justice move fast enough to anticipate revolution.'[87]

A similar opinion is held by Millikan and Rostow, and is reflected also in the Report of the 'Presidential Task Force on International Development,' an advisory committee to President Nixon on the question of foreign aid:

> 'Development can help make political and social change more orderly. There is at least a good prospect that more rapid development could facilitate more constructive social experiments, more open political procedures and less disruptive international behavior.'[88]

There is, moreover, an additional – though quite different – polemological aspect of mass organization during the early stages of development. Myrdal has seen this aspect in connection with India. He called attention to the fact that such newly activated groups tend to function rather blindly, and may become centres of action without

---

[86] C. Leys – 'What is the Problem about Corruption?,' 3 J. Mod. Afr. St. ('65) pp. 224-225; see also K. T. Young, jr. – 'New Politics in New States,' 39 For. Aff. (April '61) p. 498: 'Corruption and nepotism rot good intentions and retard progressive policies.'
[87] Ch. G. Fenwick – 'The Dominican Republic: Intervention or Collective Selfdefence?,' 60 A.J.I.L. ('66) p. 67.
[88] 'US foreign assistance in the 1970's: a new approach,' Report to the President of the US from the Task Force on International Development (March '70).

being able to benefit their members.[89] It would seem that a situation characterized by initial improvement and successive stagnation on the one hand, and by functioning but ineffective organization on the other hand, is particularly delicate.

5.3. *Rate of growth: too rapid and uneven*

When the pace of development is considerably slackened, discontent and unrest may be the results. A minimum pace therefore is a necessity. Too much pace on the other hand can become as destabilizing a force as too little.

This is one of the conclusions of the Feierabend's study, which found that the higher the rate of change, the greater the increase in political instability.[90] The correlation between rapid economic growth and instability was also considered valid (for India) by Hoselitz and Weiner.[91]

The same correlation is suggested by Huntington, who finds it 'hardly accidental that in the 1870's and 1880's a high rate of American economic development coincided with a low point in American governmental integrity.'[92]

The apparent contradiction between the theory presented under this heading and the one discussed under the previous heading might be explained by reference to the special circumstances prevailing in poor countries:

in a situation characterized by lack of resources on many levels it seems nearly impossible to achieve both rapid and over-all growth; this means that rapid growth in one sector of economy will almost certainly not be accompanied by equivalent growth on many other levels (economical and social ones). Thus, rapid growth is often bound to lead to unequal growth. While rapid growth by itself would seem to have positive results, the fact that it entails unequality on different economic and social levels may well explain its negative results in several Third World countries.

Olson holds two separate groups responsible for destabilization during a process of rapid economic growth: on the one hand the 'new rich,' the new middle class which rises like a star in the economical field, but gets disoriented socially and frustrated politically; on the other

[89] G. Myrdal – 'The Challenge of World Poverty. A World Anti-Poverty Program in Outline' ('70) pp. 425-426.
[90] Feierabend & Feierabend, p. 265.
[91] B. F. Hoselitz & M. Weiner – 'Economic Development and Political Stability in India,' VIII Dissent (Spring '61) pp. 172-179.
[92] S. P. Huntington, p. 407.

hand the 'new poor', the mobilized workers who expect too much, but become the first victims of the resulting inflation tendencies, and also become socially disoriented.[93]

The noticed phenomenon of imbalance implies a social mechanism of importance to the present context. This mechanism Johnson has called 'the process of dysfunction', defining it as 'recognition of a lack of harmony among economic, social and political system.'[94] When somebody climbs the economic ladder, but is not allowed to climb the social and political ladder as well, his new position is qualified as dysfunctional.

Johan Galtung used this mechanism as the pivot of his 'structural theory of agression.'

According to him, aggression is the result of internal imbalance within a social structure, prevailing when an actor ranks high in one social dimension but ranks low in another. Neither the topdog, nor the underdog is going to be aggressive. It is the middledog who is going to react. It is he who rises in some aspects but remains on the bottom in other aspects; he will try to level his position to a corresponding degree in other dimensions.[95] In projecting this theory on the Third World one may think in the first place of the 'new poor,' the majority of which, as Nazeer shows, consists of the younger people.[96] As soon as a promising development process starts (in the form of new factories, the construction of roads, the building of dams etc.), they tend to leave the overcrowded countryside 'en masse,' and settle in the emerging cities where jobs are plentiful. But then, they find that mere jobs are only part of the improvement they seek. They are confronted with the fact that more money to spend results in scarcity prices, because it is mostly impossible for the government to invest simultaneously in several equally crucial sectors of the economy; now that they have a little more money, the 'new poor' may still remain hungry, because the national agricultural output is not sufficient and import capacity is restricted. In stead of the

---

[93] M. Olson – 'Rapid Growth as a Destabilizing Force,' XXIII J. Econ. Hist. (Dec. '63) pp. 529 ff.

[94] Ch. Johnson – 'Revolution and the Social System' (Hoover Inst. Studies, '64).

[95] J. Galtung – 'A Structural Theory of Aggression,' J. Peace Res. 2 ('64) pp. 95-119. An addition to this theory may be suggested to the fact that it does not necessarily have to be that an actor actually ranks higher on one dimension than on another. The underdog, who is convinced that he has a definite *right* to rank high on one dimension, may by that conviction alone be stimulated to try to raise his rank on other dimensions. This could explain the fact that in some poor countries specific segments of the underdog-population, being convinced that they have an absolute *right to equal economic conditions*, try to reach a better political position.

[96] M. M. Nazeer – 'Urban Growth in Pakistan,' VI Asian Survey ('66) pp. 317-318.

expected better life, they find lack of governmental services; in general they come to realize that the promising fast industrial development is miles ahead of improvement in other sectors of development. One could speak here of 'intra-economic dysfunction.' Even though the 'new poor' are part of a rapidly expanding economy, they gain little. This shock could account for much of the discontent and civil strife which take place under circumstances of too rapid growth.

Imbalance may occur on other than economic levels, as the Ecosoc's Committee on Programme Appraisals states in one of its reports:

> 'one of the greatest dangers in development policy lies in the tendency to give mere material aspects of growth an overriding and disproportionate emphasis. The end may be forgotten in preoccupation with the means: Human rights may be submerged, and human beings seen only as instruments of production rather than as free entities for whose welfare and cultural advance the increased production is intended.'[97]

In the second place one can think of the newcomers to modern economic life, the 'new rich.' They climb fast along the economic dimension as entrepreneurs, merchants, dealers, big shopkeepers, etc., and become the new economic middle and upper class. These people, profiting from the rapid growth of industry, business, and employment, see their lucky star rising rapidly. At the same time, however, they will find in many countries a strong traditional élite opposing the corresponding rising of their social and political star. Thus, such new groups may become socially disoriented and politically frustrated.[98]

This may happen also to many of those newly educated people, who do happen to find adequate jobs. Having seen fulfilled their high expectation on the basis of their studies, and thus strengthened anew in their aspirations toward similar social and political status, they will often find heavy obstacles when entering the ruling circles.

A fourth group of importance in the present theory is formed by the military officers. In this connection there is an interesting theory of Kling concerning the military in Latin America. Concerning the question why there are so many palace-revolutions in this part of the world (31 between 1945 and 1955) he answers:

1. Ownership of the principal economic resources (agricultural as well as mineral) is concentrated in the hands of a tiny, very stable, wealthy élite;
2. The institutionalized opposition-groups, who are able to attack the élite's position, do not exist;

---

[97] UN Sales no. 60 IV 14, E/3347/Rev. 1 para. 90.
[98] M. Olson, note 93 supra.

3. For the sons of people who do not belong to the traditional élite the main road to gaining social and political rank leads via the Army, which in turn is able to capture the governmental machine. Having reached the top they enter into a coalition with that élite. They remain in their posts (as long as they do not interfere with vested interests) until they are overthrown by the next group with the same aspirations.[99]

Whatever the importance may be of other factors which may have to be taken into consideration in explaining the many Latin American coups, this aspect deserves attention.

Dysfunction is considered by Barbara Ward to be one of the disturbing factors during the 1929-crisis. She writes:

> 'The economic picture was patchy, with bits of development here and bits of development there, while social changes went forward in one sector and were quite absent in others. Young people had the feeling to belong to a dyscontinuous society.'[100]

Thus it may be suggested that inequality of rank in different social respects may lead to a disturbance, caused by those who are neither the top- nor the underdogs. In particular *rapid* economic growth, leading to the satisfaction of material demands, but (as must be expected in much of the Third World as it stands today) unaccompanied by equal satisfaction on other economic levels or on the social and political level, leads to social frustration among several groups.

Johnson concludes that the more rapid and profound the change, the stronger the dysfunction which results in a conflict situation.[101]

Opposition against rapid growth, coming from traditional élite-groups who see their positions endangered, will be discussed under heading 12.

Generally speaking, it is quite doubtful whether unorganized societies like most of the new countries would be able to endure the earthquake launched by rapid economic development.

6. *Modernization: Social disruption, alienation and urbanization*

Under conditions of rapid development in particular, modernization tends to disrupt and alienate the traditional social patterns. The additional amount of communication and education (purely psychological stimuli) may be enough to provoke disturbing social processes; for example conflict, unequal distribution of power, and

[99] M. Kling – 'Toward a Theory of Power and Political Instability in Latin America,' IX W. Pol. Q. ('56).
[100] Barbara Ward – 'The Rich Nations and the Poor Nations' ('62) p. 116.
[101] see note 94 supra.

caste interaction have all shifted with the decline of village cohesion in India. Wherever the movement toward social cohesion in the larger units of region and nation has had some success, the impact on the traditional social patterns is already felt.[102] Such processes happen to occur in particular, however, during a period of unprecedented industrialization and urbanization.

The social influence of modernization will be felt primarily in the ranks of the younger generation. A process of comparison will take place, directed both at the economic situation of their own country, and at its traditional social structure. When thoughts of modernization grip the minds of the younger population, a conflict between generations is likely to occur. At such times the traditional authority patterns are bound to be uprooted. The same may be expected from women living in paternalistic countries, who at a certain stage of modernization will break away from existing paternalistic patterns.
One should remember that the social shifts are bound to occur very suddenly and not, as in the case of many industrialized countries, as a gradual development.

The resulting situation, in which groups or entire populations have to re-orient themselves as far as social roles are concerned, may lead to psychological disturbances. Behrendt compares this state of affairs to the adolescence of the individual young man, who has to disengage himself from old securities and has to search unsteadily for new ones. During this period he is very receptive to rebellious feelings.[103] For many this re-orientation comes not as the culmination of a long process of social evolution but it comes in disconnected stages. People then are not prepared for a situation in which old securities, cultural ties, religious traditions and social patterns are broken. Social fermentation is bound to be the result; the more so when traditional ruling groups resist the re-orientation. People may either be stimulated to completely shake off all remnants of the old times in their search for new securities, or, they may return to old habits – which frustrates their courageous compatriots – because of fear. In these situations, violence may be the outcome.
The transition to modernization on the one hand and the loss of security on the other hand, apparently played an important role during the rural violence in Columbia, between 1946 and 1953. Columbia has an exceptionally strong political tradition. When the spirit of modernization descended upon the country, both parties – the Liberals and

[102] H. Orenstein – 'Gaon: Conflict and Cohesion in a Maharashtrian Village' ('64).
[103] R. F. Behrendt, p. 261.

the Conservatives – approached the peasants with symbols appropriate in attracting them: the Liberals condemned the Church and advocated a better life by way of modernization; the Conservatives – recognizing the fear of a sudden social revolution – warned the people against faulty new ideas and stuck to the old customs, old habits and religion. What then happened is very important in the present case: on the one hand, those used to following the Liberal Party thought the time had come to shake off the old social yoke, by violence if necessary; on the other hand, there were those frightened by the idea of building up new structures and of losing (even the bad) securities they had before. Caught by this fear, many poor peasants stuck to the Conservatisve and fought against their compatriots – and in fact contrary to their own interests – who were in favour of change! The result was some 135.000 deaths between 1949 and 1958 alone.[104]
A similar process took place in Indonesia during the beginning of class-struggle in the countryside during the 1960's. Part of the small peasants followed the call from the communist party to seize land on their own out of the hands of the landlords. Others – obviously unprepared for this sudden kind of social change – kept close to traditional leaders, and in fact opposed the movement organized for their own sake.[105] This might explain part of the later internecine violence, organized by the Army.

There are, of course, many important aspects of modernization – like the search for national identity or the role of new élites – which are dealt with under separate headings. Under the present heading we only deal with the phenomenon of social disruption, which may in general be expected to be intensified under conditions of urbanization and industrialization: traditional legitimacy will be most upset when people leave the countryside and move to a modern urban context. Once a certain number of people have left their village, it will be difficult for them to return again, because the overcrowded communities are glad to have lost a couple of peasants who also had to share the small amount of land and food. Besides, once they have left for the town they get eventually accustomed to new social and psychological processes, making it difficult to fall back upon old structures. Everyday practice shows, moreover, that once people take the step to leave their villages, that step is often taken for good; even if the villagers

---

[104] R. S. Weinert – 'Violence in Pre-Modern Societies: Rural Colombia,' LX Am. Pol. Sc. Rev. ('66) pp. 340-347.
[105] W. F. Wertheim – 'Agrarian Problems and Communism in Southeast Asia,' in 'Nationalism in the Third World' (Polemological Studies no. 11, in Dutch) ('70) p. 108.

have to live under miserable circumstances, the big town keeps its attraction to them. Perhaps it is somehow felt nevertheless to be the only doorstep to modernity and a better life.

Urban civilization is indeed (perceived as) the historical, economic and demographic expression of advanced industrial production; before 1800, e.g. only 8 per cent of the population of the United States and 20 per cent of the population of England lived in towns, as against 90 per cent and 80 per cent respectively in 1960.

In most cases people enter a completely new way of life, of which one aspect is that they

> 'loose and destroy the social nexus of family, village and tribe, in which they found themselves secure at least to some extent. The vacuum thus created will be filled by social unrest and political agitation.'[106]

Besides being upset by an uprooted social security-system, people are plunged as individuals into a new competitive world of individual effort with no paternalistic small group units to fall back upon. They find that their crucial values and beliefs are being constantly subjected to daily challenge: their new way of life, (if they are lucky) that of a wage-earner, also brings with it problems of adjustment and problems of a shaken identity. Even *if* the villagers find a job in the city, they will still belong to that ever growing mass of disoriented, rootless, restless, unskilled workers, who are the first to become victims of inflation and economic fluctuation. It is then that these people realize fully what it means to live in a environment in which old cushions have gone and the promised new cushions of social security are still non-existent.[107] The relevance of losening the social ties and of being plunged into a new environment to social unrest is emphasized by Kornhauser's finding that

> 'large isolated factories are more likely to give rise to extremist movements than smaller plants more closely integrated into the surrounding community.'[108]

One of the most difficult problems in this connection is, that the increased creation of jobs in the cities will often not *de*crease, but instead *in*crease urban unemployment, and this, moreover, is found to be true by people with increased aspirations: as soon as it becomes known that jobs have become easier to get, the flow of migrations

---

[106] H. Morgenthau, p. 306; for Africa see I. Wallerstein – 'The Politics of Independence' ('61) pp. 29-43.
[107] see M. Olson on 'the new poor.'
[108] W. Kornhauser – 'The Politics of Mass Society' ('59) pp. 150-158, 145.

from the countryside tends to increase by × times.[109] This could partly explain the enormous migration in some industrially expanding countries in Latin America, where the number of jobs increased in an absolute sense, but may have decreased in a relative sense.

The urban population in Brazil is growing at a rate of 6%, in Columbia 7%, in Equador 6.6%, in Chile 5.9%, in Venezuela 7.3%, in the Dominican Republic even 9.1%.[110] As a result of this migration, a parasitic population, whole 'communities of poverty' are created, encircling the cities with poverty belts of unemployed, whose number for entire Latin America at this moment averages some 20% of the labour force.

In other parts of the world this problem is even more complicated by the fact that such discouraging conditions create transients rather than permanent dwellers. These transients try to maintain links with their home areas. This is the case in African countries, for instance, with the result that frustrated communities are being organized along tribal lines. The various tribal quarters may develop feelings of hostility against each other.[111] (see section 8).

Sendut shows a comparable development in Malaysia, which might be applicable to other urbanizing countries in Asia and Africa as well: The conflict between the Malays and the Chinese escalated in the towns rather than in the villages. The reason for this being that the rural Malays had always taken for granted the privileged position of the Chinese in the village. When the rural Malays left the countryside for the town in search of a better living, and when they found that there again the Chinese occupied the better positions, they became aggressive. Thus in those countries, where ethnic conflicts exist, one might expect a heightening of tension when people are migrating from their original regions, determined to search for a better life.[112]

In general it seems beyond doubt that rapid urbanization under the prevailing circumstances in many Third World countries can hardly create a peaceful climate. Indicative of the mood is the trend towards a higher rate of delinquency under such circumstances, as found by Sendut:

> 'rapid growth of urban society in Malaysia has been accompanied by a general increase in rates of crime and delinquency'; at the same time 'it is also interesting to note that the

---

[109] W. Elkan – 'Urban Unemployment in East Africa,' 46 Int. Aff. (London) 3 ('70) p. 527
[110] A. Guillen – 'Rural Population and Urban Civilization,' XXI Rev. Int. Aff. 479 ('70) p. 22.
[111] R. J. Harrison Church – 'Urban Problems and Economic Development in West Africa,' 5 J. Mod. Afr. St. 4 ('67) p. 515; see also under Heading 8.
[112] H. Sendut – 'Contemporary Urbanization in Malaysia,' VI Asian Survey ('66) p. 490.

local distribution of delinquency is less in Kuala Lumpur city proper than in such slum areas as Besi Road, Klang Road, Tiong Nam Settlement ....'

Finally it should be recalled that modernization, even if it brings rapid material welfare to large sections of the people, may be a time-bomb if insufficient care is taken of improvement on other social levels. As Packenham says:

> 'attention just to economic growth, without outlets and channels for the psychological steam built up in the growth progress, can aid and abet the generation of powerful frustrations.'[113]

But again: urbanization and industrialization do not *have* to result in social unrest, they only may very well do so. It seems appropriate to reiterate here the possible objection that for instance in Latin America the situation in the towns is rather quiet – although misery is great, and although half of all Uruguayens live in or around Montevideo, and although 80% of all Venezuelans are concentrated in the 10% of the country between Caracas and Maracaibo, still the degree of social unrest is relatively low. The answer seems to be that generally a number of other factors must play a role before the mechanisms discussed here will lead to an explosion. We shall discuss these factors – which in themselves may be the causes of explosion as well – next.

7. *Modernization: Industrialization, social mobilization and political participation*

Sendut's study has shown that one of the reactions during an urbanization process may be a high rate of delinquency. Supporting this finding the International Encyclopedia of the Social Sciences explains:

> 'For many of the displaced, there is little social framework between the immediate family and the (possibly remote) State. If either of these links to society fails, and especially if both do, apathy, alienation, and amoral or criminal conduct are likely to ensue.'[114]

This clearly points to the inherent instability of the situation. Alienation and a high level of criminality may be serious enough in themselves, but to us in the present context they are symptomatic of the social spirit among poor city-dwellers: a spirit dominated by anger

---

[113] R. A. Packenham – 'Political Development Doctrines in the American Foreign Aid Program,' XVIII World Politics ('65-'66) p. 227.
[114] Int. Enc. Soc. Sc. 7 ('68) p. 269.

and frustration. In other words, such people form a *potential* cradle of rebellion. But in order to pass from the stage of individual irregular behaviour to the stage of collective (violent) social action, a crucial chain of interdependent conditions must have been fulfilled: class consciousness and solidarity must have emerged, and the resulting social mobilization must have realized political participation.

Let us turn to Latin America for a while. It has been pointed out before that the Latin American cities seem rather quiet, although a great misery prevails. From this some authors have concluded simply that the Latin American proletariat is not revolutionary. I disagree with that opinion, a more accurate conclusion being that *there is at present hardly any Latin American proletariat in the strict sense of the word*; and if it exists, it has certainly proved itself to be revolutionary.

This might seem to be a rather strange remark at first, but some illuminating figures may clear up the point: At this moment almost half of the industrial workers (47.3%) are artisans, working for themselves in workshops with at most five workmen. Only 5% of the working population has a job in big industries. The great mass of the poor, however, is formed by a 'subproletariat,' the mass of partially and irregularly working slumdwellers.[115] This situation, in which half of the workers is engaged in small private business, a way in which most of the poor try to scrape together some money, and in which only 5% of the regularly employed work in big industry, results rather in an individually-oriented than in a class-oriented attitude. Consequently, it has until now generally been impossible that solidarity and class consciousness should develop to such extent as to lead to big lower class organizations; and as long as the poor masses are so unorganized, scattered and divided, the risk of virulent agitation may be considered not very high.

Things are bound to change quickly, however, when substantial groups of hitherto deprived people come together because of industry. *Centralization* then occurs, contributing heavily to a growing awareness of belonging to a mass which can eventually perceive the common interest of the group. As a result of centralization, a real proletariat comes into being, and the basis for collective action is created. As a

---

[115] J. Petras – 'Klassenstruktuur en Politiek' (Class Structure and Politics), 16 te elfder ure no. 3/4 ('69) pp. 132 ff.; see also D. Goldrick et al. – 'The Political Integration of Lower Class Urban Settlements in Chile and Peru,' Studies in Comparative International Development III ('67-'68), whose findings relating to the subproletariat are very striking; 51-76% agreed strongly with the proposition that 'in general our system of government and politics is good for the country,' while 75-85% was only then in favor of social change 'if it doesn't promote disorder!' (p. 17).

country develops economically, it also develops politically in the sense of mass-participation.

Big industry is not a *sine-qua-non* for the creation of political consciousness and eventual mass solidarity (anti-colonial wars often had the same result) but it can be a very important factor in accelerating it. The more so, since in the present era mass consciousness is prepared and activated by politicians and mass media. Concerning the factor just mentioned, it was already pointed out how important growing literacy, the increasing stream of information, and the demonstration-effect emanating from political events abroad, are in reaching hitherto isolated people. Lerner sees this as a three-staged process: 'The secular evolution of a participant society appears to involve a regular sequence of three phases. Urbanization comes first, for cities alone have developed the complex of skills and resources which characterize the modern industrial economy. Within this urban matrix develop both of the attributes which distinguish the next two phases – literacy and media growth. There is a close reciprocal relationship between these, for the literate develops the media which in turn spread literacy. But, literacy performs the key function in the second phase. The capacity to read, at first acquired by relatively few people, equips them to perform the varied tasks required in the modernizing society. Not until the third phase, when the elaborate technology of industrial development is fairly well advanced, does a society begin to produce newspapers, radio networks, and motion pictures on a massive scale. This in turn, accelerates the spread of literacy. Out of this interaction develop those institutions of participation (e.g. voting), which we find in all advanced modern societies.'[116]

Concerning the first factor (politicians and mass media activating mass consciousness) politicians in Latin America have become aware of the increasing influence of the ordinary man, who until now was often excluded from politics. Both the leftist and rightist leaders are now trying to win large groups of the population over to their side. Recent events in Peru and Chile speak for themselves. Bolivia's Barrientos, loosing support among the middle class parties, mobilized campesinos, trying to find broad popular support in the countryside, while using his former supporters as a convenient group to inveigh against.[117]

In Africa and Asia similar methods have been employed by the 'populists'; to use the appropriate expression of the British sociologist

---

[116] D. Lerner – 'The Passing of Traditional Society' ('58) p. 60.
[117] Th. M. Millington – 'Bolivia Under Barrientos,' 56 Curr. Hist. (Jan. '69) pp. 28-29.

Worsley.[118] Leaders like Sukarno, U Nu, Sihanouk, Gandhi, N' krumah, or Nyerere, basing their national policies on the presumption that people are equal and that the people form a unit, all helped to prepare the mobilization of broad segments of their population. Even if some of them scarcely succeeded in activating the people politically, they roused popular feelings hitherto unknown in many of these countries. This kind of political activation of the non-élite, even if still very feeble, facilitates the arrival of collective consciousness. This process of creating underdog solidarity again will be accelerated by economic centralization in particular: industrialization and national organization of agriculture.

In order to describe the mechanisms taking place then, K. Deutsch speaks of 'social mobilization.' This is a two-staged process originating from social consciousness, in which major clusters of old social, economic and psychological commitments are broken down enabling people to become available for the new patterns of socialization and behaviour. Such mobilization again results in political participation and organization.[119] Or, to put it in the terminology of the Argentine sociologist Germani:

'Mobilization refers to the psychosociological process through which groups submerged in that 'passivity' characterizing the traditional normative pattern (the predominance of prescriptive action through the fulfilment of internalized norms) acquire a certain capacity for deliberative behavior, achieve levels of aspiration distinct from those fixed by that pre-existing pattern, and consequently succeed in becoming active in the political field. The latter step obviously produces participation, or intervention in national life.'[120]

Some authors are inclined to consider the presence of an institutional political infrastructure as an important peace-preserving factor. Gurr considers institutionalization one of the factors which decides whether civil strife will break out under conditions inviting violence. The higher the level of institutionalization (political parties, trade unions etc.), the more intensive the pressure towards change, and consequently the smaller the amount of strife.[121]

Lefever and Young consider the Belgian government partly responsible for the instability of the Congo after independence, because this

---

[118] P. Worsley – 'The Third World' ('64) Ch. 4.
[119] K. Deutsch – 'Social Mobilization and Political Development,' LV Am. Pol. Sc. Rev. ('61) p. 494; see also D. Lerner – 'The Passing of Traditional Society' ('58) pp. 48-50; and G. A. Almond & S. Verba – 'The Civic Culture' ('63) p. 4.
[120] quoted by K. H. Silvert – 'Parties and the Masses,' 357 The Annals (March '65) p. 102.
[121] T. Gurr – 'A Causal Model of Civic Strife: A Comparative Analysis Using New Indices,' LXII Am. Pol. Sc. Rev. ('68) p. 1104.

government did not prepare the Congo for independence.¹²² Sometimes India has been taken as an example of the opposite, where the British left behind a strong political infrastructural tradition, upon which the new government could build.
In the same sense an Ecosoc-study reminds us of the fact that trade unionism during the industrial revolution in the West was one of the most positive factors in the recognition and protection of social rights and thus was able to further a relatively peaceful social evolution.¹²³

Obviously such theories are based on the consideration that large groups of deprived people may become so powerful in closing their ranks, that political pressure will be enough to achieve their aims.
Yet, the present author would doubt the validity of any such theory without further conditions.
It is suggested here that at least three variables have to be taken into account, before one can put forth any hypothesis for a given political entity in practice:
1⁰. the level and rate of integration of the subject-group in the entire society;
2⁰. the existence and power of traditional opposition;
3⁰. history, i.e., the occurrence of previous negative experience.

1⁰. Beginning with the first condition, it can be said that many authors (among which Gurr should probably be reckoned here) base their positive outlook on political organization on the so-called 'social desorganization thesis.' According to this thesis, the individuals or small groups which are badly integrated within society, and which have little or no relations to primary groups and top-organizations, are less inclined to or even incapable of expressing their griefs along constitutional lines. Their organization, on the other hand, would contribute to giving them a firmer place in society, and would enhance their chance of being taken into account by the others.¹²⁴
This theory has been affirmed by investigations in relation to racial violence in the United States, where it was found that such violence is more likely to occur, when the negroes as a group are not sufficiently

[122] E. W. Lefever & C. Young – 'Politics in the Congo: Decolonization and Independence' ('65).
[123] ECOSOC – 'Preliminary Study of Issues Relating to the Realization of Economic and Social Rights contained in the Universal Declaration of Human Rights and in the International Covenant on Economic, Social and Cultural Rights,' E/CN. 4/988 (20 Jan. '69) p. 10.
[124] S. Spilerman – 'The Causes of Racial Disturbances: a comparison of alternative explanations,' 35 Am. Soc. Rev. 4 (Aug. '70) p. 649.

integrated in their local society.¹²⁵ Myrdal has shown that the lower white classes in particular support Wallace, because they are still imperfectly integrated within society, and are not effectively organized. They are, therefore, the ones who are most afraid that the black population would be in their way, a fear that could be diminished by better organization and assimilation.¹²⁶

Here one might also look at the communist parties in Latin American countries. These heavy, bureaucratic organizations, which have on the whole lost much of their effectiveness from the point of view of the non-élite, have nevertheless functioned as centers through which the voice of lower class people was channelled in a constitutional way.

Yet, it would seem that this integration theory holds true in particular with relatively powerless minority groups, and then only if integration really improves their situation to some extent. The theory would seem of doubtful value in a situation where large, relatively powerful groups opposed each other within one society. In such a situation one group rules at the cost of an other.

Deprived groups can be structured within existing social patterns only if they have to gain something from their assimilation. If the deprived groups as a minority have little to gain from those radical groups who oppose the ruling majority, then they will assimilate with the existing patterns. If one, or both, of these conditions is unfulfilled, one may expect that the internal organization of such groups will not contribute to their assimilation, but rather to their opposition.

This is the case in S. E. Asia, with substantial ethnic minority groups in India, Burma, Laos, South Vietnam, Cambodia and Thailand. In these countries ethnic groups were organized into political entities during the second World War, and afterwards during the period of decolonization. On the one hand, they generally feel deprived and neglected by the central government, and they doubt whether their integration into the nation contributes primarily to their own prosperity. North-East Thai peasants feel that their energy is used for the sake of the already more prosperous people in the South. Nevertheless, many of these groups, now that they are better organized, feel powerful enough to oppose the central government and eventually revolt violently. Those 'Montagnards' in South Vietnam, who felt

---

[125] Silverman – 'The Precipitants and Underlying Conditions of Race Riots,' 30 Am. Soc. Rev. (Dec. '65) p. 897.
[126] G. Myrdal – 'Challenge to Affluence' ('65) pp. 95 ff.; idem – 'An American Dilemma' ('44) Ch. 3.

exploited and suppressed by the Diem-government, have from the beginning supported or constituted part of the NLF (see further under heading 8 on the phenomenon of 'group-centrism').

Examples of this kind are to be found in Africa as well as Latin America. The communist parties there have been mentioned as a possible example of the positive effect of the organization of underdogs from the constitutional point of view. That remark, however, should be seen in its proper context, a context marked by hitherto scattered and divided organizations and low political participation. As soon as large segments of the urban 'subproletariat' and the small indebted peasants become mobilized, feelings of social solidarity will emerge, and substantial political participation can create powerful organization. Such organization will only then contribute to assimilation, when the ruling class realizes the strength of this new power, which in itself can pave the way for peaceful change in a more just society. In other words, under the circumstances prevailing in much of the Third World, the integration-through-organization theory by itself seems of doubtful value, because much depends on the behaviour of traditional ruling groups in a situation characterized by almost diametrical opposition between powerful traditional and powerful newly-organized groups. It would seem more important then, to turn to the second and third conditions mentioned above: prevalence of strong traditional opposition, and occurrence of previous negative experience.

2^0. It is clear that strong, well-organized, anti-status quo-movements opposing relatively small privileged groups may function as peace-preserving factors, when their strength is a sufficient threat to compel the opposition to compromise. Mass mobilization in countries where traditional interests are small or have eroded, should therefore be in the interest of development and a peaceful climate. A good example of this seems to be Tanzania since the Arusha-Declaration (1967); another example might be Mali. Such positive influence, moreover, presupposes that the process of mass mobilization is not disturbed by overwhelming internal racial or tribal contradictions. This would be a reason why for instance Kenya should not be mentioned here.

It is also clear, however, that the average picture throughout the Third World shows potential opposition between ruling groups (often by tradition) and deprived groups, and that many ruling groups must be regarded as defending the status quo – even at the risk of civil war. In particular during the earlier stages of mass organization, when solidarity and social co-operation are only beginning to emerge, the traditional opposition may try to break the new movement's neck or in any case to resist its far reaching demands. Then comprehensive trade-unions, socialist mass parties, etc. become the media through which the by now organized industrial proletariat or peasantry formulate their increasing demands of the economic élite. If the élite still considers itself strong enough to maintain the status quo, mass-institutionalization becomes quite the opposite of a peace-preserving factor: it creates the possibility of an organized revolt.

Coming back to the 'quiet' Latin American cities, some examples can be mentioned to prove that this is not just theory: wherever industrial workers were centralized and organized, they often played an important role in the case of revolutions or endeavours towards radical change: the organized workers of the tinmines were among the leaders of the social revolution of 1952 in Bolivia; the workers at the sugar centrals formed the pillars of the Cuban revolution; the industrial proletariat in Argentina supported the national front under Peron; the successful Accion Democratica in Venezuela in 1958 was supported by the workers in the oil-industry; the workers at the sugar- and cotton estates in Peru formed the mass basis for the Aprista in 1962; and the miners of Chile presently form a substantial support of the Marxists; it is reminded also the case of the rural violence in Columbia which would not have taken place if there had not existed a strong political tradition among the peasants of that country. Weinert states in this connection:

'The existence of national political parties which differ in their commitments to modernization and with which nearly all peasants identified, were thus crucial ingredients to the violence. The absence of such institutions in other countries explains why the Columbian violence has few parallels among modernizing countries.'[127]

That this violence did not result in a class struggle of exploited peasants against the existing social structure, was exactly the result of the circumstance that those peasants formed an individualistic society. The society was not organized along social lines, but merely along traditional political lines.

3°. In this connection history is also of importance; the question, namely, whether the newly-organized have tried to reach improvement before, but failed because of traditional resistance. If such is the case, those who feel that they now have the power to change an unjust structure, are less inclined to take the peaceful and constitutional path.

This was illustrated in Russia at the beginning of our century:

[127] R. S. Weinert, p. 346.

The internal situation was tense, people were incontent and impatient, and the defeat inflicted upon Russia by the Japanese in 1905 gave rise to violence, manifestations, and strikes to such a degree, that the government was compelled to install a 'doema' (a kind of parliament). When it became known in August of that year, however, that the doema would have only advisory powers, a general strike broke out, compelling the government to issue a manifest in which civil freedoms were recognized and in which the doema was extended the right to decide on new laws. When the first doema openly opposed the government, it was decomposed. The same happened to the second one. After the government had been strengthened by the appointment of Stolypin as the new Prime-Minister, the electoral system was changed in such a conservative way that the third doema became in majority a reactionary one, depriving it of any sense. With this history in mind, it may well be that many revolutionaries in 1917 distrusted any scheme for peaceful change, and that this negative experience has contributed substantially to the violent character of the Russian revolution.

A good example at present might be Tunisia. Since the achievement of independence in 1956 the development of the Tunisian political system has been basically one of mass mobilization. Continuation of a liberal 'laissez-faire' economy eventually led the party structures to loosen their grip on the political system. The absence of any kind of economic growth produced by this disorganized economy resulted in the fairly abrupt proclamation of 'Tunisian socialism' in 1961 and in national planning. At the same time mass mobilization was activated anew, now combined with more direct endeavours to break through the structure still largely dominated by traditional interests. Although both economic progress and political mobilization experienced many difficulties – to be expected in a country like Tunisia – this policy culminated in 1969 in a radical agricultural reform-endeavour. The Tunisian régime, by this reform, intended to extend re-structuring to the point where all agricultural land – most of the land best suited for agricultural diversification and intensification being in the hands of large private landowners – would be included in producers' co-operatives. Officially, this goal was to be reached before the end of 1969, but meanwhile, the entire endeavour has been abolished. It proved impossible for the time being to break through the existing structure of vested interests, and to mobilize enough people to reach a powerful mass-movement.[128] In the meantime, the

---

[128] G. Arrighi & J. S. Saul – 'Socialism and Economic Development in Tropical Africa,' 6 J. Mod. Afr. St. 2 ('68) p. 156.

people who did not own any land before, but have now received shares of previous colon, state, or collective land, form a source of inspiration to many others who hoped to profit likewise by further progressive development. In 1964 all remaining land owned by French colons or Italian farmers was nationalized and combined into producers' co-operatives. This strongly strengthened the aspirations of many poor peasants. The policy of Tunisian socialism has awakened many poor people, who saw their expectations shattered at one blow, when the clock was put back again to the times of haves and have-nots. The question is, whether in some years the deprived segments of Tunisian society will be prepared, when they are better organized, to make a new attempt on the gradual, peaceful road – keeping the disappointments of 1969 in mind. The same holds true, of course, for Latin America, where so many times activated groups have been disappointed in their reliance on those who preached and promised the peaceful way to reform.

In general, the Populist movements throughout the Third World, which are based on the mostly false assumption of classless societies, are bound to frustrate many who begin to believe in that alleged structure. African or Asian societies are not classless, and the realization of this fact may make people less patient a next time.

Even so a Marxist-tinged spokesman as Sekou Touré had to fall back upon the 'communocratic' nature of African society in order to smooth over, ideologically, certain of the potential class antagonisms in Guinean society.[129] At present such disappointed groups may fall back into apathy, but the next occasion may show that enough people's participation has been prepared now to agitate powerful mass movements then.

If things continue as they do, a process may be expected to occur which Lewis has called the 'culture of the poor.' This culture belongs to the relatively deprived groups in a socially mobilized society. They are the people who can be swept quickly into (violent) political movements that appeal to their objectives and psychological needs.[130] In times of mass mobilization much depends on previous experience with traditional élite-opposition, and the rate of socio-economic development.

The crucial question, then, is whether the disparity between economic improvement and social welfare on the one hand and the quickly

---

[129] L. Rudebeck – 'Developmental Pressure and Political Limits: A Tunisian Example,' 8. J. Mod. Afr. St. 2 ('70) pp. 173 ff.
[130] O. Lewis – 'The Culture of Poverty,' Scientific American (Oct. '66) pp. 19 ff.

escalating social mobilization on the other hand will not become too great as soon as a development process has started. Both the little improvement for the newcomers and the great resistance from the status quo groups must be feared as dominating factors in the near future. If fundamental changes do not occur, Huntington might be right in his pessimism when he says:

> 'Instability is the hallmark of a society where mobilization has outrun (governmental) institutionalization,' and 'most modernizing countries are buying rapid social mobilization at the price of political degeneration.'[131]

This certainly holds true for the present day Latin America, the object of Needler's investigation. His findings support in general what has been suggested here; he concludes:

> 'At any level of development between the extremes of the completely underdeveloped and the completely developed societies there is an inverse relationship between mass participation and constitutional stability';[132]

a conclusion which, even in such absolute terms, can hardly be called surprising.

This inverse relationship could only be decreased if mass participation were accompanied by an equivalent level of economic progress. Chile is a good example in question. This country has always been described as one of the most quiet ones, along with Urugay (the latter being one of the most prosperous countries in Latin America). This would seem rather obvious when one takes into account the present theory on the effects of organization. Chile's economic level has been relatively low, but its political participation has been low as well. The 17.9 per cent turnout of the population in the presidential election of 1958 represents the high point reached by electoral participation at that time. 'Politicization' advanced, however, as The Christian Democrats and the Socialist-Communist Alliance, FRAP, competed in organizing the masses, including the hitherto neglected rural population. The Christian Democrats made the attempt of removing the last barriers to total participation, by abolishing the literacy requirement for voting, and by organizing peasant unions. The results are clear. Chile has become an explosive society. Were it not that presently the storm provoked by mass expectations was lulled by the political success of the newly-mobilized (the election of Allende), Chile might well now belong to the *least* peaceful Latino societies. Even so, traditional opposition and a slow rate of improve-

---

[131] S. P. Huntington, pp. 417, 415.
[132] M. C. Needler, p. 95.

ment may easily turn the tide. In this sense Needler has warned that 'the new political order could only persist if it were underpinned by the higher level of economic well-being that would be demanded by the newly participant groups, who would be likely otherwise to reject the established system and turn to anticonstitutional alternatives.'[133] The emergence of strong political parties during the early stages of economic development can thus have a very destabilizing effect. Not only in Colombia, as has been described above, but also in countries like Nicaragua, Honduras and Paraguay strong party identification assumed the character of polarization of opinion in preparation for combat, rather than of preparing the way for peaceful competition.

Generally, it can be said that it depends entirely on the local circumstances whether organization will contribute to a (more) peaceful society or not.

At this place it seems appropriate to add one crucial observation for the entire picture of political consequences of development. In order to avoid conclusion by the reader that – in view of the deliberations presented under the present heading – industrialization ought perhaps to be hindered because it might cause trouble, it must be reminded what has been said under the previous headings concerning surplus-population, unemployment, urbanization and the creation of consciousness. *In the present world it may well be considered a certainty that even without any material development the increasing amount of literacy, education and mass communication will in the long run – and may be sooner than expected – add to a growing tendency of people thinking more and more in terms of class, social status and underdog solidarity.* This is true in particular for the subproletariat in the growing cities. The situation is bad enough already, but in time the word 'bad' may well be insufficient to describe it, because the population explosion only now begins to make itself felt. During the period 1958-1960 the urban population in the developing nations expanded by about 58%; by the year 2000 it is expected that the expansion will have increased up to 500%. What this means is clearly shown for instance in Latin America, where the urban population has grown twice as fast as the number of jobs. It is shown equally clearly in India where it is expected that during the period 1969-1973 the number of unemployed will increase by 4 million.[134] It would be a grave mistake to think that the growing masses of deprived people will remain as apathetic, as patient, as

---

[133] idem, p. 93; this kind of violence he calls 'representational violence.'
[134] these figures were taken from Mac. Namara, note 66 supra, pp. 14, 17.

divided, as unorganized and as unconscious of their common interest in the future as they are now. *Industrialization will soon bring about political mass participation; without industrialization growing social consciousness may be slowed down, but certainly not stopped – on the contrary, it might in the long run assume an even more grim character.* For this reason, I think, the Norwegian Parliamentary Commission awarded last year's Nobel Peace-Prize to the International Labour Organization. It is against the same background that the FAO recently warned that the problem of unemployment is seriously threatening peace and stability in the Third World, and that around 1985 this problem might become even more dangerous and more difficult to solve than the problem of feeding the world's population.

8. *Group-centrism*

Concerning the causes of economic conflict Boulding has written:

'It is only where economic development is heavily concentrated in one sector of an economy to the exclusion of the other sectors that it produces a sense of economic conflict and eventual alienation from the society of those who fail to benefit.'[135]

If a government in the developed industrialized world takes certain measures to improve the economy in general, people will in general be prepared to accept it, even if a certain sector or region mainly gets the benefits: one is used to regarding the economy as an entity and the country as a unity consisting of interdependent economic particles. But even in the industrialized countries and under relatively prosperous conditions the phenomenon of a group- or region-oriented attitude prevails, according not only to economic sectors (farmers protest if they feel that industrial development is stimulated more than agricultural development), but also according to social strata (compare countries like Belgium and Northern Ireland, where linguistic and religious conflicts are fed by economic contradictions).

Group-centrism indicates the primary loyalty to a specific ethnic, religious or other social group, rather than to the nation as a whole. It plays an even more important role in most of the developing countries – particularly the young countries – because of the crucial importance of the factors of kinship and ethnic origin.
In most of the young countries of Africa and Asia the idea of the nation as a supreme social value has not yet come into existence, or

[135] K. E. Boulding – 'The Economics of Human Conflict,' in E. B. Mc. Neil (ed.) – 'The Nature of Human Conflict' ('65) p. 189.

at least is just beginning to develop. On the one hand, people have not had enough time to become adapted to the idea of a multi-tribal or multi-racial community like the 'nation,' and on the other hand many people refuse to share a common citizenship with certain other groups. This may be the case in countries characterized by a heritage of inter-tribal hostility or by traditional hierarchic relations, where one tribe for a long time dominated or exploited the other(s) and is now being suspected of continuing that situation in the new state. Such circumstances can prevail either because a specific majority tribe dominated over its smaller neighbour tribes, or because the former colonial Power recruited native officials from specific (usually the least resistant) ethnic groups. These then became the ones to profit most from education and other socio-economic advancement.

Even in the older states of Latin America the scarcity of development, communication, and traffic left most of the population with their village – not the nation – as the ultimate social value. A few Asian states are perhaps exceptions to this situation. Their populations were mobilized 'en masse' during anti-colonial wars of liberation. There perhaps nationalism may have defeated group-centrism to a certain extent.

If people maintain the village community, the tribe, or any other restricted social group as their supreme social value, and if ideas of nationalism, national well-being and national identity have not yet developed to a substantial degree, planning for economic development should take the following three consequences into account:

1^0. During the process of modernization people will not assign priority to large-scale national development plans, aimed at future improvement for the country as a whole; instead, they want to see here-and-now results of projects aimed at bringing profit to the own ethnic community in question. Rather than being prepared to work for national transformation and general modernization of the country's economic structure, people remain focused on traditional communities and are less interested in remote plans which do not directly improve the living conditions of their own community.[136]

2^0. Being group-focused, people also tend to perceive the new national leader, however eager to develop his entire country, not primarily as such, but instead as the representative of a certain group within the nation. On the slightest occasion they mistrust the government, which they are soon inclined to see as neither just nor representative of their real interest. Each section of the new national society is fearful of exploitation and suppression by others, thereby weakening

---

[136] A. O. Hirschman – 'The Strategy of Economic Development' ('62) pp. 11 ff.

the effectiveness of government and adding to the reluctance of specific segments in participating in schemes for which the government needs the assent and the co-operation of all.[137]

3⁰. In these circumstances not only the pace of development is heavily impeded, to the frustration of those who are ready for and count upon improvement, but also – if the population at large demands better living conditions – ethnic conflict may be intensified. Modernization and development entail increasing ethnic contacts and confrontation, which in the prevailing circumstances may intensify ethnic awareness and ethnic loyalty vis-à-vis other segments of the nation rather than a national spirit. Ethnic or other inter-communal conflict may be heightened or even come into existence during the process of economic development in particular, if certain groups clearly begin to benefit before others do, or are suspected of doing so.[138] This holds true for both the entire social entities like tribes or religious minorities, and for specific segments like the newly educated élite.

If education runs far ahead of the needs of the economy, frustration on the part of the newly educated is inclined, long before the general social discontent comes to a head, to crystallize in the bitterness of tribal or religious opposition. This competition tends first to be expressed in the rush for jobs in the bureaucracy. There may be a period of opportunity for all, as the bureaucracy expands and the posts of departing expatriates become vacant. But this process creates a climate of rapid advancement that is all the more frustrating to those qualified individuals who arrive on the scene later, the number of available jobs usually being exhausted very soon. Then the real struggle starts: in many former colonies particular segments of the population have for long been more pushed by the colonial Powers than others, specific tribes have also for long been more wealthy and better educated than others. In this situation of scarcity of (official) jobs after independence such social divisions tend to be continued by the traditionally privileged groups, while the others, stimulated by the new spirit of independence, will not accept this any longer. The consequence is, on the one hand, a confrontation between lower and higher ranking members of the bureaucracy, and, on the other hand, a confrontation between the candidates for the remaining posts and promotions, all bringing their own ethnic links into the struggle. Whoever loses, tends to suspect that the ethnic affiliation of rivals has been a more decisive factor than ability. The political significance of

---

[137] E. Shills – 'Political Development in the New States' ('62) pp. 13-14.
[138] thus G. W. Skinner – 'The Nature of Loyalties in Rural Indonesia,' in idem (ed) – 'Local, Ethnic and National Loyalties in Village Indonesia; a Symposium' ('59) p. 7.

these ethnic conflicts is that they heighten social distrust among the
élite groups and damage communication between (potential) political
leaders, requiring the support of their own communities. They thus
also create or intensify inter-communal antagonisms on a vastly larger
scale.[139]

A very dramatic example of the mechanisms described here is
provided by the Nigerian civil war. An illuminating analysis by Paul
Anber is mentioned in this connection, a study of which the central
conclusion is that 'Ibo nationalism is primarily an offspring of
modernization, not a re-emergence of traditional attachments.'[140]
As recently as 50 years ago the Ibos did not even regard themselves as
one people. They consisted of more than 200 segmented groups, each
of which functioned as a separate society. Faced with internal problems of land hunger, impoverished soil and population pressure, and
driven by an innate ambitious spirit – in contrast to other Nigerian
tribes – the Ibos migrated during the colonial period in large numbers
to urban areas both in their own region and in the North and West,
in search of economic and educational advancement. They rose to
white-collar positions in a short time, quick to cultivate an intellectual
élite consisting of educators, journalists, professionals, and businessmen. Although the Yorubas led the Nigerian advance of education
because of their advantage of earliest contact with the British, the
Ibos since the 1930's shot ahead, and were the ones to profit most by
the modernization process. In 1934 an Ibo Union was formed which
later expanded into the Ibo Federal Union. At the same time tribal
friction between Yorubas and Ibos became intense, especially in
Lagos. The standard of living rose rapidly among the Ibos (most of
whom live in the East) in contrast to the Hausas and Yorubas in the
North and the West.
A tri-polarisation in Nigerian politics in fact developed during the
period 1948-1952, years of rapid modernization. It above all benifited
the Ibos, and inevitably resulted in extreme social and economic
inequalities – which then contributed to bitter tribal antagonisms.
Figures, for instance, on elementary and secundary education indicate
that the approximate ratio of teachers to population in 1963 was 1 to
every 1500 in the East, 1 to every 2500 in the West, and 1 to every
10.000 in the (most densely populated) North. Other statistics,
indicating the difference in the rise of the standard of living, reveal

[139] J. O'Connell – 'The Inevitability of Instability,' 5 J. Mod. Afr. St. 2 ('67) pp. 185-186.
[140] P. Anber – 'Modernisation and Political Disintegration: Nigeria and the Ibos,'
5 J. Mod. Afr. St. 2 ('67) p. 179.

that the East had the most extensive hospital facilities in the country by 1965, the largest regional production of electricity since 1954, the greatest number of vehicle registrations by 1963; and by far the largest membership in credit associations: in 1963 the East had 68.220 individual association members, in contrast to the West with 5.776, and the North with only 2.407.

As to be expected in this development it was not long before the educational and economic progress of the Ibos led to their becoming the major source of administrators, managers, technicians, and civil servants for the country, occupying senior positions far out of proportion to their numbers. This led to accusations of Ibo monopoly which excluded other ethnic groups from working in the Federal public service and the governmental statutory corporations. In 1966 a Northern publication, 'The Nigerian situation: facts and background,' based this fear on several other figures: the manpower situation of the public services was 'threatening to reach 60% Ibo by 1968,' while the North was credited with only 10%; three-quarters of Nigeria's foreign service came from the Eastern region, and the Universities were headed by Ibos, as were the economic centers like the Railway Corporation and the Ports Authority. It is not very surprising under these circumstances, that the North – having the absolute majority of the Nigerian population, while at the same time feeling most deprived – started a political counter-offensive, trying to gain the first place on the national scene. An important additional incentive to this struggle was the discovery of oil in the East.

The 1964-elections marked the point at which the North tried to become the dominating region, and so the first public expressions of separatist sentiment in the East were heard. The Western Region election of 1965, which allegedly was frauded, finally sparked the Ibo-coup, followed shortly after by the Northern counter-coup and the civil war.

This history clearly illustrates how the development process can create or intensify tribal nationalism. As Anber concludes:

'Tribal loyalties may develop not along with, or in spite of, modern advancements; they may in fact develop because of the nature and context of modernisation itself.' [141]

A second, and perhaps not less dramatic, example is Sudan. Many historical reasons can be mentioned to explain the hostile attitude of the South towards the North. Several of the border tribes such as

---

[141] idem, p. 168.

Luanda, Kakwa, and Zande are divided by the boundaries between Sudan, Congo, and Uganda. But most important is their belief that they have always been exploited by 'imperialist groups' from the North. During the first half of the nineteenth century the Southern provinces of Equatoria and Upper Nile were subject to the most ruthless exploitation. It was a major area for slave-raids. Still today Northern peasants in reference to the Southerner frequently use the word 'abaid,' meaning 'slave.'[142] Although Southern tribesmen fought with the Northern Mahdi against Egyptian rule, they did so for the sake of their own independence and not for a united nation.[143] There is strong evidence suggesting that the attitude of revolt against Northern imperialism remained dominating, which explains why the decision of joining the South and the North under colonial rule in 1947 received very little support in the South. Resistance grew along with the increasing influence of Northern parties at the approach of independence, and culminated in widespread violence in August 1955. During the process of modernization the (Arabic) Northern element became overwhelmingly predominant. Traditionally the major centers of the economy had been in the North, and this situation of inequality grew worse after independence. The major commercial and manifacturing centers are (still) in the North, around the Khartoum, Atbara, Port Sudan complex, where the new consumer goods industry is clustered. The major primary product, cotton, is grown in the Gezira scheme, in the North. Most irrigation projects have been installed in the North, as well as the railways. In fact, investigation reveals that almost all recent economic development has taken place in the North. Even many British schemes for Southern development were abandoned or then later carried out in the North.[144]
Southern leaders, understandably, claim that the Arabic Sudanese have deliberately continued this policy of modernisation in the North and have neglected and exploited the South.[145]
Thus we have an example of a country traditionally characterized by inter-group inequality. After independence, the continuance of inequality during the development process has become a major cause of group-hostility. The Sudanese civil war, which has been going on for years, is a grim testimony to that. Under prevailing circumstances,

---

[142] R. Gray – 'A History of the Southern Sudan, 1839-1889' ('61) pp. 120ff.
[143] R. O. Collins – 'The Southern Sudan, 1883-1898' ('62) p. 23.
[144] G. W. Shepherd, jr. – 'National Integration and the Southern Sudan,' 4 J. Mod. Afr. St. 2 ('66) pp. 193-212.
[145] J. Oduho & W. Deng – 'The Problems of the Southern Sudan' ('63) pp. 49-52.

Al-Rahim's point of view seems a rather doubtful case of wishful thinking, where he concludes:

'In the present age Africa, of which the Sudan constitutes an integral part and a uniquely representative cross-section, is moving towards unity and close association rather than in the direction of separation and Balkanisation.'[146]

A third example is Kenya. This country, which Kenyatta proudly announced as the future proto-state where all people would be equal, suffers increasingly from inter-tribal friction. Notwithstanding endeavours to prevent this, inequality of opportunity among tribal groups remains a stubborn fact of Kenyan society, causing political tensions to rise to the surface. In this country again a pre-existing domination by one tribe (the Kikuyus) is continued today. Discrepancies in education are very significant, not only emphasizing the priorities of the past, but also determining the resultant supply of skilled manpower for the future.[147] Public welfare investment went largely to the Central (Kikuyu) Province. In April 1966 the Kikuyus, constituting only 20 per cent of the male population, received 64 per cent of the industrial and 44 per cent of the commercial loans issued by the Industrial and Commercial Development Corporation. The same is true concerning the allocation of jobs. A typical charge put forward by a member of the opposing Kenya People's Union in Parliament in 1968 is:

'Today, when we look at the top jobs in the Government, we find that in most of the Ministries, including certain co-operatives, practically all these have been taken over by people from the Central Province ...... If one tribe (the Kikuyu) alone can take over about 72 per cent of the Kenya jobs, and there are less than two million people, how can you expect 25 per cent of the jobs to go to more than eight million people who belong to other tribes?'

This situation of course results in a substantial inequality of income among the different regions. This is, moreover, a self-escalating process. The consequent call for more equal representation, more equal development, more equal chances, is heard again and again. Meanwhile political tension increases. Around the time of independence in 1963 the critics assailed both Kikuyu and Luo domination of the country. Today the Luos too feel neglected and from 1966 on the Kikuyus alone have been the stone of offence. Impatience with the present state of affairs is indicated by a new term, 'Kikuyuisation.'[148] The country, where all were to become equal, gets torn by tribal rivalries.

[146] Muddathir 'Abd Al-Rahim – 'Self-Identification in the Sudan,' 8 J. Mod. Afr. St. 2 ('70) p. 249.
[147] D. Rothchild – 'Ethnic Inequalities in Kenya,' 7 J. Mod. Afr. St. 4 ('69) p. 692.
[148] idem, pp. 691-693, 696-701.

In turning to Asia, an interesting example has been described by Dasgupta, who studied religious conflicts in India.[149]

In 1964 a religious conflict broke out in Rourkela, during which 34 people were killed. Most observers saw this event merely as a consequence of the religious riots in Jessore (East Pakistan) and Calcutta in the same year. Dasgupta, however, wondered why it was exactly in Rourkela that the new riot broke out. He discovered that Rourkela was one of the places where an important industrial project had been started, bringing hope of employment to the population. However, as only few from Rourkela had been skilled and educated, most of the important positions were given to people from other regions. This aroused fury among the local population. When the local people were contracted, moreover, they happened to be Moslems in most cases, who were richer and had received on an average better education. Under these circumstances the riots of Jessore and Calcutta were perhaps little more than accelerators for the Rourkela riot. The important underlying cause was in fact group-centrism intensified by the process of economic development.

Another example of this mechanism is formed by the peasants of North-East Thailand, to which has already been referred in a previous context (see under heading 7).

Particular difficulties may arise in countries, in which the situation is further complicated by the occurrence of trans-national ethnic loyalties. If this is the case, tension between ethnic groups in one country may easily evoke similar tensions in other countries in which relatives of the victim-group live.

Whereas discrimination of a specific minority-group may contribute to secession movements, discrimination of a trans-national ethnic community may result in 'pan-movements.' The most outstanding example of this is found in the Somali's in Africa. They were dispersed and divided under colonial rule, living in five different territories (French Somaliland, British Somaliland, the Ethiopian Haud and Ogaden, Italian Somaliland, and the Northern province of Kenya). The pre-existing desire to be united into one Somali-state is intensified, notably in Kenya, because since the 1950's the pace of social and economic development of the Somali's in this country has lagged behind that of changes in Italian and British Somaliland. This situation is continuing now that independence of the respective territories has been reached.[150]

[149] S. Dasgupta – 'Peacelessness and Maldevelopment,' Proc. IPRA II ('68) pp. 33-40.
[150] K. W. Grundy – 'Nationalism and Separatism in East Africa,' 54 Curr. Hist. (Febr. '68) pp. 90-91.

Special problems may arise also in those countries in which foreign ethnic minorities live, especially in the cases where a foreign minority traditionally held a better position than the original population. The population in such countries, once they are ready for development, may be expected to put the foreigners in the low position they themselves had before, or at least to put an end to existing foreign privileges.

An example of this can be found in Ghana. Events in this country have shown that under circumstances of economic scarcity in a political system that formally incorporates some groups to the exclusion of others, strangers are likely to be among the first to be excluded from buying scarce goods. This is merely a convenient way of reducing the demands on the distributive capacity of the government. The stranger's status is inherently vulnerable, since xenophobia often occurs during periods of relative scarcity. In Ghana in recent years the category of 'strangers' or 'aliens' has been maintained or even expanded as a way of eliminating competition for scarce goods, and so of reducing popular impatience with the economic situation.

In november 1969 the newly elected Government of Ghana delivered an ultimatum to all 'aliens,' requiring those without residence permits to leave the country in two weeks. Several reasons for this action were given, but, as Schildkrout concludes, 'unemployment among Ghanians was undoubtedly one of many additional factors.'[151]

A special and very important role is played in this connection by the Chinese and Indian minorities – and to a lesser degree by Europeans – in several African and Asian countries. These foreign minority-groups in particular are a potential stumbling block, as they happen to belong traditionally to the economically more prosperous classes. In many South-East Asian and East African countries commerce is largely controlled by the Chinese, together with the people coming from India. They often constitute an important part of the relatively well-to-do middle class (shop-keepers, managers, technicians, etc.). In the eyes of the local population they are privileged people, who become rich at the cost of the natives. This view has usually been strengthened after independence, since these foreign groups – better educated and prepared for modernization – were often among the first to benefit from economic development.

During the development process conflict between these groups and the native population is strengthened by two interconnected ways.

[151] E. Schildkrout – 'Strangers and Local Government in Kumasi,' 8 J. Mod. Afr. St. 2 ('70) p. 269.

In the first place, there is a growing reluctance on the side of the latter to accept the privileged positions of the others. Now that political independence has been reached, and the national economy is theirs, they want to profit from economic progress themselves, and do not want to see the privileged continue. In the second place, if the hitherto privileged groups perceive this they will strive to maintain their economic position, while fearing at the same time social and political degradation. They may even try to compensate such degradation on one level (the socio-political one) by improvement on the other one (the economic level).[152] For such reasons one may expect Chinese and Asian minorities to use their advantages from the past in order to be the first to gain from economic development.

This indeed is what has happened in many countries:

In S. E. Asian countries the Chinese have proved to be the foremost profitgainers from Western (in particular American) aid, which is directed in particular at the stimulation of private enterprise. The accusation is often heard that under prevailing circumstances this form of aid tends first of all to enrich the already privileged Chinese.[153] This situation certainly has contributed to the intensified Malay-Chinese conflict in the Malaysian towns in recent years. The same may hold as a partial explanation of increasing anti-Indian pressures in Burma, which led eventually to the nationalization of (Indian) shops.[154] Thousands of Indians returned to India after 1962. When the situation of intolerance grew worse, the number of Indians leaving Burma each week amounted to two thousand in July 1964. It was estimated that 300.000 Indians left during the years 1963-1964 alone, and their total by 1964 was taken to be about 500.000.[155]

Similar conditions prevail in some East African countries. It has been estimated that by 1965 approximately 65 per cent of the labour force in commerce and the public sector in entire East Africa was constituted by Asians![156]

The situation in Kenya illustrates this point very well. This country is marked not only by inter-African tribal competition, as was shown before, but it is also marked by extensive competition between Kenyans and foreigners. In pre-independent Kenya, non-Africans, though few

---

[152] E. Hagen – 'A Framework for Analyzing Change,' in 'Development of the Emerging Countries' ('62) p. 23.
[153] W. E. Willmott – 'The Overseas Chinese Today and Tomorrow,' LXIII Pac. Aff. 2 ('69) p. 212.
[154] R. L. Park – 'India's Foreign Policy: 1964-1968,' 54 Curr. Hist. (April '68) p. 205.
[155] Keesings Hist. Arch., vol. XIV p. 20315.
[156] D. P. Ghai & Y. P. Ghai – 'Asians in East-Africa: Problems and Prospects,' 3 J. Mod. Afr. St. ('65) pp. 40-45.

in number, held nearly all the positions in the government and the private sector. After independence many of them stayed, realizing that their skills would be badly needed and that they were in a good position to profit by economic progress. A racial breakdown of jobs requiring university or higher education at the time of independence shows the extensive role played by non-Africans: out of 6.488 positions surveyed, 77 per cent were held by Europeans and Asians and only 23 per cent by Africans. Africans held only 2 per cent of the highest positions in leading banks and motor firms; less than 6 per cent of them were town planners, lawyers, doctors, engineers, surveyors, etc.[157]

This is a logical consequence of the colonial policy in the field of education and employment. African ambitions in those days were thwarted by colonial budgets which spent much more money on European and Asian than on African education (each being separate), even though the latter community represented 97 per cent of the total population.

Likewise, non-African leadership in the private sector of economy was buttressed by the access to capital available at home and abroad and by discriminatory legislation. Kenya's economy was and is largely dependent on private capital, which even today still comes from non-African sources, who try to fix their own prices, and continue increasing their own (non-African) capital. Until today it has proved extremely difficult for the government to break through these entrenched privileged positions.

Although the policy of Africanisation is pushed very hard, even in the public service high inequalities remain. Here in 1966 88 per cent of the African males earned no more than £ 359 per year. On the other side, among the European men 51 per cent earned between £ 1200 and £ 2399, 33 per cent earning even more than £ 2400. Of the Asian males 37 per cent earned more than £ 720. The differences in annual incomes in industry and commerce were the same in general.[158]

The majority of Kenyans, however, looks upon independence as not simply a transfer of sovereignty into African hands, but as implying emphasis on African dominance – or at least equal participation – in the bureaucracy, the Army, industry and agriculture. The Government's emphasis on Africanisation is an attempt to relieve increasing pressure on the régime and to meet the rising expectations. But, as Rothchild observes,

---

[157] D. Rothchild, p. 693.
[158] idem, pp. 694, 696.

'the extent to which the Government fails to measure up to these mass expectations will have a direct bearing upon the general public's sense of frustration and, in turn, upon the régime's stability.'

The Government in Peking has recognized, as far as the Chinese are concerned, the potential disturbing influence of the existing privileges on the relations between China and developing countries, particularly as far as Asia is concerned. Chinese leaders, therefore, have urged in recent years that the overseas Chinese should give up unjust privileges and should contribute more to the development of their resident countries; in 1958 Ho Hsiang-ning stated:

'We urge Overseas Chinese commerce to transfer to local industry, or in joint management with local national capital to participate in economic construction which will benefit the national independence of the countries of residence. Overseas Chinese children should learn the local language, geography, history and skills, so that they may be educated and make a living in the local countries.'

In a famous speech held in Rangoon, Chou En-lai payed much attention to this problem. He accused those Overseas Chinese who refused to learn local languages of 'conservatism,' 'laziness,' and 'false chauvinism.' He urged the Overseas Chinese businessmen to be honest and law-abiding in all their transactions, to improve the living-standards of their employees and to undertake social welfare work for the local communities, to invest in joint ventures, and to transfer their capital from commerce to industrial development.

Such initiatives clearly serve political objectives in the era of peaceful co-existence, but in the present context it is important to note that Peking realizes that the privileged positions held by many Chinese in developing countries are a source of unwished local (and consequently of international) conflict.[159]

A last example to be mentioned in the present context is American economic domination in Latin America.

Several studies have shown a correlation between the strong US economic presence and political instability. Some of the studies have suggested that this correlation demonstrates that clear signs of the abundant American way of life in the environment of a poor country, whose population feels exploited to the benefit of the Americans, may provoke hostility towards the US, which in turn may result in domestic violence. Both a demonstration-effect and an intensified xenophobia may be considered causative factors.

[159] S. FitzGerald – 'China and the Overseas Chinese: Perceptions and Policies,' The China Q. no. 44 (Oct-Dec. '70) pp. 30ff.

Such, for instance, is suggested by Merle Kling, who points out the relationship between chronic political instability in Latin America and the domination of the local economy by foreign economic interests.[160]

Johnson, in his case study of the Cuban revolution, has indicated that one effect of strong US economic presence in Cuba was an increase in hostility towards the US, which resulted in an increase in popular support for the revolution and facilitated Castro's expropriation of privately-owned US property. The resentment and frustration of economic dependence concerning one product (sugar), which happened to be largely controlled by American economic interests, was exploited by Castro in his fight against Batista.[161]

Carey uses Peru as an example. In 1958 a popular controversy had developed on the issue of foreign domination of Peru's national resources, because the (American financed) International Petroleum Company had gained control of the vast majority of Peru's petroleum resources. Subsequent strikes and demonstrations against the US illustrate the relation between (potential) violence and hostility towards that American-dominated enterprise.[162] Much has still to be found out in this respect, but studies like these suggest that during the period of modernization the existence of foreign privileged positions tends to become a particular stone of offense intensifying feelings of deprivation and xenophobian behavior. This may eventually result in the rejection of a local government which allowes the unjust situation to continue, and may even stimulate a climate of more general violence.

Under the circumstances prevailing at present in many developing countries, and in view of the limited possibilities of rapid general development, it seems doubtful whether the local governments will be able to avoid ethnic conflicts and will manage to lead assimilation and integration along peaceful ways.

9. *Deterioration during initial period*

Under heading 2 the psychological phenomenon was iterated that people tend to react to any deterioration of conditions. On that occasion population increase was mentioned as resulting in *relative*

[160] M. Kling – 'Towards a Theory of Power and Political Instability in Latin America,' IX W. Pol. Q. 9 (March '56) pp. 21 ff.
[161] L. L. Johnson – 'US Business Interests and the Rise of Castro,' XVIII World Politics 17 (April '65) pp. 440 ff.
[162] J. C. Carey – 'Peru and the U.S., 1900-1962' ('64) pp. 170 ff.

deterioration. The present heading deals with *absolute* deterioration. During the process of economic development under the prevailing circumstances in the Third World, we may sooner or later – even under optimal conditions – expect set-backs in one or more economic sectors, both because of the sudden character of economic growth and the limited amount of resources. Aversion to any set-back will be very strong particularly in those stages of development in which the standard of living is still critical. In the early period the majority of the lower classes is likely to suffer heavily from inflationary tendencies, as is illustrated by many food riots (a result of the rising food prices). Any deterioration then may provoke sharp reactions, since people can not afford a set-back. Inflation and depression create general unrest and may bring to the fore conflicts that in better times might have been evaded, because contending parties are then temporarily more satisfied. Political instability is the result. The critical character of the first period is illustrated by the fact that during the depression of 1929 a wave of revolutions swept, in the first place, the colonial area, as people there were not prepared to accept any deterioration of already bad conditions.[163]

In this connection attention should be payed to the correlation which was found to exist between economic deterioration and the occurrence of military coups. Needler has stressed the point saying that a military coup is seldom made by the military alone. The conspirators, he states, are invariably in touch with civilian politicians, responding to their advice, counting with their assistance in justifying the coup to public opinion, and then helping to run the country afterwards. Even the apparently internecine military struggles may often be connected with internal developments of the country.[164] Several authors have concluded that one of these developments happens to be economic deterioration.

Some good arguments can be given to explain this connection. In the first place, depression, bringing about social unrest and political conflict, may activate the military who intervene with the purpose of restoring public order. Furthermore, when social conflict becomes very intense, the military (or part of it) may side with one of the political factions. This political activity, in part stemming from a cultivated mentality 'to save the country from chaos,' may result in rejection of civilian governments, which are unable to relieve the plight of their country. At the same time the military consider them-

---

[163] E. Lieuwen – 'US Policy in Latin America' ('65) p. 67; Barbara Ward, p. 117.
[164] M. C. Needler – 'Political Development and Military Intervention in Latin America,' LX Am. Pol. Sc. Rev. ('66) p. 618.

selves as being in a better position to do something about it. In short, as Fossum puts it,

> 'there seem to be many reasons why the military should show a greater propensity to intervene in times of depression than in 'normal' times.'[165]

This author studied data from two different periods, 1922-38, and 1951-63. For the first period he took the rise or fall in the value of world export in relation to the preceding years as an index for respectively improvement- and deterioration-years, and found that the frequency of coups in deterioration years was on the average twice that in improvement years. For the second period he took the rise or fall of per capita GNP in relation to the preceding year, and found practically the same correlation, the frequency of coups in improvement years being 60% of the frequency in deterioration years.

The indices used by Fossum may be considered inadequate (it being extremely difficult to gather similar data for many developing countries over longer periods). But the use of two different indices certainly adds to the validity of his argument. His findings, moreover, have been confirmed by other investigations. E.g. Johnson has concluded likewise, that

> 'economic deterioration, if it is severe enough, will tend to invite military intervention that will have popular approval.'[166]

Needler reached the same conclusion, stating that:

> 'the available data are consistent with the hypothesis postulated, that the overthrow of a government is more likely to occur when economic conditions worsen.'[167]

Even though these studies are all concerned with Latin America (the world's traditional center of military coups), similar conclusions are drawn for African countries by Cowan. In particular the 1965-coup in Ghana is described by him as a clear example of a case where economic deterioration (even the supply of normally available consumer goods had been reduced) contributed to a military coup, which met with enthusiastic reception by the people.[168]

Deterioration of economic conditions during the early phases of development may be dangerous in itself. Deterioration which comes as a sudden break after a period of progress is even more dangerous. This will be the topic of the next section.

[165] E. Fossum – 'Factors Influencing the Occurrence of Military Coups d'etat in Latin America,' J. Peace Res. 3 ('67) p. 237.
[166] J. J. Johnson – 'The Military and Society in Latin America' ('64) p. 260.
[167] see note 164 supra.
[168] L. Gray Cowan – 'The Military and African Politics,' XXI Int. J. 3 ('66) pp. 291-292.

10. *Sudden deterioration after a period of progress*

The International Covenant on Economic, Social and Cultural Rights states in its 11th article:

'The States Parties to the present Covenant recognize the right of everyone to an adequate standard of living for himself and his family, including adequate food and housing, and to *continuous* improvement of living conditions.'[169]

Probably without knowing it, the drafting authorities layed down in this article a regulation of great polemological importance.
The necessity of *persistent* growth has been discussed already. The necessity of *substantial* growth has also been dealt. Now we come to an important additional condition: Although both continuous and substantial growth are necessary, and together serve as prerequisites to peaceful development, they carry with them an increased risk: that of *intensified frustration* if a set-back takes place.

Studies in the United States revealed that the lynching of negroes in the Southern States prior to the 1930's was the result of frustration on the part of the whites caused by *unexpected* economic hardship. This shows, as Berkowicz states, that 'the blocking of activities involving strongly held anticipations leads to more intense hostility than does the non-fulfilment of weaker expectations.'[170]

The correctness of these figures may have been doubted by other authors, who stressed other factors which accidentally played a role in the same situation – their relevance is considered beyond doubt now. Many studies have recently suggested that *politically the most critical moment exists when hope is dashed to the ground after a long period of progression, during which the hope was strongly intensified and honoured.*

Thus, the more positive the economic development, the greater the inherent danger of strong averse reactions to economic set-back or stagnation.

A prominent advocate of the present theory of political instability is James C. Davies, who developed his famous 'J-curve' in this connection, defining it as follows:

'Revolution is most likely to take place when a prolonged period of rising expectations and rising gratifications is followed by a short period of sharp reversal, during which the gap between expectations and gratifications quickly widens and becomes intolerable. The frustration that develops, when it is intense and widespread in the society, seeks outlets in violent action.'[171]

[169] Annex to G. A. Res. 2200 (XXI), 16 Dec. '66 (my italics).
[170] L. Berkowicz, p. 57.
[171] J. C. Davies – 'The J-Curve of Rising and Declining Satisfactions as a Cause of Some Great Revolutions and a Contained Rebellion,' in D. Graham & T. R. Gurr – 'The History of Violence in America' ('69) p. 690.

He is supported by Stone, who adds that the 'J-curve' is also applicable to other than purely economic satisfactions, namely in the social and political field:

> 'The recipe for revolution is thus the creation of new expectations by economic improvement and some social and political reforms, followed by economic recession, governmental reaction, and aristocratic resurgence, which widen the gap between expectations and reality.'[172]

Gurr is the author who made, in my opinion, a very important contribution to the present theory. First, he adds that not only an abrupt limitation of what people hope to achieve may arouse their fury, but also any sharp increase in people's expectations unaccompanied by an adequate increase in value capabilities. In the second place, however, he adds an important qualification, affirming what has been stressed in this study before: i.e. *the critical character of the initial development phases*. Davies states that 'the actual state of socio-economic development is less significant than the expectation that past progress, now blocked, can and must continue in the future.'[173]

It is hard to imagine, however, that a stagnation of the German Wirtschaftswunder in this time could drive the W. Germans to revolution. When people have just begun to taste the fruits of a better life, they will react furiously to any obstacle as long as they have not overcome the stage perceived as miserable. Gurr's findings affirm this hypothesis. Having analyzed the function of a number of socio-political variables in the case of civil strife, he concludes that

> 'none of the mediating variables appear to affect the relationship between *persisting deprivation* and strife, i.e. there is a certain inevitability about the association between such deprivation and strife', whereas 'the intervening variables do tend to control for short term deprivation's effects.'[174]

In other words, *short term deprivation* (the destruction of hope) is particularly dangerous in circumstances of *persisting deprivation* (existing certainly until a minimum level of prosperity has been reached). It may be assumed, moreover, that those people who have gone part of the way towards a better life, do not fall back into apathy as easily as do the people who have yet to take the first steps on that road. (see heading 1).

---

[172] L. Stone – 'Theories of Revolution,' XVIII World Politics ('65-'66) p. 172.
[173] J. C. Davies – 'Toward a Theory of Revolution,' XXVII Am. Soc. Rev. (Feb. '62) pp. 5-6.
[174] T. R. Gurr – 'A Causal Model of Civic Strife: A Comparative Analysis Using New Indices,' LXII Am. Pol. Sc. Rev. ('68) pp. 1110, 1120.

An example suggesting the validity of the present theory is provided by political events in Latin America during and directly after the World Wars. Whereas the years of these wars were marked by the lowest frequency of internal violence in 20th century Latin America, the years following the wars were marked by an extremely high frequency.[175] During the years 1916-1918 Latin America witnessed only 1 coup in contrast to 5 during the years 1919-1921; during the years 1940-1942 there were no coups at all, in contrast to 18 during the years 1943-1948. The most obvious explanation is based on the economic situation of this part of the world during these respective periods:

Both World War periods created a great demand for Latin American export products which resulted in economic booms. The demand was sharply reduced after the wars, resulting in sudden unemployment, economic depression, and hence political instability. Political instability increased again during the second World War (in 1943) because of the difficulties of transporting exports across the oceans. Exports bound for Europe came virtually to a halt, resulting in heavy economic set backs.

The high expectations created and satisfied during the years of war were suddenly broken when the wars were over. The resulting political instability can be explained in two ways; on the one hand, pre-existing political conflicts, soothed by general economic advancement to the satisfaction of different parties, by then became manifest; on the other hand, the large-scale frustration may have contributed directly to the creation of new conflicts. A similar explanation might perhaps hold for the sudden increase of political violence during the period 1961-1963 (10 coups as against 2 during the preceding period 1958-60), a period characterized by constantly declining prices of raw commodities on the world market and by rapid inflation.

Another example of the applicability of the present theory is the revolt of the Vietnamese peasants against Ngo Dinh Diem. They rejected him when he restored large land ownership (the break-effect) and thus ended a period of increasing prosperity for the small peasants, who had for the first time in history owned the land taken from the landlords by the Viet Minh (which had resulted in high expectations of continuing improvement during a time when real prosperity was still little more than a future goal).

This theory also contains an additional explanation, partly perhaps, for the beginning of rural violence in Colombia in 1946, when a Conservative assumed the Presidency after many years of Liberal rule (see section 6).

[175] E. Fossum, p. 237.

And finally there is the example of the newly educated groups in several colonies during the 1929-depression. 'A sense of isolation tended to weaken them and undermine their political confidence,' writes Barbara Ward. 'Moreover, the environment confused them further. After a number of small hopeful beginnings, colonial economies failed to move forward to sustained momentum.'[176]

To a certain extent this theory seems appropriate in explaining the behaviour of the many frustrated newly educated people in the Third World today. This important group has been discussed at length in section 3. Therefore, it will not be discussed here, although the link with the present theory is evident. The reason why it was thought more appropriate to discuss the group there, is that the newly educated élites have developed great hopes and aspirations during their studies, but that on the other hand, before they become frustrated by the incapacity of their country to provide adequate employment, the period of cultivation of their expectations has in a sense not been accompanied by an equivalent period of gratification.

Davies, while discussing his J-curve, has himself mentioned as examples among others the French revolution, the American civil war, the rise of Hitler-Germany, and the revolt of black people in the US in the sixties. As to the last event he explains:

'as in major historic revolutions, the events relating to the 1960's rebellion consist of a rather long period of rising expectations followed by a relatively brief period of frustration that stuck deep into the psyches of black people.... there was, starting notably in 1963, not the first instance of violence against blacks but a sudden increase in it. This resurgence of violence came after, and interrupted, the slow but steady progress since 1940.'[177]

Such evidence of the validity of the present theory suggests its relevance to the development process in the Third World. So much has to be done with such restricted resources, that even the lucky country that manages to perform sustained growth over a longer period must be expected to suffer from set-backs sooner or later. As long as such a country has not escaped from a state of general scarcity, averse reactions to any set-back must be expected to be very strong.

11. *Opposition: against certain aspects of development*

Until this point we have dealt exclusively with the polemological aspects of development resulting from the pressures toward improvement.

[176] Barbara Ward, p. 116.
[177] J. C. Davies, note 171 supra, pp. 722-723.

The other side of the coin is, however, that there are also polemological aspects resulting from opposition to development, either opposition to a certain aspect of development, or to the entire development process. Under this heading we are concerned with the first and under the next heading we are concerned with the second form of opposition.

The 'new rich', the new economic élite, have been referred to above. Under circumstances in which the majority of the population longs for improvement, but has not yet reached a certain minimum level of prosperity, the 'new rich' become an object of suspicion because they have advanced much too quickly in the eyes of others. If a small group of the population quickly succeeds in reaching that economic level to which all are aspiring, those who are behind compare their own position to that of the lucky few, thereby being inclined to feel deprived. The source of frustration in the town will be the new entrepreneur, the big shopkeeper, or the successful merchant. In the countryside it will be the rich farmer.

Modernizing the agricultural sector presupposes the introduction of modern machines, fertilizers etc. (the 'green revolution'). In countries where private ownership is stressed and collective ownership is mistrusted as a first step on the road to communism, only rich farmers can buy such aids and appliances. The mass of small peasants may be threatened in its very existence by the increasingly unequal character of the competetive struggle. The rich are quickly getting richer and the poor are removed from the scene. Under circumstances of private ownership and liberal economic principles (as they are stressed, for instance, by the aid program of the United States) the countryside may become explosive because of frustration of the many small peasants who had hoped to share in prosperity and who see only the already well-to-do profit from development programs. Many of the losers may even experience a deterioration of their conditions, i.e. not only a relative, but an absolute deterioration. The 'demonstration-effect' resulting from the progress of small groups may provoke both feelings of deprivation in general, and feelings of anger towards such groups. The possibility of conflict is further enhanced by the expectation that those 'new rich' who *do* manage to enter the circles of the ruling social and political élite, may soon become 'plus royaliste que le Roi,' once they finally belong to the élite. If such an attitude indeed occurs it will further intensify the jealousy and fury of the others.

In this connection we may also be reminded of what has been said in section 8 about foreign minorities which are often the first to gain the benefits of development. These groups in particular may arouse the fury of the slowly developing masses.

These are a few deliberations on situations (mostly dealt with previously and for this reason only touched upon here) in which those who are badly in need of improvement may themselves become opponents of a specific positive form of economic development, and thus may reject a government associated with that specific policy.
The opposition that originates from the traditional élite is of a different kind. This group fears that it will be deprived of its privileged positions if economic development succeeds. Thus, this group, to which we will turn in the next section, tends to oppose any form of socio-economic change.

12. *Opposition: by status quo groups, and the consequences of negative experience*

Once people have attained privileged positions, they often want to keep them and, if necessary, to fight for them. This is just another variety of the axiom that people tend to resist any decrease of what they have, or to resist any deterioration of conditions.

This rule certainly applies to those people threatened of loosing something in absolute terms. It may, however, be equally applicable in case when people perceive a relative loss, for instance if lower ranked groups are approaching their privileged position; such relative loss of position may be on the economic, the social, as well as the political dimension.

The traditional social and economic structure in much of the Third World shows a hierarchical, if not feudal, pattern, within which the gap between powerful and powerless, high and low, rich and poor, is often extremely wide. In many cases a small, strong social élite decides the course of events within the country. The majority has nothing to do with it, being more the object than the subject of decisions. Wherever and however socio-economic development starts, such rigid social patterns are fought by those who want their share of prosperity – and conversely, the traditional élite will try to keep its position and fight against development: leftist versus rightist revolution.

This is what happens in much of modernizing Africa, where it is not so much the constitution lacking adequate provisions (as is sometimes stated), but rather the profound socio-economic differences between the traditional rulers and the new national, young élite, constituting the real obstruction to necessary change.[178] Traditional loyalties are often so dominant and traditional chiefs still so powerful that they

---

[178] R. K. Woetzel – 'Political Rights in Developing Countries,' Proc. Am. Soc. Int. L. ('66) pp. 144-147.

survive in modern times as local political leaders, who in fact are the keys to failure or success. In many cases their co-operation with the central government merely resulted in new forms of old organizational structures. Thus they tend to frustrate the new national leaders, the newly educated, and all those who are 'change-minded' and in favour of modern national planning.[179]

The same holds true for much of Asia. We have noticed before the extraordinary difficulties which hinder the endeavours of India to modernize the country, and to change and democratize the existing social structures.[180] What has been said under heading 1 is equally important under this heading.

The situation in Latin America is the most clear perhaps. There, on an average, 10% of the people own 90% of the land. The circles of the rich social élite are extraordinarily strong, since they are not only very powerful by themselves, but usually have the military on their side. Several young officers may be an exception to this rule. They are seldom powerful enough, however, to challenge the old élite seriously. If one adds to this the traditional role of the Church and the support implicit in the aid programs of the United States, a hopeless picture – in terms of peaceful change-remains. It should be noted, of course, that in particular the younger part of the clergy is gradually developing a more critical attitude towards Latin American societies, and in some countries even takes sides with the opposition. Until this moment such change has only resulted, as in the case of Paraguay or Brazil, in increasing suppression – both of the clergy and of the opposition at large. Many experts, and not without reason, give rather pessimistic answers to the question whether they consider peaceful change possible. Carroll considers

'the available evidence not encouraging. In fact, on the basis of past experience alone, an outlook of pessimism is warranted. With the possible exception of Venezuela, policy tends to polarize on one side in a 'do nothing' attitude and on the other in a radical revolutionary stance.'[181]

Mason writes:

'Existing social relationship, income distributions, individual values and human motivations are so inhibiting to economic development of any sort, and the existing

---

[179] N. N. Miller – 'The Political Survival of Traditional Leadership,' 6 J. Mod. Afr. St. ('68) pp. 183-189; see also J. Kraus – 'On the Politics of Nationalism and Social Change in Ghana,' 7. J. Mod. Afr. St. ('69) pp. 107ff.; and J. Fairbairn – 'Crisis in Uganda,' New Statesman (May 27, '66).
[180] see notes 14, 15, 16 supra; and S. N. Eisenstadt – 'Transformation of social, political, and cultural orders in modernization,' XXX Am. Soc. Rev. 5 ('65) pp. 637-659.
[181] Th. F. Carroll in A. O. Hirschman (ed.) – 'Latin American Issues' ('61) p. 200.

governments so unwilling to, or incapable of, initiating change, that it is hard to see how the elementary preconditions of development can be established short of political revolution.'[182]

This picture may seem too pessimistic to those who expect much of the examples of Frei and Allende in Chile and of recent steps against vested interests by the military governments in Peru and Bolivia (the example last mentioned being obsolete in the meantime). Yet, it remains to be seen what is involved and how far they can really go until such vested interests strike back. Anyhow, keeping in mind all that has been said earlier in this Chapter, it should not be very difficult to imagine the increasingly explosive character of relations in Latin America – 'the world's powder keg,' in the words of Myrdal – as well as in other parts of the developing world; the more so, as we are confronted with a two-edged sword . When peaceful change proves impossible because of the resistance of the traditional élites, violence from anti-status quo factions must (also) be expected sooner or later; it seems just a matter of time. Moreover, the longer traditional élites resist, the greater the risk that large-scale violence will occur eventually. This is because of the influence of what might be called 'progressive negative experience,' discussed under heading 7, (pp. 54-55). The longer people's hopes and expectations are frustrated, the more they tend to reject peaceful ways to achieve their goals.
Whatever the strength of traditional groups for the foreseeable future may be, Gurr is probably right when he says that in this era 'no pattern of coercive control, however intense and consistent, is likely to deter permanently all enraged from violence, except genocide.'[183] Looking back in history it may be stated that one of the chief outcomes of the American civil war has been the removal from the national political scene of the group most inclined to obstruct a further expansion of industry based on an ideology of nationalism, more freedom, and which gradually met the challenges of workers and small peasants.

It should be remembered that it is not only the ruling élite who resists modernization. During the initial stage of development, traditional cultural, religious and political loyalties may still be stronger among deprived sections of the population than the demand for prosperity. Such was indicated by the example of the rural violence in Colombia, where large sections of the poor peasants, un-

---

[182] E. Mason – 'Economic Planning in Underdeveloped Areas' ('58) p. 27.
[183] T. R. Gurr – 'Why Men Rebel' ('70) p. 358.

prepared for and afraid of radical change, stuck to traditional political
loyalties and fought against their compatriots, who advocated
improvement of their living conditions.
Under such circumstances violence, once it breaks out, may escalate
not only into an interclass struggle but into an outright national civil
war.

13. *Military government*

The last topic to be mentioned within the framework of internal
polemological aspects of development is the military government,
an almost symptomatic feature throughout the present developing
Third World. What is the relation between the development process
and the occurrence of military political activity, and what are the
polemological consequences of a military government under the
prevailing circumstances?

As for the first question the answer would seem quite obvious.
Looking at the new countries of Africa and Asia, it can be said that
many of these countries became independent at a moment when they
were neither economically, nor socially, nor politically mature for
the heavy tasks of self-government. The resulting economic and
social problems were often intensified subsequently by the incapability
of new governments who promised much but could realize little. We
have dealt elsewhere with additional problems such as corruption
within civilian administrations, communal approach of and communal
resistance to development programs etc., and resulting political instability. A general consequence of all this is that of internal chaos.
In such circumstances the military are seduced, as it were, to take care
of their country. It is indeed not a very astonishing fact that in the
round of coups throughout the developing world the justification
most frequently heard is that military rule is needed to avert economic
chaos. 'Facing the enormous complexity and variety of economic
and social problems that are inescapable after independence,' as
Barbara Ward puts it, 'the temptation to impose the rule of a single
party and use hard discipline to solve them is obvious.'[184]
The political role of the military is of course not exclusively caused by
the socio-economic situation. This role is stimulated also by political
and historical factors. On the one hand, the new countries often lived
in a political vacuum into which the military stepped as the only

---

[184] Barbara Ward, p. 131; see also L. G. Cowan – 'Military Rule in Africa,' IX Survival
(Jan. '67) pp. 9-13.

organized national authority.¹⁸⁵ On the other hand, the new social concept of nationalism was often closely tied to the heroes of the anti-colonial struggles, mostly military officers, which made it quite natural that such military leaders should be the first to govern the new state.¹⁸⁶ Many of them, although being very reluctant to enter politics, still decided to take that step, because successive civilian governments were thought to have led the country further into social and economic problems.

Military intervention is a dominant feature of Latin American politics. Although we cannot speak here of new countries, their problems are in general the same as those in the rest of the Third World. Socio-economic problems often form the basis of a political struggle, and political parties are usually identified with specific economic interests. Military intervention usually occurs in the name of putting an end to chaos, if conflict between different parties becomes excessive – such excesses often being the consequence of socio-economic tensions. Colombia, Nicaragua, Honduras, Paraguay and other Latin American countries have been mentioned as examples where the military intervened 'to save the country.' Again, it should be added that the economic situation in Latin America is not the only factor explaining the occurrence of military coups. An important additional factor, for instance, is the impossibility of social mobility. The Army is the only institution through which the sons of the non-élite can reach the top of society. The Army is also seen by many young revolutionaries as the only career institution through which they can obtain the power to realize the needed social and political change. Yet, as has been explained in a previous section, such political activity tends to occur in particular during periods of economic tension. The extent of military political activity in Latin America is illustrated by the fact that this part of the world witnessed no less than 56 *successful* changes of government by extraconstitutional means during the period 1935-1964.¹⁸⁷

Although the military tend to play an important political role in developing countries in the effort to end conflict and chaos, and

---

¹⁸⁵ see for instance the example of rural upper Burma in M. Nash – 'Party Building in Upper Burma,' IV Asian Survey ('64) pp. 197-202; see also H. Hveem – 'Military Coups and the Political Development in Africa,' Syn Og Segn (Oslo) 5 ('66).
¹⁸⁶ J. L. Horowitz – 'Three Worlds of Development' ('66) p. 258.
¹⁸⁷ M. C. Needler – 'Political Development and Military Intervention in Latin America,' LX Am. Pol. Sc. Rev. ('66) p. 617. Similarly, during the years 1965-1969, Africa witnessed at least 9 successful military coups.

whatever the merits of some positive examples may be, they are poorly equipped to lead their countries out of such chaos.

One may argue about the pros and cons of a one-party rule under the prevailing circumstances in the Third World; but it can hardly be denied that dictatorial administration tends to create a climate of latent conflict and to be intrinsically unstable. In particular the military is bound to become a new source of conflict in developing countries.

1°. In Africa and Asia, their strong nationalistic ideology as well as their ambitious plans for modernization tend to collide with the vested interests of the traditional social rulers. The military leaders who do fight eagerly and ambitiously for national identity and national modernization, are often seen not as the representatives of the nation but as representatives of a certain tribe or region. Thus they may contribute by their powerful presence to sharper divisions along ethnic lines.

2°. In Latin America, the military are suspected of serving the interests of the traditional ruling classes and thus tend to collide with the interests of the anti-status quo groups in a modernizing society. Although the social and professional characteristics of the Latin American armed forces may have developed in ways parallel to those in which changes take place elsewhere in society, the military on the whole has acted politically in ways which frustrate these changes rather than reinforce them; indicating that military intervention here is 'pulled' by extra-military forces rather than 'pushed' by intra-military ones. In a developing society, however, as Needler observes, 'mass politicization increases even under a dictatorship. This shows itself in a high propensity to participate after the death or removal of the dictator.'[188] It is becoming increasingly more difficult to suppress political activity coming from the lower classes. At the same time the prevailing political role of the 'status quo-minded military' contributes to provoking violent solutions for socio-economic problems, as the 'change-minded' people expect traditional interests to be defended by force.

3°. They are often divided among themselves. Instead of trying to form a superpower, by creating unity whithin the ranks, the military becomes the victim of internal rivalries. In Africa, for instance, such internal rivalries can be held directly responsible for the overthrow of régimes in Algeria, Nigeria, Sudan, Central African Republic, Congo (Leopoldville), Congo (Brazzaville), Togo, Dahomey, Upper Volta and Ghana.

[188] M. C. Needler – 'Political Development in Latin America: Instability, Violence, and Evolutionary Change' ('68) p. 160.

4°. Military coups have a tendency to proliferate. Existing junta's are easily penetrated by agents, groups or ideas from the inside as well as from the outside.[189] 'A successful coup or insurrection by one party or group in one country inspires similar parties or groups in other countries to similar action,' as Huntington suggests.[190]
Using Galtung's Center-Periphery index, Fossum found a relation between coups as far as the topdog countries are concerned.[191] He did not suggest a more general relation because he approached the problem by focussing on a 'neighbour-effect.' This effect is based on the hypothesis that if any connection exists between nations in this respect, it should operate between neighbours to a greater extent than between non-neighbours. This approach, however, might be disputable: given the fact that Latin Americans perceive their continent somehow as an entity – in particular when confronted with the US – it might well be that similar socio-economic conditions (stage of development, percentage of literates, rate of industrialization and urbanization, rate of mass-organization, etc.) would be a far better point of departure for proving the relationship. Several existing studies, however, including that made by Fossum, suggest that a relationship exists, leading one to the tentative conclusion that under circumstances of potential political instability the occurrence of military coups tends to proliferate.

5°. The military may be powerful enough in cancelling democratic norms but they are often not powerful enough in maintaining social order over a long period of time. By temperament and by training, the military is more capable of preventing the exercise of political rule than of exercising such rule itself.[192] Notwithstanding their discipline, their sincerity and honest goals, they are usually not the best people to solve the complex economic and social problems of their country.

6°. By promising too much (as an endeavour to justify their power and control) and by being insufficiently capable of changing things, the military may in general contribute rather to increasing frustrations than to a better fulfilment of expectations.

7°. Finally, there is a tendency to link national greatness to military grandeur, symbolized by a modern Army, equipped with modern, expensive – and in the concrete circumstances often entirely useless –

---

[189] S. P. Huntington – 'Patterns of Violence in World Politics,' in idem (ed.) – 'Changing Patterns of Military Politics' ('62) pp. 44-47.
[190] idem, p. 45.
[191] E. Fossum, pp. 238-241.
[192] J. L. Horowitz, note 186 supra, p. 268.

weapons. Military budgets in the developing countries may still not be outrageous, but they are usually larger than the international climate seems to justify. How strong such tendencies towards the establishment of a strong Army is, may be suggested by the following quotation of former US Secretary of State Dean Rusk:

'I recall that at the time when all Members of the UN General Assembly were voting unanimously for disarmament, 70 Members were at that moment asking us for military assistence.'[193]

This constant drain on the national economy – up to 40% of the budget in some developing countries! – certainly contributes to the impedement of necessary economic programs and thus to intensification of frustration among the population.

'The successful transition of the developing countries into stable and variable societies,' as Bloomfield and Weiss write, 'is probably unattainable if arms competitions swallow up the precious margin of resources needed for development.'[194]

14. Internal prospects

At the end of this first Chapter the various relations between poverty, economic development, and internal conflict can be reproduced in the model presented at p. 102.

It is difficult to predict what is going to happen in the poor countries in the near future; the development to be achieved in the years ahead depends not only on the developing countries themselves, but also – and probably more – on the rich countries.
If present attitudes and policies of the rich countries do not change fundamentally, and if the developing countries can not achieve major improvements by themselves – and how should they? –, the following conclusions seem justified at this moment.
1. The period of 'static poverty' transcends rapidly into the period of 'dynamic poverty'; even larger sections of poor communities become aware of their relative deprivation and become conscious of their rights as human beings.

---

[193] quoted in G. Kemp – ' Arms Sales and Arms Control in the Developing Countries,' 22 The World Today ('66) p. 391.
[194] L. P. Bloomfield & Amelia C. Weiss – 'Arms Control and the Developing Countries,' XVIII World Politics ('65-'66) p. 3;
for further discussion on the influence of the arms trade to developing countries see the extensive 1910 – pages publication by SIPRI – 'The Arms Trade With The Third World' (Stockholm, New York, '71).

RELATIONSHIPS BETWEEN POVERTY, ECONOMIC DEVELOPMENT, AND DIRECT VIOLENCE IN POOR COUNTRIES

2. Apathetic reactions will become exceptional, anti-status quo reactions will be come the rule.
3. The increasing social consciousness and underdog solidarity will contribute to higher levels of organization, decreasing feelings of impotence and increasing the readiness to confrontation.
4. The longer people's hope for peaceful change is frustrated and the more negative experiences they suffer, the higher the risk that underdog-organization will contribute to the search for violent solutions.
5. While hitherto the frustration of roused expectations – in particular if some improvement has been achieved – may be considered to constitute an important cause of violent behavior, it might well be that in due course any belief in peaceful solutions is destroyed and that the mere feeling of deprivation will become the major determinant of poor people's actions.
6. Above certain minimum levels of common welfare the risk of social violence decreases; prosperity contributes to stability.
7. The development process may entail important disturbing effects; while these could be restricted or prevented at least in part through adequate planning which takes potential sources of conflict into account, however, the large-scale violence resulting from lasting poverty in this era must be feared to be unmanageable and to get out of control.

Many people in the rich countries wonder what they have to do with the developments in the Third World. The next Chapter will show that they have quite a lot to do with it: peacelessness in the poor countries constitutes, through various mechanisms, an increasing danger to world peace at large.

Chapter II

Polemological Aspects of Poverty and Development: The International Context

The present Chapter tries to analyze the international polemological consequences of lasting poverty and socio-economic development in the Third World. This analysis has been divided into three parts: first, the consequences for the relations among the donor countries, in particular the Super Powers, and the consequences from their present aid policies for the internal stability in recipient countries are discussed (A); second, the consequences for the international relations among the poor countries (B), and third, the consequences for the relations between the rich and poor countries as groups (C) are analyzed. Although in part closely interwoven, these three sets of aspects were considered to have enough specific features justifying separate analysis.

A. *Relations Among the Super Powers:*
   Intervention and the Welfare-Gap

In this section of the study, the bearing of the internal socio-economic problems in Third World countries upon world peace, more specifically the relations among the Super Powers, will be discussed. This is done by reference to their policy of intervention. Both the economic needs of developing countries and the politically instable situation in many of them offer occasions to the Super Powers to intervene, with the purpose of gaining influence in the Third World. First, however, it should be explained why the policy of intervention has become – and should accordingly be considered here – such an important phenomenon in post-War politics (A. 1.). Thereafter, this policy will be analyzed as far as it functions in particular within the present context of povertya nd economic development (A. 2.), intervention by aid.

1. *Intervention and civil strife*

When both the United States and the Soviet Union during the early fifties realized that a direct military confrontation between them would lead to the complete destruction of both of them, the Cold War froze positions in Europe – until then the political battlefield fought upon by the protagonists of democracy and those of communism.

At that time, however, developments in Africa and Asia attracted the attention of the Soviet Union and the United States. They saw two continents emerging from a colonial rule into independent entities and so recognized their interests in this: both inside and outside the United Nations Organization the increasing number of young, independent countries were to become of high political importance to both of them; inside the UN they would one day decide on a great many Resolutions brought up in the General Assembly; outside the UN their friendship would mean increased political power and strategic gain. A struggle for the support of the young states began, and the Third World became a major political battleground in the framework of the Cold War.

The strongly nationalistic ideologies of many leaders of the new countries might have provided a serious obstacle to any endeavour in this direction, had not the excessive and ever increasing level of conflict in these countries created an easy opportunity for a policy of intervention. On the one hand, the Super Powers tried to gain the favour of national leaders by supporting them in case of civil strife. On the other hand, many of these leaders themselves appealed to one of the Super Powers to intervene and save their position. An atmosphere of intense distrust arose between the two Super Powers because each of them doubted the other's objectives in the Third World. They became so anxious about the other's potential increase of influence, that intervention and counter-intervention came to dictate their relations with the Third World to such extent, that in the beginning both of them negated the possibility of neutralism. They both considered it their right to intervene in any conflict, thereby preventing the eventual 'desertion' of a country to 'the devil' – the other side; both of them considered neutralism as politically immoral.[1]

---

[1] As such neutralism was denounced by President Truman. Equally the Soviet Political Dictionary of 1956 still called nationalism (which in the Third World means in the first place independence of any block) as 'a bourgeois ideology and policy hostile to the proletariat.' Likewise China rejected the concept of neutralism until 1955 (Bandung Conference); see H. M. Vinacke – 'Communist China and the Uncommitted Zone,' The Annals (Nov. '65) p. 113.

Within the present context an extensive discussion of the topic 'intervention in the Third World,' as far as it does not function directly within the context of poverty and development, would carry us too far. Yet, it is important to recognize the fact that the policy of intervention, as it developed throughout the Third World as a practice of the United States, the Soviet Union, and later China, which confronted the world several times with dangerous hot excesses of the Cold War and sometimes may even have brought us to the brink of nuclear war, has been a consequence of the fact *that the economic circumstances in the Third World contribute to internal unrest and thus to the opportunity of intervention, while on the other hand, given the importance of interventionary practices, they provoke a specific means of intervention, namely intervention by aid.* Keeping this in mind it seems appropriate to make here a few more introductory remarks on this policy of intervention in general.

1.1. *The United States*

The way of thinking about the countries in the Third World and their involvement in the East-West conflict during the time when the Cold War was at its height, is best characterized by John Foster Dulles, who in 1956 as Secretary of State called neutralism, as advocated by many young régimes in developing countries, 'an immoral and short-sighted concept.' For several years, American officials demanded that non-aligned nations should 'choose' sides in the Cold War; legislative and public reactions to non-alignment were, and tended for a long time to remain, highly critical. Gradually, however, executive policy-makers began to modify their assessment of non-alignment, the concept gradually being perceived as a valuable obstacle in itself against communist influence.[2] The notable exception remained Latin America, but even here we were to witness a less stringent policy in the years to come.

Both the initial refusal to accept a neutralist stand, and the later approval of it, accentuate the fact that the Third World was and is considered a major target of Cold War strategy. Wherever the 'communist threat' was perceived as being too dangerous, political or even military intervention was considered and often occurred.

The American policy of intervention within the framework of the Cold War was initiated officially with the 'Truman-doctrine,' incorporated in Truman's speech on March 12, 1947, in which this President announced 'the policy of the United States to support free

---

[2] see C. V. Crabb Jr. – 'The US and the Neutralists: A Decade in Perspective,' 362 The Annals ('65) pp. 93 ff.

peoples who are resisting attempted subjugation by armed minorities or by outside pressures.' This doctrine, according to E. Rostow 'has gradually evolved, first in Europe, and then in Asia, into a kind of common law of international order.'[3]
This line of policy was extended substantially by President Johnson in 1965, when he made clear that (in connection with Latin America) an official request for American assistance by a foreign government should be no longer a prerequisite for such help. Washington announced that it alone would decide on the necessity of intervention in Latin American countries.[4]
It would seem as superfluous as it is impossible to present a list of the numerous interventions practiced by the United States in the Third World. It is superfluous because so much has been written already on US intervention in countries ranging from Guatemala and the Lebanon to Vietnam and the Dominican Republic.[5] It is impossible because so much has remained hidden and interventions often occured more in a covert than an overt way.[6] At this moment only insiders know how many revolts, civil wars, and international conflicts were used, fed, or even instigated by United States machineries abroad. What we know however, is enough. Intervention has become an every day practice. It seems even to have escalated into a moral duty. President Kennedy once said:

'We in this country, in this generation, are – by destiny rather than choice – the watchmen on the walls of freedom.'

[3] E. V. Rostow – 'Law, Power and the Pursuit of Peace' ('68)p. 43.
[4] on the 'Johnson-doctrine' see R. J. Barnet –'Intervention and Revolution' ('68) pp. 10, 174.
[5] just to give some examples:
on Guatemala see E. Lieuwen – 'US Policy in Latin America' ('65) pp. 90ff; and Ann Thomas & A. J. Thomas – 'Non-Intervention' ('56) pp. 161;
on the Lebanon see Q. Wright – 'US Intervention in the Lebanon,' 53 A.J.I.L. ('59) pp. 112-125;
on the Dominice Republic see J. P. S. Mc Laren – 'The Dominican Crisis: An Inter-American Dilemma,' IV Can. Y.I.L. ('66) pp. 178-193.
[6] see for instance D. Wise & Th. B. Ross – 'The Invisible Government' ('60); they begin their book as follows: 'There are two governments in the United States today. One is visible. The other is invisible. The first is the government that citizens read about in their newspapers and children study about in their civics books. The second is the interlocking, hidden machinery that carries out the policies of the United States in the Cold War. This second, invisible government gathers intelligence, conducts espionage, and plans and executes secret operations all over the globe.' In the same sense the former head of the CIA, Dulles, described the Russian KGB (Committee of State Security) as a 'multi-purpose, clandestine arm of power..... more than a secret police organization, more than an intelligence and a counter-intelligence organization.... It is an aggressive arm of Soviet ambitions in the Cold War'; A. W. Dulles – 'The Craft of Intelligence' ('65) p. 84.

In this sense the 'Captive Nations Week' was announced on July 17, 1959, as a warning to the 'communist oppressors.' In the proclamation it was said that 'the submerged nations look to the US as the citadel of human freedom, for leadership in bringing about their liberation and independence.'[7] Intervention eventually became considered necessary, just, and even stabilizing world peace, often without having made an enquiry into the dangers of this policy. Brzezinski witnessed this view when he said:

> 'Our global involvement and our preponderance of power is such that our disinvolvement would create international chaos of enormous proportions. Our involvement is a historic fact. There is no way of ending it........ intervention is justified whenever its absence will create regional instability of expanding proportions.'[8]

The amount of instability resulting from this policy was often discounted because the idea of counter-balancing perceived communist aggression throughout the Third World seems to have obscured consistent and rational thinking: although poverty was considered by officials as the most important cradle of communism, the basic reaction has been to prepare the military for the fight against its political consequences, instead of removing that creadle. Instead of helping consistently to build the underdeveloped countries, US policy has rather been marked by the endeavour to strengthen the military of rightist governments.

The illogical character of this US policy towards the Third World becomes clear from a consideration of two opposite dicta determining that policy. On the one hand, there was the dictum that 'poverty breeds communism' – ergo that it is an internal problem –; on the other hand, there was the supposition that 'no people votes itself into communism' – ergo that it is an external problem. The second dictum seems to have become, however, the dominant one.

In respect to Latin America especially the answer to the perceived communist threat was not sought for in fundamental socio-economic transformation and economic development, but instead in military preparations directed at foreign aggressors. The result has been, on the one hand, a half-hearted measure (that failed) like the Alliance for Progress, and, on the other hand, a full-scale preparation for war.

Fort Gulick in Panama functions within this context. This was the place where until the beginning of 1968 some 25000 Latin American

---

[7] for a criticizing comment on this event see Q. Wright – 'Subversive Intervention,' 54 A.J.I.L. ('60) pp. 521-536.
[8] Z. Brzezinski – 'The Implications of Change for US Foreign Policy,' Dept. State Bull. (July 3, '67) p. 22.

officers were trained in the techniques, methods and ideology of the anti-guerrilla. The task of the Special Forces 'educating' those officers has been described officially as 'to advise, train and aid the Latin American military and paramilitary forces to conduct counter-insurgency activities, and to do so in support of the objectives of the United States within the framework of the Cold War.'[9]

Another aspect of the same preparation has been the spending of millions of dollars on social science-projects, executed by Universities by order of the Pentagon, the State Department and the AID. In 1967 alone about $ 40 million were spent on research entitled 'Social Factors Relevant to Military Civil Action Doctrine.'

The famous project Agile ($ 38 million a year), which was officially said to be intended to strengthen and support pro-United States régimes, provided studies for Bolivia, Columbia, Equador, Guatemala, Honduras, Panama, Peru and Venezuela.[10]

The policy of intervention has become a principal answer of the United States to perceived threats from communist side, and has dictated to a large extent its policy towards the Third World.

1.2. *The Soviet Union*

The same can be said of the policy of the Soviet Union. In the beginning the Soviet ideology left no place for relations with non-socialist governments. Economic interests and commerce as well as the alliance with the West during the second World War practically dissolved that principle, but theoretically it was maintained for a while. There was said to be little justification for extensive contacts with the emerging countries of the Third World. As in the case of the United States, no third camp was recognized for years, and the granting of independence to countries like India and Burma was regarded as spurious in Moscow. Instead of showing interest in closer contacts with the new governments, Moscow preferred to assist communist centers in developing countries. In 1948 communists in Burma, India, Indonesia, the Philippines, and Malaya, were urged to adopt insurgency tactics.[11]

During the Korean war, however, the USSR first recognized the importance of neutralist countries sympathizing with its position.

[9] see Ph. Nourry – 'Camping Tonight,' Atlas (May '68) pp. 18-20.
[10] see C. Brightman & M. Klare – 'Campus Counterinsurgency. Focus: Latin America,' Viet Report (April-May '68) pp. 22-23.
[11] J. S. Reshetar – 'The Soviet Union and the Neutralist World,' 362 The Annals ('65) p. 104.

On that occasion it was realized that the 'national governments' in the Third World might be valuable partners against the US.

Such reorientation of its approach of neutralism was advanced during the fifties, when the USSR recognized with increasing unrest the growing activities of the US in the Third World, and also when another Super Power (China) began to emerge on its borders. In particular Pakistan's alliance with the West, ostensibly directed against the Russian-led communist bloc, seems to have stimulated Russia to formulate a clear-cut policy of friendship with neutralist countries, in particular with regard to India.

Once the Soviet philosophy had thus to be adapted to practical reality, there was no reason for not going further on that road. The Soviet Union realized that by supporting neutralism in the underdeveloped countries it would gain support from those countries which were not fully resolved with their ties to the west. It was thus considered not only politically and economically sound, but it could, moreover, be depicted as morally superior, since it did not expose the Soviet Union to charges of neo-colonialism.[12] Soviet appreciation of neutralism began to manifest itself after Stalin's death. The theoretical line for this new aspect of Soviet foreign policy was first laid down by Khrushchev at the twentieth Party Congress in 1956, and was developed further in the 1961 Party Program.[13]

In the Spring of 1962, after the twenty-second Congress, a conference of the Soviet Institute for World Economy and International Relations invented the concept of 'positive neutralism,' the outposts of which were said to be the UAR in Africa and India in Asia. The definite acceptance of neutralism was marked as a welcome concept: During earlier periods, Soviet policy was dictated by the demand that the Soviet side should be chosen. Now the principal demand had become that the Western side should not be chosen.[14]

This new approach eventually led to the adoption of two new theoretical concepts, enabling the Soviet Union to compete with the United States in the Third World. First the concept of 'national democracy' was introduced, concerning those young countries which took an anti-imperialist stand, and were on the road to socialism. At the outset 'national democracy' appears to have projected an alliance between nationalist élites and the still disorganized but

---

[12] S. P. Seth – 'Russia's Role in Indo-Pak Policies,' IX Asian Survey (Aug. '69) pp. 614-615.
[13] J. S. Reshetar, pp. 104ff.
[14] W. A. C. Adie – 'The Communist Powers in Africa,' Conflict Studies, No. 10 (Dec.-Jan. 70/71) p. 4.

(presumably) developing mass movements – not unlike the 'united front from above' of the 1920's. In due course, the assumption was held, that the nationalist leadership would yield to the greater sense of direction and purpose of the Marxist – led proletarians. As the meeting of 81 communist parties, held in Moscow in 1960, made clear, such states were to be isolated from the non-communist world, to become economically dependent on the communist world and so inevitably to develop along the path of 'scientific socialism.'

Since it was recognized soon that many countries would thus remain outside the scope of Soviet relations, – because the supposed progressive bloc often remained imaginary – a second concept was introduced later. The concept of 'revolutionary democracy' was aimed at those young countries with progressive leaders which were anti-imperialist but not (yet) on the road to socialism.[15] Thus practically the entire Third World was included and the theoretical foundation of extended relations was created, with the aim of competing against the US.

In the West we know less of Russian interventions in the developing countries – and probably there have been far less of them – than we know of the American interventions. What is important to recognize here is that the *Russian intentions as perceived by the Americans* have been sufficiently important in leading to such crises as the Lebanon and Vietnam ones. The Russians themselves have in part helped to create that picture of their intentions by often repeated ambiguous statements; e.g. Khrushchev said during the 21st Party Congress:

'The Soviet Union will participate in the joint struggle with the dependent peoples.'

Similarly during the 22nd Party Congress he said that it was Russia's obligation

'to strengthen proletarian solidarity with the working class of all working people of the world, and to render the fullest moral and material support to peoples fighting to free themselves from imperialist and colonial aggression or to consolidate their independence.'

Concerning the last words, Brezhnev let everyone know that real independence cannot exist as long as socialism has not been reached. In this light, he repeated at the 23rd Party Congress that

'the communist party of the USSR regards as its international duty continued allround

---

[15] Ch. B. Mc Lane – 'Soviet Doctrine and the Military Coups in Africa,' XXI Int. J. ('66) pp. 304-305;
Ph. E. Mosely – 'Soviet Policy in the Developing Countries,' 43 For. Aff. (Oct. '64) pp. 97ff.; and idem 'The Kremlin and the Third World,' 46 For. Aff. (Oct. '67) pp. 64-77.

support to the people's struggle for final liberation from colonial and neo-colonial oppression.'[16]

The Pravda, finally, left no doubt about the way the Soviet Union looks at the development of the Third World. On Sept. 14, 1966, it wrote:

> 'The national liberation movements are an organic element of the epochmaking process of the revolutionary transition from capitalism to socialism.'

In trying to gain the sympathy from anti-American factions in developing countries by propaganda and support, the Soviet spokesmen have often used the argument of 'the common interests.' As Rymalow puts it: 'Die KPD SU betrachtet das brüderliche Bündnis mit den Völkern, die das koloniale und halbkoloniale Joch abgeschüttelt haben, als einen Grundpfeiler ihrer internationalen Politik. Dieses Bündnis beruht auf der Gemeinsamkeit, die zwischen den Lebensinteressen des Weltsozialismus und der weltumspannenden nationalen Befreiungsbewegung besteht.'[17]

1.3. *China*

The same argument of 'common interests' has often been used by the Chinese. The speech made by Lin Piao in 1965 is most famous in which he appealed to the peoples of the Third World to unite and stand up together against the rich and in which he predicted the encirclement of the cities (the rich nations) by the countryside (the Third World).[18]

At first, China – like the United States and the Soviet Union – negated the possibility of neutralism as a valid concept in international relations. This point of view was expressed in Mao's address 'On the People's Democratic Dictatorship' (July, 1949), in which he said:

> 'You lean to one side! Precisely so..... the experience of forty years and twenty-eight years, respectively, show that, without exception, the Chinese people either lean to the side of imperialism or the side of socialism'.

This would hold for others as well, Mao said; there could be no middle course:

---

[16] see the accounts of the Party Congresses edited in English by Novosti Press Agency House.
[17] W. W. Rymalow – 'Die UdSSR und die wirtschaftlich schwach entwickelten Länder' ('64) p. 6.
[18] Lin Piao – 'Long live the Victory of the People's War,' 8 Peking Review 36 (Sept. 3, '65).

'To sit on the fence is impossible; a third road does not exist'.[19]

Thus, initially, Communist China's policy was opposed to non-alignment and directed toward alignment with the Soviet Union. Peking refused, for instance, to establish relations with Yugoslavia because of Tito's breach with Stalin.[20]

Eventually, both the military encirclement by the United States and the rupture with Moscow initiated China's change in this respect. China recognized that its political interests were contradictory to its anti-neutralist campaign, especially as China – unlike the Soviet Union – was in no position to engage in nation-to-nation competition with the United States. It could only compete by putting forth its advocation of global revolution, and by gradually enticing Third World countries away from Western or Russian influence.[21]

Since the time of the Bandung Conference in 1955 China accepted non-alignment as possible, legitimate, and profitable to Cold War objectives; first vis-à-vis the United States, later also vis-à-vis the Soviet Union. For this purpose the concept of 'new democracy' was introduced, as a banner under which to enrol as many compatriots as possible for their ostensibly nationalist cause; theoretically, communists were expected to take a leading role in national struggles of liberation and subsequently to carry on with the true socialist revolution as advocated by China. Thus Chou En-lai during his tour in 1963 praised the achievement of independence in Africa and added that 'an excellent revolutionary situation exists in Africa.' He expected the 'new democratic revolutions' to develop into socialist revolutions, a hope which has proved idle and which had its theoretical consequences as far as neutralism is concerned: today a new approach can be witnessed, characterized by global activity and diplomatic initiatives without any obvious discrimination as to ideological stand.

China joined the competition for the Third World in 1956, when the UAR (then still Egypt) was the first African State to enter into diplomatic relations with China. From that moment the Chinese endeavours to win the support of the young countries and to aid pro-Chinese factions became ever more intensive.[22] Rumours about

---

[19] C. Brandt, B. Schwartz and J. K. Fairbanks – 'A Documentary History of Chinese Communism' ('52) pp. 453-454.
[20] H. M. Vinacke – 'Communist China and the Uncommitted Zone,' 362 The Annals ('65) p. 114.
[21] see R. A. Scalapino – 'The Sino-Soviet Conflict in Perspective,' 351 Annals ('64) p. 9.
[22] see G. T. Yu – 'Sino-African Relations: A Survey,' V Asian Survey ('65) pp. 321-332; and idem – 'China's Failure in Africa,' VI Asian Survey ('66) pp. 461-468.

Chinese intervention practices became manifold,[23] such rumours being intensified by acts of overt interference in internal affairs as in the case of Burma in 1967.[24] China's Prime Minister Chen Yi reportedly said that Thailand was the next target on China's list.[25]

Whatever the real intentions of the Chinese in the Third World are, it is important to realize again how the United States (as well as the Soviet Union this time) perceive such intentions. This perception happens to be very negative, intensified by the fact that in 1965 and in 1966 many African countries broke with China just because of alleged undermining activities.[26]

Just as in the case of the United States and the Soviet Union, official statements have been taken as a warning signal by the other side(s); in the case of China they have indeed been quite radical. General Lo Jui-ching compared the American foreign policy with Hitler's and appealed to the Soviet Union to accept the necessity of war and violent revolutions[27]; and Lin Piao repeated in his afore mentioned speech the often expressed statement, that 'the socialist countries should regard it as their internationalist duty to support the people's revolutionary struggles in Asia, Africa and Latin America.'

The cadres of the People's Liberation Army are instructed how to assist Wars of Liberation abroad, as became clear from secret Journals[28]; and just as the American Special Forces and Russian instructors do, Chinese military specialists are training young Africans for a future struggle in their country.[29]

---

[23] these rumors often related to undermining activities by Chinese embassy-personnel, as was recently the case with the peasant unrest in Cambodia.

[24] on that occasion the activities of the Chinese embassy resulted in anti-Chinese riots during which many people were killed. The population was called upon 'to master the great thought of Mao Tse-tung,' and Radio Peking appealed to the pro-Chinese Communist Party of Burma to start violent insurrection against the bourgeois-government, while it was said that the Chinese Central Party Committee would assist: 'We regard such support as our bounden international duty'; see P. Boog – 'People's War in Burma,' Far Eastern Economic Review (Nov. 16, '67); reprinted in Survival (April '68) pp. 123-126.

[25] O. E. Nuechterlein – 'Thailand: A Year of Danger and Hope,' VI Asian Survey ('66) p. 122.

[26] see on this for instance P. Andrews Poole -"Communist China's Aid Diplomacy", VI Asian Survey ('66) p. 626.

[27] Lo Jui-ching — "China's Military Doctrine", VII Survival (August '65) p. 201.

[28] Tsang Tson & M. Halperin -"Mao Tse-tung's Rezolutionary Strategy and Peking's International Behavior", LIX Am. Pol. Sc. Rev. ('65) p. 83.

[29] see Musosa Kazembe – 'Why should I die?,' Atlas (June '68) pp. 19-21.

1.4. The new arena of the Cold War struggle

The three Super Powers use the same phrases, but they mean different things. They all speak of freedom, justice and self-determination, but they look at the world through their own glasses. Taking the concept of self-determination for instance, it would seem quite encouraging to hear President Eisenhower say that 'any nation's right to form a government and an economic system of its own choosing is inalienable. Any nation's attempt to dictate the other nations their form of government is indefensible.' These words are based, however, on the dubious assumption 'that no nation will ever vote itself into Communism' and thus a nation's free choice is guaranteed and self-explanatory as long as that choice is a non-communist one.[30] This kind of thinking becomes apparent when we add to those words of Eisenhower the following words of Rusk in 1951:

> 'We do not recognize the authorities in Peiping for what they pretend to be. The Peiping régime may be a colonial Russian government, a slavonic Manchukuo on larger scale. It is not the government of China. It does not pass the first test. It is not Chinese.......'[31]

Indeed, a somewhat narrow concept of 'self-determination.'

The same can be said of the other side. The Russians too have their own concept of the fundamental principle of self-determination. Take Stalin, who quite frankly said:

> 'The principle of self-determination must be a means in the struggle for Socialism and must be subordinated to the principles of Socialism.'[32]

This way of thinking has not changed since Stalin's days – and how should it? This can be concluded e.g. from communist literature dealing with international law; cf. Mampel writing:

> 'Nicht irgendein beliebiger Wille des Volkes soll zum Ausdruck kommen, sondern der geschichtlich notwendige Wille, der der Wille der Marxistisch-Leninistischen Partei ist, weil nur sie wisse was die Zukunft mit Notwendigkeit bringe und das eintrete, weil allein dieses im Interesse des Volkes liege.'[33]

---

[30] 28 Dept. of State Bull. 599 ('53);
S. Hoffman – 'The American Style: Our Past and Our Principles,' 46 For. Aff. 2 ('67) p. 371.
[31] R. Harris – 'A new 30 years' war?,' The Times (Febr. '68).
[32] translated from German: 'Das Prinzip der Selbstbestimmung muss ein Mittel im Kampf für den Sozialismus sein und den Prinzipien des Sozialismus untergeordnet sein,' 'Gesammelte Werke' (E. Berlin '52) IV p. 27.
[33] S. Mampel – 'Das Selbstbestimmungsrecht der Völker', Jahrbuch für Ostrecht 1/2 ('60) p. 58.

The same kind of argument is used by Arzinger concluding from it that the people in the DDR have expressed their free will contrary to the people of Western Germany, who are still oppressed by the 'devilish capitalists.'[34]

What remains thus of the usefulness of concepts like self-determination, freedom, independence etc.? The answer seems very obvious. When McKinley annexed the Philippines he justified that by explaining that 'the Lord told him it was America's duty to educate the Philippines, and uplift and civilize and Christianize them,' or, as F. Schuman reminds, 'by solicitude for the little brown brothers for whom Christ also died.'[35] Today America's concept of 'manifest destiny' has been proliferated: we have now an American destiny, a Russian destiny, and a Chinese destiny. As far as neutralism is concerned, the three Super Powers have all come to accept it as a valid political concept, as long as it constitutes a barrier against extension of influence by the opponents. But in practice their acceptance is only conditional, because they all try to get any neutralist country on their side before the others do.

In the meantime the intervention policy of the Super Powers is extremely dangerous since the risk of direct confrontation – avoided so far in Europe – is always present. They keep their devilish perceptions of each other, which leaves no room for an attitude of expectation. The fear of intervention by one side has often been enough to provoke a preventive intervention by another. The one reacts to the other and vice versa. It is like a vicious circle: the Americans intervened in the Dominican Republic, 'to prevent some Communist take-over'; the Soviets build up their armed forces 'to counter the imperialist strategy of local and restricted wars with its own weapons, the weapons of the selfsame local and restricted wars';[36] Kosygin warned China against any further intervention in Burma, 'pledging full support and sympathy for Burma in its trouble with China;'[37] the Chinese usually accuse the other two Powers of imperialistic interventions, which China will not tolerate.

What we have today is an international situation characterized by the fact that Great Power conflict has been transferred from the formal military level to the level of political, economic and indirect paramilitary confrontation. Every internal conflict today is of potential

---

[34] R. Arzinger – 'Das Selbstbestimmungsrecht im Allgemeinen Völkerrecht der Gegenwart' ('66) pp. 339-359, and 364 ff.
[35] F. L. Schuman – 'International Politics. The Destiny of the Western State System' ('48) p. 535.
[36] A. Gabelic – 'New Accent in Soviet Strategy,' Survival (Febr. '68) pp. 45-46.
[37] P. Boog, note 24 supra.

international importance because of intervention. The occasions to intervene are numerous enough.

'Given the certain connection between economic stagnation and the incidence of violence,' as McNamara put it, 'the years that lie ahead for the nations in the Southern half of the globe are pregnant with violence'; and because of the Great Power struggle, 'violence anywhere in a taut world transmits sharp signals through the complex ganglia of international relations; and the security of the United States is related to the security and stability of nations half a globe away.'[38]
This point of view, moreover, is held by the other Big Powers as well.
'In the past,' as Rothstein writes, 'the influence of small powers rose only when they were sought as allies on the eve of a great-power conflict. But now, with great-power military conflict limited, they are still sought as allies or friends – but in place of, not because of, an imminent great-power war.'[39] In the same sense the policies of intervention make Henkin state:

> 'In part, perhaps, because war is less likely, the disorders of the future which must be feared and faced are subversion, revolution, insurrection and civil war.'[40]

This is not only so because the Great Powers intervene as they think necessary, but also because sometimes the leaders of young countries invite them to do so, asking them to support their personal position and offering their political sympathy in return. How dangerous to international peace this can be, was illustrated when Kasavubu and Lumumba asked the Russians to intervene against the Americans during the Congo-crisis. On July 16, 1960, the Russians warned: 'if the States which are directly carrying out the imperialist aggression against the Congo Republic and those inviting them continue their criminal actions, the Soviet Union will not hesitate to take decisive measures to stop the aggression.'[41] On that occasion things changed in a positive way. One wonders what could have happened otherwise.

'We have now come to a stage', says U Thant, 'where all ideological concepts ... will become meaningless if their pursuit involves a third world war'.[42]

---

[38] N.Y.T. (May 19, '66).
[39] R. L. Rothstein – 'Alignment, Nonalignment and Small Powers: 1945-1965', XX Int. Org. ('66) p. 407.
[40] L. Henkin – 'Force, Intervention, and Neutrality in Contemporary International Law,' Proc. Am. Soc. I.L. ('63) p. 154.
[41] D. Morison – 'The USSR and Africa' ('64) pp. 37-38.
[42] UN Monthly Chronicle (June '66) p. 67.

This crucial insight should be kept in mind whenever one thinks of intervention. Intervention can only occur as long as the Third World is the scene of riots, strife and civil wars. That scene again is strongly influenced by economic conditions.

Having considered the international framework of the Cold War and having observed how the socio-economic situation in the Third World contributes *indirectly* to intervention, we can now turn to a special 'weapon' within this framework: the medium of economic aid. In the next section it is discussed how poverty and development *directly* provoke intervention and international destabilization.

2. *Intervention by aid*

The fear of direct confrontation caused the shift of Cold War manoeuvers to be moved from the European to the Third World scene. Likewise the fear of direct confrontation there contributed to the acceptance by the Super Powers of the politically convenient concept of neutralism. Acceptance of neutralism in its turn meant a shift from direct military intervention to more subtle methods on the political and the economic level. Under pressure of the nuclear threat, but eager to prevent any gain by the adversaries, the Super Powers substituted their original Cold War struggle for a more peaceful Cold War competition.

The economic needs of the developing countries constituted a welcome basis on which to build the structures of such indirect policy. It did not take long before the Super Powers recognized their interests in a policy directed at winning friends, by extending economic assistance and exploiting economic relations. Just as the Cold War contributed to the process of decolonization, it also stimulated the concept of foreign aid. Today it can be said that economic aid has become one of the most important means of foreign intervention.

Of course it would be incorrect to state that aid has been given for political reasons only – economic and humanitarian considerations have played their role also. Taking all the evidence that follows into account, however, one must inevitably conclude, that the political motives have been the most important arguments in deciding whether and how aid should be given.

We shall now turn to the polemological aspects of both economic and military aid.

First, the question concerning the motives for assisting the developing countries and the role of aid in the setting of the Cold War is dealt with (2.1.). Second, some special features of present bilateral aid are considered, which are thought to be of polemological importance with respect to the internal stability of developing states; the factors of discontinuity (2.2.1.) and waste (2.2.2.). Under 2.3. we shall deal with military aid. Under 2.4., finally, we shall try to reach some conclusions, and discuss the official presupposition according to which the donor can influence the political development of the recipient by way of the aid he gives.

It should also be remembered that when bilateral aid is mentioned in this book, only bilateral *governmental* aid is meant, unless it is stated otherwise.

The term 'aid' as used here should, moreover, be understood to include trade transactions with developing countries, as far as their economic effects are presented as being one-sidedly profitable to the developing countries in question.

2.1. *Economic relations with the Third World*

Within the setting of the policy of intervention as it was developed after the Second World War, it may be unsurprising that the United Nations has never become the real center of aid distribution, once the desire for development swept through the Third World. The United Nations is supposed to be neutral, and so the Super Powers soon recognized the potential political importance of playing Father Christmas: when his arrival is expected, the children are nice and willing. This largely explains that the bulk of economic aid – some 85% on average – went through bilateral channels; e.g. in 1963 it was 84%, in 1968 it was 88%.[43]

Economic aid and trade have become important political tools in the hands of the donors. This becomes clear when one takes a look at the motives behind the aid programs as put forward by the United States, the Soviet Union, and China respectively, and when one compares their aid activities against the background of the Cold War competition.

2.1.1. *The United States*

Beginning with the United States as the most important donor, it seems appropriate to state first that American aid activities are not discussed within a context of mere economic imperialism. One line of thought on this subject tends to reduce all American economic

---

[43] according to the DAC of OECD. For earlier periods see OECD-Report 'The Flow of Financial Resources to Less-Developed Countries, 1956-1963' ('64).

relations (including aid programs) to a network of economic imperialism. Another line of thought, negating the imperialistic setting, is inclined to stress political and strategic (or even humanitarian) motives exclusively.

In the opinion of the present author this discussion would seem to be mainly an academic one: whatever may be true of the alleged necessity of capitalist imperialism (this is not the topic of the present study and is therefore not discussed here), within the context of the Cold War it simply is impossible to distinguish between economic and political factors. It cannot be maintained that economic deliberations alone can explain America's international economic activity now that it is confronted with socialist adversaries, nor the other way round. From the American point of view a 'one-ness' of national security and business interests exists: the size of the 'free' world and the degree of its 'security' define the geographic boundaries within which American capital can be freely invested. Such a point of view is supported by Magdoff in his book on American economic imperialism, where he states:

'Just as the fight against Communism helps the search for profits, so the search for profits helps the fight against Communism. What more perfect harmony of interests could be imagined?'[44]

On a more official level Rostow made it clear that this is indeed the case:

'The location, natural resources, and populations of the underdeveloped areas are such that, should they become attached effectively to the Communist bloc, the United States would become the second Power in the world....... If the underdeveloped areas fall under Communist domination or if they move to fixed hostility to the West, the economic and military strength of Western Europe and Japan will be diminished, and the Atlantic world will become, at best, an awkward alliance, incapable of exercising effective influence outside a limited orbit..... In short, *our military security and our way of life* as well as the fate of Western Europe and Japan are at stake in the evolution of the underdeveloped areas. We evidently have a major interest, then, in developing a free world coalition which embraces in reasonable harmony and unity the industrialized states of Western Europe and Japan on the one hand, the underdeveloped areas of Asia, the Middle East, and Africa, on the other.'[45]

Clearer testimony to the inseparability of economic and political-strategic interests from the American point of view can hardly be imagined. Whatever the main objective of America's economic

---

[44] H. Magdoff – 'The Age of Imperialism' ('69) pp. 200-201.
[45] US Cong., 84th Conf. 2nd. Sess., Hearings before the Subcommittee on Foreign Economic Policy of the Joint Economic Committee (Dec. '56) pp. 127, 131.

relations may be, given the Cold War struggle against communism in the Third World, economic motives become at the same time political ones, and vice versa.

Given this situation, the American aid policy can justly and will be treated here from the political point of view, since mainly political motives have officially been put forward to explain its purposes.

On many occasions, official spokesmen of the United States have stressed the political importance of economic aid in relation to the national security of the United States and the interests of democracy. Quite typical of this way of thinking about aid are the following introductory words of Secretary of State Rusk, speaking on the Foreign Aid Program to the House Committee on Foreign Affairs:

> 'I appreciate the opportunity to meet once again with the Committee to discuss one of our vital contributions to the security of the free world.'[46] 'The US,' Rusk said on another occasion, 'must play the leading role in shaping the history of our time in that direction. This is both the burden and opportunity of our generation in this country.'

Equally characteristic was the speech of President Kennedy on March 20, 1963, during his visit to Costa Rica. He spoke on the purposes of the Alliance for Progress and mentioned: (1) political freedom and independence; (2) democracy; (3) social justice; and (4) economic progress – in this very order![47] On another occasion the President said:

> 'Foreign aid is a method by which the United States maintains a position of influence and control around the world, and sustains a good many countries which would definitely collapse, or pass into the Communist bloc.'[48]

Likewise a former member of the AID, Nelson, summarizes the military and political objectives of foreign aid as:

> 'continued access to military bases and other strategic facilities located in specific developing countries; maintaining ties with formal allies and strengthening their defense capacity; delaying recognition of Communist China, and its admission to the United Nations; discouraging trade, particularly in strategic goods, with Communist China, Cuba, and North Vietnam; more generally, encouraging independence or a pro-Western alignment in the foreign policy positions of developing countries.'[49]

---

[46] Dept. State Bull. (April 29, '63) p. 664.
[47] Dept. State Bull. (April 8, '63) p. 519.
[48] US Senate, Committee on Foreign Relations – 'Some Important Issues in Foreign Aid,' a report prepared by the Legislative Reference Service of the Library of Congress ('66) p.15.
[49] J. M. Nelson – 'Aid, Influence, and Foreign Policy' ('68) p. 11.

It was found that among high officials the main purpose of aid is believed to be the creation of a world community of free and independent nations; free in the American sense of the word.[50]

Thus the medium of aid has been thrust into the arena of the Cold War, as it was once clearly indicated by Stevensen on American TV: 'The importance of the great struggle of the future is to gain the sympathy of the mass of neutral countries and territories, which try to escape from hunger, misery and ignorance.'

This argument is also revealed in the motivation of concrete aid-programs. From the beginning, the government of the United States assumed that technical assistance would contribute to political stability and resistance against Soviet penetration, and for this reason these objectives have never been absent from considerations about US aid programs.[51] Steel concludes that the survival of foreign aid programs is almost entirely dependent on the Cold War.[52]

The concept of foreign aid became related to the question of national security with the Lend-Lease Act of 1940, in which Roosevelt modified the definition of non-intervention in order to assist beleaguered Britain in resisting Nazi-Germany. This relation was reinforced during the War, when large shipments of supplies of all kinds were sent to Europe, and it was continued after the War as a feature of the emerging Cold War.

This began with the Marshall-plan for European recovery. While applauding its favourable economic consequences, several observers have failed to notice how the principle aim of the Marshall-plan was circumscribed in the Economic Cooperation Act; it clearly being a political aim:

'Recognizing the intimate economic and other relationships between the United States and the nations of Europe, and recognizing that disruption following in the wake of war is not contained by national frontiers, the Congress finds that the existing situation in Europe endangers the establishment of a lasting peace, the general welfare and national interests of the United States, and the attainment of the objectives of the United Nations. The restoration or maintenance in European countries of principles of individual liberty, free institutions, and genuine independence rests largely upon the establishment of sound economic conditions, stable international economic relationships, and the achievement by the countries of Europe of a healthy economy independent of extraordinary outside assistance. The accomplishment of these objectives calls for a plan of European recovery.....'[53]

[50] see R. A. Packenham – 'Political Development Doctrines in the American Foreign Aid Program,' XVIII World Politics ('65-'66) p. 210.
[51] see G. Ohlin – 'Foreign Aid Policies Reconsidered' ('66) p. 16.
[52] R. Steel – 'Pax Americana' ('67) p. 254.
[53] Economic Co-operation Act of 1948, in 'Documents on International Affairs 1947-1948' ('52) p. 76; issued under the auspices of the Royal Institute of International Affairs.

There are several indications showing that economic assistance was intended primarily as a *means* to political ends, i.e. the security of the United States and the survival of democracy in Europe.

The purpose of the so called 'Mutual Security Programs' from 1951 on was very obvious. It combined economic aid with military assistance within the framework of the policy of containment. This kind of 'defence support' became the primary form of US aid.[54] About 80% of the total US aid after 1945 went to Europe, South Korea, South Vietnam and Taiwan.

In the Foreign Assistance Act of 1961 it is said that 'the survival of free institutions in the United States can best be assured in a worldwide atmosphere of freedom.' The AID Program Guidance Manual for 1963 states that the goal of aid is 'the development of a community of free nations...... basing their political systems on consent and progressing in economic welfare and justice. Such a world offers the best prospect of security and peace for the United States.'

The same motives we find again in the numerous reports on development assistance. The Randall-Commission, for instance, recommended in its Report to the President and the Congress:

'No further aid is justified unless it contributes to the security of the United States..... In cases where our security is importantly involved, the Commission believes that moderate grants in aid may serve the national interests of the United States.'[55]

In 1957 a voluminous report (1500 pages) was delivered by a special Sub-Committee to the Senate Committee on Foreign Relations. 'The reason for this massive enquiry,' said its Chairman Senator Green, 'was the increasing opposition to the foreign aid programs, which seemed to indicate either that their purposes have not been clearly understood, or that there is a growing belief that they have in some way failed to serve the national interest.' In the same sense the Report itself says:

'Since the end of World War II, US aid programs have included rehabilitation, restoration of economic stability in key countries, the supplying of arms and economic aid to halt Communist encroachment, the rebuilding of the armed forces of allied countries threatened by Communist aggression, the encouragement of technical cooperation, the promotion of economic development, and the expression of humanitarianism.'[56]

---

[54] see for instance U.S. Congress, 83 d. Cong., 2nd Sess. – 'Mutual Security Act of 1954,' P.L. 665, ('54).
[55] Randall-Commission – 'Report to the President and the Congress' ('54) p. 8.
[56] US Congress, 85th Cong., 1st Sess. – 'Foreign Aid Program, Compilation of Studies and Surveys' ('57) p. 4.

Finally the Clay-Report of 1963 is mentioned. Its purpose again was 'to determine whether scope and distribution of military and economic assistance programs was effectively contributing to the security of the United States and the economic and political stability of the free world.'[57] In this report the pursuit of that basic purpose was indicated among other things by the high concentration of assistance to countries on the Sino-Soviet border (72%).[58]

Recently, the debates on the American aid program for the year 1972 have revealed the same. The major argument used by the government to persuade the Congress to anull its original decision to cut off the entire aid program has been the political one. Phrases like 'the survival of democracy,' 'American security' etc. were not from the air. It was said on many occasions by White House spokesmen that a suspension of the American aid program would severely harm the free world, that it would interfere with President Nixon's successful foreign policy, that it would endanger the prospects of ending the Vietnam war, and that it would provoke severe disturbances in countries like Thailand, Cambodia, S. Korea, and Jordan. This kind of argumentation was continued by some Members of Congress, it being brought to extremes by Senator Aiken, who said:

'As I look at the amendent offered by the Senator from Colorado, there are some remarkable possibilities in it which will perhaps solve all our problems. For example, if we wipe out the FAO, we can let famines take over the countries of Asia and let them go over the hill into the camp of the Communist philosophy . . .'

In the light of all this it seems rather superfluous to cite a large number of authors explaining and analyzing the purposes of the aid-programs of the United States in similar terms. Allen speaks for all of them when he says:

'US foreign assistance, at least in part, serves the purpose of preventing those conditions from arising which the Soviet Union can exploit to its advantage..... The United States is interested in economic development, hoping thereby to create conditions helpful to United States interests in terms of economically and politically stable democratic régimes'.[59]

Whatever the significance of the humanitarian and economic motives may have been, the policy of anti-communism has determined the American aid program to a more than considerable degree.

[57] G. Ohlin, p. 21.
[58] Committee to Strengthen the Security of the Free World (Clay-Committee) – 'The Scope and Distribution of US Military and Economic Assistance Programmes: Report to the President of the United States' (March 20, '63).
[59] R. L. Allen – 'Soviet Economic Warfare' ('60) p. 249.

Anti-communism has permanently been a crucial factor determining the scope and volume of US aid. A change has taken place in the choice of bulwarks to be defended. Like for example twenty years ago we still hear about the defence of democracy and freedom, but the practice has evolved to the point where every régime, however oppressive and dictatorial, is considered good enough to be supported as long as it takes an anti-communist stand. 'To save the world for Democracy' has become 'to fight Communism at any price.'[60]

The deliberations described above have indeed decided in practice on both the quantity and the quality of U.S. aid. To reinforce this, some examples will be given, first concerning the quantity – in terms of geographic distribution of aid (1) –, second concerning the quality (or purpose) of specific aid programmes (2).

1) From the beginning, American post-War economic assistance has been geographically concentrated in key countries along the Sino-Soviet border, indicating its primary political and strategic function within the context of the containment policy. The following list shows that (with the only exception of Brazil as the most important Latin American country) all major recipients of U.S. aid from 1946-1965 are part of the circle of countries surrounding the communist bloc:

Major recipients of U.S. economic aid, FY 1946-FY 1965

Country	Amount (in millions of US dollars)
1. India	6.318
2. S. Korea	4.081
3. Pakistan	3.035
4. Brazil	2.622
5. S. Vietnam	2.397
6. Turkey	2.279
7. Taiwan	2.273
8. Greece	1.934
9. Philippines	1.442

Source: Agency for International Development – 'U.S. Overseas Loans, Grants and Assistance from International Organizations, July 1, 1945 – June 30, 1965' (USGPO, '66).

[60] see for instance W. W. Kretzschmar – 'Auslandshilfe als Mittel der Auszenwirtschafts- und Aussenpolitik' ('64) pp. 130-136.

The relevance of this list gains even more weight if one takes into consideration that the total aid to these 9 countries ($ 26.681 billion) represents well over 50% of the entire amount of $ 44.4 billion extended to some 90 countries.

We could have a closer look at specific recipients within this picture of geographic distribution, but this can be done just as well when we deal with the quality or purpose of specific aid programs (geographic distribution and purpose of aid being two sides of one coin).

2) The *quality* of U.S. economic aid programs is clear evidence to their political and strategic background in two ways. In the first place, many specific projects have in fact served ultimately political and strategic aims rather than economic progress (see examples 1^0-4^0 below). In the second place, those projects which indeed served economic purposes were fitted into the general scheme of promoting the private sectors in recipient countries and served in general in trying to develop their economies in such a way as to tie them more closely to the Western economic system (example 5^0).

1^0. Several aid projects formed an integral part of anti-insurrectionary or containment programmes. 'Economic' assistance was extended within the framework of the Pacification program in South Vietnam, where funds were extended to assist in solving refugee problems in Vietnam and Laos (as part of an endeavour to attract the civilian victims of the war), and 'economic' aid was made available to the government of Thailand for increasing its border security. These are clear examples in question.

We shall have a closer look at a few important recipients of such aid.

1^0.1. In addition to the Marshall-plan for Europe, South Vietnam should be mentioned first here as the most outstanding example. It is the country that received the bulk of American aid. Almost half of the overseas personnel of the A.I.D. are working in Vietnam. More than $ 500 million, over 20% of the total of American aid funds, was expended annually in this country already by 1968. In addition $ 200 million worth of U.S. agricultural implements was being supplied that year under the 'Food for Peace Program.' The United States has intervened so thoroughly in the Vietnamese economy, that it operates, in effect, as an American organization parallel to the Saigon government, which controls and checks the use of aid funds. American economic aid to South Vietnam was intended to finance what was called 'the other war.' It tried to attract the population by supplying the civilian imports – cement, fertilizer, petroleum, industrial machinery, raw materials, food – required to maintain minimal stability in a hyper-inflated economy. Furthermore, Saigon's Pacification-program and its resettlement of refugees were to be financed through U.S. aid. In short, this is the most outstanding example of a 'mutual security program.'

10.2. Thailand is another clear example of a situation, where economic aid has been heavily influenced by the containment-policy. Bangkok faces the problem of a communist-supported insurgency in the northeastern part of the country, adjacent to the Laotian frontier. This happens to be the poorest part of Thailand, to which the government has devoted little attention. By instigation of the Americans, the government has now begun to pay more attention to this region. Because of American aid, agricultural, health, and educational services in the North have been expanded. The logical basis of American aid grants of about $ 40 million annually to Thailand is clearly strategic and political, rather than economic. Besides, part of the *economic aid-*funds is spent on the improvement of rural security by training and equipping the local police-forces.

10.3. The Philippines, a SEATO-member, because it was suffering from the pro-communist Hukbalahab revolt, was granted over $ 800 million for reconstruction and rehabilitation in the post-War period. Subsequent economic aid until 1968 has amounted to about $ 400 million in grants, loans, and agricultural implements, and other very substantial technical assistance.

10.4. For over ten years the United States has maintained the economy of Laos by large-scale economic assistance amounting to about $ 60 million annually. This was done because Laos forms a buffer between China and Thailand. American assistance, in addition to financing Laos' imports, and subsidizing the governmental budget, has provided for the needs of refugees from the eastern part of the country (which is heavily bombed by the U.S. Air Force).

10.5. U.S. economic assistance to Cambodia from 1953 to 1963 resulted in an extensive program of technical aid in the fields of education, health, and agriculture. It financed the construction of a major highway and other public works, and supplied economic support to the Cambodian Army.

10.6. Indonesia, being the most populous nation in South-East Asia, has always ranked high on the American list of priorities. But Sukarno's line of policy did not allow big offers from the Americans. Between 1949 and 1963 the United States furnished a total of $ 278 million for economic assistance, in addition to which $ 262 million worth of food and fibers were supplied within the agricultural commodity program. Such assistance was given with the purpose of convincing the population of the generosity of the big Western friend, an endeavour clearly expressed in the $ 10 million emergency-loan after Sukarno's fall.[61]

2⁰. Many specific economic projects have served in fact ultimately military aims. Roads (like the highway from Saraburi to Ban Phai in Thailand, or the highway through Cambodia), airports, seaports, and communication centers are frequently geared primarily to military needs.
A Library of Congress Report concludes in general, that only

> 'between one quarter and one third of the $ 115 billion that has been spent for foreign aid since the close of World War II – including food for peace, Export-Import Bank loans, and other categories – has been devoted to economic development as such.'[62]

3⁰. South Korea and the Philippines are examples of countries which received economic assistance in exchange for specific military duties within the context of communist containment, in this case the sending of troops to Vietnam. As the Economist observes:

> 'South-Korea... is putting a price on the military help it is giving to the Americans in Vietnam.... (it) has asked the United States for certain quid pro quos for the troops it has sent. These include... a rise in American military and economic aid.'[63]

Thus it got what it had asked for. Similarly Marcos, of the Philippines, has profited from sending troops to Vietnam. Three days after the first 800 Army engineers and security troops had left Manilla for Saigon, Marcos arrived in Washington, where one 'felt under some obligation to provide Mr. Marcos with an economic counterweight to the political capital he was obliged to sacrifice to get his Congress to authorize the troops.'[64] Again two days later, it was announced that the United States would 'make a heavy increase in its economic assistance to the Philippines.'[65]

4⁰. Turkey and Spain are clear examples of countries receiving economic assistance in exchange for American military facilities.
Turkey's willingness to take part in NATO and CENTO have helped 'to qualify Turkey highly for whatever foreign assistance might be offered,'[66] while Spain has presented a clear bill for American military presence in the country. The use of Spanish bases between 1953 and

---

[61] on such and other examples see A. Rosenau – 'US Economic Commitment in Southeast Asia,' 54 Curr. Hist. (Jan. '68) pp. 7 ff.
[62] note 48 supra, p. 32.
[63] The Economist (Febr. 9, '66) p. 791.
[64] N.Y.T. (Sept. 14, '66).
[65] N.Y.T. (Sept. 16, '66).
[66] H. L. Haskins – 'Aid and Diplomacy in the Middle East,' 53 Curr. Hist. (July '66) p. 15.

1963 was approved in an agreement that coincided with Export-Import Bank loans amounting to $ 500 million. The new five-year agreement in 1963 was reinforced by a further loan of $ 100 million. Until 1962 alone, U.S. aid to Spain of all kinds totalled $ 1.695 billion, nearly three-quarters being in the form of grants.[67]
Besides these non-Third World countries, Nelson has concluded that

'more than half a dozen developing countries received substantial economic assistance annually as more or less explicit rental for U.S. military bases or communication centers on their soil.'[68]

5⁰. Since the mid-1950's (the time when geographic emphasis of U.S. aid programs shifted from Europe to the developing countries), a theme underlying development assistance (and one of the major contrasts to the Soviet program) has been the emphasis put on the growth of private sectors in recipient countries. Two considerations formed the basis of this preoccupation. On the one hand, it was thought that economic progress would enhance the chances of democracy and prevent communism in the developing countries. On the other hand, it was supposed that by stimulating free enterprise systems the developing countries would be tied closer to the West. Thus American aid programs have witnessed an almost holy respect for economic liberalism and private enterprise.
In 1951 the Benton-Amendment was introduced to the Senate and was incorporated in the Mutual Security Act. According to this amendment the promotion of private enterprise became an obligatory condition before America would grant aid.[69]
An official report of 1957 suggests accordingly:

'Development achieved under State direction absorbs more scarce resources per unit of achievement and cements fewer strong ties with the United States than development achieved largely by the activation of latent private resources in the less developed countries.'[70]

The Foreign Assistance Act of 1961 likewise expresses American dependence on the way of development in the Third World and states that 'the survival of free institutions in the United States can best be assured in a worldwide atmosphere of freedom.'
In 1963 the Clay-report warned that nevertheless too much U.S. aid

---

[67] J. D. Montgomery – 'Foreign Aid in International Politics' ('67) p. 16.
[68] J. M. Nelson, p. 112.
[69] see W. W. Kretzschmar, p. 127.
[70] U.S. Congress, Gen. Comm. on For. Rel. – 'American Private Enterprise, Foreign Economic Development, and the Aid Program' ('57) p. XIII.

had been granted to public enterprises and that not enough consideration had been given to the 'interests of our economic system.' The report urged more aid for the private sector, which 'alone could make the greatest contribution to rapid economic growth and overall development.'[71]
In practice this preoccupation has had different effects, positive or negative, depending on the recipient country in question.
Latin America in general, and the Alliance for Progress in particular could be treated here as an outstanding example. The maintenance or development of free enterprise systems in this case, however, have led to an enormous waste of funds and energy, and can be regarded as having contributed to internal instability in Latin American countries. The Alliance will therefore be treated in section II A 2.2.2.

What has been said may be sufficient to show how important the Cold War aspect of American foreign economic aid has been. Several other aspects of U.S. aid might well have been treated here as additional evidence. There are, for instance, the 'timing' of specific aid-programmes at politically most convenient moments (e.g. $ 10 million loan to Indonesia directly after Sukarno's fall), and the suspension of aid for political reasons (e.g. the sugar boycot of Cuba). Because these aspects of aid, however, are of specific importance for the direct confrontation of the competing Super Powers, and have specific consequences for the internal stability of the recipient countries respectively, they will be treated below under sections II A 2.1.5. and II A 2.2.

2.1.2. *The Soviet Union*

The Soviet Union's entrance in the market of economic aid for developing countries dates from the period after Stalin's death. Stalin had been too occupied with Europe to pay much attention to the developments in the Third World. An important additional reason for this initial position, however, must have been Russia's own economic position. Because 'national liberation' of colonial peoples and their eventual absorption in the communist world has always held high priority in Russia's strategic thinking, and because the Russian policy in relation to aid to the Third World changed fundamentally after its own economy had been strengthened, it may be assumed that the original position was perhaps as much a conse-

---

[71] Committee to Strengthen the Security of the Free World – 'The Scope and Distribution of the us Military and Economic Assistance Programs' ('63) p. 19.

quence of Stalin's political orientation as it was a pure financial necessity.

This is indicated by the fact that it was Stalin who gave the first aid to Turkey in 1934 when this country was developing its system of state enterprises. Furthermore, under his direction the USSR offered assistance to the Economic Commission for Asia and the Far East (ECAFE) in 1951 and again at the World Economic Conference in Moscow in 1952.[72]

Thus it may be assumed that the Soviets recognized their interests in the Third World and the political profit to be expected from assistance quite early, but on the other hand the large demands of communist régimes in Europe and China for assistance in consolidating their positions were probably during this early period preventing the USSR from initiating a large-scale program.

This could probably also explain their original universalistic line on the subject of aid. During early deliberations on development assistance in the United Nations the Soviet delegate insisted on the axiom that 'any technical assistance should be given with participation of the United Nations as the body best fitted to safeguard objectivity.'[73]

The United States, for one, took Russia's economic and financial inferiority vis-à-vis the U.S. as the reason behind this moralistic position, its representative replying with the accusation that the Russians in fact did not contribute 'one red ruble' to the UN Technical Assistance Program.

Things changed drastically after Stalin's death. While the USSR was achieving a stronger position by the mid-fifties, its leaders at that time saw the beginning of large-scale American endeavours to attract the new governments in the Third World by its economic assistance-programmes. The Russians provided some indication in 1954 that the extension of economic relations with developing countries was to receive a higher priority (e.g. by offering its first contribution to the UN Expanded Program of Technical Assistance, by offering large assistance to Egypt, and by extending Soviet Membership in International Organizations like ILO and UNESCO to show its interest in increased contacts with neutralist countries).[74] They eventually invented the new concepts of 'national democracy' and 'revolutionary democracy' to permit them theoretically to achieve close relations

---

[72] US Dept. of State – 'Communist Economic Policy in the Less Developed Areas' ('60) p. 6.
[73] A. Z. Rubinstein – 'Soviet Policy Toward Underdeveloped Areas in the Economic and Social Council,' IX Int. Org. 2 (May '55) p. 236.
[74] S. Reshetar, p. 104.

with non-communist régimes. The year 1955 witnessed the big change. The immediate cause for this change again confronts us directly with the Cold War. The foundation of SEATO and in particular the membership of Pakistan in that Organization offered the Russians a great opportunity for closer relations to India. Having suddenly taken a firm stand on behalf of India by voicing unequivocal support for that country on the Kashmir dispute, the Russians offered a major aid agreement to New-Delhi.[75] Furthermore, the USSR found a receptive atmosphere in which to nurture neutralism emerging from the Bandung Conference, and offered similar agreements to Afghanistan, Burma, Indonesia, and Egypt.
From that time on the Soviet program has rapidly expanded.

As in the case of the United States, important economic motives underlie Soviet economic relations with the developing countries. While the Russians still assign the highest priority to the development of heavy industry, increasing attention is being paid to the expansion of and the availability of agricultural and other consumer goods. Consequently, trade with the developing countries can be advantageous to the USSR, because the import of consumer goods enables the USSR to increase consumption faster than domestic production facilities would permit. This is true, in fact, for the entire European communist bloc, which forms an important market for many agricultural raw materials and minerals. Export credits extended to developing countries, furthermore, permit the Soviet Union to expand their industrial sectors by creating an international market for their products.
Yet, the most important motives have probably been political and strategic ones, and – as has been pointed out in the case of the United States – it would seem artificial to make a distinction between long-term political and economic interests. While restriction of the private sectors of economy in recipient countries constitutes an economic interest for the Russians – and a set-back for the Americans –, it constitutes at the same time a political interest because it may help to draw away such countries from the Western economic system. Soviet economic relations with these countries are, in the words of one author

'as much a political as an economic phenomenon..... a curious amalgam of politico-economic considerations which makes impossible any meaningful distinction between the two.'[76]

---

[75] on the volume of this Russian aid to India see S. S. Harrison – 'Troubled India and her Neighbours,' 44 For. Aff. (Jan. '65) p. 323.
[76] M. Kovner – 'The Challenge of Coexistance' ('61) p. 52.

Although thus important economic interests are certainly at stake for the Soviet Union, their aid program plays an important political role in the Cold War competition for the friendship of the Third World, and it can properly be treated in its political context.

This political function has been stressed from the very beginning of the Program, and has been presented as part of the anti-imperialist struggle. Time and again official statements have been based on anti-Western sentiments in former colonies, and have presented Soviet aid as the only alternative enabling the young countries to struggle against imperialism and neo-colonialism, and enabling them to reach real independence. This has been a recurring theme at every Party-Congress, the records of which are full of such statements. Likewise it has been stressed in direct confrontation with Third World representatives, such as during the Afro-Asian Conference in Cairo in 1957. On that occasion Arzumanian, for instance, developed an elaborate doctrine of 'economic independence,' which was to be won in collaboration with the Soviet Union. He explained how Western aid was bound to deprive the young countries of whatever independence they might have; how real independence demanded a break with those old economic ties with the West which supported the basis of the unequal division of labour between advanced and backward countries (a situation continued by Western aid and trade policies); and how real independence could only be reached by accepting Soviet assistance and by establishing a new division of labour in collaboration with the Soviet bloc.[77]

Soviet literature has consistently depicted Western aid, in particular private investment, as the long arm of imperialist foreign policy, whereas Soviet aid is described as the very paragon of aid.[78]

In general it can be said that analysis of the political function of Soviet aid reveals two policy lines.

In the first place, a distinction can be made between a long-term strategy and short-term tactical measures (the latter fitting, however, into that strategy). In the second place, a distinction can be made between measures aimed at a mere loosening of ties between recipients and the West by offering an alternative source of aid, and measures meant to tie recipients closer to the Soviet system. Although the last distinction is a vague one, it is supposed to be valid by several authors. That the Soviet Union tries to create an international economic system

---

[77] R. Loewenthal – 'China,' in Brzezinski (ed.) 'Africa and the Communist World' ('63) p. 156.
[78] S. Charkson – 'The Soviet View of Aid to India', XXVI Int. Journal ('66-'67) pp. 254 ff.

with Russia in the center seems to be confirmed by statements like that of Khrushchev where he said:

'Our supreme aim is to make socialism, as practiced in the Soviet Union, the economic system of the whole world';[79]

or that by Kim, who said:

'The growth of economic relations between the former colonial countries and the socialist countries noticeably constricts the sphere of the world capitalist market and expands the sphere of activity of the world socialist market.'[80]

It should be noted, furthermore, that this Russian strategy has moved from a one-front policy to a two-front policy. Initially only the United States was the objective, but the rupture with China and the entrance of that country into the Third World resulted in an anti-China strategy as well.

The relevance of this short introduction to the political background of Soviet assistance is confirmed in practice both by the geographic distribution of aid 1), and by the quality (or purpose) of specific programmes 2).

1) The strategic reasons behind the Soviet aid program become clear in the first place from the high degree of concentration in a few strategic key countries.

During the early period 1954-1964 about $ 4 billion worth of grants and credits were offered (of which amount only about $ 1.5 billion was actually received), 80% of which went to the Arab-Mediterranean area and South Asia alone. This percentage even increased to 90% during the period 1965-1967, when the USSR was able to offer more substantial assistance, though several new recipients were added.[81]

Of the total amount of $ 5 billion having been made available to twenty-eight developing countries until 1967, no more than three key countries – India, the U.A.R., and Afghanistan – together received 51%. The addition of four more recipients – Algeria, Indonesia, Iran, and Turkey – raises this proportion to 72%.

---

[79] quoted in R. L. Allen, p. 1.
[80] quoted in L. Tomsky – 'US and USSR aid to Developing Countries' ('68) p. 12.
[81] US Congress, Joint Economic Comm. – 'Current Economic Indicators for the USSR' ('65) p. 174;
US Dept. of State – Communist Governments and Developing Nations: Aid and Trade in 1965' (Res. Mem. RSB-50, '66); idem '... in '67' (Res. Mem. RSB-120, '68).

Major recipients of USSR economic aid, 1954-1965
total: $ 5.030 million

Country	Amount (in millions of US dollars)
1. India	1.022
2. United Arab Republic	1.011
3. Afghanistan	552
4. Indonesia	372
5. Iran	330
6. Algeria	230
7. Turkey	210
8. Iraq	184
9. Syria	150

source: L. Tansky – 'U.S. and U.S.S.R. Aid to Developing Countries,' pp. 18-19.

All other recipients lagged far behind.
These figures clearly illustrate that the Arab world from Morocco to the Persian Gulf, and South Asia from Iran to India, have consistently represented high-priority targets for Russian aid efforts.
Latin America, Subsaharan Africa, and South-East Asia (apart from Vietnam) were clearly assigned lower priority.
This high measure of selectivity might be explained both as a consequence of strategic thinking and as a consequence of relatively scarce resources. The strategic deliberations are nearly self-explanatory: while three major recipients are important neighbours to the Soviet Union (Afghanistan, Turkey, and Iran), the others represent important countries, which all have in common the fact that they are quite independent of the United States and critical towards Western policies.
Generalizing on the Soviet strategy in this respect, an interesting theory is suggested by Beim, based on the Indian political thought of 'mandala,' the principle of alternating rings of friends and enemies, of encircling an encirclement.[82] Apart from extending considerable aid to specific important neighbours (here Beim's figures are even insufficient, as he assumes that Turkey and Iran receive only light tactical aid), major recipients are indeed often situated directly behind Western allies. Such is the case with Syria and Iraq behind CENTO,

[82] D. Beim – 'The Communist Bloc and the Foreign Aid Game,' XVII W. Pol. Q. ('64) p. 790.

Egypt, Yemen, Ethiopia, Sudan and Somali behind the pro-Western considered countries Lebanon, Israel, Jordan, and Saudi Arabia, and of India and Indonesia behind SEATO.

Whether such motives have indeed underlied Soviet decisions, strategic considerations seem indisputable. This is confirmed also by recent adaptations of the Soviet aid program to its policy-change towards worldwide military presence. This new policy, indicated e.g. by the Soviet naval entrance into the Mediterranean and the Indian Ocean, and new diplomatic and political initiatives in S.E. Asia (probably directed against China, advancing American withdrawal from that region), is accompanied by the extension of aid programmes to hitherto neglected areas, notably South-East Asia and Subsaharan Africa. Concerning South-East Asia, the new course of interest was shown by Breznhev's call for a new 'Asian Security System.' Concerning Africa, recent ties with many states – Chad, Central African Republic, Zambia, Togo, Somalia, Sudan, Mauretania, to mention a few –, in which Moscow's ideological interest must be considered to be minimal, have been accompanied by a substantial increase in aid to and trade with such countries. The increase in aid programs suggests, that the USSR is trying to play its role of Big Power in a more worldwide sense and is trying to build reservoirs of goodwill throughout the Third World.[83]

The strategic and political backgrounds of the Soviet aid program become clear not only from its geographical distribution, but it is also elucidated by the quality and purpose of specific programmes.

2) The quality and purpose of specific aid programs show their strategic or political objectives in three ways: first, there are economic projects aimed at (or entailing) Soviet military profit (1^0); second, there are projects offered in order to make friends or obviously set up because of their propaganda value (2^0); third, the economic objectives of aid- and trade agreements are part of the endeavour to further economic structures based on state control, and, if possible, make them similar to the Soviet economy ($3^0.1$), and these agreements are often meant to create greater dependence of recipients' economies upon the Soviet Union ($3^0.2$).

1^0. Part of several economic assistance programmes has allegedly been intended to serve Soviet military interests. More specifically, Soviet assistance in the building or reconstruction of seaports, airports, and other facilities along important air and maritime routes, is considered by many observers as part of the Soviet drive to establish

---

[83] Ch. B. Mc. Lane, pp. 298-299.

a worldwide military presence and to obtain more tangible advantages in the event of conflict.

In 1958 the USSR built a complete modern port for Yemen at Hodeidah on the Red Sea, which becomes of great importance in view of the recent activities of the Soviet fleet in the Indian ocean. Since that year, the Russians have been extending Aeroflot lines, beginning with the modernization of Conakry airport in pro-Russian Guinea, and have been building or modernizing ports and maritime facilities from Singapore to Senegal.

Early in 1968, Moscow persuaded Jordan to accept economic aid for a number of unspecified 'maritime projects,' thereby extending the Soviet presence into the Gulf of Aqaba. No longer satisfied with its power in Iraq and the use of the port of Basra, Moscow has sought to increase its influence in the Persian Gulf and the Indian Ocean. Projects have been started in Kuwait, and an offer has been made to modernize the port of Aden (a port of call for Soviet warships cruising from Vladiwostok).[84]

Western military experts aren't the only ones who see this kind of economic assistance as a replacement moving in the vacuum created by the withdrawal of British presence east of Suez by 1971. Peking has denounced such activities as an attempt to restrain China and has charged that the Russian Navy has become a tool for establishing the naval supremacy of a new colonial empire.[85]

Another example, of a project serving the Russian Army, might be the construction of a mountain – highway over the Hindukush on the Russian-Afghanistan border. This road and its bridges have been observed to be strong enough for the biggest Russian tanks.

2⁰. In the second place, it can be said that many offers have been made to special countries and at a certain time, suggesting strongly the predominance of political motivations, namely the buying of friendship. Moreover, several projects seem to have been set up for propaganda effects rather than for their contribution to the recipient's economy.

2⁰.1. As examples of the first effort (buying friendship), Indonesia, the Middle East, and Guinea will be mentioned:

Indonesia, initially a high ranking recipient of Western aid, increasingly disturbed the West, which has led to repeated reappraisals of policy towards this country. The West was disturbed because of Sukarno's

[84] E. K. Valkenier – 'Sino Soviet Rivalry in the Third World,' 56 Curr. Hist. (Oct. '69), p. 205.
[85] see N.Y.T. (May 18, '69); and 'Batchers of the People's Revolution in Southeast Asia,' Peking Rev. (May 16, '69) pp. 24 ff.

independent ways and in particular because of his increasingly friendly relations with the PKI. By 1956 the internal and international policies of Indonesia were such as to invite the USSR 'to come in,' which it did without hesitation as the country is of enormous importance to all Big Powers. Sukarno's visit to Moscow was followed by an extensive Soviet-Indonesian trade agreement in mid-August 1956, followed again in mid-September by a $ 100 million loan, repayable over twelve years at $2\frac{1}{2}$ per cent interest. With the gradual rupture of relations between Indonesia and the West, Russian activities in that country increased accordingly. In October 1959 the Soviet credit was expanded to $ 117.5 million, and, although only part of this sum seems to have been expended (reportedly it has been used largely to cover sales of Russian military material), Krushchev's visit to Djakarta in February 1960 was highlighted by another loan of $ 250 million to be spent on economic projects.[86]

A main thrust of Soviet endeavours in respect to economic assistance has been directed towards the cementing of political friendship with the Middle Eastern countries, apart from Israel.

Here Soviet aid policy to developing countries began (with the 1955 arms agreement with Egypt), and here the largest amount was spent.

To begin with the principal recipient, Egypt, the Russians themselves have confirmed from time to time the political character of their economic assistance, be it mostly in an anti-Western context. The very beginning of the Russian aid program is marked by its political background: Nasser developed an increasingly anti-American policy because of his resistance to the Western-sponsored Baghdad Pact (which he saw as a hindrance to his Pan-Arab plan). At the same time, the USSR feared becoming entirely encircled because the Badghdad Pact would fill up the gap between NATO and SEATO, thus completing the chain of anti-Soviet military Alliances along its Western and Southern borders, and Nasser's socialist programs were in bad need of economic assistance (a situation the Western Powers hoped to exploit). Thus a sudden convergence of Egyptian and Russian political interests coincided with a proper occasion for the USSR to get a stronger foothold in this important Arab country.[87] This temporary coincidence of political objectives, from early 1955 onwards, clearly called for some form of joint action that would leave the Turkish-Iraqi Pact a still-born creation, weaken Western influence in the Arab world, and isolate Iraq. What seemed to be required, were

---

[86] for further information on the political backgrounds of this assistance see U-Ra'anan – 'The USSR Arms the Third World' ('69) pp. 178-185, 187-188.

[87] on the political context of this Soviet aid program to Cairo see Ra-anan, pp. 14-26.

'measures that would demonstrate incontrovertibly that the West, in spite of its commanding political presence in the region, did not have a monopoly of control over the balance of forces there. If it could be shown that the USSR, an outsider, was in a position to hand out meaningful rewards or punishments to Near Eastern governments, then the local governments would have no particular incentive to go along with Western plans.'[88]

Accordingly, Soviet diplomatic support to Cairo during the Suez crisis was combined with the undertaking of building the Aswan Dam. The latter was presented as a highlight showing the friendship of Russia towards the Arab countries, and as evidence of the advantage of having a big socialist friend. An eloquent example of this presentation of aid is provided by Belyayev, who stated:

'The Aswan building site is an arena where socialism and capitalism compete, and the outcome of this competition is to the indisputable advantage of socialism.'[89]

From that time on Soviet ties with Egypt have steadily been strengthened. Soviet economic assistance was coupled with Egypt's willingness to serve as a transit route and a starting point for political and military initiatives in Yemen, South Arabia, and Africa. The endeavour to gain influence by economic assistance was enhanced particularly after the five days – war of June, 1967.

Substantial Soviet efforts were also made in Syria after 1957 and in Iraq after the revolution of 1958. In both cases political and diplomatic initiatives were combined with economic assistance. The case of Syria may be mentioned in particular, since the more favourable treatment of communists in that country (Syria's leading communist, Khaled Bakdash, was allowed to return from exile in the Soviet Union, and to make public statements; it was even possible for two new members of the cabinet to be communists) coincided with Russian development of Syrian oilfields and their undertaking to supervise the construction of the Euphrates Dam.

A similar pattern was followed in relation to Algeria and Republican Yemen, where the same statements, containing the political vocabulary of a common struggle against imperialism and Zionism, were applauded with offers of economic aid.

Similar motivations can also be traced behind the aid programs to Turkey and Iran. The improvement of political relations between the USSR and Iran was used to offer a comprehensive aid agreement in 1966, whereas Turkish reaction to the much criticized American neutrality in the Turkish-Greek conflict over Cyprus can partly be

[88] idem, p. 26.
[89] quoted in D. Morison, p. 16.

held responsible for Kosygin's visit to Ankara and the signing of new economic co-operation agreements.[90]

Finally, the example of Guinea can be mentioned (as one among many African countries according to Erlich and Sonne).[91] Soviet relations with Guinea began with diplomatic recognition two days after its citizens voted for the rejection of de Gaulle's association plan. On December 4, 1958, the Soviet Union sent a delegation and shortly after a Russian aid program for this pro-socialist country, which seemed to offer (together with Mali and Tanzania) the best prospects for close political collaboration, was initiated.

2⁰.2. As examples of the second effort (to set up propaganda-projects mainly for their political pay-off) many projects have been mentioned by anti-communist authors, the economic value of which, however, can not be denied. It is easy to denounce projects like the Aswan Dam, the Euphrates Dam or the Bhilai steel mill as 'propaganda projects,' but this would not do justice to their real economic value, even if Russian officials boast of them that way.[92] Notwithstanding such usual denunciations, even pro-American authors like Tansky have admitted that such projects 'are relatively few. The bulk of Soviet assistance actually is being channeled into basic industrial facilities and overhead investment.'[93] Nevertheless there are examples of projects presented as economic aid, which can be considered to have served little more than their propaganda effect. Such projects usually can be completed rapidly and seem appropriate in leaving a profound impression on the local population without really serving the recipient's economic needs.

Among the examples often cited are a bakery complex and the paving of streets in Kabul, huge hotel accomodations in Burma and Ghana, swimmingpools and parks in Afghanistan, and impressive sports stadiums in Indonesia and Guinea. Such projects may be considered to have served political interests in the first place.

Within this context it would perhaps also be appropriate to say that it is a usual practice of the USSR first to announce a large, generous, but vague framework-agreement (which seems very impressive), but then, later, to proceed step by step, project by project, which involves

---

[90] see G. Lenczowski – 'Soviet Policy in the Middle East,' 55 Curr. Hist. (Nov. '68) pp. 268
[91] A. Erlich & Ch. R. Sonne – 'The Soviet Union: Economic Activity,' in Z. Brzezinski (ed.) – 'Africa and the Communist World' ('63) pp. 49 ff., p. 72.
[92] like Khrushchev, who hailed Bilai during his visit to India as 'not simply a stage in India's industrial development but also a symbol of co-operation of Soviet and Indian specialists,' V. V. Rymalov – 'The USSR and the Economically Under-Developed Countries' ('63) p. 88.
[93] L. Tansly, p. 29.

not only that such specific second level agreements are announced one by one as if they were new aid packages, but also that very seldom the sum of such specific agreements comes up to the magnitude of the basic framework-agreement. Billerbeck has pointed out that this practice has often led to double-counting and over-estimation of Soviet aid.[94] Such risk becomes clear if one compares the $ 4 billion worth of grants and credits announced between 1954 and 1964, and the $ 1.5 billion actually drawn.

3⁰. In the third place, the economic objectives of the Soviet aid program are evidence to its political motivation; on the one hand as far as this program tries to further economic systems based on state control (1); on the other hand as far as specific agreements serve to tie recipients more closely to the Soviet Union economically, and consequently also politically (2).

3⁰.1. It is part of the USSR's long-term objectives to convince the non-Western world that communism offers the only means for rapid economic growth, as Khrushchev used to say: 'fast tempo's are a general law of socialism.'
This endeavour is reflected by the quality of Soviet assistance. Whereas typically private sector projects were entirely neglected, assistance to the rapid development of the state-owned production sector is the most important form of USSR aid; 53% of all aid has been allocated to expansion of state-owned industry, while another 35% was expended on the construction of hydro-electric, irrigation, and transportation facilities – indicating a total of 88% for the public production sector. Other projects have included municipal and public utilities, public health, medicine, and tourism (hospitals, for instance, were built in Burma, Cambodia, Guinea, and Nepal).
A good example in question is India, the main recipient of Soviet aid. Almost all of the aid given was used for public industrial development. The only non-industrial aid (worth $ 2.7 million out of a total of $ 1.022 until 1966) was planned for the construction of two technological institutes and an experimental farm. One of the major projects was the construction of an enormous steel plant at Bhilai (whose capacity of 2.5 million ton provided one-third of India's total iron and steel production in 1965). 'Steel,' as one author observes, 'spells heavy industry for the Marxist-Leninist and 'heavy industry' means the creation of the means of production – essential requisites of a nation's economic independence.'[95] This independence is meant to be

---

[94] K. Billerbeck – 'Die Auslandshilfe des Ostblocks für die Entwicklungsländer' ('60) p. 41 ff.
[95] S. Charkson, p. 258.

independence of the Western imperialist system. That is why the Soviet Union has also begun to develop the public Indian oil industry (in order to break the Western monopoly in oil import), as it did in Afghanistan, Syria and Iran. In short, it can be said that the emphasis on the public production sectors serves Russian political interests as far as it helps to develop economies based on state control (if possible along Soviet lines), and further serves to harm Western interests, as far as private enterprise becomes restricted and Western import monopolies are broken. This effort is strengthened by Russian encouragement to nationalize foreign private investment (both in words and in practice by showing the advantages of public enterprise). Furthermore, nationalization or the prospect of nationalization of foreign investments inhibits Western investors from pumping additional capital into these countries, which offers the Soviet Union more opportunities. Thus, the Russians seem to hope that the developing countries will not only become independent of and destroy their economic bonds with the West, but also that they will develop along Soviet lines and become more dependent on the Soviet Union. As one author observes:

> 'By weakening the ties between these areas and the Western powers, the Soviet Union seeks to achieve a decisive leverage effect upon the advanced industrial nations, in the expectation that the 'inevitable' crisis of capitalism will be hastened as markets and sources of raw materials are cut off.'[96]

The Bhilai project also shows another feature of the Soviet aid program, strengthening the perception of its purposes as expounded above. This feature is that part of the construction process of this project was the training of Indian engineers, cadres, and workers both in Russia (about 700 engineers and skilled workers) and on the spot.

Both by sending large numbers of Soviet technicians to the developing countries, and by inviting their nationals for study and training in the USSR, recipients of aid are exposed to its ideas, techniques and methods. Since 1960 technical assistance and the 'program of cultural exchange' have had top-priority. Whereas by the end of 1957 1110 Russian technicians were employed on projects in developing countries, this number had by 1963 multiplied nearly eightfold, rising to 8625.[97]

---

[96] M. D. Shulman – 'The Real Nature of Soviet Challenge,' N.Y.T. Magazine (July 23, '61) p. 43.
[97] W. A. Nielsen & Z. S. Hodjera – 'Sino-Soviet Bilateral Approach,' CCCXXIII The Annals (May '59) p. 41;
US Dept. of State – 'The Communist Economic Offense Through 1963' ('64).

On the other hand, while in 1957 about 200 nationals from developing countries received training in the USSR, by 1964 this number had risen to about 11.900.
At the end of 1965 about 5000 students from Africa alone were reported to have been trained in Russia (an important center is the People's Friendship University at Moscow, named after Patrice Lumumba.)[98]
In view of the non-communist (if not anti-communist) structure of society in many developing countries, an important part of the effort has been directed at the training of trade unionists. On the one hand, many nationals of developing countries were invited to take courses in trade union schools in communist European countries, such as a WFTU school in Budapest, the Fritz Heckert High School in E. Berlin, the Institute for Foreign Students in Leipzig, and the Central School of the Revolutionary Trade Union Movement of the CSSR in Prague. On the other hand, such institutes have been set up in Africa itself, e.g. in Guinea, Ghana, and Mali, at which the teaching was to be done initially by Russians.[99]
Moscow evidently hopes that this expanded program of technical assistance to (future) élite representatives may further the aims sought by the development of the public production sectors.

3⁰.2. Another pattern of Soviet aid, considered by many to be part of the effort to tie recipient countries economically more firmly to the USSR, is that nearly all aid agreements include trade clauses.
Such clauses stipulate that credits must be spent in the Soviet Union, which implies that certain sectors of the recipient's economy eventually become dependent on Soviet techniques and advice, and Soviet substitution material (this would hold, of course, likewise for Western supplies). It is also usually stipulated that repayment must be done either in convertible currency (which is mostly impossible for the recipient) or (and thus in practice most often done) in local commodities. Such trade clauses commit the recipient to many years of economic contact with the Soviet bloc, while under circumstances such trade connections may become the heart of economic dependence. Who, moreover, is going to buy the new production when the debt will have been payed off, and an equivalent internal market does not yet exist? By then the Soviet Union can fix a new (political) price.
It has been estimated that the benefit to the Soviet Union from repayment of debts in local commodities seems more apparent than

[98] Ch. B. Mc. Lane, p. 299.
[99] see W. A. C. Adie – 'The Communist Powers in Africa,' Conf. St. no. 11 (Dec./Jan. '70/'71) pp. 5-6.

real, since such repayment would constitute only a relatively small part of recipient's export in many cases. Together with other trade clauses and increasing dependence on the USSR once production has outgrown the capacity of internal markets, this may, however, become quite substantial. By 1958, for instance, 50% of Afghanistan's, 44% of Egypt's, and 32% of Syria's export went to the Soviet Union. Thus long-term loans, combined with extensive trade clauses, can tie a recipient rather firmly to the USSR.[100]

One could go on, of course, providing additional evidence or supposed evidence, for suggesting the political and strategic background of the Soviet aid program. One might, for instance, point out the strikingly low interest of long-term loans (usually 2.5%), which could of course be considered a proof of Soviet generosity, but might as well be regarded as an effort to beat Western donors. All the 'evidence' presented here can be called into question, but in general it seems justified to say that it is difficult to dispute the fact that political and strategic motivations play a role behind the curtain. Additional evidence could be supplied further by analyzing the timing of offering or suspending specific aid programs; because this aspect, however, faces us directly with the East-West confrontation in the Third World, it was thought more appropriate to treat this aspect in sections 2.2.1. and 2.2.2.

Generalizing it can be said that the short-term and long-term objectives of the Soviet economic aid program have served three purposes, all being part of the same over-all anti-Western and later also anti-China strategy:

1. to receive recognition throughout the neutralist world as a Big Power, able to compete with the United States and to eclipse China;
2. to loosen the ties between Third World countries and the West, and to prevent too close contacts between them and China, in short, to offer an alternative;
3. to tie recipients to the Soviet bloc through economic relations and by stimulating economies based on state control, while at the same time harming Western capitalist interests.

According to Beim the last mentioned objective would be the most important one; for the year 1961, for instance, he concludes that 85% of Soviet aid was devoted to establishing or maintaining economic dependence of recipients on the USSR.[101]

---

[100] D. Beim, p. 792.
[101] idem, p. 794.

A question often raised in literature, but of less importance in the present context, is the question whether the political and strategic purposes of Soviet foreign policy must be considered primarily as an ideological or as a national phenomenon. Since the rupture between the USSR and China this question would seem to be mainly an academic one; events such as the invention of new concepts like 'national democracies' and 'revolutionary democracies,' such as the Russian hostility to China (which was openly witnessed throughout the Third World), and such as the maintenance of extremely close relations to a country like Egypt where communists are prosecuted and put in jail, strongly suggest, in any case, that the Soviet Union is pursuing a foreign policy based mainly on the nationalist interests of a Big Power.

2.1.3. *China*

Like the Soviet Union, China began to extend some economic aid in 1953, first exclusively to communist countries. Beginning in 1956, non-communist countries were also included; first Ceylon, Nepal, and Cambodia. From 1960 on a larger program was developed for the Third World in general, communist and non-communist countries alike.[102]

When dealing with the Chinese aid program within the context of the Cold War, it should be observed, that China had to cope with two major handicaps: on the one hand, it could not afford the large amounts spent by the other Super Powers, and on the other hand its prospects for trade with the Third World were rather meagre, as its own products and those of developing countries were not complementary and to a large extent similar. That explains why China's aid policy has been marked by the 'do-it-yourself' slogan.

The unfavourable situation of China's possibilities of trade with developing countries vis-à-vis the other Powers is expressed by the figure indicating that China's trade with the Third World constitutes only 18 per cent of its total trade. Its restricted financial possibilities are indicated by the figure showing that China's part in the total communist aid to developing countries has been only 5%.[103] One of the centers of Chinese aid, Africa, for example was promised a total amount of only $ 850 million until the end of 1968, of which less than

---

[102] A. G. Marsot – 'China's Aid to Cambodia,' XLIII Pac. Aff. 2 ('69) p. 189.
[103] figures are estimated as follows: 1953-'54 $ 118 million; in 1955 $ 166 million; in 1956 $ 171 million; in 1957 $ 192 million; in 1958 $ 116 million, in 1959 $ 253 million; in 1962 finally a top of $ 350 million. see Marsot, note 102 supra; as to Africa particularly see G. T. Yu, pp. 326-327; W. A. C. Adie, p. 11.

$ 200 million was actually spent. If China were to compete for the friendship of the Third World with the United States and (later) the Soviet Union as its opponents, it had to search for alternative methods. Such an alternative was found in the proposition that the Third World could only become really independent by developing through its own efforts with the advice of China, and at the same time radically breaking off ties with the imperialist West. Thereby China presented itself as the historical example in showing the developing countries the way.

> 'Mao Tse-tung's theory of the Chinese revolution is a new development of Marxism-Leninism in the revolutions of the colonial and semi-colonial countries (to the last category China counts all developing countries except the few communist ones) ..... (It) has significance not only for China and Asia, it is of universal significance for the world Communist movement..... the classic type of revolution in colonial and semi-colonial countries is the Chinese revolution.'[104]

The Chinese do not accept the idea that this revolution can or should be exported, but they claim that the Chinese revolution serves as a paradigm for all anti-imperialist liberation movements, and that China should support these movements with aid and advice. An essential part of this national liberation throughout the Third World should be the indigenous effort, and thus 'do-it-yourself.'

A good example of this is to be found in a Joint Communiqué of China and Tanzania, of February 24, 1965, issued at the conclusion of Nyerere's visit to Peking:

> 'The two parties agreed that in order to consolidate their political independence and shake off poverty and backwardness, it is necessary for the new-emerging countries in Asia and Africa to make energetic efforts to develop their national economies on the principle of mainly relying on their own strength. The two parties pointed out that the Asian and African countries, with their industrious and talented people and rich natural resources, are fully capable of developing their countries by their own strength.'[105]

This approach was stressed in front of a large audience at the Afro-Asian Conference in Cairo in 1957. In contrast to the Soviet promise of large-scale assistance which pledged to help the developing countries reach economic independence, the Chinese delegates said that this aim could only be reached by self-help, assisted slightly by stringless Chinese aid: 'We advocate that the Asian and African countries be economically independent and rely on their own efforts, and that we co-operate, aid each other, and develop our trade relations

---

[104] Speech of Ting-yi, (June 25, '51); C. P. FitzGerald, p. 42.
[105] quoted in H. M. Vinacke – 'Communist China and the Uncommitted Zone,' 362 The Annals (Nov. '65) p. 119.

on the basis of equality and mutual benefit.'[106] The encouragement to nationalize and eliminate foreign private business is part of the approach. To sustain the Chinese point of view, Chou En-lai, while in Mali in January 1964, laid down 'eight principles' governing the CPR's economic aid program:
1. a goal of self-sufficiency rather than dependence; 2. stringless aid (which only China intended to offer); 3. mutuality of benefit; 4. low or no interest; 5. emphasis on light industry (N.B. China cannot afford to offer large heavy-industry projects like the USSR); 6. valuations at international market prices; 7. Chinese training of local personnel to operate the enterprises constructed with Chinese aid; 8. living standards of Chinese personnel no higher than those of corresponding personnel of the recipient country in question.[107]
Chinese officials have often expressed that their foreign aid is part of the anti-imperialist struggle, directed at the isolation of the Western capitalist system, and more recently also at the prevention of an alleged neo-colonialist Soviet empire. The political and strategic backgrounds of their aid program are further illustrated by its geographical distribution (1), and by its quality and specific purposes (2).

1) In the first place, it is noteworthy to remark that, whereas Chinese assistance until 1956 went to communist countries exclusively, the open rupture with the USSR and the beginning of the economic competition between the U.S. and Russia in the Third World coincided with a drastic change in Chinese aid programs. From 1956, and more clearly from 1960 on, practically the entire Third World was gradually included in China's aid program. Until 1960 roughly one quarter of Chinese activity in the fields of aid and trade was aimed at countries outside the communist world. Since then, the main emphasis has shifted to non-communist countries. Between 1956 and 1964 about half a billion dollars were extended to non-communist recipients such as Burma, Laos, Cambodia, Indonesia, Ceylon, and Nepal in Asia; and Yemen, Algeria, Ghana, Mali, Nigeria, Somalia, Zanzibar, Kenya, and Tanganyika in Africa.[108] This important shift suggests China's endeavour to become the Power center of the poor Third World united against 'the rich capitalist and revisionist system.' This doesn't mean that China does not also have key regions on its list, like the other Super Powers. It is obvious that on the one hand its Asian neighbour countries, and on the other hand leftist African

[106] D. S. Zagoria – 'The Sino-Soviet Conflict 1956-1961' ('62) p. 264.
[107] G. T. Yu – 'China's Failure in Africa,' VI Asian Survey ('66) p. 467.
[108] H. C. Hinton – 'Communist China in World Politics' ('66) pp. 119-120.

countries have had priority. This reflects China's endeavour to reach or maintain friendly relations with neighbour countries, stimulating their pro-Chinese or at least neutralist course, and the endeavour to obtain strongholds in specific African countries, all of which are considered favourable for China's political objectives. Examples of the first priority-group are North Korea and South Vietnam (as communist neighbours), and Pakistan, Nepal, and Burma (as neutralist neighbours). Examples of the second category are Algeria, Mali, Guinea, and Tanzania. There would be little point in presenting a division in percentages in the case of China, since the amounts spent were so relatively small.

We shall have a closer look at China's aid to these countries below. Because specific aid programs reveal much of the Chinese purposes behind them, they are discussed under 2).

2) The purpose and quality of Chinese economic aid programs betray their political and strategic background again in three ways: in the first place, there are projects destined to serve military purposes (1^0); in the second place, many offers have been made for political reasons (the endeavour to buy friendship) (2^0); in the third place, the quality of economic projects suggests the intention of strengthening the bond between the recipient and China, and the purpose of injuring Western or Soviet interests (3^0).

1^0. Various projects announced as 'economic aid' have probably been intended to serve mainly military interests, either those of China, or those of its allies.

Examples of such projects are the Chinese construction of roads in North Laos and North Vietnam; the construction of a new railway connecting Hanoi and Nanning (in Kwangsi); the provision of non-military supplies to regions in Burma where communist rebels are active;[109] and the construction of a highway linking Pakistani-held Kashmir and Sinkiang across the Pamirs.[110] Projects of this kind in Africa include a highway from Hodeidah to Sana'a, the inland capital of Republican Yemen;[111] the construction of a harbour at Dar-es-Salaam, from which Chinese supplied gunboats can operate;[112] and the offer of economic assistance to Morocco, thus facilitating the establishment of diplomatic relations in 1959 with the aim of obtaining a second base (besides Egypt) from which to support the Algerian FLN.[112]

[109] Th. W. Robinson – 'Peking's Revolutionary Strategy in the Developing World: the Failures of Success,' 368 The Annals (Nov. '69) p. 69.
[110] H. C. Hinton, p. 456.
[111] D. Beim, p. 790.
[112] R. Loewenthal – 'China,' in Z. Brzezinski, pp. 164-165.

Apart from supplying military aid to allies or liberation movements (see section 2.3.3.), such economic assistance can be considered at least in part to have served military purposes.

2^0. The political purposes of China's aid program can also be understood from their obvious function as part of the total of China's foreign policy. To illustrate this, a division is suggested in (1) Asian recipients, and (2) African recipients. The Asian recipients, moreover, are divided in neighbours and non-neighbours.

$2^0.1$. Although China's policy with respect to Asian countries is marked by its unconditional support of neutralism and of any nationalist policy aimed at removing Western influence from this part of the world, its policy towards its direct neighbours is also marked by the endeavour to create a 'cordon defensif' of countries friendly towards Peking.

$2^0.1.1$. To begin with the first category, the non-neighbours, it may be observed that China's aid policy has been aimed at gaining recognition as a Big Power, and at the same time removing Western (especially American) influence by 'rewarding' those governments which live up to their declared neutralist and anti-imperialist policy.

$2^0.1.1.1$. A good example of this is provided by China's aid to Ceylon from 1956 onwards. In the spring of 1956, Ceylon's internal and external orientation drastically changed to a leftist and neutralist direction. When Prime Minister Bandaranaike came to power, he began soon to demand the withdrawal of British bases from the island, and an agreement to that effect was signed in 1957. This remarkable course was 'rewarded' in January, 1957, by a visit from Chou En-lai to Ceylon, resulting in the establishment of diplomatic relations and a declaration of political support. The visit was crowned shortly after with a grant of $ 15 million for purposes of economic development, which in turn was followed a year later by a $ 10 million credit at very low interest. [113] After Mme. Bandaranaike succeeded her murdered husband, Ceylonese-Chinese relations cooled down because of her pro-Indian stand in the Sino-Indian border dispute. But relations improved again after Ceylon began to nationalize American investments followed by her refusal to accept further American aid. This resulted eventually in another visit by Chou En-lai, at which time he cancelled Ceylon's interest payments on Chineese credit.[114]

$2^0.1.1.2$. Another example is Indonesia. Indonesia, the most important South-East Asian country, has been a favourite of China as long

---

[113] A. Doak Barnett – 'Communist Economic Strategy: the Rise of Mainland China' ('59) p. 75.
[114] N.Y.T. (May 6, '64).

as Sukarno adhered to his anti-Western, nationalist policy. By supporting all of Sukarno's claims (from West Irian to Malaysia) China had completely won Indonesia from both the U.S. and the USSR by 1965.[115] China's political support was supplemented by economic support, the most illustrative example of which is the offer of $ 50 million made by Chen Yi during his visit to Djakarta in December 1964. This sum turned out to be roughly the amount of the United Nations aid that Indonesia forfeited by withdrawing from the UN in January, 1965.[116] A clearer example of economic aid aimed at furthering a specific policy line by the recipient could scarcely be found.

2⁰.1.2. Stimulation of nationalist and anti-imperialist policies has been of an even more intense character as far as China's neighbours are concerned. China's policy in respect to them has been marked by the endeavour to create a ring of friendly nations on its borders, and if they were communist neighbours, encourage them to side with China in the Sino-Soviet dispute. Part of this endeavour, again, has been shown in China's aid policy. It is noteworthy that the Afro-Asian Bandung Conference of 1955, where China stressed the principles of anti-imperialism, neutralism, and peaceful coexistence (the USSR not being invited as a white European country), was followed some years later by the open rupture between China and the USSR. On that occasion China clearly advocated its support to an independent Asia, free both from Western imperialism and from Russian influence.

2⁰.1.2.1. First we will say a few words on China's aid to its communist neighbours, North Korea and North Vietnam. We can be rather short on this, since this part of China's aid policy places us directly in the context of the Big Power struggle, which is treated more thoroughly in section 2.1.5.

Both North Vietnam and North Korea have found it difficult, but have somehow managed to sail between the USSR and China. The communist competition for these important countries on China's borders has led to a real 'aid race,' one Super Power trying to beat the other in generosity, and sometimes trying to hinder the other's aid activities. Concerning the last method it should be remembered that China tried to prevent Russian goods destined for North Vietnam from reaching that country by refusing the right to transport these goods over Chinese territory. Concerning the first method two examples can be mentioned. On July 7, 1955 (the anniversary of the Japanese attack

---

[115] H. M. Vinacke, p. 120.
[116] H. C. Hinton, p. 440. It should be remembered that during this time the Chinese were fervently opposed against the UN as a 'by imperialists dominated organization,' and came up with their proposal for a new UN of the developing countries and China.

on China) Vietnam's Ho Chi Minh, having been invited to Peking, was promised full support in his endeavour to organize general elections in Vietnam (as promised at the Geneva Conference) and was offered economic and industrial aid in the form of a grant of the unusual magnitude of 800 million yuan (approximately $ 338 million). He then moved on to Moscow, where he received comparablep olitical and economic commitments, including a grant of 400 million rubles (approximately $ 100 million).[117] The other example is related to North Korea. In September, 1953, North Korea had been promised a grant of $ 250 million by the USSR. Two months later North Korea was promised a grant similar to the amount later promised to North Vietnam, about $ 338 million.[118]

Such aid activity of China, marked by the endeavour to equal Russian offers (an endeavour made nowhere else by China) indicates how important a part its aid policy towards its communist neighbours is in its general effort to win these countries over to its side.

2⁰.1.2.2. China's policy towards its non-communist neighbours has not been so consistent. It can be said, however, that in general this policy has been marked – apart from stimulation of neutralist and anti-Western policies – by the endeavour to create friendly ties and to keep SEATO as far from its borders as possible.[119] When relations with official neighbour governments deteriorated too much (as in the case of Burma for some time, or recently Cambodia), China has sometimes offered assistance to 'liberation movements' within such countries.

We shall have a closer look at China's aid programmes to the countries Pakistan, Nepal, Burma, and Cambodia respectively.

Pakistan, SEATO-member and ally of the US, expressed on many occasions its protests against the massive US supplies of military material to India, notably since 1962 (the year of the Sino-Indian border conflict). American assurances that India would not be permitted to use its Western arms against Pakistan were not accepted in Rawalpindi as credible. When Indo-Pakistani relations grew seriously worse because of the Kashmir dispute, so did Pakistan's relations with the West; an outstanding chance for China to improve its relations with that country. While Pakistan tried to influence the American policy towards India by making the Americans worry about the future of SEATO, China saw its chance to get some foothold in Pakistan; when Pakistan took sides with China on several political questions, Foreign

[117] A. B. Cole (ed.) – 'Conflict in Indo-China and International Repercussions: A Documentary History 1945-1955' ('56) pp. 238 ff.
[118] Survey of International Affairs ('53) pp. 240-241.
[119] R. Loewenthal, 146 ff.

Minister Bhutto implied publicly that China had concluded a tacit alliance with Pakistan against India ('an attack by India on Pakistan involves the territorial integrity and security of the largest state in Asia.....').[120] It was not long before Chou En-lai paid a visit to Rawalpindi, followed shortly after by the completion of the highway linking Pakistani-held Kashmir and Sinkiang, which in turn was followed by the offer of a $ 60 million interest-free economic credit, a reward for Pakistan's anti-imperialist policy.[121]

Nepal, a country situated at a strategic position between India and China, has been the recipient of economic assistance both by India and China. When in 1956 Nepal became concerned about incursions on its territory by Tibetans, China made clear that Nepal had nothing to fear. Peking showed its interest in maintaining friendly relations by inviting Nepal's Prime Minister to the CPR, where he was offered a Chinese grant of $ 12 million (by then China still considered Nepal an independent state, and part of the Indian sphere). In 1960, when political events evoked an outburst of anti-Indian feeling in Nepal, the CPR was again quick to offer a border agreement and a grant of $ 20 million for economic development.[122]

Burma has been one of the most independent countries on China's borders, and from time to time too much Chinese interest in this country has led to serious difficulties. China has tried on the whole, however, to cultivate friendhsip with the government in Rangoon, making this obvious by official visits and economic assistance.

One offer of economic assistance was so exceptionally high, that it seems to call for some comment. It was related to an agreement of January, 1961, by which China was to grant an interest-free loan of £ 30 million to Burma. The immediate political purpose of this loan probably was to make the Burmese government as co-operative as possible with respect to a problem then perturbing the CPR; the possibility that the right-wing coup of December, 1969, in Laos might lead to fighting near the Chinese border. The collaboration of the Burmese Army in preventing the hostilities from extending to China's border was considered as a valuable asset, and it seems to have been forthcoming.[123]

Cambodia, it was hoped by the Americans, would join SEATO, but Thailand's adherence to this Organization automatically alienated Sihanouk from it. This was the first issue that stimulated Cambodia

---

[120] for text see 5 Survival 5 ('63) pp. 220-223.
[121] N.Y.T. (Aug. 1, Aug. 7, '64).
[122] H. C. Hinton, p. 459-460.
[123] idem, p. 418.

to follow a neutralist course and that rendered it receptive to Nehru's alternative of cultivating good relations with China.[124] When relations with Thailand deteriorated seriously, during a period when Sihanouk expected the eventual Vietnamese general elections to give the DRV control over entire Vietnam, Sihanouk went to Peking. The Prince having established, moreover, diplomatic relations with the USSR in May, 1956, China – probably both to reward and stimulate his anti-SEATO course, and to prevent substantial Russian influence – offered Cambodia a grant of £ 8 million for equipment and technical services needed for its economic development program.

2⁰.2. Africa has been the second important region for Chinese aid activities. Although many African countries were included in the program, as was pointed out above, it can be said that this program has been aimed mainly at those countries which seemed to offer the best prospects for close political ties with China; i.e. Algeria, Mali, Guinea, Tanzania, Ghana, and – to a lesser extent – Egypt, being the most 'socialist' of the African states.

We shall have a closer look at some of these aid agreements, namely those with Guinea, Ghana, Tanzania, and Egypt.

2⁰.2.1. Immediately after its break with the French Community, Guinea became the object of intensive endeavours by the USSR and China, both of which wanted to get a strong foothold in this country. Sekou Touré, having old ties with communist parties and leftist front-organizations outside Africa, was expected to become a highly important friend. Guinea, moreover, was rapidly becoming a refuge for the exiled leaders of opposition groups from various French colonies, as well as a training ground – at the UGTAN school at Dalaba, this school being supported with money and materials from the WFTU (World Federation of Trade Unions) – for cadres. Here, then, a big chance was offered of gaining direct influence in the training of future African leaders. Accordingly, the first visit to Conakry by the new Chinese ambassador to Morocco took place immediately after his arrival in Africa in April 1959. With him he brought a gift of 5000 tons of rice for the hungry population. Both China and the Soviet Union were not slow to establish diplomatic relations with the new régime, and the Soviet Union tried to beat its concurrent by offering a loan of 140 million rubles. Shortly after Sekou Touré was invited to Peking, where he was offered an equivalent loan of 100 million rubles, but – in contrast to the Russian offer – free of interest. 'Clearly' as Loewenthal suggests, 'these terms were intended to suggest that the Soviets were moved by material self-interest in their aid agree-

[124] M. Leifer – 'Cambodia and her neighbours,' XXXIV Pac. Aff. 4 ('61-'62) p. 364.

ments whereas the Chinese were motivated only by the spirit of fraternal solidarity.'[125]

2⁰.2.2. N'krumah of Ghana was another promising new leader in the eyes of the Chinese. Like Sekou Touré he was soon invited to Peking where a Joint Communiqué was issued condemning the West and calling its imperialism 'the plague of humanity.'[126] Two days later China announced a $ 20 million loan to Ghana, again interest-free.

2⁰.2.3. Tanzania was honoured by the Chinese offer to construct the Tanzanian railway (intended among other things to take Zambia out of the South African economic orbit). It has been calculated to cost $ 167 million, and is now combined with the construction of a new harbour at Dar-es-Salaam, to be realized by the Chinese as well. Although Nyerere and his socialist ideas may not entirely fit into the Chinese concept for Africa, he certainly belongs to the leaders most independent of Western Powers and is as such a potential friend of China.[127]

2⁰.2.4. Finally there is the example of Egypt, in which Peking hoped in vain to find a very close friend. China presented itself directly after the Suez crisis with a gift of $ 4.7 million. Later developments, however, made the Chinese shift over to Algeria and the Subsaharan countries.

3⁰. The quality of specific aid agreements also shows their political purpose. Two aspects are mentioned here; trade clauses (1), and industrial projects (2).

3⁰.1. As in the case of the Soviet Union, it is a usual Chinese practice to include trade clauses in aid agreements, which tend to create some measure of dependence of the recipient on the donor. This would seem to be the case in particular where it concerns products which cannot easily be sold on the world market, and for which the internal market of the recipient is still too small. The development of such sectors and the initial Chinese promise to accept such products as repayment for debts, places China – intentionally or not – in a favourable position once the debt has been paid off.

This became clear in the case of Ceylon, which was presented with a $ 16 million loan for improving Ceylonese rubber plantations. In return, Ceylon promised to reduce its import restrictions on Chinese goods, while China promised to accept part of Ceylon's increased rubber supply. Later, China announced its refusal to accept this rubber

---

[125] R. Loewenthal, pp. 157, 166, 183.
[126] 'Peiping and Ghana Set Up Closer Ties,' N.Y.T. (Aug. 19, '61) p. 6.
[127] W. A. C. Adie, p. 13.

at any price higher than the falling world price, and was thus in a position to exert substantial pressure on the Ceylonese government.

In 1957 China extended two credits totalling $ 36 million toward the expansion of Indonesia's textile industry. The agreements were linked with trade, and repayment was to be partly in textile products. Since these are among China's chief import products, and in view of the problem of selling such products on the world market, stimulation of Indonesia's textile branch would seem to create some economic dependence of Indonesia on China's willingness to buy an increased supply.

3⁰.2. China's strategy in the field of industrial development is far more important. Unable to afford the large funds usually needed for heavy industrial plants, the Chinese have concentrated on light industry. Light industrial projects do not only require less investment, they also yield quicker results, and as such are expected to carry faster political impact. Among the 'eight principles of assistance,' as outlined by Chou En-lai, however, were two others of importance within the present context. In the first place, it was demanded that Chinese technicians should train the local personnel to operate the enterprises constructed with Chinese aid. In the second place, it was stipulated that these technicians and experts should earn as much as the corresponding personnel of the recipient country.

By assisting the development of industrial centers, the Chinese (intend to) create centers of workers and beginning mass movements where these did not exist before. Moreover, by sending their own experts and technicians with the supplies, and by demanding that they should live under the same circumstances as the local population – in contrast to Americans and Russians – an excellent basis is created for personnel contacts and for initiating local workers into 'the great thought of Mao Tse-tung.' Another advantage is that, in countries where this seems profitable, a large economic mission constitutes an appropriate channel for getting in touch with the indigenous Chinese community (as it has occurred in Cambodia).[128] These motives can probably in part explain the Chinese emphasis on industrial projects, particularly if a finished project bears the name of 'Sihanouk-Chou En-lai factory' (as one was called in Cambodia) or something of the like.[129]

This observation of political backgrounds has often been confirmed by conflicts between recipient governments and Chinese personnel, occurring if the latter were urged to stop their political propaganda among the local population. In some cases, as in that of Burma, such

---

[128] R. G. Boyd in G. Modelskie (ed.) – 'SEATO: Six Studies' ('62) p. 175.
[129] idem, pp. 194-197.

activities contributed to serious political friction with Peking. Peking itself has shown clearly how it understands the fear of recipients in this respect. When in October, 1956, an aid agreement was offered to Nepal, it was stipulated that no Chinese technicians were to be sent with the supplies, an indication that China at that time respected Nepalese and in particular Indian feelings about this. When the crisis with India on the Sino-Indian border question approached, China offered a new loan to Nepal; this time, however, explicitly to be accompanied by the acceptance of Chinese technicians.[130]

Another part of the endeavour to create state-owned industrial centers in developing countries is the encouragement given to the nationalization and elimination of all private business. It was on Chinese advice that Zanzibar, for instance, decided to do so (although the measure failed).[131]

The other side of the coin has been the emphasis on China's cultural exchange program, which gives opportunity to masses of technicians, students, trade unionists and officials to visit China and become convinced of the superiority of Chinese society. Bulk invitations were issued, for instance, to students from countries that were just gaining independence – for example in 1960 from the Belgian Congo and from Somalia.[132] Many hundreds of Asian, African and Latin American students are controlled by the 'Institute of Foreign Students' in Peking and in April 1961 an Association of African Students in China was formed.[133] This is not a technique solely employed by the Chinese – the United States and the Soviet Union are doing the same, probably even on a vastly larger scale –, but it is noteworthy to see how important this 'program of cultural exchange' is thought to be by the Chinese.

Many additional arguments could be brought up to indicate the political and strategic aims of Chinese economic aid activities. For instance, one could point out the propitious moments the Chinese usually choose for making specific offers. China displayed e.g. an intense aid activity during the first six months of 1965 in order to build up its prestige on the eve of the scheduled Afro-Asian Conference at Algiers.[134] One could also show that this 'timing' includes the practice of making use of international tensions, particularly if one of

[130] H. C. Hinton, pp. 459-460.
[131] E. Valkenier, p. 206.
[132] see G. Brook-Shepherd – 'Red Rivalry in the Black Continent,' The Reporter (Jan. 10, '62).
[133] New China News Agency (April 13, '61).
[134] P. Andrews Poole – 'Communist China's Aid Diplomacy', VI Asian Survey ('66) p. 626.

the Super Powers is involved on one side, and a potential recipient on the other. Such an analysis, again, leads us to the direct confrontation between the Super Powers, and will therefore be treated in section 2.1.5.

In general, it would seem that the analysis presented above is enough to suggest the prevailence of political and strategic motivations behind China's aid program, which is directed at:

1) achieving recognition as a Big Power by, and if possible as the leader of, the Third World. To achieve the last purpose China has consistently put forward the thesis of 'the common colonial heritage' of the developing countries and China. Furthermore, as far as the more progressive developing countries are concerned, China has tried to eliminate Russia as a leader by introducing a racist element into its propaganda.

Having managed to keep the USSR from the Bandung Conference in 1955, succeeding Afro-Asian meetings were marked by a radical racist stand of the Chinese. For instance, at the Afro-Asian Writers Conference at Cairo, in 1962, a Chinese delegate is reported to have said: 'These Europeans are all the same, whether they are French, Americans Russians, or Poles: We non-whites must get together.' More recently, in Moshi, the Chinese declared to their African colleagues that the Russians will let them down:

'whites will back whites, but we are coloureds and your blood brothers in the struggle. Only we can understand your problems.'[135]

2) stimulating nationalism and neutralism in Asia, and at the same time cultivating friendly relations with it, in particular with neighbour countries, in order to expel American influence from that part of the world, and eventually to become accepted as Asia's 'natural leader.'

3) eliminating Western imperialism from the Third World in order to accelerate the pace of the alleged doomsday of the capitalist system, and, at the same time, preventing the 'revisionist' Soviet system from building an alleged new neo-colonialist empire.

2.1.4. *Other donors*

Of course the three opponents in the Cold War, China, U.S.A. and U.S.S.R., are not the only states who use economic aid for political purposes. But for the others such political purposes are of a different kind. England, France, Portugal, Holland and some other countries extend most of their aid funds to their existing or former colonies in

[135] for sources (Kenya Daily Nation) see C. P. FitzGerald, p. 48.

order to keep some influence there and to retain their power and prestige; e.g. France in 1962 spent $ 850 million out of a total of $ 880 million on former French territories. This is a clear proof of the political importance of aid; it is, however, not directed as such against another aid-giving nation within the arena of the Cold War and therefore it is considered of less importance within the present context.

2.1.5. Cold War Confrontation

There is a heap of bones. Three dogs stand around it, watching each other's steps. Carefully each of them takes a bone from its own side of the heap. Nothing happens. Then they come back and take another one. They are already grimly tense, as the heap becomes ever smaller. The game may remain peaceful until the strongest dog does not accept any further steps from the others. If there is no strongest one, a moment will come when no dog can take another bone without touching one of the others and then a fight is inevitable.
The world of Walt Disney and that of politics are often alike. In our days we can witness dangerous struggles in and because of the Third World. Some countries have been tied to one of the Super Powers, others have not. Asia has been the most important issue at stake during the last years, but Africa might well become the next.

2.1.5.1. Economic aid has become an obvious weapon, shown to and raised against the adversaries.
Walter Lippmann has warned: 'the Communists are expanding in Asia because they are demonstrating a way, at present the only obviously effective way, of raising quickly the power and the standard of living of a backward people. The only convincing answer to that must be a demonstration by the non-Communist nations that there is another and more human way of overcoming the immoral poverty and weakness of the Asian people.'[136]
Chou En-lai has presented his eight points of development assistance in order to show that the United States and Russia have neo-colonial objectives in mind but that Chinese aid alone guarantees development and independence.[137]
The Russians boast of the glorious successes of Russian aid by putting a finger on the failures of the Chinese. On November 16, 1967, Radio Moscow said: 'in the six years since the signing of the Sino-Burmese

---

[136] cited in X Bulletin of the Atomic Scientists I ('59).
[137] see note 107 supra.

co-operation agreement China has completed only two of eleven projects envisaged in the agreement..... Realizing that they could not achieve their aims despite their provocation and their pressure on the Burmese government, the Chinese leadership ordered the Chinese technicians in Burma to stop their economic co-operation.'[138] As such it is dramatically enough to see that economic aid has become a political tool in the Cold War. One of the means in creating a more peaceful world has turned out to be a threat to it.

Economic competition is certainly preferable to outright fighting, which today could end in nuclear war and total destruction. Yet, it is not a funny thing to hear Khrushchev say: 'I declare war on the United States in the peaceful field of trade,' or to hear Kennedy explain: 'the Third World is the great battleground for the defense and expansion of freedom today.'

It would be frivolous to underestimate the threat to world peace inherent in this 'peaceful' competition, which not only stimulates and maintains an atmosphere of enmity among the nuclear opponents, but also entails direct confrontations among them throughout the Third World. It has been shown before, that numerous developing countries accept aid from different sides, which thus become unintentionally the object of Cold War manoeuvers. Russia contends with China for the favour of North Korea, Noth Vietnam, Yemen, Guinea, Mali. The US contends with the USSR for the favour of India, Iraq. China competes with the U.S. for the favour of Pakistan, Laos, Cambodia. All three of them are or have been involved in the struggle for Indonesia, Egypt, Laos, Vietnam, Korea, to mention a few only.

This situation has resulted now and then in 'aid races,' one donor trying to beat the other in offering assistance.

Examples of this are the U.A.R., where the years 1964 and 1965 witnessed a competition in aid between the USSR and China in connection with the second five-year plan; North Vietnam, being the recipient of Chinese aid when it received Russian aid and vice versa -e.g. when the USSR in 1965 supplied a large amount of medicaments and transport material, China did not hesitate to send its own supplies of rice, medicaments and transport material; then, North Korea often saw Chinese assistance offered or increased together with Soviet assistance, if necessary beyond the limit of China's financial capacity.

Another well-known example is Afghanistan, once significantly called by US-ambassador Byroade 'the economic Korea.' The struggle for the sympathy of this country is even unique in the sense that it was the object not only of a race in money but also of a race in prestige-

[138] P. Howard – 'Soviet Policies in Southeast Asia,' XXIII Int. J. ('68) p. 441.

projects: the Americans began to build in the middle of this underdeveloped country a prestige project for the workers of a non-existing industry – a beautiful bungalow park with a fantastic swimming pool – so, then the Russians built a second fantastic swimming pool. The Russians modernized the existing airport – so, the Americans built a new one with all the glamour one can imagine. It was never used, however, because modern airplanes no longer needed to refuel in Afghanistan en route between India and East Asia (by the way, 400 people are contracted to keep this splendid useless project clean). The Americans made serious mistakes during their work on the development of the big Helmand-valley – so, the Russians learned from their mistakes and took over, partly with more success. The Americans built a Technical High School – so, the Russians built a second one. One could go on presenting examples of this kind.[139]

The picture of a struggle becomes even clearer from the figures relating to the funds spent throughout the years: until 1955 US aid was rather small, because the Soviet Union did not extend any substantial aid to Afghanistan. Things changed with the strengthening of the American position in Asia by the foundation of SEATO, and with China's rise to power. After Russia had begun to extend substantional aid to India, it joined the game in Afghanistan a year later. During the years 1950-1953, when no Soviet aid was extended, American aid amounted to $ 1,2 million a year. Since 1955, when Soviet aid increased suddenly, American aid increased accordingly to $ 16 a year, reaching even $ 38 million in 1962.[140]

2.1.5.2. The disadvantages of such a competition are apparent, and their potential dangers – once the opponents perceive real interests to be defended vis-à-vis each other – need little comment.

Such dangers become particularly clear if one takes into consideration a specific method practiced by all three of the Super Powers. This is the custom of exploiting specifically propitious moments for offering assistance, in particular at a time when the recipient in question has conflicts with its original donor. By offering assistance under such circumstances the Super Powers directly confront each other in a conflict situation. Some examples will be mentioned:

1°. The Soviet Union used this method when Egypt came into conflict with the Western Powers because of the nationalization of the Suez Canal Company, and America's endeavour to create CENTO. The

---

[139] these facts were revealed in a documentary, made by a W. German TV-team on the spot.
[140] see on this G. Nollau & H. J. Wiehe – 'Russia's South Flank' ('63) pp. 124-148.

U.S.S.R. did not hesitate to exploit the situation for its own profit by extending the generous offer to take over the construction of the Aswan dam, when the Western Powers cut off their assistance to the project.[141]

2°. Equally well-known is the example of Cuba: the United States tried to instigate a revolt in Cuba against Castro's régime by entirely cutting off the import of Cuban sugar (on which the countries' economy depends). It is difficult to say what the result of that boycot would have been, had it been succesful. But the Soviet Union stepped in and bought the sugar, about six million tons, even though the amount of sugar derived from internal resources (beet sugar) was more than the Russians needed. So it was clearly a political manoeuvre.

3°. Pakistan began a flirtation with Peking in 1963, increasingly upsetting President Johnson; to such an extent that he cancelled Ayub Khan's visit to Washington, in April 1965, and the consortium meeting which was planned to allocate funds for Pakistan's third five-year plan. Ayub Khan was promptly invited to Moscow, where he was offered an agreement to carry out – among other things – 30 major projects in the framework of the third five-year plan.[142] Again, in 1966 and 1967, substantial aid was extended to Pakistan, this time perhaps in order to neutralize Chinese rather than American influence.[143]

4°. The same method was used to attract Indonesia in 1956. By then Sukarno's internal and international policy had led to a virtual break with the Western Powers, until then Indonesia's main donors. Sukarno was invited to Moscow, where he was offered an extensive trade agreement, followed shortly by a $ 100 million loan.[144]

5°. Similarly a temporary alienation between Turkey and the US, because of the Turkish reaction to America's neutrality in the conflict with Greece over Cyprus, was used by the Soviet Union to strengthen its improving relations with Turkey by offering new economic co-operation agreements.[145]

6°. The USSR offered aid to Tunesia directly after the French bombing of Bizerte, trying by that method to get a stronger foothold on North Africa's coast.[146]

---

[141] see p. 139 above.
[142] M. A. Chaudhri – 'Pakistan's relations with the Soviet Union,' VI Asian Survey ('66) p. 497.
[143] S. P. Seth – 'Russia's Role in Indo-Pak Politics,' IX Asian Survey ('69) p. 619.
[144] see note 86 supra.
[145] see note 90 supra.
[146] J. F. Triska & D. D. Finlay – 'Soviet Foreign Policy' ('68) p. 267.

7⁰. One of the Russian steps used to improve its image in India was the take-over of the construction of the Bokaro steel plant, over which a conflict had risen with the United States.[147] From that time dates the expression 'Russkiy Da, Yankee Nyet!.'

8⁰. Recently the Soviet Union has tried to gain more sympathy with Burmese authorities. When in 1968 relations between Burma and China deteriorated once more, a Russian trade delegation was sent to Rangoon with generous offers. The Russians will have been pleased to see 'New Times of Burma' write: 'what the British withheld us during 100 years, we got finally from our Russian friends.'

9⁰. In order to conclude the Russian examples, the recent Russian move in the case of Indonesian rubber can be mentioned. After Indonesia expressed its concern about the alleged American intentions to depress the world market price for natural rubber by selling its bufferstock (which, according to Indonesia's Minister for Trade, Sumitro, would cause a loss to Indonesia of $ 50 million), the USSR offered to buy much more rubber than it had done before in order to avert Indonesia's problem.

10⁰. China has also often used the above mentioned tactics (being of special importance to this Power, in view of its restricted resources). The first time China did so, was in 1952. On that occasion the United States refused to pay more than the (falling) worldprice for rubber from Ceylon. It was noted before that Ceylon was one of the first objectives of Chinese aid. So, it does entirely fit into the picture that China took over the American offer and paid a much higher price in the form of rice.[148]

Again, after 1962, when a conflict arose with the US on nationalization of American investments, China reacted by cancelling Ceylon's interest debts to Peking.[149]

11⁰. Another example is the trade agreement with Pakistan of January 5, 1963. This was an offer made by China after the relations between Pakistan and the United States had deteriorated because of American military aid to India in 1962. Pakistan tried to put pressure upon the United States by improving its relations with China, which did not hesitate to exploit the situation by offering an interest-free loan of $ 60 million in July 1964.[150]

12⁰. A third example is the railroad from Zambia to Dar-es-Salaam,

---

[147] D. Rothermund – 'India and the Soviet Union', 386 The Annals ('69) p. 85.
[148] J. S. Berliner, p. 20.
[149] see note 114 supra.
[150] G. J. Lerski – 'The Pakistan-American Alliance: A reevaluation of the present decade', VIII Asian Survey ('68) p. 410.

which was a fervent wish of President Nyerere. Having sent a team of experts, the World Bank refused to extend the money because the report enquiring into the possibilities had been quite negative. Notwithstanding the assumed economic irresponsibility of the project, the Chinese stepped in and offered to fulfil Nyerere's wishes.[151]

13⁰. A further example is China's exploitation of the Suez crisis in 1956. Recognizing a chance to enter the struggle for the African continent, China granted Egypt a generous gift of $ 4,7 million in hard currency.[152]

14⁰. When Cambodia conflicted with the United States on the occasion of Thailand's adherence to SEATO, and Cambodia accordingly refused to become a member of this organization, it tried to put pressure upon the U.S. by improving its relations with China. Peking, recognizing a unique chance to get some foothold in Pnom Penh, and fearing too much influence of the USSR (with which Sihanouk had established diplomatic relations in May, 1956) rewarded Cambodia for its neutralist course with a $ 8 million credit for its economic development program.[153]

15⁰. Immediately after its break with the French Community, Guinea – recognized both by the Western and by the Eastern Powers to be a potential center of revolutionary activities in Africa – was to be boycotted by Western Powers, and accordingly became the object of assistance of the Chinese: first 5000 tons of rice were shipped to Guinea, then an interest-free loan of 100 million rubles was offered.[154]

16⁰. The same happened in the case of Ghana, whose leader N'krumah was invited to Peking shortly after the country reached independence. A communiqué was issued in which Ghana adhered to Peking's cruisade against the West and its imperialism ('the plague of humanity'), two days after which a $ 20 million interest-free loan was announced.[155]

17⁰. The United States, extending aid to some 90 countries, has not used such tactics as regularly as its opponents.
The US has rather been in a position to suspend promised assistance with the aim of putting a recipient under pressure (see section 2.2.1.). There are, however, some examples, like the $ 10 million emergency loan to Indonesia directly after Sukarno's fall, obviously intended to attract the new government in Djakarta.[156]

[151] V Kron. Afr. 4 (Dec. '65) p. 249.
[152] P. Andrews Poole, p. 625.
[153] see note 124 supra.
[154] see note 125 supra.
[155] see note 126 supra.
[156] see note 61 supra.

The atmosphere of hostility resulting from this kind of competition, in particular when the Super Powers try to expel each other from a specific country by exploiting conflict situations, entails the potentialities of less peaceful confrontation. The relevance of such fear is accentuated by three considerations.

1) The aid competition may provoke internal rupture in recipient countries, because some indigenous groups will profit from and accordingly favour a Western-style development, whereas others have more to gain from a socialist development. Even regular contacts with or temporary dependence on one of the donors may activate people's political radicalism in opposite camps, even though ultimately their interests might converge. It has been reported, for instance, that when Tanzania's two big transport projects – the railroad constructed by the Chinese, and the highway constructed by the Americans – crossed each other, indigenous workers came to blows.

Such internal instabilities, being the result of economic assistance, bear the risk that the Super Powers may get involved.

2) The more so – this being the second consideration – since it is quite clear that economic assistance may create political and strategic interests where these did not exist before. The more money a country invests in another country, the more prepared it becomes to defend such investments and the more unwilling it becomes to accept influence from the other side. Long-termed common experience and co-operation, moreover, tend to create emotional ties, and friendly relations based on the donor-recipient relationship may eventually lead, by pressure of the first and inclination of the second, to the establishment of military relations as well, and thus to the creation of a new strategic interest.

'It is becoming increasingly clear,' Bloomfield writes, 'that definition of vital interests and subsequent intervention have sometimes taken place *as a result* of arms or expertise transfer to the developing countries, rather than vice versa.'[157] The awareness of this danger is expressed by a sentence in the American Foreign Aid Bill of 1966, determining that 'the authorization of military and economic aid shall not be construed as creating a new commitment or as affecting any existing commitment to use armed forces of the United States for the defense of any foreign country.'

3) The aid competition on the part of the Super Powers commits the Third countries to an involvement in the Cold War.

It may be true that Cuba, Afghanistan, Indonesia and Pakistan have

---

[157] L. P. Bloomfield – 'Future Small Wars: Must the US Intervene?,' XII Orbis 3 (Fall '68) p. 679.

somehow managed to keep their independence by playing off the Super Powers against each other, but many examples to the contrary indicate that this has rather been a coincidence than their own merit. The examples of Guinea which was offered further assistance on the condition that it would break with the United States,[158] the construction of ultimately military projects (sometimes, as in Laos or Afghanistan, by opposite camps in the same country), and South Korea and the Philippines (which became directly involved in the East-West conflict by sending troops to Vietnam in exchange for economic aid) suggest so. There are even examples of leaders who, so to speak, brought the Cold War home during times of internal conflict, as Ojukwu did by inviting the Chinese to support him against the aid extended by the Americans and the British to the other side during the civil war.[159] One Third World country – being a first-rank recipient – has itself taken sides in the Cold War by playing the role of donor. This is India, which is trying to compete with the Chinese in respect to a leadership in the Third World. Recipients of Indian assistance, offered in order to decrease Chinese influence, have been for example Yemen (since 1965), Bhutan, Nepal, and Somalia (since 1964). Another very important recipient of Indian assistance has been Indonesia, which for a long time was a close friend of China and a supporter of Pakistan in the conflict on Kashmir; when in 1966 Indonesia got its new government and broke its ties with China, India stepped in without hesitation with a Rs. 100 million loan.[160]

May this suffice to show that economic aid has become a new form of Cold War intervention, a kind of 'informal attack' as Scott puts it, which has introduced an important additional element of instability in international politics.[161]

A crucial factor for the future might be the threatening increase of food scarcity throughout the Third World coupled with its rapidly growing population. If no solutions to this problem are found, food might well become a principal 'weapon' in the Cold War. This has been suggested by the former US Secretary of Agriculture, Freeman. He has stated that the Cold War might be waged more with food than with armament, and he speakes already of food as 'America's secret

---

[158] Le Monde (Dec. 21, '66).
[159] VIII Kron. Afr. 4 ('66) p. 246.
[160] see Ph. M. Phibbs – 'India's Economic Aid Programs,' 54 Curr. Hist. (April '68) pp. 232 ff.
[161] see M. M. Scott – 'Internal violence as an instrument of cold warfare,' in J. N. Rosenau (ed.) – 'International Aspects of Civil Strife' ('64).

weapon,' while predicting that 'the United States is dominant not only in firepower, but also in food power.'[162]

2.2. Consequences for the internal stability in recipient countries

2.2.1. Discontinuity

Apart from introducing the Cold War into the Third World, present bilateral economic aid as a function of the national policies of the donors has other aspects of polemological importance, which have consequences for the internal scene of the recipient country.

Under this heading it is important to remember what has been said in section 10 of Chapter I: people who have become conscious of relative deprivation, and then see their lot improved, want to amend their situations as quick as possible. They want to shake off all remnants of their previous misery, desiring to achieve a better life as soon as possible. The resulting intense expectations entail high risks since such expectations, if followed by deterioration or stagnation, tend to result in intense frustrations and thus to contribute to aggressive behaviour. This should be kept in mind, when we deal with the following feature of present bilateral aid:

Being based on political rather than on economic or humanitarian considerations, foreign aid becomes extremely dependent on political developments for its very survival in the long run. Several authors have pointed to this feature of politically determined aid programs. One of them, Steel, writes in connection to the American program:

> 'Born of the Cold War and perennially justified to Congress and the taxpayers as a weapon in the arsenal against communism, foreign aid has been one of the least understood and one of the most maligned forms of American intervention. Unloved by those who pay for it, and distrusted by those who receive it, the aid program has been subject to scepticism and abuse that continually threaten its survival.... Whatever attitude we now take toward it, foreign aid in its present form grew out of the Cold War, was nourished by it, and is almost totally dependent upon it for survival. Every year since 1948 the President has gone before Congress with a foreign aid request which he had defined as being absolutely vital to the national interest. Every year the Congress nips away at the aid budget, never quite convinced of the argument, never sure it is totally wrong, and grudgingly passes a hacked-up aid bill in the belief that it is helping to fight the Cold War. But the growing belief in continued 'peaceful coexistence' between America and Russia has undermined much of the support for foreign aid as a Cold-War weapon, and the disappointing experience of the new nations has dampened enthusiasm for aid as a cure-all for instability.'[163]

---

[162] O. L. Freeman – 'Food – American's Secret Weapon,' US NWR (July '67) pp. 40-44.
[163] R. Steel – 'Pax Americana' ('67) pp. 253-254.

This long quotation was given here, because it expresses so clearly how unstable a basic political justification is bound to be. In the long run the donor country is bound to be disappointed and bitter about the results, believing the aid-receiver to be not grateful enough. On the other hand the attitude in the recipient country is bound to be that of mistrust and averse reactions. As Myrdal puts it:

> 'in present political conditions unilateral aid on large scale is bound to have the most serious effects both in the United States and in the receiving developing countries; at home it can hardly be motivated except as a political device in the Cold War; this lowers moral and economic standards in the distribution, direction, and utilization of aid, creates resentments and splits in the developing countries, and *will in the end only provide valid reasons in the United States for radically cutting down the appropriations.*'[164]

The same argument would hold true in the long run for the other donors. Failures and mistakes seem to be inevitable consequences of an aid policy based not on economic rationalism but on political salesmanship. Such failures will have a negative impact on the readiness to continue the aid program. Moreover, as soon as the political motivation becomes weaker, the readiness to continue foreign aid will also become less.

It is not only this long-term process, however, which endangers the continuity of foreign aid. The political background of aid programs has also consequences for their continuity in daily practice. On the one hand, the political function implies – as has been illustrated above – that aid is offered to specific countries under specific circumstances profitable to the donor. On the other hand, it implies also that aid may suddenly be suspended in order to put an unwilling recipient under political pressure. In other words, recipients can never be sure of continuous assistance, a situation seriously restricting the possibility of planning, and forming a serious obstacle to the possibility of continuous growth. The additional risk being, moreover, that a recipient itself will suddenly decide to refuse any further assistance, when it fears that its independence will be threatened.

Such sudden suspension or refusal of long-term aid programs occurs quite regularly. A few examples will be given to illustrate the importance of first, the suspension of aid by a donor (1^0), and second, the refusal of further aid by a recipient (2^0).

$1^0.1$. At the beginning of 1965 the U.A.R. extended military assistance to the Congolese rebels, whereas the United States supported Tsjombe. As a result, American-Arab relations deteriorated to such

---

[164] G. Myrdal – 'An International Economy: Problems and Prospects' ('56) p. 329.

an extent that in February of that year the American Ambassador warned President Nasser that if the U.A.R. would continue its support to the rebels, the American wheat supplies (amounting to about 40% of the U.A.R.'s need!) would be suspended. And this was indeed done, until the U.A.R. stopped its assistance.[165]

1⁰.2. The example of Pakistan has been discussed before. The United States cancelled its funds for the third five-year plan, because Pakistan had improved its relations with China more than the Americans liked.[166]

1⁰.3. When Indonesia under Sukarno took too much of an anti-Western road, this resulted in a virtual stop of Western aid by 1963, thus preventing the Indonesians from bringing progress to the economy.[167]

1⁰.4. The best known example is America's boycot of Cuba. This country, economically almost entirely dependent on its sugar export to the United States, became the object of an endeavour to starve it by a sudden total embargo on imports from Cuba. Had it not been that the USSR and China took over Cuba's export, the endeavour – intended to stimulate a counter-revolution against Castro – might have succeeded.

1⁰.5. Within the framework of the Cold War on the Western side one might also refer to the relations between the German Bundesrepublik and developing countries under the Hallstein-doctrine. When President Nasser invited Ulbricht to visit the U.A.R. in January 1965, the Bundesrepublik threatened to stop economic assistance. The same happened in the case of Tanzania, when it refused to break with the DDR.[168]

1⁰.6. A recent example is related to the conflict with Equador concerning the latitude of territorial waters. Equador, claiming the enormous distance of 200 miles for its territory (like many other Latin American countries do) came into conflict with the U.S. by seizing American fisherboats sailing for tunafish. America's first reaction was to cut off its military aid to Equador, and in December 1971 it decided to cut its entire economic assistance (an amount of $ 15,5 million) as well.

The most notorious example is, of course, the recent decision taken by US-Congress on October 29, 1971, to cancel the entire original aid program for the year 1972, the immediate motive for which has been

[165] V Kron. Afr. I ('65) p. 12; N.Y. Herald Tribune (April 24, 25, July 12, '65).
[166] M. A. Chaudhri p. 496; G. J. Lerski p. 411.
[167] D. Hindley – 'Indonesia's Confrontation with Malaysia: a Search for Motives,' IV Asian Survey ('64) p. 910.
[168] V Kron. Afr. I ('65) p. 13; idem p. 30; idem 2 ('65) p. 108.

said to be the expulsion of Taiwan from the UN. Now that the threat to cancel the largest foreign aid program of all has been removed by a later decision of Dec. 8 to extend a total of $ 3.003 billion this year on economic and military aid together, several comments have been forthcoming claiming that it has never been seriously considered to stop American aid. This interpretation of events, however, seems hardly in accordance with the actual debates in the Senate (see the Int. Her. Trib. of Nov. 3, '71 p. A 14). These discussions, indicating a general frustration caused by the fact that the political aims pursued by the aid program are not forthcoming, rather reveal that Senator Javits was right in stating that the original refusal 'represented a thorough feeling throughout the country.' It could also hardly be explained otherwise why the government had to make such an unusual campaign in favour of the continuance of the program, bringing up all the political, the strategic and the economic self-interests of the United States that officials could invent. An additional reason for the later decision to continue with the program seems to have been, moreover, the maintenance of employment of thousands of people during a period characterized already by large-scale unemployment and dismissals; 3297 American employees in the United States, a further 597 American employees abroad, and 632 foreigners were threatened to be dismissed immediately, while a total of 12.000 AID-employees were confronted with very insecure prospects. Whatever the real risk of a stop of the American aid program may have been, and whatever the chances of the opposition which allegedly wanted to introduce an alternative plan to extend economic aid through UN channels, the events in October and November 1971 are a sign on the wall and have at least confirmed the very insecure character of aid programs connected with foreign policy.

1⁰.7. Concerning the Soviet Union, the reader might be reminded in this connection of the usual trade clauses, included in aid agreements – stimulating particular sectors of production both by the Soviet credits and by the possibility of exporting such products as repayment of debts to the USSR – which may cause a sudden stop of increased production, when the debt has been payed off and the Soviet Union is not prepared to buy such products in succeeding years. This holds also for China, which uses similar trade clauses).

1⁰.8. In general the Soviet Union has indicated in 1960 how much present foreign aid is dependent on political factors. It appears that the Soviet effort to foster economic dependency in the late 1950's was supported by the expectation of a steady growth of ideological compatibility. To the dismay of the USSR, the anti-imperialist dynamics

which made early Soviet aid successful was not extended to the adoption of Soviet economic or political forms. On many occasions, it did not even lead to support of Soviet international positions. For example, Nasser maintained his refusal to adopt a benevolent attitude toward domestic communists (on the contrary, he suppressed the C.P. in Egypt), while Iraq as well became resistant towards a perceived internal communist threat. The list of disappointments could be a long one. Let it be sufficient to say that, late in 1960, the USSR abruptly suspended any new aid commitments while evaluating the returns on its investments. On the other hand, after China entered the market in 1962 with substantial offers, Russia could not afford to maintain this negative position and resumed making new aid commitments. Some figures clearly illustrate this:
during 1960 a peak of $ 1.154 million had been committed by the USSR in the developing countries (a commitment which in terms of Soviet GNP matched the U.S. foreign aid commitment); in 1961 and 1962 the totals dropped precipitously to $ 171.4 million; but in 1963 the amount rose sharply again and by 1964 Russia announced extensions up to $ 890 million.[169]

1⁰.9. An example to be mentioned apart is the withdrawal of all Soviet experts from China, when that country was still an important recipient of Russian assistance. Political and economic contradictions had gradually led to hard polemics. Although the USSR in the agreements of 1958 and 1959 undertook to assist the process of rapid economic expansion envisaged by the Great Leap Forward (in this case assistance in the contruction of 125 industrial projects in addition to 211 Soviet-aided projects in progress or completed), the virtual rupture between the communist rivals became apparent by a decline of over 50% in Sino-Soviet trade in 1961, the withdrawal of all 1.390 Soviet specialists, and a drastic suspension of aid.[170]

1⁰.10. Cameroun, which became independent in 1960, traded with the USSR without any formal arrangements until 1962. Apparently hopeful of closer relations after that country's independence, the Soviet Union made large purchases of coffee and cocoa in 1958 and 1959, but – disappointed by Cameroun's political course – cut down sharply in 1960 and did not trade at all with this country in 1961.[171]

1⁰.11. The relations between the Soviet Union and India were negatively affected when Mrs. Ghandi's government displayed greater

---

[169] see G. F. Triska & D. D. Finlay, pp. 267-271.
[170] J. Gittings – 'Survey of the Soviet-Sino Dispute 1963-1967' ('68) pp. 129-131.
[171] A. Erlich & Ch. R. Sonne – 'The Soviet Union: Economic Activity,' in Z. Brezezinski, pp. 70-71.

flexibility regarding the role of the private sector in industrial development and was prepared to invite private American capital into hitherto closed sectors. Moreover, an Indian request for a re-examination of the cost structure of the Russian-aided Bakaro Steel Plant, following a detailed project study and caried out by a private Indian firm, was considered an insult and is believed to have caused a good deal of bitterness in official Russian circles. At that time, however, the Soviet Union could not afford to endanger its relations with India too much, which circumstance declares its careful reactions on this very occasion.[172]

1⁰.12. Concerning China, there is first the example of Cuba. Since 1960 (when the United States broke its economic relations with Cuba) China concluded commercial deals with that country. In 1966, however, the Chinese decided to 'punish' the Castro régime for denying them the right to distribute propaganda material. Peking cut down its purchases of Cuban sugar and reduced its sales of rice to the country.[173]

1⁰.13. The great political disillusion China had to digest in Africa during the year 1965 resulted in a drastic cut of Chinese aid from $ 330 million in 1964 to $ 50 million in 1966.[174]

1⁰.14. The withdrawal of Chinese experts and the cancelling of Chinese funds to Burma is well-known. This happened after serious anti-Chinese riots in Burma, caused by the Chinese refusal to stop propaganda actions in the schools and factories.

These were some examples of the suspension of economic aid because of political conflict *by the donors*. As serious a measure as this, however, can be the refusal to accept any further aid *by an insulted or anxious recipient*. Some examples are mentioned pertaining to the latter case:

2⁰.1. In 1953 Burma terminated the American aid program in order to minimize Cold War manoeuvres and threats to its neutralist course.

2⁰.2. The same happened in Cambodia. Initially Cambodia had not accepted any aid from communist countries. Relations with the United States deteriorated, first because of America's alliance with Thailand and South Vietnam in SEATO, later (in 1963) because Prince Sihanouk believed Americans to be involved in South Vietnamense incursions on Cambodian territory and the CIA to be attempting to

---

[172] see S. P. Seth, p. 618.
[173] P. Andrews Poole, p. 625.
[174] J. E. Khalili – 'Sino-Arab Relations,' VIII Asian Survey ('68) p. 688.

oust him. As a result, Cambodia broke diplomatic relations with the United States and terminated its economic aid program.[175]
China's aid to Cambodia neither has ever had a regular or continuous character, because the Cambodians, anxious to preserve their neutralist stand, did not wish to tie themselves too firmly to their powerful neighbour.[176]

2⁰.3. Tanzania came into inflict with the Bundesrepublik, because it refused to break off official relations with the DDR in 1965. When Bonn cancelled its military assistance on February 26, President Nyerere answered by denouncing all German aid, which happened to be quite substantial at that time.[177]

2⁰.4. On January 6, 1966, the Central African Republic cancelled all contacts with China, after munition depots and training camps set up with Chinese assistance had been discovered.[178]

2⁰.5. The conflict between Ceylon and the U.S. over its political course in general, and its nationalization of American investments in particular, ended up in February 1963 with a refusal of further American aid.[179]

One could go on like this for a long time. Many leaders of Third World countries distrust this form of aid because of its political implications, and they are often proud enough to denounce even the most badly needed assistance in order to retain their feeling of independence. Significant of this attitude is a Joint Communiqué published after a meeting of the Presidents of Yugoslavia and Egypt and the Prime Minister of India, in October 1966, in which neo-colonialism and imperialism were called the principal sources of international tension:[180] this is how these countries experience present bilateral aid. Indeed, the political overtones, the sense of rivalry, and the pressure with which so much aid is beset, adds enormously to the political and economic dilemmas of the poor nations. It is understandable that young countries, having just received their independence after so many years of subjugation, should defend this independence rather than work towards economic development at any price.

[175] W. C. Johnstone – 'Political Commitment in Southeast Asia,' 54 Curr. Hist. (Jan. '68) p. 12.
[176] L. P. Singh – 'Die Ausstrahlung des Vietnam Krieges auf Laos, Kambodscha und Thailand,' XX Eur. Arch. ('68) pp. 159 ff.
[177] A. M. Mohiddin – 'Report on Tanzania,' VIII Kron. Afr. 2 ('68) p. 133; see also in idem V 2 ('65) p. 108.
[178] VI Kron. Afr. I ('66) p. 20.
[179] H. C. Hinton, p. 464.
[180] see VI Ind. J.I.L. ('66) p. 560; see also M. V. Subba-Rao – 'Neo Colonialism: The Invisible Government,' IV Afro-Asian World Affairs I ('67) pp. 73-77.

Their independence is holy to them; a fact which the rich countries have to accept. But instead, the rich countries sometimes go as far as the United States did in the case of Brazil from 1965 on: since this year the 'International Federation of Petroleum and Chemical Workers' and the 'American Institute of Free Labor Development' have been active in Brazil with CIA funds to encourage Brazil's petrochemical Unions to affiliate with their North American counterpart. This is part of the CIA's continuing effort to influence Latin American Trade Unions to be primarily a-political craft guilds, on the assumption that the policies of Latin American Unions will be anti-United States.[181] This case of interference was considered so serious that even the Brazilian government ordered a profound investigation, during which the accusations were verified as correct.
This happened in Latin America, where things like that are still possible without evoking very serious reactions, but what would have been the reaction in Africa or neutralist Asia?

Some developing countries like Cuba or Afghanistan have been quite fortunate in being able to play the Super Powers off against each other. But most of them have become a political football in the stadium of the Cold War. In the meantime much has been promised, much has been offered, and some things have been done. Many people, especially those in the cities, have noticed the first fruits of development. Exactly because of this reason present bilateral aid, with its intrinsic danger of an abrupt halt, and consequently of averse reactions, is too unstable a basis upon which to build the hopes of global economic development.
The increasing internationalization of aid operations has been widely greeted as a means of avoiding the often irrelevant political restrictions put on American funds by Congress. Bilateral aid, as it functions within the framework of the Cold War, involves too great a risk of stagnation and intensified frustrations.

2.2.2. *Waste*

Besides the danger of frustration resulting from discontinuity as a hallmark of today's bilateral aid, there is an additional risk of frustration resulting from stagnation by waste. Just as too many interruptions endanger the continuous character of economic growth, so too much waste makes a heavy obstacle to its substantiallty. Both elements are – as has been suggested in Chapter I – of importance to the internal

[181] E. Garvey – 'The CIA bungles on,' LXXXVII Commonweal (Febr. 9, '63) p. 553.

stability of a developing nation. If there is some truth in the story of the 'empty bucket,' it is not because development is impossible, but because too much of it has been done in the wrong way. The present waste of money and labour, both by donors (1^0) and recipients (2^0), is again first and foremost a corollary of bilateral aid as a function of the Cold War.

$1^0.1$. In this connection the common practice of many donors who tie aid to exports should be mentioned. Most of them do this for economic reasons mainly, as indicated, for instance, by the former British Minister of Overseas Development, Earl Grinstead:

> 'About two-thirds of our aid is spent on goods and services from Britain... trade follows aid. We equip a factory overseas and later on we get orders for spare parts and replacements.... We shall spend on aid because it is right and because it is in our long-term interest..';

and a Parliamentary Committee stated more bluntly:

> 'aid should be increasingly concentrated in those countries which offer the greatest potential markets for goods originating from Britain.'[182]

Similar arguments have been put forward recently by President Nixon in his campaign to prolong the Congress-vetoed American aid program (see p. 169). For the Super Powers, however, an additional stimulus for tying their aid programs to export provisions is the resulting dependence of the recipient on the donor in a political sense. They hope that they will later be in a position to exert pressure upon the recipient once he has become dependent on their supplies, replacements and technical assistance. Such motives may be supposed to play a role behind the American, Russian, and Chinese practice.

This means, however, waste and loss for the recipient, as Myrdal observes:

> 'tying aid to exports implies a curtailment of the aid-receiving underdeveloped country's freedom to buy the most suitable commodity and at the most favorable price. In the latter respect it has been estimated variously to increase costs by 20 to 40 per cent.'[183]

In the same sense it should be observed that the politically motivated stipulation of sending experts with the supplies as part of the aid package (practised by all three Super opponents, but this remark is not applicable to China for reasons outlined above) can mean severe additional loss to the recipient. A Pakistani government report of

---

[182] Report in 'Overseas Development' (Nov. '68) p. 9; IV 'Survey of International Development' 1 ('69).
[183] G. Myrdal – 'The Challenge of World Poverty' ('70) p. 349.

1958 has shown that the American experts placed at the disposal of the Pakistan government – although they were not irreplaceable by indigenous experts – were calculated to cost on the average $ 40.000 a year. It was implied that Pakistan could buy equivalent services much more cheaply elsewhere, if instead the money would be given for free use. The new government, however, repaid the friendly reception the 1958-putsch was given by Washington by suppressing the report.[184] This clearly suggests the political importance, to the donor, of expensive economic advisers sent to the recipient.

1⁰.2. In the second place, reference should be made to the likewise common practice of 'rewarding' friendly governments or individual politicians for their friendship and political services with funds to be spent on economic assistance. Part of such aid funds has been entirely' lost' in corruption. Whatever happened with the money given by Khrushcev when he arrived in Djakarta in 1960, where he was proud to announce an 'additional' $ 250 million loan, is uncertain; it has been estimated that one third of the original $ 117.5 million credit may have been expended on activities not covered by the protocols.[185]

1⁰.3. Since propaganda effects are an underlying objective of specific development projects, several of them have been set up without contributing to the fundamental needs of the developing countries in question. Some examples in this connection have been mentioned before.

Afghanistan has been presented with magnificent bungalow parks and swimming pools for the workers of non-existing industries, built both by the Americans and the Russians. It was also supplied with the brilliant new airport, which was never used, built by the Americans.

To Burma the Russians made an offer in March 1956, of building a theater, a sports stadium, a cultural center, buildings for exhibitions, a conference hall, a 206-room hotel and a swimming pool. Similarly, some American projects were designed principally to counteract the propaganda effect of the Russian gifts.[186]

Guinea witnessed the construction by the Soviet Union of an entirely useless 700-hectare state rice farm at La Fié, which so far has yielded no results despite the expenditure of a large part of the planned investment.[187]

---

[184] idem, p. 350.
[185] U. Ra-anan, p. 188.
[186] J. D. Montgomery, pp. 41, 43.
[187] A. Erlich & Ch. R. Sonne, p. 73.

1⁰.4. Then there are the many offers to extend aid for the realization of projects which are refused (sometimes on economic grounds) by the other: here we may think of China's offer to help build the railroad through Tanzania, after the World Bank had come to a negative report concerning the economic soundness of the project on December 7, 1964.[188] The same happened when the United States refused to pave the streets of Kabul because the money would be wasted on that economically useless project. This time the Russians came in and did it nevertheless.[189] This kind of taking over of projects constitutes a political rather than economical activity, and it means nothing less than waste of money which could have been spent more profitably elsewhere.

1⁰.5. The same can be said of the policy of 'buying as a last resort' practiced by China and the Soviet Union. Thinking of the money spent by the Soviet Union for the purchase of Cuba's sugar in 1960, one may argue that without that the Cuban economy would have collapsed. But let us not forget then, that it was by the permission of a strictly bilateral system of aid and trade that something like the American boycott could occur without provoking serious international conflict. Considering that, one may say that this Russian money could have been spent more constructively.

It should be made clear at this point that the present author is certainly not trying to denounce bilateral aid *per se* as wasteful. His only intention is to make clear that because present bilateral aid was used as an instrument in the Cold War, too much money and energy has been spent in vain.

2⁰. Concerning the other category of states, the recipient countries, the same remark is valid: too much has been wasted.

First, there has been waste because of ignorance, lack of know-how, and lack of additional means to make a project run within an established infra-structure.

Second, much has been wasted because of corruption.

Third there has been waste because of the urge towards prestige vis-à-vis the own population as well as the outside world. Many governments in developing countries are receptive to the (understandable) urge of realizing as soon as possible some projects which are believed to show that they are on their way to becoming a modern state. They first want to have magnificent governmental palaces,

---

[188] V Kron. Afr. 4 ('65) p. 249; also idem V I ('65) p. 30.
[189] H. Morgenthau – 'A political Theory of Foreign Aid,' LVI Am. Pol. Sc. Rev. ('62) p. 304.

impressive Court buildings, and of course a national airline. Such projects may have a certain positive effect on formerly apathetic sections of the population; yet, it means that a lot of money is spent on non-priorities. Neither their economy will get a push forward, nor their international position will be changed by them.

In the fourth place there is the obstacle of the traditionally ruling élite. Wherever these social groups still decide on the way their country is going to develop, they may accept economic aid intended to bring about change, but use it for such projects which will not endanger the status quo.

Under the prevailing circumstances it seems hardly surprising to see a recent World Bank study reveal that in 1965 the developing nations spent $ 2,1 billion in domestic resources, to manufacture industrial products at a world market value of only $ 800 million.[190]

Of course, one must consider the afore-said factors causative to the waste of so much money. But again, one could state not without reason that such factors *can decide on the fruitfulness of aid owing to the present form of bilateral aid*, i.e. because they are inherent to the present bilateral aid system. Because the donor countries want to win political friends in the Third World, and because they have often enough experienced the pride and distrust of the new governments, they will rather offer the money without any comment than demand that it be spent on economically justified projects. Besides, even if they feel unhappy about wasting their money, there is always the fear that the adversary will step in and exploit the resulting conflict to his own political advantage.

On the other hand, the recipient countries are often anxious for similar reasons. India for example refuses to accept foreign experts payed by their own government. Although this system might be most convenient, the Indian government keeps to the fundamental rule of paying all foreign experts in American dollars in order to avoid any feeling of dependence.

3⁰. Another typical feature of present bilateral aid is the fundamental lack of co-operation and co-ordination, an absolute *sine qua non* to any successful development program. Within the framework of an organized and co-ordinated multilateral development aid system much duplication of effort could be prevented.

4⁰. Attention should be payed to one more aspect of Cold War-oriented aid, resulting in waste and frustration; i.e. the donor's endeavour to export his own socio-economic system.

[190] See MacNamara's Address as the President of the World Bank (Sept. 29, '69) p. 20.

Each of the three Super Powers tries to use its aid, whenever it can decide on those projects to be set up, in order to transplant its own socio-economic structure in the recipient country. Sometimes this policy may not impede real development, but on other occasions it certainly does. Whether a negative effect on development will occur, depends mainly on the characteristics and the level of development of the recipient country in question.

The intrinsic disadvantage of bilateral aid in this respect is that the Super Powers are so preoccupied with the endeavour to export their own socio-economic values, that they are often unable to adapt their way of contributing to development to the local needs. For the Americans it is inconceivable to promote state- or community-ownership at the expense of private enterprise, whereas to the Russians and the Chinese it is inconceivable to accept the principle of private ownership at the expense of central authority. Kennedy said that the developing countries should be allowed 'to discover that economic and social advantages can best occur under free institutions;' so Chruschev asserted that 'fast tempos are a general law of socialism,' and thus they both stuck to their own conviction. Whereas the Clay-Report claims that 'aid to the private sector alone could make the greatest contribution to rapid economic growth and overall development,'[191] it is a recurring theme in communist publications that the most important form of economic assistance is to stimulate the rapid development of the state sector.[192]

It has been shown before how China provoked trouble with African and Asian countries, by the endeavour to use its aid projects for propaganda purposes. The Chinese have cultivated the art of propaganda on the micro level. In April, 1965, to mention another example, the Chinese Embassy in Congo (Brazaville) employed 30 'officers' and 180 'diplomats' whose duties were entirely obscure.[193] The Chinese almost exclusively built industrial projects, to be operated by the State. Thus they create a working proletariat where it did not yet exist. By sending Chinese experts, who are to live under the same circumstances as the local population, they try to exploit the eventual ties of co-operation and friendship in order to transfer the thoughts of Mao Tse-tung.

Likewise, 53% of the entire Russian aid is extended to industrial projects run by the State. It must be observed, however, that these

---

[191] Clay-Report, note 58 supra p. 19.
[192] see for instance V. Vershinin & V. Demidov – 'Disinterested Aid,' Int. Aff. (Moscow. Jan. '60) p. 35.
[193] Daily Telegraph (April 27, '65).

projects have generally contributed in a positive way to economic development, because the circumstances in many Third World countries are asking for a rather high degree of centralization and control to make development proceed rapidly enough. It is highly problematic, if rapid growth is needed, to build the necessary infra-structure on the foundations of private enterprise. If one has to start from practically zero and has to work as quickly as possible towards *general* development and a higher standard of living for everybody, economic liberalism can hardly solve the problems.

That is why the greatest mistakes in this connection have been made by the United States. From the beginning, American aid programs have shown a holy respect for economic liberalism and private enterprise.[194] This ambition has occasionally led to serious frustrations. Latin America in particular has become the victim of fundamental errors. A closer look at the famous Alliance for Progress, as the outstanding example, is used in illustrating this point.

On the one hand, the Alliance was intended to contribute to Latin America's economic development. On the other hand, however, this economic objective was subordinated to the supreme goal of consolidating regional security against alleged communist aggression and subversion. President Kennedy often stressed this point; for example when he said:

'A wisely administered US-aid program can help to build nations that are increasingly prepared to defend their independence against totalitarian enemies – external or internal, overt or covert – and increasingly willing to work with us as partners on common projects which may lead the world a little closer to peace.'[195]

This perception of the tasks of the Alliance and this fear of communist agitation of any kind has made it impossible for the United States to support any necessary fundamental change in the socio-economic field.[196] Privileged groups throughout Latin America denounce anyone who dares to ask for fiscal or land reforms as a communist, and the United States government tends to agree with them. Accordingly, the principal result of the Alliance has been the maintenance of a highly unjust system, which sometimes made the privileged élite even more privileged. The economic and the political aim of this 'revolutionary plan'

[194] see above section 2.1.1.
[195] cited in Ch. Bowles – 'Why Foreign Aid?,' Dept. State Bull. (May 20, '63) p. 778.
[196] see R. F. Smith – 'Social Revolution in Latin America; the role of US policy,' 41 Int. Aff. (London, Oct. '65) pp. 635 ff; see also W. F. Barber – 'Can the Alliance for Progress Succeed?,' 351 The Annals ('64). On p. 85 he says that 'it would indoubtedly come as a traumatic shock to a number of S. American governments to learn of this purpose of the Alliance.'

(as it was called), were incompatible; the former was sacrified for the benefit of the latter. Aguilar writes:

> 'In synthesis, the Alliance does not pretend to cope with the principal historical causes of backwardness, nor with the poverty of Latin America, but merely attempts to preserve law and order and to apply the brakes to any popular movement which might cause damage to the powers that be.'

El Alianza para el Progresso is first of all a political program,

> 'an instrument in defense of the ruling classes, an exposition of Monroism and an outpost of anti-Communism, an answer to popular discontent, a barricade against any desire for emancipation, an alternative and a check to the Cuban revolution, and a new Holy Alliance directed against the revolutionary struggle of our people.'[197]

These are the bitter words of a Latin American Professor of Economics, and in general they are correct. Much of the money spent has been more or less wasted if one looks at the innumerable fundamental projects, vainly waiting for a solution. Less aid, but better management, would certainly have had a more beneficial effect than the haphazard, incoherent and contradictory programmes of the past. 'Some intelligent Columbians had hoped that an 'old' Nixon would lend less and be less stultifying,' as one author observes.[198]

The Alliance, like so many moderate initiatives, has raised hopes which were to be seriously frustrated, mainly because political and strategic objectives did not allow those fundamental socio-economic changes to occur which are a *sine qua non* for Latin American progress. In this light one should see the significance of Aguilar's remark: 'the conclusion is telling: every day they talk more and more of the need for such and such a reform, and every day they move further away from any possibility of carrying out any type of reform.'[199]

Lieuwen, one of the outstanding experts on Latin America also stresses the incompability of the two objectives; he says:

> 'The subsequent social crisis in Latin America has made the military considerations increasingly untenable. The political freedom, social reform, and economic development principles outlined in the Alliance for Progress program appear to be inconsistent with our military assistance programs in Latin America. Unless this inconsistency is removed, frustration and failure may crown our whole Latin American policy.'[200]

---

[197] A. Aguilar – 'Latin America and the Alliance for Progress,' Monthly Review Pamphlet Series No. 24 ('63) pp. 30-31.
[198] M. Deas – 'Columbian Prospects,' XXIV Int. J. (Summer '69) p. 513.
[199] A. Aguilar, p. 20.
[200] E. Lieuwen – 'US Military Assistance of Doubtful Value in Latin America,' in 'A Strategy for American Security' ('63) p. 16.

Finally, there is one other specific peace-disturbing effect of US aid programmes to be remembered. In dealing with countries with privileged foreign minorities (like Chinese in S. E. Asia, Indians in E. Africa) we observed that these groups often control economic life to a considerable extent. If development programmes in such countries have to be based on free enterprise and economic liberalism, they tend to intensify ethnic conflict, because in this system such foreign minorities are the first to profit from development.[201]

Generally speaking, it can be said that bilateral aid within the framework of the Cold War has been characterized by too many promises, too much waste and stagnation, and the lack of a sound development strategy. The Cold War has both created and hindered economic assistance. Apart from some positive experiences, this kind of aid has eventually contributed to disappointment and frustration (both in the rich and in the poor countries), and to poisoning of the international atmosphere.

Concerning the point last mentioned, the negative influence of economic aid has been intensified by the fact that economic aid has often been connected with or even been subordinated to military aid, thereby strengthening its Cold War character.

2.3. *Military aid and the Cold War*

Although military aid somewhat exceeds the context of this book, two reasons made the author decide to pay attention to it. The first reason being that it is part of the donor-recipient relation and as such – like economic aid – a corollary to the developmental process in the Third World. The second reason being that economic aid has often been so much interwoven with military aid, that a distinction could scarcely be made (see section 2.2.).

The developing countries can be said to have spent, in view of their economic needs and capabilities, generally quite a lot on their military sector. Most African states spend 10-15% of their total budget on military affairs.[202] Some Latin American countries sometimes passed 25%, as in 1959 under the Mutual Security Program; in that year Argentina spent 21.5%, Brazil 29.1%, and Paraguay 32.7%. In 1963 it was somewhat less, though still significant; at that time, Argentina

---

[201] D. P. Ghai – 'Asians in East-Africa: Problems and Prospects,' 3 J. Mod. Afr. St. ('65) pp. 40-45; and W. E. Willmott – 'The Overseas Chinese Today and Tomorrow,' LXIII Pac. Aff. 2 ('69) p. 212; see also Ch. I under Heading 8.
[202] N. Brown, W. F. Gutteridge – 'The African Military Balance,' Adelphi Papers no. 12 ('64) p. 4.

spent 15.6%, Brazil 11.4%, Paraguay 27.5% and Peru 28.5%.[203]
Why do developing countries themselves want to spend so much on armament?

1°. There is the argument of prestige vis-à-vis the outside world: a modern Army is thought to be a proof of national strength, trustworthiness and 'civilization.'

2°. There is the argument of prestige vis-à-vis the inside world: many young political leaders do not enjoy enough sympathy initially and think they can attract or deter their own population by making a deep impression with a strong, modern military apparatus.

3°. As a consequence of the two former factors, governments in the Third World are inclined to buy heavy material and modern equipment, which is in most cases as expensive as it is useless. Aircraft, missiles, tanks, etc. are particularly regarded as symbols of power and independence.[204]

4°. Many leaders in the Third World are military men themselves, which contributes naturally to substantial emphasis on the Army as a socio-political institute.

5°. Many governments fear internal difficulties during the process of political and economic development. They want to possess a strong arm for resisting internal upheavals.

6°. Manifold are regional conflicts such as border conflicts throughout Africa, Asia and Latin America, andc onflicts with colonial administrations and white minority governments in Africa.

7°. An important additional factor is the process of escalation and proliferation; if one state raises its military expenditures, or increases its military power by way of military grants from a rich donor country, its neighbours tend to do the same.[205]

---

[203] see D. Wood – 'Armed Forces in Central and South America,' Adelphi Papers no. 34 ('67) p. 24. Comparing the monetary costs of defense-spending as a percentage of the Gross National Expenditure, we find the poor countries of the Middle East even highest on the list. But this is because of the permanent war and it would diminish in times of peace. As to comparison of military expenditures to GNP see 'The Military Balance,' edited by the Institute for Strategic Studies (London); see also M. Thomson – 'Militarism 1969, A Survey of World Trends,' II Peace Res. Rev. 5 (Oct. '68).
[204] for a country as big as India these symbols may not even be sufficient in the long run. Some writers fear that the lack of nuclear weapons deprives India of prestige and demoralizes its Army. See B. Singh – 'National Defense in Nuclear Age: Dilemma of India,' in Political Scientist (Jan./June '66); and S. K. Shastri – 'A Possible Strategy,' Seminar No. 83 (July '66).
[205] here again (see note 204 supra) nuclear weapons may be in the game. Thus Ayub Khan said that when India would make an A-bomb, Pakistan would follow. See R. Stephens – 'Vietnam War May Last 50 Years, says Ayub,' London Observer (Febr. 12, '67).

Such are probably the main reasons which made Rusk remark:
'I recall that at the UN General Assembly, at the time when all members were voting unanimously for disarmament, 70 members were at that moment asking us for military assistance.'[206]
Many poor countries were eager to obtain an impressive military apparatus, but could not afford it. So, they turned to the rich world, where many countries were equally eager to supply it. Why were these prepared to extend the weaponry and, although they all spoke of the necessities of economic development, ready to support the efforts of the poor to waste so much on armament? We shall again have a look at the policies in this respect of the United States, the Soviet Union, China, and others respectively. This will confront us with quite another motive behind the arms traffic to the developing world; i.e. the rich nations are themselves stimulating the build-up of a military apparatus in the poor countries.[206a]

2.3.1. *The United States*

The extension of military assistance has obviously been a very important tool of foreign policy to the United States, as is indicated by the following figures:
Since 1954 the United States has supplied military aid to the amount of some $ 50 billion (about 90% of the sum of military aid supplied by all countries). US-assistance (grants + sales) averaged more than $ 2 billion a year.[207] During the years 1953-1956 the amount of military aid surpassed the amount of economic aid by far. What have been the reasons of this massive transaction?
The main reason, as many observers think, has been political; namely, to use military aid as a weapon in the Cold War, supplemented by economic aid. This political objective has a twofold character. On the one hand, it is to strengthen the military power of friendly governments as a bullwark against perceived communist aggression or subversion. On the other hand, it is to use weapon supplies as a means to obtain influence in recipient countries, in order to bind these to the United States. As Lieuwen writes:

---

[206] G. Kemp – 'Arms Sales and Arms Control in the Developing Countries,' XXII The World Today ('66) p. 391.
[206a] recently SIPRI has published an enormous study on the arms trade – 'The Arms Trade With The Third World' ('71). Since my study had been finished by the time, it could not take profit of this tremendous work realized by the colleagues at Stockholm.
[207] G. Thayer – 'The War Business: the international trade in armaments,' ('69) p. 19.

'Though expressed in military terms, the objectives of the US military assistance program for Latin America are primarily political... the US, during the past decade, has been granting military assistance primarily as a quid pro quo for Latin America's friendship and co-operation.'[208]

Simarly Hoogland, who thinks there are other reasons as well, states that 'far more compelling, particularly to the competing superpowers, have been the political motives associated with the Cold War and the encounter of ideologies.'[209] Sutton and Kemp agree with him when they write:

'America and Russia have used military aid as a political lever to influence the foreign policies of recipient states. The international arms trade has been a central factor in Cold War policies for over a decade.'[210]

Thus it is assumed that the United States, recognizing the military needs and wants of governments who could not afford the money and were incapable of manufacturing arms themselves, exploited the opportunity by selling weapons in order to buy friendship and to strengthen anti-communist countries. A lot of arguments, indeed, can be mentioned supporting this opinion.

1°. There are the *official Acts* concerning foreign assistance: the Military Defence Assistance Act of 1949, the Mutual Security Acts of 1951 and 1954 (amended), and the Foreign Assistance Act of 1961 (amended). All of them clearly link military aid to the prevailing Cold War objective of communist containment. In the basic legislation authorizing the Military Assistance Program, the US Congress has proclaimed its intention to promote:

'the peace of the world and the foreign policy, security, and general welfare of the United States by fostering an improved climate of political independence, and individual liberty, improving the ability of friendly countries and international organizations to deter or, if necessary, defeat Communist or Communist-supported aggression, facilitating arrangements for individual and collective security, assisting friendly countries to maintain internal security, and creating an environment of security and stability in the developing friendly countries essential to their more rapid social, economic, and political progress.'

Particularly during the decade after the second World War this political objective was considered to be so fundamental that economic aid was ordered to be subsidiary and supplementary to military aid. The concept of 'defence support' was created, a clear indication that

---

[208] E. Liewen pp. 13-14.
[209] J. H. Hoogland – 'Arms in the developing world,' XII Orbis (Spring '68) p. 182.
[210] J. L. Sutton and G. Kemp – 'Arms to Developing Countries, 1945-1965,' ('66), Adelphi Papers no. 28, p. 31; see also XXIII Bull. At. Sc. 7 ('67) p. 45.

economic aid was designed to provide the supplementary economic resources required in order to enable the recipient countries to carry out adequate defence efforts. 'Defence support' in due course became the principal form of economic aid: in 1956, for instance, the sum of economic aid given to the Far East amounted to $ 763 million, $ 724 of this sum being 'defence support' concentrated in the countries along the borders of China.[211]

2⁰. There is the geographical distribution. On the one hand the *number of recipients*, on the other hand *their quality* is indicative of the political and strategic motives underlying the military aid program.

2⁰.1. Concerning the *number of recipients*, it is noteworthy that anno 1950 the US extended military assistance to some 14 countries only. After the USSR entered this market (by 1955), however, the number of recipients increased rapidly: in 1957 there were already 42 of them, and in 1963 their number amounted to 69. In total, about 80 countries have received American military assistance during that period.[212]

Such figures suggest that US aid does not only go to countries allied or sympathetic to American aims and values, but also to countries tending to oppose US policies. The United States expects that countries receiving American aid are at least stimulated to preserve their independence and thus to contribute to communist containment.

2⁰.2. Then there is the *quality of recipients*. The Lend-lease expired at the end of June 1946, but arms worth $ 800 million were sent to Chiang Kai-shek in China between 1946 and 1949 to support his campaign against the communist troops. When the communist rebels in Greece got support from Yugoslavia, Albania and Bulgaria – not, as was alleged at that time, from Russia –, the Truman-doctrine was put into practice in 1947. In this year Greece and Turkey received military assistance worth $ 497.6 million.[213] From that time on military assistance has been concentrated in countries encircling the 'communist bloc' or other countries of particular strategic importance to the United States, such as those countries in Europe, the Middle-East, S.E. Asia and Latin America. For instance, before the United States became involved directly in the Indochinese conflict, it payed nevertheless 80% of the French war costs in Vietnam.[214] Today military assistance grants amounting to approximately $ 55 million annually, and credit sales to approximately $ 25 million annually are

---

[211] J. S. Berliner p. 66.
[212] G. Thayer p. 38.
[213] H. A. Hovey – 'United States Military Assistance' ('65) p. 5.
[214] W. D. Verwey – 'Bombardments on the North after Tonkin and Pleiku: Reprisals?,' V. Rev. belge dr. int. 2 ('69) p. 467.

extended to Latin America. Very recent examples constitute e.g. Jordan and South Korea. At a time when the entire aid program for the year 1972 seemed to be cancelled, White House spokesmen mentioned these nations – together with S. Vietnam of course – as countries which might be coerced to follow a 'wrong course' if aid were to be stopped. Jordan, it was explained, might follow a leftist course if the promised $ 9.6 million worth of military aid would be refused. S. Korea might suffer from a severe political crisis if the envisaged $ 642,3 million worth of military aid – making possible the withdrawal of 20.000 American soldiers – would not be extended. The following table listing the main Third World recipients of us military aid – even when omitting the countries completely identified with the us, in this case S. Korea, S. Vietnam, and Taiwan – illustrates its containment function. It is noteworthy that the only exception to this (Brazil) was found to be also the only exception among the main recipients of us economic aid: clear evidence of the close connection between military and economic aid programs.

Main Third World Recipients of US Military Aid: FY 1965-FY 1967

Country	Amount (in millions of us dollars)
1. Turkey	1735.5
2. Pakistan	750.0
3. Iran	627.6
4. Thailand	600.0
5. Philippines	262.5
6. India	200.0
7. Brazil	160.8
8. Laos	150.0

All other recipients received amounts under $ 100 million.

Source: U.S. Dept. of Defense – 'Military Assistance Facts' (USGPO '68) pp. 14-15.

In the fiscal year 1965 military aid amounted to $ 1.215 billion; $ 861.6 million (or ± 70%) went to only 11 countries, all of them situated on the Chinese and Russian borders (Greece, Turkey, Laos, S. Vietnam, Pakistan, S. Korea, Taiwan, Philippines, Thailand, India, Iran).[215]

---

[215] H. A. Hovey, pp. 12-13.

3⁰. Then there is the *quality of military aid projects*.
3.1. Part of the military aid-complex is made up of offers to build or reconstruct harbours, airports, roads and other useful military facilities in countries of strategic importance to the United States. Particularly Asia shows many examples of this, such as the harbour and the airports in Thailand from which B-52's are flying their raids over Vietnam, and the maritime bases in Japan and the Philippines. Since the United States has a second strike capability against any adversary by its nuclear ICBM's, the importance of having 'forward facilities' throughout the world may have diminished, but the need to keep conflicts non-nuclear makes the argument far from obsolete, as the example of Thailand indicates.
3⁰.2. Also relevant is the *way of extending aid*, namely, the high amount of *grants* during the years before the thaw in the Cold War. Between 1945 and 1955 the United States gave away most of the material supplied. Until 1966 the amount of grants reached some $ 33 billion.[216] This policy of generous granting has a threefold political implication: first, it enables poor countries to arm or re-arm; second, it brings them under obligations to the United States because of its generosity; third, by supplying the military equipment, the recipient becomes dependent on the United States for advice and replacements (which has a political as well as an economic aspect).
3⁰.3. Military assistance does not exclusively mean supplies of arms. It also means training and advising, as is done in the Panama-school or by special forces in the recipient countries themselves. Today MAAG-officers are operating in most non-communist countries, overtly or covertly.[217] Training foreign officers – especially in the United States, where 10-15,000 foreigners annually are taught in military affairs and come into touch with 'the American way of life' – is considered to be an excellent medium for interventionary purposes.

2.3.2. *The Soviet Union*

The Soviet Union started its military assistance program to the Third World in 1955, and has by now become the second important supplier of arms after the United States. The Soviet Union's share of communist military assistance amounts to ± 95%, averaging some $ 500 million a year.[218]

---

[216] Int. Her. Trib. (22, 23 July '67).
[217] American military are stationed in 119 countries. See Gen. D. M. Shoup & Col. J. Donovan – 'The New American Militarism,' The Atlantic Monthly (April '69) p. 51.
[218] G. Thayer, pp. 38, 315.

The main reason behind Soviet military assistance, as in the case of the United States, is thought by many observers to be the political one. In this respect the opinions of Sutton, Kemp and Hoogland have been mentioned already.[219] Likewise Ra'anan considers political objectives the most important motives behind Russian military assistance.[220] He points out that, in contrast to the United States, the Soviet Union focussed its attention in this respect immediately on the countries of the Third World, beginning with Egypt in 1955.

Russia's main political aims have been twofold: on the one hand, Russia tried to neutralize countries and to draw them away from the Western sphere of influence; on the other hand, Russia tried to build a bullwark against increasing Chinese influence in the poor countries while at the same time, of course, increasing its own influence.[221] Both aims have often overlapped. The USSR has also covertly and overtly assisted national liberation movements; the latter, however, very selectively, notably when Russia had nothing to lose by a conflict with an already anti-Soviet official government, and when it could expect political profit by assisting the liberation movement in question. Again some arguments supporting this opinion are mentioned:

1⁰. Beginning with the official documents, I had, for linguistic reasons, to rely on articles like one by Gilbert, who studied several such documents and concluded that, like the United States, the USSR officially declares that its military aid program is intended to support its foreign policy objectives in the Third World.[222]

2⁰. In the case of the USSR also, geographical distribution is a relevant indication. On the one hand the *number of recipients* and on the other hand *their quality* is indicative.

---

[219] see note 209, 210, supra.
[220] U. Ra'anan – 'Tactics in the Third World; contradictions and dangers,' Survey (Oct. '65) pp. 26ff.
[221] Frank sums up six goals of Soviet arms experts, which in fact are a subdivision of the same two central goals: a. to extend Soviet influence in the less developed countries of the world; b. to extend and reinforce the image of Soviet leadership of the Communist World vis-à-vis China; c. to support 'wars of national liberation' such as those in Vietnam, consistent with Soviet interpretations of Marxist-Leninist ideology; d. to extend Soviet defenses beyond its immediate borders; e. to deny the West access or to hamper Western access to strategically important areas such as the Suez-Red See zone, the straits of Malacca and Gibraltar, the Baltic-North Sea approach, the Gulf of Tonkin, and the see of Japan atwarth Korea; f. to prevent the re-introduction of Western military power into areas formerly held by it in the middle East, Africa, and Southeast Asia. L. A. Frank – 'The Arms Trade in International Relations' ('69) p. 84.
[222] S. P. Gilbert – 'Soviet-American Military Aid Competition in the Third World,' XIII Orbis ('70) p. 1130.

2⁰.1. As to the number of the recipients the most notable thing is that, although the total amounts involved are equivalent to those of the U.S., the Soviet Union has strongly concentrated its assistance on some key countries. Whereas the U.S. distributed its $ 5.399 billion extended during the period 1955-1967 among fifty-four recipients (notwithstanding the concentration of a large part of this amount in the ring around the Sino-Soviet border), the USSR concentrated its $ 5.768 billion during the same period on twenty-four recipients. These figures suggest that the Soviet Union focusses its military aid on those countries that may be expected to agree with Soviet policies or which may maintain friendly relations with the Soviet Union, or where the USSR may at least hope to gain direct political profit.[223]
2⁰.2. Such a conclusion is confirmed by analyzing the quality of its recipients. The program started in 1955 with Egypt, which was by then trying to shake off the remnants of Western influence. The Russians stepped in and offered military assistance amounting to $ 300 million.[224] From then on many Soviet supplies were extended in order to function against the interests of the West, and some time later these supplies were also used to function against the Chinese. These were the momentous motives behind the weapon supplies to the Zanzibar rebels, the Vietnamese (North Vietnamese as well as the NLF), the rebels in Eritrea and Yemen.[225] The sale of Mig-15 jets and T-34 tanks to Morocco in 1961 was partly intended to undermine American influence. The Algerian FLN was supported in order to expel French influence from North Africa and to prevent Chinese endeavours. Weapon supplies amounting to $ 100 million were given to Iran with the purpose of promoting Iranian non-alignment. The liberation movements in Angola and Mozambique were and are supported with the purpose of creating friendly ties with the Soviet Union which thus anticipates their independence. Cyprus received assistance worth $ 14 million in order to isolate Makarios from the West. Under N'krumah Ghana received assistance to diminish English influence as well as to counterbalance Chinese aid. The Army of Afghanistan was completely modernized and became dependent on Soviet supplies, before the Americans or Chinese entered that market. Likewise, weapons were supplied to India and Pakistan in order to counterweigh American and Chinese influence.[226]

---

[223] idem, p. 1122.
[224] K. Billerbeck – 'Soviet Bloc Foreign Aid to the Developing Countries' ('60) p. 68.
[225] An AFP-report of January 4, 1968 states that probably not only airplanes but also pilots had been supplied to the Yemeni Republicans.
[226] see G. Thayer pp., 322ff.; K. Billerbeck, p. 69.

In general the political and strategic function of Russia's military aid program can be gathered from the following list of main recipients, the direct allies – Mongolia, N. Korea, and N. Vietnam – again being omitted.

Main Recipients of Soviet Military Aid: 1955-1967

Country	Estimated amount (in millions of US dollars)
1. United Arab Republic	1.500
2. Indonesia	1.200
3. Cuba	750
4. India	700 (or somewhat less)
5. Iraq	500 (or more)
6. Syria	300 (or more)
7. Afghanistan	260
8. Algeria	200

Two more recipients received up to $ 100 million (Iran and Yemen), all others far less than $ 50 million.

Sources: U.S. Dept. of State – 'Communist Governments and Developing Nations: Aid and Trade in 1967.' Res. Mem. RSE-120 ('68);
W. Joshua & S. P. Gilbert – 'Arms for the Third World: Soviet Military Aid Diplomacy' ('69) pp. 23, 45, 73, 102.

As was found to be the case with their economic aid program – which is strikingly similar – this list clearly shows Russia's concentration of military aid in those countries friendly with the USSR, and which are either situated along its border, or are of high strategic importance (Cuba versus the U.S., Indonesia versus China).

3^0. Then, there is the quality of specific aid programs. Again several aspects can be distinguished in this connection:
$3^0.1$. In the first place, several projects serve the military interests of the Russian Armed Forces. One could think here of the highway across the mountains between the USSR and Afghanistan, and the construction or modernization of harbours like one for U-boats in Cuba. At present the Soviet Union is trying to counterbalance the Western fleets in the Mediterranean and the Indian Ocean, while reinforcing its naval force in other parts of the world as well. For this it needs advanced facilities, the number of which is increasing. Examples of this (apart from Cuba) are Algeria, Egypt, and Guinea.

3⁰.2. In trying to withdraw developing countries from Western influence, but eager to retain the image of the disinterested, morally superior friend, the USSR did not extend its assistance in the form of grants (as the United States did) but in the form of credit sales at very low interest rates (2-2.5%). Thereby the Russians hoped perhaps to avoid any feeling of dependence on the side of the recipient, while at the same time hoping to bind those countries in a more subtle way by creating strong economic ties.

3⁰.3. Another practice of importance in this connection has been the use of intermediaries. Bulgaria, E. Germany and Czechoslovakia have often supplied weapons to liberation movements as intermediaries for the Soviet Union.[227]

Another form of the same practice was planned re-sale. Russian weapons were sold to Egypt, Algeria, Guinea, and Ghana, who were to function only as intermediaries. They then re-sold them to the ultimately intended recipients. By way of this indirect policy the Soviet Union tried to avoid political reactions from official governments when it assisted liberation movements. It also tried to avoid difficulties with the U.S. when it operated in an American sphere of interest.[228]

4⁰. A final observation is that the Soviet Union has sometimes tried to annul the existing influence of an adversary by creating new military services which would make the recipient friendly to and dependent on the Russians. The most important example of this is Indonesia under Sukarno. The Army was reinforced by the Chinese and Sukarno cultivated friendship with Peking. So, the Russians decided to supply material for a Navy and an Airforce on a huge scale ($ 1 billion between 1958 and 1964), thus establishing two new services which practically did not exist before. While these became dependent on Soviet supplies and advice, they had nothing to gain from the Chinese.[229]

---

[227] see U. Ra'anan note 220 supra. Czechoslovakia acted as an intermediary in the case of weapons supplies to Guatemala and Egypt; the DDR did the same in the case of the Zanzibar rebels, Poland for the NLF in Vietnam, and Bulgaria in the case of the rebels in Yemen and Eritrea. On one known occasion the United States also used an intermediary: that was when W. Germany supplied weapons to Israel in 1965.
[228] for the use of military aid to support wars of liberation, see S. P. Gilbert – 'Wars of Liberation and Soviet Military Aid Policy,' IX Orbis ('66) pp. 839 ff.
[229] G. Thayer, p. 327.

2.3.3. China

China has only just begun to compete with the other Super Powers in the field of military assistance. At this moment China's share in the total military assistance by communist countries is estimated at a little more than 5%. Because of its economic position China has not been able to take very big jumps, and, as in the case of economic assistance, China works more on the micro level, often more covert than overt. While concentrating on specific promising key recipients, the Chinese have extended military aid throughout the Third World. The political motives behind this assistance may be summarized as: (1) to fight 'Western imperialism,' (2) to counterbalance 'Soviet revisionism' and (3) to further Afro-Asian-Latino solidarity under China's leadership.

China's main tactics have been to extend military supplies in times of conflict – such as its supplies to Indonesia, Egypt, Yemen and Pakistan indicate – since the recipient's need and gratitude are then greatest. Frequently the recipient has been a participant to some internal conflict; a few examples of this will now follow:

Concerning Asia, China has been accused of supporting the guerillas in Northeast Thailand, and it is certainly lending support to Sihanouk's troops in Cambodia. The Naga and Mizo rebels in India have reportedly received Chinese military assistance, which also holds for the White Flag rebels in Burma.[230]

Concerning Africa, the Algerian FLN has been a main recipient, and so has the Republican faction in Yemen. The Chinese are known furthermore to have supported the armed rising of the UPC in Cameroun. Gizenga was supported during the Congo crisis, while in Angola and Mozambique China competes with the USSR in providing military assistance.[231] China has financed arms purchases for an irredentist movement in French Somaliland, and weapons were sent to support revolts in Zanzibar, Kenya, Burundi, Uganda, and Guinea.[232]

Another method indicating China's political objectives is the endeavour to gain influence in friendly Armies, notably by providing supplies and by providing training and technical assistance.

Examples of the first are the Indonesian Army under Sukarno, and at present all three services of Tanzania. In relation to the second point, training, the Chinese do not deny that they are involved in military

---

[230] Th. W. Robinson – 'Peking's Revolutions Strategy in the Developing World,' 286 The Annals (Nov. '69) p. 69.
[231] R. Lowenthal, pp. 192-193.
[232] R. Counts – 'Chinese Footprints in Somalia,' The Reporter (Febr. 2, '61); see also G. Thayer, p. 315, 344.

training of various revolutionary groups, apart from training friendly official Armies, like the Tanzania one. They have been reported to train Thai rebels, as well as Burmese insurrectionists and people from Portuguese colonies. In July 1961, a group of Camerounians was arrested on their return from China, where they admitted to have been trained in the tactics of guerilla warfare.[233] Ghana has likewise complained that the Chinese were instructing military saboteurs. The Central African Republic broke off its relations with Peking after training camps had been discovered, and after it had been ascertained that revolutionaries were trained in China. For similar reasons Chinese diplomats were expelled from Burundi in 1965. In the Congo the rebels of Olenga, Soumaliot and Mulele were instructed.[234]

Such examples suggest that, in contrast to China's economic aid policy, its military assistance has been much more radically destined to serve revolutionary purposes with the aim of undermining rightist official governments.

2.3.4. *Consequences for the developing countries*

If the rich countries honoustly try to support the poor countries in their endeavour to reach a human level of welfare, their military assistance programs run contrary to that goal. It may be true that the initiative has often come from the poor countries themselves, but no less important has been the stimulus given by the rich countries as donors.

First, by granting, or selling at very low interest rates, the rich countries offer many governments the opportunity to build up an Army of their own as a symbol of national identity and as a precautionary measure against eventual conflicts.

Secondly, by assisting one country, they incite its neighbours to build up an Army as well: these, however, often have to pay the full price. Latin America provides examples of such a regional arms races. E.g. within the framework of the 'policy to strengthen the defensive capabilities of our allies,' the United States supplied A-4B Skyhawks to Argentina. Chile, perceiving this as a potential threat to its own security and having failed to obtain what it wanted to get in turn from the United States, bought English Hawker Hunters. This measure, however, was reason enough for Peru to enlarge its equipment in turn, since it has a border conflict with Chile. When thus three

---

[233] Details from their diaries were quoted in the Sunday Telegraph (London, July 23, '61).
[234] VI Kron. Afr. I ('66) p. 20; see also P. Alexandre – 'Note on the Activities of the Communist Powers in French Speaking Africa,' in 'East-West Confrontation in Africa' ('66).

countries were busy increasing their military strength, very soon Venezuela and Brazil followed.[235]
This is what has also occurred in Asia and may occur in Africa as well. If one country gets something, its neighbours try to get it from somewhere else or will buy it.
Such local arms races have a threefold polemological effect:
1°. They constitute a permanent and serious drain on the countries' meager budgets. Economic high-priority projects have to be cancelled or broken off. At the same time the donors reckon their grants and credit-sales among their posts of 'foreign aid' and thus the more they give or lend as military assistance, the less remains for badly needed economic aid. Consequently, this policy of weapon export contributes to the frustration of all those who urge and wait for economic progress. This may explain why Brown and Gutteridge reach the conclusion that 'undue smallness of local forces may be a cause of political instability in one way, but correspondingly excessive expenditure on weapons and equipment and the development of a large and self-willed military élite are likely to contribute to economic and political instability in another.'
2°. Arms transfers tend to imply factual or perceived political dependence. This may have consequences in the economic field: when a donor supplies military assistance for political reasons and the recipient does not follow the expected political line, not only military assistance will be suspended but economic aid may be cut as well, be it by the donor or the recipient. Thus the political background of military assistance may easily result in a halt of economic projects already in process.[236]
3°. Local arms races tend to cause an atmosphere of regional instability and to hinder the prospects of peaceful (economic) co-operation (which can be very important to economic progress). They stress nationalism, and in case of existing conflicts – and there are so many border conflicts alone at present – they tend to intensify them. Arms races have as serious destabilizing aspects in the North as they have in the South.

---

[235] G. Thayer p. 234 ff. The State Department, recognizing the contradictions within the aid program, has been unable to give priority to the economic interests of the poor countries 'at the expense' of the economic interests of the United States itself. 'The Power of the Defense Department over a long period of time, has been so overwhelming, that many State Department officials think in Defense Department terms. They are prostitutes to the rich uncle' (p. 194).

[236] In the UN, representatives of young countries have often complained of political blackmail by the donor when the recipient country is in need of assistance, see for instance Mr. Sharif (Indonesia) GA/C 1 Off. Rec. 1456 (Nov. '66) p. 180.

4°. It needs little comment to observe that arms supplies to conflicting political factions in developing countries have often stimulated internal violence. Weapons supplied by the C.I.A. to rightist factions, and weapons supplied by the USSR and China to leftist factions, have in many countries at least prolonged fighting. In connection to the most dramatic example, Nigeria, many observers do not doubt that the civil war was sustained by foreign supplies.[237] The incredible human suffering during that conflict makes all other considerations seem rather unimportant. Yet, it should not be overlooked that this drama also proves the detrimental effect weapon supplies can have upon economic progress.

2.3.5. Consequences for international peace in the Third World

Local arms races fed by military assistance tend to destabilize the international relations among recipients.
Some politicians seem to understand the risks very well. For instance Katzenbach, speaking on arms trade at the Institute of International Relations of Stanford University said:

> 'Any arms build-up, once begun, takes its own dynamic shape and logic. It gets easily out of hand. The acquisition of new arms in one country leads to demands for new equipment by its neighbours, whether for reasons of prestige, national pride, or simply what they see as a satisfactory military balance..... the tension resulting from an arms race in an area may increase the power, stature, or belligerency of a nations military leadership.'[238]

Many observers are inclined to consider military assistance – usually far exceeding internal needs – a contributing or even causative factor in the outbreak of local violence. Hoogland states that 'in many such conflicts there are grounds for suspicion that the influx of weapons from a major power provided the aggressor with the confidence he needed to start the fighting';[239] while Taylor concludes that 'an increase in the availability of weapons is concomitant with an increase in their use.... the upward curve (of arms sales and grants) would closely parallel the curve on the incidence of violence since 1945.'[240] He considers the influence of American weapons instrumental to the outbreak of the 1965 Kashmir war. The same conclusion is reached

---

[237] see a.o. J. M. Lee, p. 117.
[238] N. Brown & W. F. Gutteridge – 'The African Military Balance,' Adelphi papers No. 12 ('64) p. 3; Under-Secretary Katzenbach – 'US Arms for the Developing World: Dilemmas of Foreign Policy,' Dept. State Bull. (Dec. 11, '67) p. 795.
[239] J. M. Hoogland, p. 182.
[240] G. Thayer, p. 20.

by Galbraith, former US Ambassador to India, who declared to the Senate:

'The arms we supplied under this policy caused, and I underline the word, the war.'[241]

It will always be extremely difficult to prove to what extent the influx of weapons stimulated or caused local conflicts. 'What evidence there is,' says Kemp, 'is inconclusive; it is difficult to draw conclusions about the effect of arms transfers except in regional contexts.' But he also points to the dangers of the arms race in the horn of Africa. Somalia, Ethiopia and Kenya have plunged into 'an embryonic arms race that shows all the signs of developing into a more serious affair.'[242]

Few will maintain that the rapid armament of the poor countries, partly as a consequence of political and economic interests of the rich countries, has contributed to international stability in the Third World.

2.3.6. Consequences for world peace

1°. It may be fairly clear from what has been said above about the motives behind the military assistance programs of the Big Powers, that this race in arms supplies contributes little to a better understanding among them. Perhaps even more than in the case of economic aid, military aid creates and intensifies a sphere of competition and distrust.

When Argentina turned to the English to buy British Hawker Hunters, the Soviet Union saw a chance and stepped in with an offer to supply fighting and bombing planes at prices lower than production costs. A clear endeavour to turn the country away from the Western market and to gain some influence in Latin America.[243]

The races between the Americans and the Russians in arms supplies to Afghanistan, Pakistan and India have increased suspicion on both sides of the 'evil objectives' of the other. Moreover, American assistance to India in 1962 ($ 40 million) was directed against the Chinese and intensified the Sino-American conflict.

Another example of such a race is Iran. In July, 1966, Iran was reported to have considered a purchase of Soviet missiles. Promptly the Americans started a diplomatic initiative and in September they had convinced the Shah that he had better buy a squadron of American F-4 Phantoms, at the very moment these planes were in exceedingly

---

[241] US Cong., 89th Cong., 2nd Sess., Hearings before the Senate For. Rel. Committee, ('66) p. 234.
[242] G. Kemp – 'Arms Transfers to Developing Countries,' Proc. IPRA II ('68) pp. 262-263.
[243] J. S. Berliner, p. 20.

short supply in Vietnam! Yet, in February 1967, it became known that the Shah had accepted Soviet equipment amounting to $ 110 million as well.[244] Again, when King Hussein of Jordan went to Moscow in October 1967 to ask for military assistance, the United States lifted its Middle East embargo in February 1968, by sending F-104 Starfighters and M-48 Patton tanks.

2⁰. There are two specifically dangerous aspects connected with this East-West competition in the Third World.
In the first place, there is an economic aspect. After East and West have both tried to outsell the other for some time, the economic interest of keeping the market in question and the investments made may become so important, that they might be seduced to making a less careful but more aggressive policy when they fear the other party is winning.
In the second place, there is a political aspect. Given the fact that the Super Powers are trying to buy influence by extending military aid, and given the fact that the resulting arms races have an intrinsically disturbing effect on local stability, the risk always exists that somehow this competition in military assistance may drive the Super Powers into political conflicts in the Third World. Their awareness of this danger, by the way, is indicated by the joint calls for peace made by the Soviet Union and the United States during the Kashmir war and in relation to the conflict in the horn of Africa.
It is of importance to note in this connection that there is indeed a tendency to 'meet' each other, i.e. the tendency to extend the largest amounts of aid to countries in one region, or to the same countries in different regions. Such is indicated by the table presented at p. 198, with regard to the U.S. and the U.S.S.R.

The great risk of creating new interests and becoming involved in local or regional conflicts by the policy of military assistance seems clear enough if one thinks of S. E. Asia. When for instance in Indonesia internal trouble became serious, China supplied Sukarno's army, the Soviet Union supplied the Navy and the Air Force, and the American C.I.A. supported anti-communist rebel groups. What would have happened if Indonesia would have had a new pro-Russian or pro-Chinese leadership? Enough has been written about the dangerous situations in Vietnam, Laos, Cambodia and Thailand. The issues at stake are so important and involvement is so serious that the risk of a direct confrontation is inherent.

[244] N.Y.T. (July 14, Sept. 19, 1966; Febr. 8, 1967).

Comparison of Regional Priorities in Soviet and United States Military Aid: 1965-1967

Region	Estimated Total Aid (in millions of US dollars)		Percentage of Total Program		Number of Recipients	
	USSR	US	USSR	US	USSR	US
Middle East	2,748	2,602	48	48	8	10
South/Southeast Asia	2,185	2,148	38	40	6	10
Latin America	750	523	13	10	1	21
Africa	85	126	1	2	9	13
Totals	5,768	5,399	100	100	24	54

Source: S. P. Gilbert – 'Soviet-American Military Aid Competition in the Third World, XIII Orbis ('70) p. 1121.

With the (self-explanatory) exception of Latin America, the similarity is remarkable.

It is not Asia alone anymore. The Middle East shows races in assistance between the United States and Russia, as well as between Russia and China. Gradually Africa is becoming the next scene of this kind of competition. When the French left Guinea in 1958, the Russians were quick to step in. When the French left Mali in 1961, the Americans stepped in together with the Russians and the Chinese.[245] All of them were equally involved in the Nigerian war, while at the same time Russian and American involvement in the horn of Africa is assuming dangerous proportions. They are both trying to keep the conflict between Somalia on the one hand and Ethiopia and Kenya on the other hand restricted; but they have already chosen opposing camps: the Americans supplied $ 88 million worth of military equipment to Ethiopia between 1953 and 1965 and they have built a military airport less than 140 kilometers from the Somalian border; the Russians offered a $ 30 million long term credit to Somalia in 1963 and Somalian officers are trained in the Soviet Union.[246]

Sometimes the leaders of young countries, because they are pressed from different sides, intensify the East-West competition themselves. Thus Morocco turned to the United States in February 1967, after Algeria (with which Morocco has a boundary dispute) had received new Soviet equipment. Morocco threatened the United States that,

[245] J. M. Lee, p. 116.
[246] see Helga Haftendorn – 'Stabilität und Unsicherheit im Horn von Afrika,' XXII Eur. Arch. ('67) p. 715; G. Kemp in Proc. IPRA II ('68) p. 263; and VI Kron. Afr. 3 ('66) pp. 244-245.

if it would not get the demanded $ 100 million worth of arms, it would go and get them 'from somewhere else.' Likewise Pakistan and formerly Indonesia tried to play off the Super opponents against each other, obviously underestimating the risks to their own security.[247] Colonel Ojukwu, feeling threatened by British, American and Russian arms, called upon the Chinese for support. On September 29, 1968, he thanked Peking in a letter in which he said he was obliged to China, for its sympathy and understanding 'for our struggle against Anglo-American imperialism and Soviet revisionism........ In this struggle Biafrans count on the co-operation of all Socialist progressive peoples, in the forefront of which are the government of the People's Republic China.'[248]

3⁰. The Super Powers – and this seems the most crucial observation – are not always able to see and know the limits of their involvement. It is not always realized that when a conflict escalates higher and higher, it becomes even more difficult to withdraw; a dilemma, which is described so well by Osgood:

'Military escalation produces the very conditions, both internally and externally, which make it harder and harder to stop and de-escalate. Internally, if early escalations fail and produce counter-escalation, anger and frustration impel one upward; and if escalation succeeds, one is learning to use this means at the expense of others, until we find ourselves trying to police the world. Externally, the early stages of escalation are more likely to produce hardening rather than softening of the opponent's resolve, thus forcing us to higher steps on the ladder than we had originally intended to reach,'[249]

What this means and how right Osgood's opinion is, became clear in the year 1954 in Vietnam. When it became evident that the French would lose their Indo-Chinese war – the American government had by then payed 80% of the French war costs, but could not sell to the American people an overall involvement yet – Dulles, during this stage of escalation, offered the French twice the use of an atomic bomb against the Chinese and the Viet Minh. This occurred, moreover, at the height of the Cold War.[250]

---

[247] M. A. Chaudhri pp. 496-497; S. P. Seth pp. 616ff.
[248] VIII Kron. Afr. 4 ('66) p. 246.
[249] Ch. E. Osgood – 'Escalation as a Strategy,' W. P. Rep. (Sept. '65) p. 13.
[250] R. Drummond & G. Coblentz – 'Duel at the Brink: J. F. Dulles' Command of American Power' ('60) pp. 121-122. They were told this personally by Bidault. See also G. Warner – 'Escalation in Vietnam – the Precedents of 1954,' 41 Int. Aff. 2 (London '65) p. 173. Other versions of the story state that the French asked for it, but Dulles' offer has recently been confirmed by the Pentagon.

2.4. Bilateral aid: does it pay?

2.4.1. A Russian spokesman once said to an audience of Afro-Asian people:

'The Soviet Union offers you loans and technicians to speed your development. For this you are grateful. But you should be equally grateful to Moscow for whatever aid the Americans give you. They are quite frank in saying that if they were not so frightened of us Communists, they would give you nothing....'[251]

This humerous way of expressing dramatic things leads to an argument raised in favour of Cold War aid. A system of bilateral aid has often been commended as advantageous because the amount of money donated to the countries in need was raised as a result of the Cold war. In relation to economic aid Ohlin states:

'Criticism of bilateral aid programmes sometimes simply amounts to the reproach that they do not sufficiently partake the character of multilateral aid. But the variety of objectives and practices that mark actual programmes of development aid is probably neither a weakness nor a fault: it is in the first place the inescapable consequence of the fact that decisions about public uses of resources fall upon national governments, and secondly it is a factor of strength without which the flow of funds to the poorer countries would be a good deal smaller than it is.'[252]

In another sense, when speaking of military assistance, Kemp states:

'it could be argued that the costs of fighting wars with the latest equipment may deter the smaller Powers from embarking on extravagant military adventures.'[253]

Such opinions referring to the positive aspects of Cold War bilateral aid seem, however, to neglect or minimize its important negative aspects:

1°. It may be true that the Cold War created large aid programs, but it should not be forgotten that exactly because of that background its continuity is also extremely dependent on the fluctuations in international political relations. Since foreign aid programs have been sold to the tax-payer as weapons in the Cold War, any major change in East-West relations, or any disappointment in its results, endangers the programs' continuation. The intellectual duplicity implied in identifying a political and strategic aid policy in the national interest with a program for aiding the developing countries has removed more

---

[251] quoted by Ch. Bowles in Dept. State Bull. (May 20, '63) p. 778.
[252] G. Ohlin – 'Foreign Aid Policies Reconsidered,' OECD ('66).
[253] G. Kemp – 'Arms Sales and Arms Control in the Developing Countries,' XXII The World Today ('66) p. 389. Kemp adds on p. 393, however, that 'it is clear that the continued input of armaments (in Ethiopia and Somalia) has done nothing to stabilize the conflict.'

sensible arguments (long-term interest to the welfare of all, and humanitarian considerations) from the scene.

2⁰. In view of the fact that both continuous and substantial growth are prerequisites for peaceful development, one may even doubt whether any system of bilateral aid could achieve what a system of multilateral aid within a framework of global economic co-operation could bring about. In general, bilateral aid – if it is not subordinated to multilateral planning – entails the intrinsic disadvantage of lack of co-ordination. Much duplication of effort results which implies waste of funds and energy.²⁵⁴

3⁰. Remembering the waste, a system of bilateral aid which functions within a political context, lacks any possibility of control and evaluation. The West did not interfere with Russian supplies of batteries to Tanzania or cement to Guinea – which was to them obviously useless after a few days in tropical climate – as such mistakes can only harm the Russian image. On the other hand, the use of large funds for private purposes by recipients, e.g. the famous 'golden bed story,' or the seizing of milk powder, granted to the undernourished children of a country whose government sells it for the highest price to merchants, is the result of the political context of present bilateral aid: since a protest by the donor country is feared to be considered intervention, it is 'wisely' omitted (see section 2.2.2.). This situation certainly has harmed the image of the usefullness of aid and has contributed to frustration in large circles. One may wonder whether such events would happen – at least to such an extent as they do today – if the extension of aid were a multilateral affair.

4⁰. At the same time economic progress is bound to be uneven, since a strategic key country with important contacts will have more chances of development than an unimportant country. In this connection one may be reminded of Boulding's conclusion that inequality of development within a country leads to conflict.²⁵⁵ There is no reason to suppose that this rule would not apply equally to the international scene.

5⁰. Bilateral aid extended within the framework of the Cold War may create Big Power interests where there were none before. It results in involvement of the Third World in the Cold War, thereby increasing the number of political or potentially military confrontations among the Super Powers. It also creates regrettable obstacles to any substantial endeavour to bridge the welfare gap.

[254] to all this we come back in Chapter III.
[255] K. E. Boulding – 'The Economics of Human Conflict,' in E. B. McNeil (ed.) – 'The Nature of Human Conflict' ('65) p. 189.

2.4.2. Whatever the advantages of bilateral aid in the present world may be, they are obviously overshadowed by its dangers and disadvantages. Having reached that conclusion, one may ask whether the political aims pursued by the donor countries by way of their aid programs can be expected to be realized. If this major 'justification' for the continuation of the present aid race – whatever the secondary motives may be – would prove to be not valid, then the claim to change present aid policies would even become stronger, and perhaps acceptable in some ruling circles. Let us turn, therefore, to the question: can donors by their aid programs dictate the political and socio-economic development of recipients?

Some investigations have been made which indicate a positive relationship between wealth and democratic institutions. Almond and Coleman found a correlation between certain indices of wealth and the degree of free enterprise in Latin American countries. Lipset found that, according to his indices of wealth, the countries of Latin America he classified as democracies and unstable dictatorships ranked higher on the scale than those he called stable dictatorships. Wolff suggests a relation between 'political vulnerability', on the basis of three economic indices, and communist voting.[256]
What has in this respect been analyzed so far, however, is so incongruous and so uncertain, that general conclusions can not be reached. This is the opinion of most authors writing on the subject. They are quite cynical about the ascertainments characterizing official statements which declare that economic progress will bring democracy, or that economic progress will lead to communism. Billerbeck calls it,

'a somewhat provincial attitude, which insists that the system which has proved practicable and is regarded as right in one's own country should be established in all other countries.'

We are inclined to forget, he says, that

'Asia and Africa must develop their own systems and forms of organizations, which do justice both to their economic and political evolution.'[257]

---

[256] G. Almond – 'The Political System of the Developing Areas,' in G. Almond & S. Verba – 'The Politics of Developing Areas' ('60) pp. 538-544; S. M. Lipset – 'Political Man: The Social Basis of Politics' ('60) Ch. 2; Ch. Wolff – 'Foreign Aid: Theory and Practice in Southern Asia' ('60) p. 408; see also E. E. Hagen – 'A Framework for Analyzing Economic and Political Change,' in R. E. Asher a.o. – 'Development of the Emerging Countries; An Agenda for Research' ('62) pp. 1-8.
[257] K. Billerbeck p. 113.

Mozingo writes:

'the foundations of transplanted Western political and social ideas in Asia are weak. Constitutions based on them have already been overturned in Burma, Korea, Pakistan, Laos end Indonesia, they have hardly existed in other countries of the Far East';

and the same holds for communist constitutions. Whatever system they are going to set up, it

'must ultimately reflect their own diversity, peculiarities, needs, traditions and aspirations.'[258]

Benham points to the strength of new nationalism and states:

'However this may be, if the West wishes to prevent a particular country from going Communist, the appropriate weapon is seldom foreign aid. Countries have their national pride; they are not going to be tribed by a few dollars a year per head of population into following political or economic policies of which the West approves, if they believe that a different course would be in their interests.'[259]

Others point out that even if it would be possible to transplant one's own socio-political system to another country, one would not know in the least how to do it. Mason explains:

'It needs to be said that much too little is known about the process of economic development and the relation of economic and political development to permit firm pronouncement..... (It is) an area of great uncertainty';[260]

Likewise Packenham states:

'Reliable studies about how aid, or any foreign policy instrument, has actually been used in relation to political development are practically nonexistent.'[261]

Ann Ruth Willner has significantly called it the 'underdeveloped study of political development' and says

'Gap analysts list the obstacles to democratic functioning and development; requisite analysts begin by specifying the 'prerequisites' or attributes of democratic societies. In either case, they mainly tell us about the absence or weakness, in neither case do they tell us much of what these countries have or are, except indirectly and inferentially.'[262]

---

[258] D. P. Mozingo – 'Containment in Asia,' VII Survival (July '67) p. 236.
[259] F. Benham – 'Economic Aid to Underdeveloped Countries' ('62) p. 89.
[260] E. E. Mason – 'Foreign Aid and Foreign Policy' p. 37.
[261] R. A. Packenham, p. 205.
[262] Ann Ruth Willner – 'The Underdeveloped Study of Political Development,' XVI World Politics ('63) p. 472.

In these circumstances it is not very surprising to see an expert like Myrdal state:

"I have little use for the highly simplified, general models for political development in underdeveloped countries which have recently been worked out.... These models have no predictive value. I have already stated my considered opinion that it is not possible to predict the type of government any single underdeveloped country will have five years from now."[263]

This list of quotations from experts has been given here to indicate how fundamental the lack of understanding and knowledge in this field is – apart from the basic question whether it would at all be possible to transplant political systems. And yet – many examples have been given in the opening sections of this Chapter – in so many official statements one finds an absolutely positive conviction on the question of the political results of aid. Part of the explanation of this phenomenon might be the firm belief in the goodness of one's own side and the badness of the other, so well expressed in relation to the 'Pax Americana' by Steel:

"The fact that this aim has twice failed in Europe has not prevented it from being pursued in Asia. It does not seem to matter that it has failed in Europe or that it is failing in Asia. And it does not matter because it is basically an act of faith, an expression of America's image of herself, not a program relevant to the world at large. It is an acting-out of the American Dream on a global scale."[264]

The general scepticism characterizing expert literature has indeed often been confirmed by practice. Before turning to that, however, it might be appropriate to point to contradictions in the official policies of the three Super Powers themselves:
An investigation concerning the opinions of AID-officers in the United States revealed that they show a strong tendency to limit the meaning of 'political development' exclusively to the leading élite in the existing central governments or to those chosen few, immediately surrounding the governments, who might succeed them. Such 'political development' appears to have little in common with the 'democratic evolution.' This contradiction is reflected in the American aid program, which shows a tendency to give more support to anti-communism than to democratic reform.[265] Brzezinski is one of the officials who has not hesitated, moreover, to admit that aid cannot influence the cause of political developments.[266]

[263] G. Myrdal – 'The Challenge of World Poverty' ('70) p. 411.
[264] R. Steel p. 257.
[265] see R. A. Packenham p. 214.
[266] Z. Brzezinski – 'The Politics of Underdevelopment', World Politics (Oct. '56).

Concerning the Soviet Union, there is also a contradiction not only in its practical policy, but even in its ideological foundation. The Soviets state that their assistance will help the recipient countries to find the right path to (Russian) socialism. On the other hand, however, many statements were issued which pointed out the practical impossibility of exporting the socialist revolution. For instance Potekhin in 1958 stated in relation to Africa that 'any industrialization in the true meaning of the word (basic for a socialist development in Russian eyes) is out of the question,' and Staruschenko explained:

> 'While giving moral and political support to revolution in other countries, the Soviet C.P. does not in fact export revolution.... to give a push to revolution is anti-Marxist adventurism which can only damage the cause of the working class.'[267]

The same holds true for China. Although China tries to gain influence in the Third World mainly by organizing local Chinese-oriented communist groups, Lin Piao made it clear that

> 'revolution or people's war in any country is the business of the masses in that country and should be carried out primarily by their own efforts; there is no other way..... If one does not operate by one's own efforts..... but leans wholy on foreign aid – even though this be aid from socialist countries which persist in revolution – no vinctory can be won, or be consolidated even if it is won.'[268]

Governments may not be very interested in contradictions between the theoretical foundations of their policy and the actual policy in practice. They should, however, be interested to know that there is no proof whatsoever that their policy will ever work. It has been noticed that there is no verified evidence at all that *political systems* can be transplanted. It can be added, moreover, that there is not even evidence that a *temporary political line of action* will be followed by the recipient because of the aid given to him. The experience gained, by the Western as well as by the Communist world, has been that the rewards in terms of friendships are often inversely proportional to the assistance given. Some speak of a 'mysterious law' or draw attention to the 'truism that for a complicated set of reasons the giver of aid often makes more enemies than friends in the process.'[269] Suspicions of 'neo-colonialism' and averse reactions resulting from the benefactor-recipient relation have probably something to do with it. Some examples, first in connection with economic aid, second in relation to military assistance, may illustrate the point.

[267] quoted in Z. Brzezinski, p. 57; G. Staruschenko – 'Peaceful Coexistence and Revolution,' Kommunist 2 ('62) p. 86.
[268] Lin Piao in 6 Peking Review 36 ('65) pp. 41-42.
[269] J. S. Berliner, p. 60.

1⁰. As far as economic aid is concerned, one should first be reminded of the many occasions in which recipients refused further aid, or even broke off their relations with a donor entirely, when they felt their independence to be in danger. Such events – they are not reiterated here – clearly indicate the fervent wish of many developing countries to prevent the donors from having too much of an influence on their internal affairs (see section 2.2.1).

Many are the examples of the expulsion of foreign personnel accused of unacceptable interference into the internal affairs of Third World countries. E.g. when Guinea seceded from the French Community, its relations with France became strained and many of its new leaders had Marxist sympathies. Technicians and advisers from the USSR poured into the country, and its economy was slowly being moved into a communist direction. Nevertheless, when Ambassador Daniel Solod was found to have been instrumental in fomenting a teachers' strike, he was expelled by the Guinean authorities in 1961. The USSR was not slow to send Mikoyan on a goodwill tour through W. Africa, and in Guinea he emphasized the general absence of interference in the internal affairs of other countries characterizing Soviet foreign policy, while stressing that Soviet ideology is not to be exported, and that 'each state is sovereign.'[270]

Furthermore, even such projects as the cultural exchange programs might have negative results in the long run. As Clemens observes:

'the training of African students at Lumumba University in Moscow might be conceived as a way to turn them into revolutionary or at least anti-Western élites, but in practice could prepare them for a status quo or even anti-Soviet orientation. Thus, the results of a program may not square with its supposed objectives.'[271]

Even specific economic projects, serving at first sight a specific economic course, can have opposite results. For instance, many American financed projects in the private sector have later been nationalized. On the other hand, the final result of Russian assistance to the public steel industry in India (meant to raise the importance of the public sector to the detriment of the private one) turned out to be subsidizing for the private steel sector, which was thus encouraged to expand.[272]

The 'political sailors,' like Indonesia, N. Korea, N. Vietnam, Cuba, and Afghanistan are further testimonies to the unpredictability of the political pay-off of economic aid programmes.

---

[270] IV Neues Afrika 2 (Febr. '62) p. 47.
[271] W. C. Clemens – 'The 1970's,' XIII Orbis 2 ('69) p. 479.
[272] Ph. Mosely – 'The Kremlin and the Third World,' 46 For. Aff. (Oct. '67) p. 71.

An interesting test has been made in order to measure the political success of Russian and American aid programmes by analyzing roll-call votes in the United Nations of Third World recipients.'[273] A rather high correlation was found to exist between aid policy and attitudes towards political and security questions, but this proves little. Cold War problems may be of paramount importance to the Super Powers, but the Third World countries are more intensely concerned with other problems. They may, therefore, be rather easily won for a specific vote on such questions. The fact, that many anti-imperialist and anti-Western countries still prefer to side with the West in some questions where they might have been expected to join the USSR, has been explained by FitzGerald in the same way as he explains the anti-Labour Party attitude among poor voters in England during the early days of that Party: 'these states, however critical and secretly resentful of the rich, think it wiser and more practical to vote for them rather than for the champions of the poor, simply because they 'have the money'.'[274] As far as problems like economic and colonial issues are concerned, it was found that nearly all of the recipients of American aid disagreed sharply with the US (the USSR votes with the developing countries on such questions). This indicates that if really crucial problems are at stake, recipients do not allow the donor to dictate their vote.

On several occasions the Big Powers have indicated that they seem to realize the negative results of their aid programs as far as their foreign policy aims are concerned.

After some years of tremendous effort in the field of foreign aid in the late fifties, the Soviet Union sharply cut its assistance in 1960, obviously disappointed by the results.[275] Likewise China sharply cut back its foreign aid in 1965, the year in which it suffered such heavy political set-backs in Africa and Cuba. Again, since the late sixties, the amounts (and rates) of economic assistance given by Moscow and Washington to the Third World have steadily declined.[276] Economic considerations may have contributed to this, but increasing impatience with the political results of their efforts may be supposed to have done so as well.

2⁰. The same negative conclusion can be drawn from an analysis of the impact of military assistance. It is particularly noteworthy that

---

[273] S. P. Gilbert, pp. 1130-1133.
[274] C. P. FitzGerald – 'The Sino-Soviet Balance Sheet in the Underdeveloped Areas,' 351 The Annals (Jan. '64) p. 41.
[275] see note 169 supra.
[276] W. C. Clemens, p. 481.

many arms supplies have not been used to serve the purposes they were intended to. Again a few examples will be given:
The United States supplied arms to India and Pakistan on the understanding that they were to be used exclusively against 'communist aggression'. In 1965, however, US Sherman tanks belonging to the Indian army battled against US Patton tanks belonging to the Pakistan army. The Indians were transported to the front in American C-130 B air plaines and the Pakistani in American C-119's and C-47's. The same happened by the end of 1971.
In 1967, American tanks supplied to Greece were supposed to function against communist aggression, but insted were used during the anti-democratic Greek colonels' coup.
In the same year American Patton tanks of Jordan (again supplied to neutralize communist influence) faced American Patton tanks of Israel.
One can find many examples of this also in Latin America. Often enough Latin American military have not hesitated to use American equipment (intended to be used against communist aggression or subversion) to conduct internecine warfare:
During the November 1961 political crisis in Equador, US-supplied Air Force Jets battled US-supplied Army tanks and troops in downtown Quito.
In June, 1962, Army tanks and troops and Air Force jet-fighters battled against a marine corps battailon for the control of the Puerto Cabello Naval Base in Venezuela.
In the same year the Cavalry and the Air Force successfully fought the Infantry and the Navy in Buenos Aires for the control of the Argentine government.
Moreover, in general military assistance is not used to stop 'communist aggression from without' but rather to suppress democratic change from within.[277]

The Soviet Union has often enough experienced the same. Russian weapons, intended for Cuba, finally landed via this country in Latin America, although the Russians reject guerilla activities there and prefer to support instead the moderate communist parties.
Like the United States, the U.S.S.R. saw its weapons, supplied to Pakistan against China or at least to compete with China, used against one of its own major recipients, India.

---

[277] see H. Hanning – 'Insurgency and World Order'; XIII Disarmament (March '67) pp. 5-8; G. Thayer pp. 21; D. Wood – 'Armed Forces and South America,' Adelphi Papers 34 ('67) pp. 3-4, 6-7; E. Lieuwen pp. 14-15; and idem – 'Generals versus Politicians: Neo-Militarism in Latin America' ('64).

The Soviet Union has even witnessed pro-Soviet governments in Indonesia, Ghana and Algeria overthrown by dissidents armed with Soviet weapons. This was what Galbraith tried to make clear to the Senate Foreign Relations Committee in his very special way:

'It was Soviet tanks that surrounded Ben Bella's palace in Algiers when that Soviet supported leader was thrown out. It was a Soviet and Chinese equipped army which deposed the Indonesian communists, destroyed the communist party in that ruthlessness on which one hesitates to dwell and which left Sukarno's vision of an Asian socialism in shambles. It was a Soviet trained praetorian guard which was expected to supply protection to the government of president Nkrumah and which did not. One can only conclude that those who worry about Soviet arms wish to keep the Russians out of trouble. This could be carrying friendship too far.'[278]

It is hoped that enough evidence has been presented in order to show that if the Super Powers want to win the Third World countries' friendship it is doubtful whether their foreign aid programs are a good method in achieving this. Even if they could achieve some ad hoc-results of minor importance, they can not decide in the long run the political or economic course or measures that the Third World countries should take, merely by giving aid. Sihanouk once made this clear by his phrase 'our socialism stems not from Marx, Engels, Lenin, Stalin, or Mao Tse-tung; it stems from Buddha.....'

In relation to the American endeavour to stop communism and introduce democracy, Mozingo has pointed out that the most politically significant defeats inflicted on communist movements have come at the hands of non-aligned nationalistic governments, and these defeats were brought about without the assistance of the United States. 'The fear,' he says, 'expressed in the argument that neutralism or non-alignment is simply a temporary way-station on the raod to communism, that Peking and other communists can push over popular nationalist régimes like 'dominoes' once a communist revolution succeeds somewhere else, is overwhelmingly contradicted by the proven vitality of Asian nationalism, in the last twenty years.'[279] Some authors go even further – and it is difficult not to agree with them – by pointing out that the principal aim of US policy, containment of *exported* communism, has been realized in those areas, where the United States did *not* intervene. Thus, the Chinese were thrown out of many African countries when they did intervene, whereas the Americans did not; conversely, a direct correlation has been found to exist between American interference in and from Thailand and the

---

[278] cited in XXIII Bull. At. sc. 7 ('67) p. 48.
[279] D. P. Mozingo, p. 234.

emergence of communist guerilla activities in that country.[280] As far as the United States is concerned, Feinstein concludes that 'the foreign economic and military practices in the US have not addressed themselves successfully to the key problems of the 1950's and 1960's. Chaos, instability and the threat of nuclear war, based on the poverty in the underdeveloped countries is increasing';[281] and one might add that this conclusion holds true for the other Super Powers as well.
As far as endeavours to export communism are concerned, Sékou Touré – though one of Africa's most left-wing leaders – has said: 'Communism is not the way for Africa. The class struggle is impossible here for there are no classes, but only social strata. The fundamental basis of our society is the family and village community.'
Whatever may be true of his assertion that Africa is classless, his description of the central place of family, village (and tribe) is valid, and both the USSR and China seem to have understood that a European-type and a Chinese-type communism belong to Europe and China respectively.

Because there appears to be little chance that the Big Powers can influence the long term course of events in the Third World by manipulating through foreign aid, the question presents itself whether other urgent motives behind their present aid policies remain which might constitute an important obstacle in deciding that these policies should be fundamentally changed. Only one important ratio would seem to remain in this connection, that of *economic profit*. This argument used to continue the system of bilateral aid is applied by all donor countries, large and small.

1⁰. As far as economic aid is concerned, the argument has been well explained for all by the former President of the World Bank, Eugene Black (even though he was specifically referring to the US): 'Our foreign aid programs constitute a distinct benefit to American business. The three major benefits are: (1) Foreign aid provides a substantial and immediate market for U.S. goods and services. (2) Foreign aid stimulates the development of new overseas markets for

---

[280] see W. Friedmann – 'Interventionism, Liberalism and Power Politics; the Unfinished Revolution in International Thinking,' LXXXIII Pol. Sc. Q. ('68) p. 184; P. Fistié – 'Communisme et indépendence nationale: le cas thailandais (1928-1968),' XVIII Rev. Franc. Sc. Pol. ('68) p. 713.
[281] O. Feinstein – 'Which Way Security? How we can counter growing instability in the Underdeveloped Countries,' in 'A Strategy for American Security; an Alternative to the 1964 Military Budget' ('63) p. 9.

U.S. companies. (3) Foreign aid orients national economies toward a free enterprise system in which U.S. firms can prosper.'[282]
The third point again implies the questionable argument that foreign aid stimulates a particular economic system favourable to the economic interests of the donor.
Then, there is the direct profit derived from extended loans. During the years 1962 to 1966, for instance, the average annual service payments on the external public debt of all Latin America to the United States came to $ 1.596 billion; during this period, the average annual assistance given by the U.S. to Latin America, in the form of loans and grants, amounted to $ 1.213 billion.
Besides, the binding of the loans to export conditions has helped to increase the export of all donors to the developing countries, much more than the other way round. The annual rate of growth of exports during the period 1950 to 1965 shows that the figure for the exports from the developing countries to the rich countries – excluding the major oil producers – has been 4.2%, whereas on the other hand the figure for the exports from the rich countries to the poor has been 6.2%.[283] Indeed, many aid programs have been 'paid back' by providing the donor with export opportunities.
Furthermore, grants may create future markets: when receiving free projects, the recipient becomes dependent on the donor for spare parts and replacements. E.g. the replacements and additions for India's railroads have to be bought mainly in the United States at steep prices, since it was the U.S. which provided the locomotives as long ago as the 1950's.[284]
In general, the relevance of economic profit to be gained from foreign aid programs was discussed at length by the White House and the State Department during the talks in November 1971 on the threatened prolongation of the American aid program. Several arguments were put forward as part of the endeavour to mobilize trade unions and public opinion in favour of continuation of the program: it was calculated that extended loans had resulted in a total export to the amount of $ 2 billion; in 1970 nearly half of America's steel export, worth $ 130 million, and export of fertilizers worth $ 100 million had been financed by foreign aid. Important American concerns had received large assignments through the aid program; e.g. Caterpillar during the first half of 1971 for $ 9.8 million, International Harvester annually for $ 2.9 million, Chrysler for $ 9.5 million, Betlehem steel

[282] quoted in H. Magdoff, p. 176.
[283] H. B. Lary – 'Import of Manufactures from Less Developed Countries' ('68) p. 2.
[284] see note 282 supra, p. 133.

for $ 7.1 million. The relevance of such and other figures was underlined by Senator Church, who based his opposition to the proposed aid program, apart from his objections to 'the preposterous scandal' of the military aid program, upon the following deliberation:

'I can no longer cast my vote to prolong the bilateral aid program, as it is now administered. I could understand – though perhaps not condone – a foreign aid program that is essentially self-serving. We live, after all, in a selfish world. But the present program is designed primarily to serve private business interests at the expense of the American people. In far too many countries, as in the case of Brazil, we poured in our money for one overriding purpose, to furnish American capital with a 'favourable climate for investment...'

2⁰. The same holds for military assistance, in this case witnessing a rather grim atmosphere.
Concerning the United States, the importance of economic motives is indicated by the fact that the U.S. granted most of its assistance until 1955, whereas since that year more and more was sold. The policy of granting has an important economic aspect in itself, since it enables poor countries to build up an Army which later becomes dependent on America for replacements, by then to be bought. Thus the basis of a world wide American arms market is created. Taking a look at some figures, the shift from grants to sales becomes very clear: during financial year 1953, the American military assistance program offered $ 1.96 billion in grants, whereas only an amount worth $ 230 million was sold. Today it is the other way round; during financial year 1968 grants amounted to $ 466 million, whereas an amount worth $ 1.5 billion was sold. Since 1962 sales have eclipsed grants. During the period between fiscal years 1962 and 1966 only, the United States sold over $ 11.1 billion worth of military equipment.[285]
According to Kuss, us chief arms salesman, since 1962 75% of the sales went to Canada and Europe; 12% to the Far East (except Vietnam); 10% to the Near and Middle East; 2% to Latin America and 1% to Africa. Only 6% would have been sold to the developing countries. These figures seem rather strange, however. For instance, there is the dubious fact that Vietnam is not included, and the rest of the Far East seems to exist, according to these figures, from the developed instead of developing nations. But apart from this there are grounds for serious doubt as to the validity of these percentages. Perhaps 25-30% is nearer the truth than 6% as far as the developing countries are concerned.[286] Today economic motives are an important

[285] see XXIII Bull. At. Sc. 7 ('67) p. 45.
[286] see G. Thayer, pp. 180-182.

factor behind the increasing arms transactions, according to Krippendorff may be even the most important one. In the United States alone, 1,2 million people's employment depends on that business.[287] Fullbright called it 'one of our main export sources,' and Thayer concludes that 'over the past years emphasis in the United States shifted from strategic and political to economic and political objectives, as the character of the Cold War changed.'[288] This opinion is supported by an article on American arms sales policy in the British Daily Telegraph in 1965, in which it charged:

'Growing resentment is being expressed by British defence experts at the effects of ruthless American high pressure salesmanship of arms and aircraft. This has already cost Britain a £ 40 million tank order from Italy.'

The same holds true for the USSR. In order to be able to compete with the United States, the Russians carry on, as the Americans do, with weapon-research and improvement. Consequently, they permanently have, like the Americans, masses of obsolete material for which developing countries are ready to pay. The Russian practice of demanding repayment in commodoties, moreover, helps to raise the standard of living in the Soviet Union.

During the last few years many other countries have entered the weapon market as suppliers. The most important ones are England and France, each of them selling weapons to an amount of $ 400 million annually. By 1962 Western Germany, Czechoslovakia, Belgium, Sweden, Switzerland, Israel, Italy and Canada had joined them. After them came Poland, the DDR, Bulgaria, and many others may fall upon this field as well, such as Japan, Denmark and Holland. To this number of State-suppliers one must add the private dealers, both the legal and the illegal ones, whose annual contribution amounts to some $ 30 million. Most of them, however, operate in close connection with certain governments today.[289]

There seem to be two main motives behind the military assistance given by the minor Powers. The first is an economic one. Many smaller countries are eager to make their own weapons, but find the process too expensive since the internal market is too small. They are able, therefore, to produce their own military material only if they can sell their new and/or old weapons to foreign countries. When

---

[287] Int. Her. Trib. (July, 22, 23, '67).
[288] G. Thayer, pp. 213-214. Chapter IV of his book contains many convincing data supporting his statement. See also E. Krippendorff – 'Waffenhandel', Atomzeitalter ('67) pp. 353-356.
[289] See generally L. A. Frank, Chapters 3 and 4.

the English government installed its first 'super salesman of arms,' it was said in his directive:

'He will ensure, within the limits of government policy, that as much military equipment is sold overseas as possible and also develop research to stimulate interest of potential buyers'.

Explaining this task, Defence Secretary Healy said in the British House of Commons:

'While the Government attaches the highest importance to making progress in the field of arms control, and disarmament, we must also take what practical steps we can to ensure that this country does not fail to secure its rightful share of this valuable commercial market.'[290]

It is an undeniable fact that the market in weapons exists and that it is a self-sustaining process since one supplier creates or maintains others. Yet, it is shocking to realize that the rich countries have come to consider the selling of bullets as 'their rightful share.'
In addition to the doubtful character of such economic interest, some minor Powers have supplied military assistance for political reasons as well. Such is the case with the former colonial Powers who use this medium to retain some of their vanishing influence. England, France and Belgium are examples in question.[291] Other countries have used military assistance as a means to gain support of the recipients in relation to some specific political conflict. In this respect one can think of Israel, which extends assistance as part of its campaign for votes in the UN on the Middle East dispute; and of both Germanies, which try to avoid and to further recognition of the DDR respectively. One may also think of Cuba which does this by exporting some weapons and sending military advisers to Latin American countries, Congo, and Portugese Guinea and Mozambique.[292] On May 18, 1967, Radio Havanna announced that Cuba would begin to assist all liberation movements throughout the world.

It is an irrefutable fact that the rich donor countries have gained economic profit by the bilateral aid system. Yet, the conclusion has been drawn, that it is at least doubtful whether the principal economic aim pursued by the US – i.e. to create a Third World market open to private foreign investment –, and the principal aim pursued by the

---

[290] quoted in J. L. Sutton & G. Kemp, p. 31.
[291] see J. M. Lee – 'African Armies and Civil Order' ('69) pp. 113-125.
[292] J. Biggs-Davison – 'Portuguese Guinea, a lesser Vietnam,' 13 Nato's Fifteen Nations ('68) pp. 24-25.

USSR and China – i.e. to prevent that market – can be achieved by foreign aid.

Moreover, all donors, the big ones as well as the smaller ones, might be adviced to asks themselves whether in the long run their own prosperity is not bound to become ever more dependent on the prosperity of the other part, the poor part of the world, and whether it is not very short-sighted of themselves to continue a system that may bring short term profits, but that tends to keep the gap between rich and poor wide open (see Chapter III below).

But quite apart from such economic considerations, on the basis of the total of deliberations presented here, the Super Powers in particular might be adviced to reconsider the fundamentals of their present aid policies, and ponder the question whether the economic profits resulting from their present aid policies are not eclipsed in the long run by the serious dangers involved – both from the point of view of East-West relations and from the point of view of events in the Third World. We are saying more precisely, that *they might realize that in the end they have much more to gain from a serious common endeavour to bridge the gap between rich and poor – both in the interest of their own prosperity in the long run, and in the interest of survival.*

This insight is expressed in the words of India's Ambassador to the United States, Kerim Chagla, speaking at the University of Boston:

'I hear very much around here about the dangers of world Communism. But I hear nothing about the much more serious dangers of poverty......'

In this light it is noteworthy and encouraging that the three most important reports on a future development strategy – those of the 'Pearson-Commission,' the 'Tinbergen-Committee' and the 'Peterson-Commission' – all plead for increasing internationalization of development aid. The first and second reports having originated from an international organization, the third seems most important here, since it is the report of an advisory committee to the President of the largest donor country in the world. Although it seems rather traditional in its recommendation to restrict the bilateral aid program to countries of particular importance to the United States, it clearly pleads for a predominant role of internationally organized economic assistance:

'The Task Force believes that more reliance on international organizations should be built into all US policies relating to international development – whether they concern development assistance, debt rescheduling, tying trade, investment or population. This is basic to the new approach to foreign assistance we recommend. A predominantly bilateral US program is no longer politically tenable in our relations with many developing countries, nor is it advisable in view of what other countries are doing in international development.'[293]

B. Relations Among Developing Countries Inter Se

Poverty and economic development may also contribute to *international conflict among developing countries inter se* in several ways, both directly and indirectly.

On the one hand, hunger and scarcity may directly contribute to conflicts over disputed territory which is rich in resources. The 'football war' between Honduras and El Salvador, for instance, can largely be explained as the result of a protracted conflict on fertile soil along the border.[294] The Nigerian civil war, protracted in part by the discovery of rich oilfields in the eastern part of the country, could be said to hold a warning signal that – in view of the disputed character of many frontiers throughout the Third World – the discovery or exploitation of resources may provoke future international conflicts.

Similar conflicts may be expected sooner or later between several African countries, if, for example, wandering tribes, being dependent for the feeding of their cattle on grass-land at the other side of a border are refused entry into such land in future – for instance, when the country develops so far that it needs new grass-lands itself. The possibility of such conflict situations is implied by the temporary character of regulations in this respect included in some border treaties.

On the other hand, poverty and development may contribute to international conflict between Third World countries in a more indirect way. This may occur along several lines.

1°. The interventionary policy of the Super Powers may result, as has been pointed out at length before, in the involvement of poor countries in the Cold War. When neighbouring countries sympathize

---

[293] Commission on International Co-operation ('Pearson-Commission') – 'Partners in Development' ('69);
UN Committee on Development Planning ('Tinbergen-Committee'), Report on the 4th. and 5th. sessions, E/4682 ('69); Report on the 6th. session, E/4776 ('70);
US Task Force on International Development ('Peterson-Commission') – 'US Foreign Assistance in the 1970's: a new approach' ('70).
[294] XXIII Bull. At. Sc. 7 ('67) p. 48.

with opposing Powers, this may lead to a confrontation between them.

2⁰. There is – largely as a consequence of socio-economic chaos – the widespread phenomenon of the military government. Several authors perceive the foreign policies of many Third World governments primarily as 'domestic policy by other means,' or, as Lagos puts it, 'systems of action oriented to enhance the real status of the nation in a stratified world, dominated by the values of wealth, power, and prestige.[295] The foreign policies of these governments are largely determined by the endeavour to level their positions vis-à-vis their own populations as well as vis-à-vis neighbouring countries.

In this connection Galtung's theory of structural aggression may be reiterated: these governments, knowing their countries to be legally independent and equal to the rich nations, but in fact politically and economically inferior – the typical middledog position –, try to evade their identity crisis by levelling their positions in the economic and political fields. As far as endeavours on the economic level are concerned, they soon become disappointed and recognize their incapabilities; thus, they tend to throw themselves primarily into the task of achieving a better political position among the nations.

In the case of military governments – which control large parts of the Third World –, this tendency is often combined with an almost natural fervent nationalism, because many military leaders fought in national liberation movements before independence was reached. These military leaders are inclined to link national greatness to military grandeur, and their way of evading their identity crisis is sought primarily in obtaining a strong Army equiped with expensive and modern weapons.[296]

They tend to overlook, however, that by pursuing such micro power policy they prompt their neighbours to do the same, for two reasons: first, many people from the military have received their educations in Western or Eastern academies and have learned from the rich countries to think in terms of balance of power, deterrence, etc.; second, the colonial era has left dozens of uncertain and artificial frontiers, so that many local conflicts are waiting for a solution. The resulting 'arms walks' may become arms races, which show the same characteristical destabilizing elements as in the rich world. (See note 238 supra).

---

[295] G. Lagos – 'International Stratification and Underdeveloped Countries' ('63) p. X.
[296] see J. L. Horowitz – 'Three Worlds of Development' ('66) pp. 261-269; see also note 238 supra.

Militarism in the Third World may have perhaps even more serious and dangerous consequences than it already has in the rich world, since the people from the military in the Third World are often the only ones who decide on foreign political affairs.[297]

Apart from the military themselves, frustration on the part of other social groups (like the newly educated) may result in the search for an 'exhaust-valve' which can also be found in fervent nationalism. Such groups will then support a hard foreign policy of their military leaders.

Moreover, many deprived people may come to consider the Army a way out as a last means: for the many men who are incapable of feeding their hungry families, the Army holds the promise of at least some material improvement, and as such these people add to the militarization of their society.

3°. A relation exists between internal conflict and international conflict, in two different ways:

On the one hand, specific forms of internal conflict may provoke intervention by neighbouring countries. On the other hand, the creation of a foreign enemy may help to maintain internal cohesion when this is threatened by dissension.

In view of the circumstance that both lasting poverty and economic development must be expected to contribute to different forms of internal ruptures, it may be appropriate to pay some attention to the relationships mentioned.

3°.1. In case of internal conflict, a foreign Power can become involved in two ways: either the foreign Power itself wishes to exploit the situation in order to further its own specific foreign policy objectives by joining one of the fighting factions; or a minority in need of assistance invites a foreign government to intervene. In the first case the *opportunities*, in the second the *motivations* of intervention are dealt with.

Concerning the first, opportunities, the general discontent with economic and social progress, the many one-party or no-party systems and authoritarian government structures, the lack of national cohesion and frequency of political suppression, are all factors which contribute to the emergence of many dissident groups. Such dissident groups, finding their state of affairs unacceptable, and willing to act in such a manner as to alter the authority structure within their respective states, constitute appropriate channels through which intervention may occur. Kwame N'krumah's continual invectives against neo-

[297] see M. Thomson – 'Militarism 1969; A survey of World Trends'; Peace Research Reviews (Oct. '66) pp. 37 ff.

colonialist forces and their 'puppets' in Africa were intended in part to provide a justification for interventions, in which he exploited existing rivalries in those countries which he tried to combine in his Pan-African movement.

Concerning the motivations of intervention, four main categories can be discerned: ethnic irredentism, religion, ideology, and anti-colonialism. In relation to the last two motivations, it may suffice here to say that a number of African states, proclaiming that the liberation from white colonialism is to be pushed on by some kind of socialist revolution, have based their interventionist policies on an 'implicit ideology.'[298] A very important justification has been ethnic irredentism, indicating a situation in which an ethnic movement aims at becoming politically united to the other members of their race or tribe, who live in other states. Both in Asia and Africa political boundaries rarely coincide with ethnic boundaries, but often cut across them. It has been pointed out in Chapter I that under circumstances of relative scarcity the process of economic development tends to intensify group-centrism and ethnic conflict. Ethnic minorities may then apply for help to their 'compatriots' in neighbouring countries, thus provoking international conflict. The situation in countries like Kenya and Ethiopia (the Somali problem) has been discussed at length before. Similar problems exist or may arise in Mauretania, in Cambodia and Vietnam (the Thai problem), as in many other countries. The overseas Indians and Chinese, who are a stumbling-block in many developing countries, may become a particular source of international conflict.

The situation is quite similar concerning religion. Muslim groups, supported by their religious brothers in other countries, form a continuous problem to Ethiopia and Chad. The largely Muslim 'Eritrean Liberation Front' and the Chadian 'Islamic Government in-Exile' have at various times operated from the Sudan, whose position has varied from condemnation to outright support.[299] A similar situation prevails in S. Sudan itself and in Nigeria. The relations between India and Pakistan at this moment need no comment. All such potential justifications of cross-national solidarity should be kept in mind when trying to understand the high level of internal conflict in Third World countries.

It has, moreover, been argued, that 'the longer the domestic violence continues, the more likely a foreign government is to become in-

---

[298] J. Wallerstein – 'Implicit Ideology in Africa. A Review of Books by Kwame Nkrumah', XI J. Confl. Res. ('67) pp. 518 ff.
[299] R. O. Matthews – 'Domestic and Inter-State Conflict in Africa,' XXV Int. J. 3 ('70).

volved. A corollary to this might read: the shorter the internal war, or merely the threat of one, the less likely there is to be outside intervention.'[300] This is a conclusion to remember, when more and more evidence can be given to prove that poverty breeds unrest, and that the Big Powers easily get involved both in internal and in international conflict in the developing countries.

3⁰.2. The connection between internal and international conflict resulting from the endeavour, by governments faced with internal opposition, to exploit real or imaginary outside opposition in an attempt to transfer internal hostility from themselves to an external object, is the other side of the coin. We deal here with an ancient phenomenon, indicated today by the term 'displacement,' the idea being based on the following assumptions:

1) The unity of a group is frequently lost when it does not have an outside opponent.

2) Hostilities directed at the outside world help to maintain group-boundaries, and groups may accordingly look for enemies who help maintain or increase internal cohesion.

3) Exaggeration of outside dangers serves to maintain the group structure when it is threatened by internal dissension.

Such relations are focussed upon by Wright, when he says:

'By creating and perpetuating in the community both a fear of invasion and a hope of expansion, obedience to a ruler may be guaranteed,' and when he concludes that 'rulers have forestalled internal sedition by starting external wars.'[301]

When writing about Napoleon he states that 'in the later stages of the Napoleonic wars, Napoleon began to appreciate the value of war as an instrument of internal solidarity.'[302] Similarly, Rosecrance asserts that over time there is a tendency for international instability to be associated with the domestic insecurity of ruling élites.[303] This conclusion is supported by Huntington, who suggests the practical relevance of this theory by having found a contrario, that a decrease in the frequency of inter-state conflict is likely to lead to an increase in the degree of domestic violence.[304]

Although precautions might be of minor importance in practice, since governments tend to overlook potential negative effects, both Simmel and Coser have added an important condition to this thesis: internal

---

[300] idem, p. 473.
[301] Q. Wright – 'A Study of War' II ('42) p. 1016; I, 140.
[302] idem, II, p. 725.
[303] R. N. Rosecrance – 'Action and Reaction in World Politics' ('63) pp. 294, 304.
[304] S. P. Huntington – 'Changing patterns of Military Politics' ('62) pp. 40-41.

cohesion may be expected to increase only if there is a basic, pre-existing consensus.
Thus Simmel states:

> 'A state of conflict pulls the members so tightly together and subjects them to such uniform impulse that they either must get completely along with, or completely repel, one another. This is the reason why war with the outside is sometimes the last chance for a state ridden with inner antagonism, to overcome these antagonisms, or else to break up definitely';

but in general,

> 'outside conflict will strengthen the internal cohesion of the group and increase centralisation.'[305]

Coser observes that

> 'internal cohesion is likely to be increased in the group which engages in outside conflict,' but 'the degree of group consensus prior to the outbreak of the conflict seems to be the most important factor affecting cohesion. If a group is lacking in basic consensus, outside threat leads not to increased cohesion, but to general apathy, and the group is consequently threatened with disintegration.'[306]

The relevance of this remark would seem to be confirmed by the American people's stand on the Vietnam war: on the one hand, the election of President Nixon indicates a movement to the right, a combination of formerly opposing nationalist groups; but on the other hand, the war seems to have resulted in rapid disintegration as far as black people and dissident groups (mainly among the younger generation) are concerned.

Haas and Whiting bring the thesis directly in the present context by contending that the élite from any populations try to shift the attention of a discontented population into some outside target, in particular if they become fearful of losing their domestic positions during periods of rapid industrialization and widespread social change.[307]
The view has also been expressed that this theory would be applicable in connection with the Third World, because, much more than in the case of the rich nations, the foreign policy of the new states must be perceived as 'domestic policy pursued by other means..... beyond the boundaries of the state.'[308] Their foreign policies, it is argued, can not be fully understood unless they are placed in the

[305] G. Simmel – 'Conflict and the Webb of Inter Group Applications' ('55) p. 87.
[306] L. A. Coser – 'The Functions of Social Conflict' ('56) pp. 92-93.
[307] E. R. Haas & A. S. Whiting – 'Dynamics of International Relations' ('56) pp. 61-62.
[308] R. Good – 'State Building as a Determinant of Foreign Policy in the New States,' in L. Martin (ed.) – 'Neutralism and Nonalignment' ('62) p. 12.

perspective of the overwhelming domestic tasks that confront them. A major task is the attainment or maintenance of internal integration.
Various tactics are employed to assist governments in achieving this goal. Attendance at international conferences and widespread publication of the leaders' speeches, the convening of conferences in pursuit of some highly respected goal like African unity, Asian solidarity, etc. are all examples of the various ways used. Such measures may, however, be insufficient at critical moments. Then the more drastic endeavour to identify external Powers as enemies threatening the state may be made, which creates international conflict.[309] A few examples of this process are mentioned here:
In the beginning of 1958 the king of Morocco brought up the Mauretanian question again – having been silent for some time on the issue of Morocco's alleged historic claims to large parts of Algeria, Mali, and the whole of Mauretania. His commitment to the Mauretanian cause at that time has been explained by many by referring to the increasing internal difficulties in Morocco.[310] Ashford explains that 'the Mauretanian question became a national issue only when the difficulties of ruling a developing nation became fully apparent to the Moroccan leaders, and when the complex problems of independence had become so numerous that distraction served a purpose.'[311]
Similarly, it has been argued that Somalia's hostility towards Ethiopia and Kenya has not only served the Pan-Somali movement, but that it has also served as a factor creating national integration which in turn controlled the centrifugal forces of clanism and North-South rivalry within the country. Decraene even predicts that, in view of the almost insurmountable economic difficulties facing Somalia, its government will progressively pursue a more aggressive foreign policy.[312] The increasing acrimony between Somalia and Ethiopia in 1962 and the outbreak of hostilities between these countries in 1964 have been attributed to internal events in Somalia: an internal crisis in 1962, and the approach of general elections in 1964.[313]

---

[309] R. O. Matthews, pp. 475-477.
[310] see D. Wild – 'The Organisation of African Unity and the Algerian-Moroccan Dispute', XX Int. Org. ('66) pp. 18 ff.
[311] D. Ashford – 'The Irredentist Appeal in Morocco and Mauretania,' XV W. Pol. Q. ('62) p. 643.
[312] Ph. Decraene in Problèmes africaines No. 181 (May 6, '63) p. 10.
[313] A. A. Castagno – 'Somalia Republic,' in J. S. Coleman & C. S. Rosberg (eds.) – 'Political Parties and National Integration in Tropical Africa' ('66) pp. 548-558; M. Wolde Marian – 'The Background of the Ethio-Somalia Boundary Dispute,' I J. Mod. Afr. St. ('63) p. 212.

The same has been contended in connection with Algeria. A direct relationship is said to have existed between internal disorders – economic disorganization, increasing opposition against Ben Bella's rule – and the clashes between Algerian and Moroccan troops along their common border, resulting eventually in a higher level of Algerian integration.[314]

Another example is Ghana's conflict with Togo, the Ewe dispute, which has been explained 'as an instrument for both sides in their efforts to consolidate their régimes and divert dissatisfaction over internal conditions to external problems.'[315]

Some authors also point out that the Indonesian confrontation with the Dutch and Malaysians took place during periods of economic stagnation. These conflicts could thus be explained in part by the necessity of maintaining national unity and turning down domestic conflict by way of the creation of a foreign enemy.[316]

In this sense some authors also refer to the 'developing' Super Power China. The Japanese Esaki, for instance, who had the opportunity of travelling through China and talking to its leaders, replied to the question whether he minimized China's war talk in this way:

> 'To a considerable degree, yes. It's all part of their house-cleaning program: to get the Chinese people to make greater sacrifices. They believe that strong verbal attacks on the United States are the easiest way to unify public opinion behind them... they will probably maintain a belligerent attitude for a long time as a means of keeping their people keyed up, even though they have no intention of fighting.'[317]

Some authors have expressed their doubts whether all the examples given in literature are valid. E.g. Matthews shows that N'krumah's foreign adventures served to weaken rather then strengthen his internal support. He also thinks that the governments of new states, 'lacking the necessary information and diplomatic specialists to formulate meaningful policy and to implement it, ... tend to take decisions on the basis of almost random pressures.'[318] Even if he is right in his

---

[314] J. J. Chouet in Problèmes africaines No. 204 (24 Oct. '63) p. 3.
[315] I. W. Zartman – 'International Relations in West Africa' ('66) p. 112.
[316] see D. Hindley – 'Indonesia's Confrontation with Malaysia. A Search for motives,' IV Asian Survey ('64) p. 908 ff. One wonders whether the terrible massacre of 500.000 communists during the 1965-1966 rage in Indonesia itself has perhaps partially the same cause. Hundreds, perhaps thousands of prisoners are being shot today; the anti-communist hysteria goes on and seems the more 'misplaced' now since almost all of the communist leaders who survived have now been captured or killed. See the London Economist – 'Deadly Echoes of an Old Communist Witch Hunt' (Dec. '68).
[317] see M. Esaki – 'China's Military Preparations,' IX Survival (Jan. '67) pp. 6, 8; also US News and World Report (Oct. 24, '66).
[318] R. O. Matthews pp. 482-483.

conclusions – which may seem doubtful as far as his perception of the inability of new leaders is concerned – this does not have to mean that there is, as he says, 'a need to qualify any expectations of widespread use of displacement.' On the one hand, it is questionable whether leaders opting for this policy realize the possible negative effects of it. On the other hand, the fact that personality factors play such an important role in the Third World could stimulate rather than hinder such foreign policy moves.

In these ways poverty and development may either directly or – via internal destabilization – indirectly cause or contribute to international conflict in the Third World.
Whatever the importance of other peace-disturbing factors is, it may be assumed that without economic misery and underdevelopment the political climate in the Third World would be almost certainly much more moderate than it is now.

C. *Relations Between Poor and Rich Countries*

Considering the relations between the rich and the poor countries as groups, a clear tendency towards polarization can be observed.
The group of rich nations has by and large for two decades been unanimous in preserving their privileged position on the world market, at the same time being very reluctant to offer the poor countries a better position. Too much priority was given to internal economic problems in the rich countries over the problems of the Third World as to change this position.
The poor countries, on the other hand, have been divided for years; partly because they have suffered from many political conflicts and partly because the emerging nationalism did not allow the pursuance of their common interest as a supreme political goal. During the last few years, however, a tendency to unite in order to form a common front against the rich nations becomes manifest on their side as well. The 'Charter of Algiers,' which was intended to be the common base of interests at the second UNCTAD in New Delhi, may have been a turning-point. Whereas the Bandung Conference of 1955 failed to create political unity, the Algiers Conference established to some extent economic unity, which clearly distinguished the 'group of 89' in New Delhi from the 'group of 77' in Geneva four years earlier.
Recently, on Nov. 7, 1971, the 'group of 77,' having become extend-

ed to a 'group of 96,' issued the 'Declaration of Lima' at the end of a meeting of the developing countries held to prepare their activities at UNCTAD III, to convene at Santiago in April 1972. This Declaration, which is supplemented by an 'Action-programme,' warns that it is no longer possible for poverty and affluence to co-exist in this world. The countries participating in this conference, representing a total population of 1.6 billion, hold the present structure of international economic relations responsible for the poverty in the Third World, and – although the developing countries accept primary responsibility for their own development – their efforts are considered fruitless by the present policies of the rich countries. In any case the poor countries want to unite their ranks closer than ever in Santiago. An additioned sign of their closer co-operation was the establishment, in Dec. '71, of an Intergovernmental Monetary Committee, to counter-balance the 'group of ten,' the forum in which the rich countries discuss their monetary problems and the poor countries have no role to play; they feel themselves the foremost victims of the monetary manipulations of the rich countries, against which they try to defend themselves by uniting in this new committee in which 15 of them are represented.

OPEC (the organization of Oil Products Exporting Countries) is further testimony to the fact that the poor countries are beginning to realize their need of closer co-operation. OPEC points also to their growing resistance to accept that the rich countries receive the major profits from their resources. Both the governments and, increasingly, the mass of the populations perceive their misery as mainly resulting from colonial and neo-colonial policies of the rich countries. At the opening of the Algiers Conference which included 86 developing countries, on October 10, 1967, President Boumedienne of Algeria said that 'Europe and the U.S. have plundered the natural wealth of the Third World... we should consider whatever contribution the industrialized countries make as a simple restitution of a tiny part of the debt the Western countries contracted by their odious exploitation.' Likewise, Peru's José Antonio del Pando pointed out, 'we are here because the have's won't let us into the twentieth century.'[319] The question whether the Western nations are indeed imperialistic is not discussed here; what is important here is that the poor countries do feel that Western imperialism has been the cause of much of their misery.

The foreign firm, hiring cheap labour from the local population,

---

[319] quoted in R. P. Anand – 'The development of a Universal International Law,' in 'The Search for World Order' (Festschrift for Quincy Wright, ed. Lepawsky, Buehrig, and Lasswell, '71) p. 169.

choosing new sites for plant facilities, often deciding the market prices by itself, and at times acting without virtual restrictions imposed by the local government, is often a source of irritation to a local population which is already disappointed with the ways of the rich. These firms are increasingly considered as masters unto themselves, because they exploit the people, export the money, and act without consideration for the welfare of those who claim the resources to be theirs. It would not be without reason to predict that large-scale nationalization of foreign investments will occur shortly, and that the example set by one nation – the copper mines in Chile constituting an outstanding one – will encourage others. In this respect also poor countries are closing their ranks and voicing their common interest, in order to stand the resulting conflicts with the rich.

An intensified polarization, dividing rich and poor, is emerging and will certainly be sharply increased if important social changes take place in poor countries – at present, one should not forget, that the ruling circles of various developing countries are profiting too much from prevailing circumstances as to desire real confrontation. Together, the poor countries, forming a large part of the world's population, may initiate a new era in international relations: the Cold War between rich and poor. This Cold War will not be characterized by nuclear deterrence, but by dramatic intolerance. Even if the Resolutions of Geneva and New Delhi may have failed to produce a substantial effect, they are nevertheless becoming the standards of frustration. If the gap between rich and poor continues to widen and if, consequently, the poor close their ranks, an atmosphere of hatred, accusation and conflict may dominate all over the world. Ogmal Ali from Pakistan significantly called UNCTAD II 'the Conference of Frustration' and Azedero da Silveira from Brazil said on the closing-day:

'The disappointing results of New Delhi have convinced the developing countries of the necessity to unite or to starve.'

The importance of decreasing the welfare gap to secure friendly relations between rich and poor has been stressed during the debates of the International Law Association on peaceful co-existence. Many representatives of poor countries referred to the mistake of thinking only in terms of East-West relations instead of paying more and more attention to North-South relations.

'Co-exister,' Boutros-Ghali warned, 'c'est d'abord aider les nations pauvres à exister.[320]

---

[320] B. Boutros-Ghali (UAR) in Proc. ILA ('60) p. 343; see also Khambatta in idem ('62) p. 34.

The young countries are weary of Northern paternalism, of benevolence from the rich world. They are not begging anymore, they are demanding. Sometimes one hears people talk about some future aggression of the poor towards the rich. In the present era this is nonsense. What might perhaps be a worrying thought is that many poor countries might acquire chemical (and biological) weapons, which as such is quite possible and would add seriously to the instability of the world. Some speak in a somewhat exaggerated way of the 'poor man's atom bomb' in this connection.[321] We may also expect new forms of violent action by terrorist groups, which in times of formal peace would intensify hatred and tension.

What might also become problematic is the role of China, which is trying very hard to become accepted as the leader of the poor in the struggle against the rich. Whatever China's chances in this respect may be in the future, the prevailing distrust on the side of the United States and the Soviet Union is alarming enough. Manifold are the official Chinese statements concerning China's duty and determination to support and lead the poor masses of the Third World, and concerning the common heritage of the colonial era. Neo-colonialism is said to kill the poor and keep their countries emprisoned:[322] 'The majority of our Asian and African countries,' Chou En-lai said at the Bandung Conference (for China the first symbol of identity with the Third World), 'are still very backward economically, owing to the long period of colonial domination.'
China is trying – at least so it says – to transplant the class struggle from the national to the international scene, which may be an unrealistic aim, but Lin Piao's prediction of the encirclement of the cities (the rich) by the countryside (the poor) has aroused fear in the North, which in itself may be important enough to provoke averse reactions.
In 1965, China first gained a maximum popularity among Third World countries. In that year the vote on China's admission to the UN General Assembly was 47 against 47 (by 20 abstentions). Encouraged by Chou En-lai's successful trip through Africa, however, the Chinese made some serious mistakes by intervening altogether too openly in the internal affairs of African and Asian states. The result was a serious set-back. Yet, at the Havanna Conference in 1966, China again successfully fought the proposal, made by some Afro-

---

[321] H. Bull – 'The Control of the Arms Race' ('61) p. 132.
[322] for instance an article in Renmin Rihbao of Dec.17,1965, entitled: 'On the Relationship between Political and Economic Independence'; cited in G. T. Yu – 'China's Failure in Africa,' VI Asian Survey ('66) p. 466.

Asian states, to replace the Afro-Asian Solidarity Conference (under China's leadership) by a new Organization of Solidarity among Latin American, African and Asian nations.[323]

In 1970, the so-called 'Albanian Resolution,' according to which China should take the place of Taiwan in the UN, and the government of Taiwan should be expelled entirely from the organization, got for the first time in history a majority of the votes (51 against 49 by 25 abstentions), many developing countries being among those who voted in favour of Resolution 2624 (XXV). In December 1971, finally, the die was cast with the admission of China to and the expulsion of Taiwan from the UN, provoking a dance of joy among the representatives of several developing countries.

China once proposed to create a new United Nations of the poor peoples under China's leadership. At the time, in 1967, this initiative failed. Still, notwithstanding the failures of the past, many hold that 'there have been enough successes to sustain her in the belief of the applicability of Mao's revolutionary strategy and tactics to the international arena.'[324]

Whatever China's real intentions and chances to become eventually the leader of the poor countries, its alleged endeavours in that direction are arousing fear among many Americans and Russians, and it is this perception that counts. *Increasing solidarity among the poor countries combined with these perceptions of China's intentions can easily result in more interventions and more Cold War confrontations.*

It is against the background of the international setting as described in this Chapter, that emotional warnings for the future should perhaps be considered more serious than they often are. The entire set of situations which together constitute this background explain the relevance of the feelings of many Third World people as expressed by Liberia's Romeo Horton at Algiers in 1967:

'The removal of inequities between rich and poor is the key question of our time; it will decide the issue of war and peace.'[325]

---

[323] VI Kron. Afr. 1 ('66) p. 3.
[324] see Tang Tson & M. H. Halperin – 'Mao Tse tung's Revolutionary Strategy and Peking's International Behavior,' LIX Am. Pol. Sc. Rev. ('65) p. 97.
[325] quoted in A. de Borchgrave – 'Scandal of the Century': Rich and Poor,' Newsweek (Oct. 30, '67) p. 26.

RELATIONSHIPS BETWEEN POVERTY, ECONOMIC DEVELOPMENT, AND CONFLICT (INTERNAL AND INTERNATIONAL)

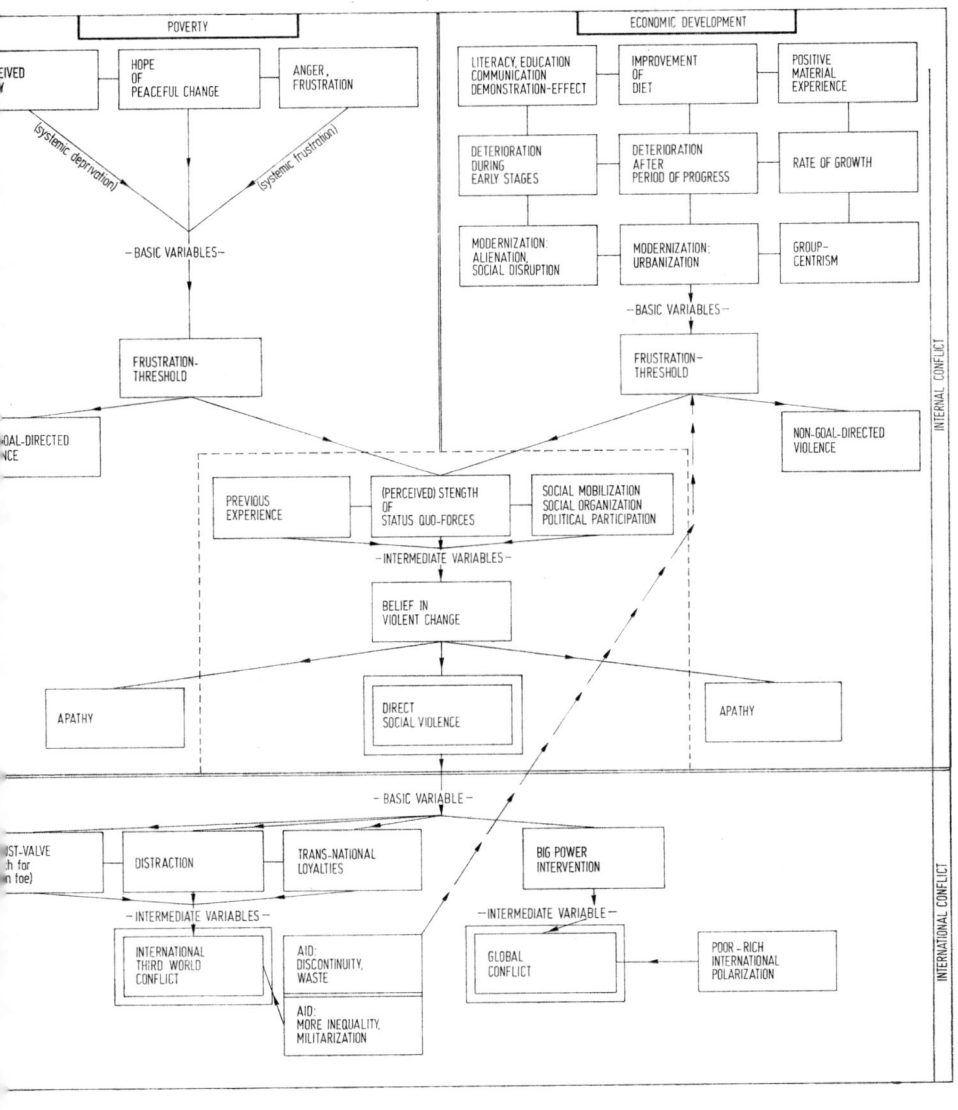

Chapter III

The Role of International Law: An Outline

The purpose of this Chapter is to find a connection between the conclusions which can be drawn from the preceding Chapters and international law as a peace-promoting factor in international relations.
The peace-promoting function of law (1), the present position of international law in relation to questions of poverty and development, and the challenge to its rules (2), and a new legal strategy (3) are discussed. In section (3) an endeavour is made to develop a legal framework aimed at the promotion of world peace by the advancement of universal welfare. After the roots of such a structure in present international law have been explored, the strategy itself is outlined.
In an Appendix the international legal aspects of intervention are discussed against the background of this general context.*

Peace Through Welfare: Towards a Development Strategy on the Basis of Law

1. *International law as a peace-promoting factor: from negative peace to positive peace*

The endeavour to give international law a peace-promoting function is as old as the international anarchy of sovereign states. Large-scale efforts on an international scale, however, have been made only in this century. Before the emergence of the nuclear arms race, endeavours were made to strengthen the peace-promoting role of law along two interrelated paths. The first path tried to rule out war as a means of national policy by way of general treaties prohibiting the resort to armed force (the Briand-Kellogg pact of 1928). The other path has tried to strengthen the organizational structure of international society by creating a permanent framework for discussing international conflicts and by creating a system of collective security (the League of Nations). In 1945, both endeavours were united in the Charter of the United Nations. Article 2, para. 4 of the UN Charter ruled out

---

* where italics are used in the text of UN-Resolutions in this Chapter, they are – unless indicated otherwise – mine.

war as a means of national policy, while at the same time a new framework for the peaceful settlement of disputes and eventual sanctions was brought into existence.

The development of nuclear stores, however, did not allow – at least as far as the Super Powers are concerned – the system of collective security to become more than a blueprint. None of the Super Powers can be controlled by collective action – their military power being too deterrent, and any action against the will of a Super Power entailing the risk of total destruction. The Super Powers, therefore, who could not rely upon the Charter's collective legal system anymore, sought their security in the military framework of nuclear deterrence. During the last few years, however, they seem to have begun to fear the shortcomings and destabilizing effects of this system. Notwithstanding the temporarily peace-preserving effect of nuclear deterrence, they are beginning to realize that this mechanism entails an ever lasting arms race. Any arms race having potentially destabilizing effects, the consequences in the case of an unlimited nuclear arms race are beyond imagination. Obviously becoming aware of the grave dangers of further escalation in this field, the Super Powers developed international law as a peace-preserving factor in a third manner: the achievement of agreements on arms control and disarmament. Successes of some kind have been scored – the Antarctic Treaty, the Space Treaty, the Nuclear Test Ban, and the Non-Proliferation Treaty being the results of world-wide awareness of the nuclear threat. However, concerning the direct relations between the Super Powers (mainly the U.S. and the USSR for the moment), little progress has been made as yet. Whatever concessions they are prepared to make, will come in the future and will, moreover, mainly have consequences for their *bilateral* relations, making little difference to the outbreak of violence elsewhere in the world (e.g. in the Third World).

For this reason, and in view of the remaining risk that the Super Powers might always become involved in conflicts on opposite sides, the maintenance of peace *in general* has been and remains mainly dependent on the scheme envisaged in the U.N. Charter; the combined system of the prohibition of war and the procedures for conflict resolution.

Developments after the second World War have seriously frustrated the 'well' believers and amused the 'ill' predictors. The former tried by means of the 'Uniting for Peace' Resolution to re-inforce the peace-preserving capability of the U.N. by putting the General Assembly partly in the place of the veto-deadlocked Security Council. The latter tried to convince the others that the time is not yet ripe for such Utopian jumps. Opinions now diverge widely concerning the question of the contribution and the role of international law in the arena of international politics.

Much has been written about the manner in which the rule prohibiting war and the system of the U.N. failed. Little, however, has been written about the fundamental causes of these failures. Is there only the choice between the pessimists, who depict any such structure as Utopian, and the optimists, who say that the main problem is to find the right structure?

Until now, much of the discussion among international lawyers has pertained to the structural aspects of the peace-promoting framework. But it has often neglected the much more crucial aspects of its foundations. With the absolute prohibition of war and the organizational framework for discussion and sanctions one has created a system that lags behind the events, instead of keeping abreast with them. A conflict situation is brought to the attention of the United Nations only when a violent conflict threatens immediately or has already broken out. If, however, discussions start at the moment violent conflict is apparent, when positions have stiffened, when hatred has been roused and populations have been mobilized, the room left for a peaceful solution is bound to be extremely narrow. Therefore, in many cases the United Nations can only observe the violence rather passively and hope that the Big Powers will not become involved.

Now that it is clear that every conflict, anywhere on earth, becomes – because of close interdependence of states and because of the Cold War – automatically a matter of concern to all; that it is clear furthermore, from the policy of intervention and the mechanisms of escalation, that every conflict carries with it the potential danger of a Big Power conflict; and because it is clear that it is often too late for the United Nations to act when the concrete conflict is just apparent, a rational conclusion is that the United Nations system can only be strengthened through valuable endeavours to *prevent such conflicts from arising*.

With the Covenant of the League of Nations and the Charter of the United Nations a framework has been created which constitutes in essence a system of *'negative peace,'* a system in which merely fighting is avoided. But, as Röling puts it,

'if we try to confine ourselves simply to banning war, as by a prohibition such as occurs in Art. 2 subpara. 4 of the United Nations Charter, what we are really doing is excluding war as a way of resolving conflict situations, yet without removing the conflict situations and without providing any alternatives to war. This is an impossible situation, because the conflict situations must become so tense that they *necessarily erupt into violence*.'[1]

A system of negative peace cannot operate successfully in the long run – as recent history has sufficiently shown – without being supplemented by a system of '*positive peace*,' meaning that accommodations between groups are created so that they can live together within a mutually accepted system of values, i.e. *solving the problems which are causative to violent conflicts*. The Constitution of UNESCO begins with the words: 'Since wars begin in the minds of men, it is in the minds of men that the defences of peace must be construed.' This is only half the truth, however, since this point of view overlooks the more fundamental problem behind the question: why are the minds of men so full of violent thoughts?

The UN Charter speaks in art. 1 of the maintenance of 'peace and security,' the first term implying the mere absence of war, the second term relating to 'positive peace'[2]; an interpretation which is at least supported by the practice of this organization (see below, sections 3.2.1.-3.2.4.). In this light the pledge embodied in the Preamble of the U.N. Charter 'to establish conditions under which justice and respect for the obligations arising from treaties and other sources of international law can be maintained,' is of crucial importance. In a world full of conflict and torn by rivalries it is neither sufficient to declare that war should be outlawed, nor is it sufficient to create an organizational structure where existing conflicts are discussed and a system of collective deterrence and security. As long as those conflicts in which vital interests are at stake remain unsolved, the prospects of peace remain uncertain. In an era, characterized by the threat of nuclear war and complete destruction, survival can only be assured by removing those roots of conflict whose continued existence is bound to end in violence.

In order to deal effectively with the realities of the present-day world, new patterns of co-operation are needed, and some of the principles that have governed international society for a long time have to be re-evaluated.

---

[1] see B. V. A. Röling – 'Peace Research, the Science of Survival'; XVIII Impact of Science on Society 2 ('68) p. 75.
Galtung defines 'negative peace' likewise as 'absence of war or more generally absence of organized violence between groups,' and 'positive peace' as 'presence of patterns of co-operations, of harmonious living together and in general integration between groups;' J. Galtung – 'International repertory of institutions specializing in research on peace and disarmament' (UNESCO-paper no. 23, '66) p. 5.
[2] see R. S. MacNamara – 'Security in the Contemporary World,' 54 Dept. State Bull. (June 6, '66) p. 878.

'Each nation,' says Hambro, 'must learn to accomodate itself to common interests of the world community. We must realize that our mutual interdependence will demand greater international solidarity in the future. The fragmentary international society of yesterday is obsolete.... International law must deal more thoroughly with those basic faults of contemporary society which lead men to violence in desperation over their condition.'[3]

Many governments in the rich part of the world, among them the Super Powers, show little intention, however, of changing their present 'security policies' and to establish their security on the basis of a new body of law, creating positive peace. Although realizing the shortcomings of the present peace-preserving system, they remain almost exclusively concentrated on East-West relations, continuing to base their security and, indeed, world peace primarily on the maintenance of negative peace through nuclear deterrence. In view of the obvious dangers and shortcomings of this system, and in particular in view of the fact that it does certainly not prevent all those conflicts in the Third World in which the well to do lands may become involved, it might be said, that they seek their long-term security in a wrong direction. While attaching so much weight to East-West nuclear deterrence exclusively, they do not seem to realize that a cornerstone of their security also lies in the North-South dimension.
Because poverty in the present era breeds conflict, and because the Cold War has a grip on the Third World to such an extent already, it is not exaggerated to state that the security of the rich is becoming increasingly dependent on the prosperity of the poor.
A common endeavour, therefore, to help the poor countries reach prosperity and to assist them in developing their economies, constitutes a fundamental contribution to the security of the rich.
While talking on the relation between internal peace and prosperity, MacNamara once said: 'If security implies anything, it implies a minimal measure of order and stability'; and, since he dealt with internal security, he went on, 'without internal development of at least a minimal degree, order and stability are simply not possible. They are not possible because human nature cannot be frustrated beyond intrinsic limits. It reacts because it must.'[2]
These words, being applicable without condition to the international level as well, clearly suggest that 'security' means more than the mere absence of violence or war. The importance of the poverty problem in this respect has been stressed likewise in the encyclical 'Populorum Progressio,' in which Pope Paul VI declared:

[3] E. Hambro, Address at the opening of the 25th Session of the UN Gen. Ass., A/PV 1839 (Sept. 15, 1970) pp. 22 ff.

'Development is the new name for peace.'

Of course, the process of development entails many destabilizing effects. Whereas one can try, however, to control these effects by taking them into consideration in planning, the violence resulting from lasting poverty and desperation may soon get out of control and turn the Third World into a scene of large-scale civil wars, with all its consequences to world peace at large.

For the security of the rich nations the solution of both problems – the nuclear arms race and the poverty problem – is of tremendous importance. It can certainly be said that the presence of weapons may contribute to the outbreak of conflicts, but it can also be maintained that the presence of conflicts prevents disarmament.

While efforts to reach a safer negative peace system – through measures in the fields of arms control, disarmament, and conflict resolution – are necessary, the realization of positive peace constitutes the only long-term basis on which to build a safer future. It has often been indicated that these two aims might merge, in particular in Resolutions of the U.N. General Assembly. Res. 724 (VIII) of 1953 states:

> 'We, the Governments of the State Members of the United Nations, in order to promote higher standards of living and conditions of economic and social progress and development, stand ready to ask our peoples, when sufficient progress has been made in internationally supervised world-wide disarmament, to devote a portion of the savings, achieved through such disarmament to an International Fund, within the framework of the United Nations, to assist development and reconstruction in underdeveloped countries.'

Res. 2542 (XXIV) of 1969 likewise urges that efforts should be made to achieve

> 'general and complete disarmament and the channeling of the progressively released resources to be used for economic and social progress for the welfare of the people everywhere and, in particular, for the benefit of developing countries.'

What international law should advocate today, is the realization of a global welfare strategy. It is important that this security strategy be based on a set of principles which fulfil the conditions that can be derived from an analysis of the polemological consequences of the development process which have tentatively been drawn in the preceding Chapters; these principles are, among others:
1. The principal aim must be to reduce to a considerable degree the welfare gap between rich and poor countries.
2. The development process in the Third World should have a continuous and uninterrupted character.

3. Improvement should be substantial on several levels, and not piecemeal.
4. Development assistance should be donated in such a way that political – in particular Cold War – manoeuvring is prevented.
5. Both aid and trade should be adapted in ways which serve the purpose of achieving world-wide welfare.
6. For each developing country specific studies should be available indicating its specific needs, possibilities, and potential causes of conflict during the development process. Programs should be devised in order to minimize the occurrence of internal conflicts.
7. In view of the restrictedness of resources and the need of maximum effectiveness of measures to be taken, maximum co-operation among the rich countries, among the poor countries, (both in general and regionally), and between the rich and poor countries 'en bloc' should be realized.
8. To achieve this, a world center is needed, where decisions on a world-wide scale are to be made, the working-out of which can be transferred to regional and other lower levels.

The specific economic and financial measures to be taken in order to realize global welfare should be in accordance with such principles. They will be discussed below in section 3.3.

2. Present rules and principles: effects and challenge

The history and development of international law can be divided into three major phases.

1. The period of the 'Christian Nations,' from 1648 – the West-Phalia Peace Treaty, when the system of independent sovereign states succeeded the system of the 'two swords,' the Pope and the Emperor – to 1856, when Turkey as the first non-Christian state was allowed to become a member of the community of nations under international law.
2. The period of the 'Civilized Nations,' from 1856 to 1945, when the United Nations were established.
3. The period of the 'Peace-loving Nations,' from 1945 on. The term 'civilized' was not incorporated anymore into the UN Charter like it was in the Covenant of the League of Nations. The basic condition required for states to become a member of the family of nations united in the United Nations Organization, according to art. 4 of its Charter, is that of being 'peace-loving.' The importance of this distinction is threefold:

In the first place, the common values – originally that of 'being Christian,' then that of 'being civilized,' and finally of 'being peace-loving' –

determined the size of the circle of subjects adhering to international law. Now, the condition of 'being peace-loving' does not determine the size of the circle any longer. The circle is approaching universality.

In the second place, the common values served to legitimatize the subjugation of other peoples – the colonial empires were legitimized originally according to the argument 'to Christianize barbarians,' and later according to the argument 'to aim at instructing the natives and bringing home to them the blessings of civilization' (Congo Conference at Berlin, 1885). The legitimization of the following inequal positions – Christians versus non-Christians; Civilized nations versus non-Civilized peoples; strong Powers versus small Powers (here we may think for instance of the privileged position of the big Powers in the Security Council of the UN and in the Non-Proliferation Treaty, both based upon the deliberation that such inequality is in the interest of peace) – was also justified according to the just mentioned common values.

In the third place, the common values constitute a basis for the substance of the rules of law. Even if one might say that the 'Christian Nations' have been rather un-Christian at times, that the 'Civilized Nations' were rather un-Civilized now and then, and that the 'Peace-loving Nations' behaved rather un-peacefully, the relevance of the common principles cannot be denied. In our times many legal or semi-legal documents within the sphere of negative peace have been adopted, like the Antarctic Treaty of 1959, Resolution 1653 (XVI) of the UN General Assembly condemning the use of nuclear weapons, the partial Nuclear Test-Ban of 1963, the de-Nuclearization Treaty of Latin America of 1967, the de-Nuclearization of Outer Space and the Non-Proliferation Treaty of the same year, and the exclusion of the Sea-Bed from uses for military purposes in UN-General Assembly Resolution 2479 (XXV); at the same time the beginning of an enormous endeavour to achieve more social and economic justice in the world, and thus within the sphere of positive peace, is undertaken, nearly all the major documents adopted by the United Nations in the field of Human Rights and welfare containing a provision that their realization is in the interest of peace.[4]

Yet, the question should be answered to what extent the present rules and principles of the law of the 'Peace-loving Nations' are indeed appropriate to promote a more peaceful world, and to promote the interests of the major segments of the subjects of inter-

[4] on the significance of these three periods see further B. V. A. Röling – 'International Law in an Expanded World' ('69).

national law. Since social and economic justice and a minimum level of welfare and equality constitute crucial conditions for a lasting peace (positive peace), the first question to be answered is, to what extent present international social and economic law stimulates such conditions.

What are the principles underlying international law in the field of international economic relations at present? The theoretical basis of present-day economic international law finds its origins in the 19th century. International law, as it was developed after the Vienna Congress, was founded on four axioms, which determined the scope and substance of its rules:

1°. The principle of the sovereign state as the supreme political value;
2°. The endeavour of states to increase their power;
3°. The balance of interests to keep the system going and to avoid its destruction;
4°. The requirement of being European (except for the United States) and Civilized.

All states willing to become subjects of 'international law' in those days, had to accept the rules established by the original circle. This was the main condition when the first non-Christian and non-European States were invited to join the circle. Concerning the newcomers (Turkey in 1856 and Japan in 1899) Hall tought in 1924 that 'States outside European civilization must formally enter into the circle of law-governed countries. They must do something with the acquiescence of the latter, or some of them, which amounts to an acceptance of the law in its entity beyond all possibility of misconstruction.'[5]

The term 'civilized' acquired more and more an economic meaning during the second half of the 19th century. The industrial revolution had started, and the Southern half of the globe, pressed by the rival interests of the industrializing imperialist nations, became ever more important as the supplier of raw materials. The great importance of economic gain and progress and the dependence on foreign resources left its mark upon the term 'civilized.' The value of this term was measured by industrial development and a capability to guarantee the protection of life, liberty and property of foreigners.[6]

The foundations of international law were determined by sovereign European states, which were industrializing and in need of raw materials. They advocated a liberal economic system at home as well as abroad. Economic international law was characterized by the

---

[5] W. E. Hall – 'A Treatise on International Law' (8th ed., '24) p. 47.
[6] Rosalyn Higgins – 'Conflict of Interests; International Law in a Divided World' ('65) p. 39.

principles of liberal capitalism and colonial imperialism. 'Laissez-faire' became the dominant credo; old customs which inhibited trade had to be abrogated, and business had to be free from supervision and notions of morality which might clog the automatic adjustments of the free market.[7] 'Laissez-faire,' the idea of a harmony of interests based on the thought that the common interest is best served by the pursuit of individual interest, made international law congenial to the needs of the industrial pioneer and the capitalist investor.[8]

The replacement of the ethical jurisprudence of the 17th and 18th centuries by the positivism of the 19th century has in fact determined the development of economic international law until today. Under this system liberalism and sovereignty reigned supreme, leaving no place for a duty of co-operation and reciprocal assistance, i.e. the concept of collective responsibility for the well-being of all the members of the international society.

It was recognized gradually, however, that a system of liberalism without restrictions would ruin many and enrich only a few. The industrializing states returned to a decentralized system with the national state as the center and protector of national economic interests. This ran counter to optimal progress as seen from a liberal transnational point of view, but there was room enough for economic expansion resulting in prosperity for many nations. Wherever international trade relations were upheld, however, the principle of liberalism remained inviolable. One clear example of this is the 'most favoured nation clause': protection by the state is allowed, but as far as the doors to foreign imports are unlocked, they should be open to all on an equal footing.

This trade system may have worked well for the industrialized nations at the time. It was to become highly questionable, however, when the newly independent countries of Africa and Asia, and the underdeveloped countries of Latin America, entered the scene and were promised to be helped in developing. The question was, whether such help could be realized under the prevailing system of international rules. The answer soon became very obviously a negative one. One can observe in this connection indeed a very strange thing: international economic inequalities, supposed to get overcome in due course, have been increasing for a long time and still

---

[7] M. A. Kaplan & N. de B. Katzenbach – 'Political Foundations of International Law' ('61) p. 66.
[8] G. Schwarzenberger – 'The Standard of Civilization in International Law,' VIII Current Legal Problems ('55) p. 220.

keep increasing. After the liquidation of colonial structures since the end of the second World War, the development toward increasing inequality even assumed dramatic proportions and became an ever more pressing concern in international politics. At this very juncture of world history, as Myrdal puts it,

> 'the theory of international trade has increasingly stressed the concept that international trade initiates a tendency toward a gradual equalization of incomes as among different countries – under assumptions that should stand out as obviously unrealistic and against all experience.... this biased bent of international theory – and its implicit predilection for harmony of interests, laissez-faire, and free trade – undoubtedly influenced the way in which the problems of the underdeveloped countries were advised.... the fact is that, contrary to that theory, international trade – and capital movements – will generally tend to breed inequality and will do so the more strongly when substantial inequalities are already established... I characterize this strange direction of theoretical interest as a bias, *opportune to people in the developed countries.*'[9]

The rich countries continued to honour liberalism in their relations with the poor in spite of their promises of help to the poor countries and in spite of the killing effect that their present principles had to the developmental efforts in the Third World.

The explanation for the rich countries' actions may be found in Myrdal's accusation, that the principle of non-discrimination is only maintained because it is to the interests of the rich. Again, as in the nineteenth century, when the first non-European nations entered the realm of international law, the pre-existing circle of its subjects demanded that the new members should accept the existing rules, even if the consequences were negative to them; as an Indian official once put it: 'equality of treatment is equitable only among equals.' The Kennedy-Round, announced to help the poor countries in the first place, is testimony to the factual unwillingness of the rich nations to help them, by its acceptance of non-discriminatory liberalism.

A typical example of Western legal thinking in this respect is a study by Scheuner. In writing about economic international law today, he deals with three traditional topics mainly: freedom of trade; protection of foreign property; and national measures influencing international trade.[10] The way of thinking, as expressed in this incidentally skilled study, shows a fundamental lack of insight into the new problems of our present world.

It is commonplace to say that the rules of international law have their origin in the needs of the international community at large. With

---

[9] G. Myrdal – 'The Challenge of World Poverty' ('70) pp. 278-279.
[10] U. Scheuner – 'Die Völkerrechtlichen Grundlagen der Weltwirtschaft in der Gegenwart' ('54), Sonderdruck aus 'Verhandlungen des 40. Deutschen Juristentages,' B. II.

that axiom in mind it must be recognized clearly that, although the circle of subjects of international law is no longer merely European but global, and although the interests to be defended are no longer those of the industrial capitalist society alone but those of quite different societies as well, the foundations of economic international law are still those of the Western industrial society – by now a minority of the world's population.

The emancipation of former colonies, leading to the emergence of young independent states in Asia and Africa after the second World War, confronted the closed group of law-creating states with a majority of poor countries whose peoples often live on the margin of existence. In particular because of the specific economic needs of this new group, existing international law – which was designed to serve the needs of the developed, industrial countries – could hardly serve any longer as a basis of common standards for the 'expanded world.'[11] Under the prevailing circumstances the sociology of international law demands a qualitative change of the rules because both a quantitative and qualitative change has taken place in the circle of its subjects: the common concepts of 'Christian nations' and 'Civilized nations' being no longer relevant, the most important remaining common interest defended by traditional international law is the avoidance of international war, as embodied in the rules of negative peace. Particularly in the socio-economic field, the old rules have become contradictory to the sociological environment in which they have to operate. Accordingly, a struggle for the 'democratization' of international law has begun.

Weak as they were, in the economic as well as in the political field, the new countries initially were unable to change those foundations of international law which were often contrary to their interests. Yet, after they had been Members of the United Nations for some years, the new countries began to recognize their common interests and to realize their combined strength. They started their campaign of challenging those principles of international law, which inhibit their status as equal, vital, prosperous states, and which are destined to serve exclusively the interests of the 'old circle' of developed industrialized nations. In general, the developing nations have urged

---

[11] as Röling has called it, see note 4 supra; for an excellent discussion of the problem of assimilation of the new countries in international law in general see R. A. Falk – 'The New States and International Legal Order,' Hague Rec. Cours II ('66) pp. 10ff.; concerning the present context see in particular pp. 26-43.

that the following major changes in the field of political, social and economic international law be made:
1. In the political and social field, they have tried to outlaw colonialism, to establish the principle of non-discrimination, and to achieve recognition of universal Human Rights.
2. In the economic field, they have tried to replace the principle of liberalism with that of *protection*:
in stead of rules which merely restrict national activities, they demand rules of *co-operation*, and *aid* for the sake of the weak members of international society;
in stead of free competition and liberalism, they demand privileges and *inequality* for the sake of those who can not compete with the rich nations;
in stead of protection of foreign investments, they demand the right to dispose freely of their own national resources.

Being dependent on the rich nations for the achievement of the most of these aims, the developing nations were able to handle the latter one themselves. Consequently, they first challenged those rules of international law, which inhibited the free use of their national resources for their development, both within and outside the territorial borders as defined by traditional international law, by extending their 'sovereign rights' in a qualitative or quantitative sense.
To do this, they used, first, the concept of 'domestic jurisdiction.' This concept, indicating the exclusive competence of the sovereign state concerning a specific matter of law, was at the time introduced by President Wilson in the Covenant of the League of Nations in order to appeace internal American opposition to the League, basically by economic considerations.[12] Again in 1945, as a result of the extension of activities of the United Nations in the economic and social fields, the scope of 'domestic jurisdiction' was widened. By replacing the phrase 'a matter which by international law is solely within the domestic jurisdiction' (art. 15, par. 8 of the Covenant) with 'matters which are essentially within the domestic jurisdiction of any state' (art. 2, par. 7 of the Charter), the term was given a broader theoretical meaning.[13]
The initiative to stress the claim once made for economic reasons by the rich countries, was taken over by the poor. As soon as they began to use the claim against the interests of the rich, the last mentioned began to fight it. The developing countries took economic measures

[12] D. H. Miller – 'Drafting of the Covenant' (I. '28) p. 227.
[13] L. Preuss – 'Article 2, paragraph 7, of the Charter of the UN and matters of domestic jurisdiction,' 74 Rec. Cours ('49) p. 582.

which they considered to be outside the scope of international law, whereas the rich countries rejected them as violations of it.

The main source of legal conflict in this connection became the large-scale practice of nationalization of foreign property. In previous times such practice might even have provoked foreign military intervention. By now, nationalization of foreign property has become accepted by the rich countries as legal, but only under specific conditions, notably that expropriation be contributory to the economic development of the nationalizing country, and that it conforms to what they call 'the international standard,' requiring payment of what has often been described as 'prompt, adequate and effective compensation.'

The developing countries have put the entire question of nationalization within the larger question of 'the principle of self-determination.' In 1955, largely by the votes of these nations and in spite of the opposition of many Western states, the General Assembly's Third Committee adopted, for inclusion as part of what was to become in 1966 Article 1 of both International Covenants on Human Rights, the following provision:

> 1.1. 'All peoples have the right of self-determination. By virtue of that right they freely determine their political status and freely pursue their economic, social and cultural development.'
>
> 1.2. 'All peoples may, for their own ends, freely dispose of their national wealth and resources without prejudice to any obligations arising out of international economic co-operation, based upon the principle of mutual benefit, and international law. In no case may a people be deprived of its own means of subsistence.'

The statement also implied that the scope of the right of capital-exporting countries to protect the investments of their own nationals should be limited.[14] This endeavour was worked out in further Resolutions – e.g. Res. 1314 (XIII) and Res. 1515 (XV) – and resulted in Res. 1803 (XVII) of 14 December, 1962, the 'Declaration On Permanent Sovereignty Over Natural Resources,' in which, among other things, it is said that

> '1. The right of peoples and nations to permanent sovereignty over their natural wealth and resources must be exercised in the interest of their national development and of the well-being of the people of the State concerned'; and
>
> '7. Violation of the rights of peoples and nations to sovereignty over their natural wealth and resources is contrary to the spirit and principles of the Charter of the United Nations and hinders the development of international co-operation and the maintenance of peace.'

---

[14] see J. N. Hyde – 'Permanent Sovereignty Over Natural Wealth and Resources,' 50 A.J.I.L. ('56) p. 854.

This Declaration, moreover, paid direct attention to the problem of nationalization of foreign property. In traditional international law the 'international standard' was a device by which the more advanced states sought to safeguard the property of their citizens who invested capital in less developed parts of the world. In 1917, Mexico, however, adopted a socialist-inspired Constitution that paved the way for expropriation of foreign agrarian and oil properties without any such guarantee, which gave rise to heated diplomatic controversies. Although Mexico paid some compensation, it declared that no rule of international law required payment of compensation for expropriations of a 'general and impersonal character' that affected citizens and foreigners alike.[15] Thus the claim was introduced that nationalization be in fact a matter of domestic jurisdiction, and that the only standard to be accepted be that of non-discrimination between nationals and foreigners. At the 1930 Hague Conference for the Codification of International Law, the doctrine that aliens were entitled to an absolute 'international standard' – implying an international legal duty to pay compensations independent of national laws – was upheld by the narrow margin of 23 to 17 votes. The 17 anti-votes came from the seven Latin American nations that took part in the vote, four Asian and African nations, five successor states of central and eastern Europe, and Portugal.[16]

The norm of 'prompt, adequate and effective compensation' was further weakened after the second World War by the practice of many developing countries. In 1966, the Asian African Legal Consultive Committee, with Japan as the only dissentient, rejected the principle of an 'international standard' in favour of the 'equality of treatment doctrine,' and drafted a convention providing for payment for expropriated foreign property 'in accordance with local laws, regulations and orders.'[17]

The 'Declaration On Permanent Sovereignty Over Natural Resources' of 1962 has in fact left the question unsolved. During the discussions on this matter the Soviet Union tried to push the conflict to extremes by introducing an amendment, according to which would have been confirmed 'the inalienable right of peoples and nations to the unobstructed execution of nationalization, expropriation and other measures.' The amendment was rejected by 48 votes to 34, with 21 abstentees. Among the negative votes were those of ten African and Asian states (including India) and sixteen Latin American nations

[15] G. Withe – 'Nationalisation of Foreign Property' ('61) pp. 183 ff.
[16] G. H. Hackworth – 'Responsibility of States for Damages Caused in Their Territory to the Person or Property of Foreigners,' 24 A.J.I.L. ('30) p. 500.
[17] O. J. Lissitzyn – 'Int. Law in a Divided World,' 542 Int. Conc. ('63) p. 43.

while nineteen African and Asian and two Latin American states abstained.[18] The fact that so many developing countries were not prepared to vote in favour of the amendment should probably be explained by their fear that such a radical statement might endanger the future flow of any foreign capital. In the end, the wording of the Declaration has become as moderate, as it has become dubious: 'Nationalization, expropriation or requisitioning shall be based on grounds or reasons of public utility, security or the national interest which are recognized as overriding purely individual or private interests, both domestic and foreign.' But, whereas it is stated on the one hand that 'in such cases the owner shall be paid appropriate compensation, in accordance with the rules in force in the State taking such measures in the exercise of its sovereignty' – thus introducing the 'domestic jurisdiction claim' and the 'equality of treatment doctrine' –, it is added on the other hand, that such measures shall also be 'in accordance with international law' – thus leaving the question entirely open. It is of importance to note, however, that the rule of 'the exhaustion of local remedies' has been accepted; the Declaration states that 'in any case, where the question of compensation gives rise to a controversy, the national jurisdiction of the State taking such measures shall be exhausted,' which would seem to be to the favour of the developing countries, since the obligation to accept arbitration or international adjudication was made dependent on agreement.
The Declaration is absolutely clear in one thing, which is found in a provision in the Preambula. No responsibility is accepted in connection with foreign property acquired during the colonial period:

> 'nothing in paragraph 4 below in any way prejudices the position of any Member State on any aspect of the question of the rights and obligations of successor States and Governments in respect of property acquired before the accession to complete sovereignty of countries formerly under colonial rule.'

Thus it may be concluded that, although the legal conflict goes on, the developing countries have managed at least to put the formerly accepted rule in doubt. The doctrine of 'state responsibility' and the 'international standard,' considered by them merely as 'the legal garb that served to cloak and protect the imperialistic interests of the international oligarchy during the nineteenth century and the first part of the twentieth,'[19] is now challenged by the developing countries' extension of the doctrine of 'domestic jurisdiction.'

[18] UN Doc. A/PV. 1193 (14 Dec. '62) pp. 71 ff.
[19] J. Castañeda – 'The Underdeveloped Nations and the Development of International Law,' XV Int. Org. 1 ('61) p. 39.

Another example of the endeavour to extend their 'sovereign rights' over natural resources is the legal conflict provoked by the proclamation of exorbitantly wide territorial seas by many poor countries, the width of which has been determined by traditional international law to range between three and twelve miles.

The developing countries refer to the crucial importance of the sea as the solution of their existing and future nutrition problems. Besides, several of them try to build up a fishing industry as one of the solutions in solving their employment problems (in view of the usually overcrowded agricultural sector). Thus, many of them extend the width of their territorial seas as a solution for the problem of their need of maritime resources and as a solution for the problem of their inferiority in the competition with the fleets from the industrialized states.[20]

Some of them, like Indonesia and the Philippines, have done this by claiming that all of the waters between the islands of the archipellagoes constituting their territory are theirs.

Others have gone further, and have, like Equador, Peru, and Chile did twenty years ago, extended their territorial seas to 200 miles. In order to enforce their position vis-à-vis the industrialized states, they concluded a joint South Pacific Treaty. Later, another six Latin American States have adhered to the 200-miles concept, and in 1970 at a maritime Conference at Lima, where all but two Latin American States were represented, this proposal gained five new supporting countries. Incidents at sea have occurred, mainly with the United States, including the sequestration and fining of foreign fishing trawlers, in one case leading to the 'Tuna-war' between Equador and the United States, which resulted in severe deterioration of relations between the two countries. In the meantime, fishing has indeed become one of the major economic activities in these countries, Peru even having become the world's most important manufacturer of fishmeal.[21]

At the Geneva Conferences on the law of the sea of 1958 and 1960, the views on this question were so diverse, that it proved impossible to reach an agreement. However, not all developing countries are in favour of such enormous territorial seas, which they would be

---

[20] see J. J. G. Syatauw – = Some Newly Established Asian States and the Development of International Law' ('61) p. 199;
G. M. Abi-Saab – 'The Newly Independent States and the Rules of International Law: An Outline,' 8 Howard Law Journal (Spring '62) p. 111;
for an example of an equal claim at the Geneva Conference on the Law of the See (1958), see UN Doc. A/Conf. 13/41, p. 4.
[21] J. Lobos – 'The Sea, Development and Latin America,' XXI Rev. Int. Aff. 493 ('70) pp. 22 ff.

unable to control. A compromise proposal to extend the territorial waters to six miles, with a further six-mile zone in which the coastal states would have exclusive control of fisheries after a ten-year period, fell only one vote short of the two-thirds required for adoption.[22] Whatever the chances for some future agreement, it is evident that the challenge by the developing countries of the traditional three-mile zone, considered as harming their interests, has put this rule of international law in question as well.

Yet, it can be said that on the whole, notably in these fields in which they are dependent on the co-operation of the rich part of the world, the developing countries have achieved little.
Partly this is because they are only beginning to realize the necessity of a closer co-operation. Anxious, as they were, to build up and defend their national independence, they have stressed national sovereignty to such an extent that they often neglected the cooperation necessary in order to be powerful enough to change the rules to their advantage. What they achieved was little. What they tried to achieve was often not part of a coordinated effort. On every occasion (even within the framework of UNCTAD) they tried to gain what they could, often without basing their demands on a comprehensive strategy. Because they are divided among themselves and their endeavours are scattered, they have generally become disappointed by their incapacity to change existing rules, they remain most confused about the value of present day international law. Their attitude has approached voluntarism. A significant example of their existing doubt of the relevance of international law to their interests, is the constitution of India, whose article 51 (c) states: 'The State of India shall *endeavour to foster respect for* international law and treaty obligations in the dealings of organized peoples with another.'[23] This formulation is clearly distinguished from usual formulations, like 'the State conforms to the rules of international law.'

The developing countries, however, can not be blamed primarily. The major cause of their frustration has been the unwillingness of the rich countries to carry out their promises.
While the smaller countries of Europe saw their interests safeguarded to a considerable degree against the overwhelming economic power of the big industrial giants, they (and the larger rich nations) were not prepared to take similar protecting measures to benifit the non-industrialized poor countries of the Third World. The relations

[22] UN Doc. A/CONF. 19/8, 13th Plenary Mt. (26 April '60) para. 18.
[23] quoted in D. R. Deener – 'Some Post World War II Trends in the Relationships of Municipal Law to Treaty Law,' V Ind. J.I.L. ('65).

between rich and poor remained dominated largely by laissez-faire liberalism and remained oriented towards the needs of the industrialized, at the expense of the poor.

What we have today is a body of international law which is not only the product of the conscious activity of the European mind, but which has also drawn its essence from a common source of European beliefs and interests; in both of these aspects it is still mainly of Western European origin. The fundamental contradiction between this origin and today's world in which the body of law has to operate, however, is too often overlooked.[24] Perhaps, in the rich part of the world, many still think too much in terms of the 'civilized' if not in terms of the 'colonial' Power. Many international lawyers obviously have great difficulty in accepting the consequences of the idea of equality of all peoples, although they pay lip-service to the principles of the UN Charter. A notable example of the difficulty to adapt oneself to changing circumstances is the European Convention on Human Rights of 1950, which in art. 7 still speaks of 'general principles of law recognized by civilized nations.' On the other hand the (Universal) International Covenants on Human Rights of 1966 speak, like the Universal Declaration, of 'all members of the human family.' Also article 38 para 1c of the Statute of the Court of International Justice still speaks of 'the civilized nations,' a phrase dating from 1920.

Many scholars seem incapable of accepting any doubt as to the righteousness and permanent usefulness of the rules they helped to create. Thus, one of the outstanding Dutch teachers, Verzijl, comes to the conclusion, after having noticed the European foundation of the system of international law, that

> 'all the newcomers to the international community' (note the word 'community' in this context!) 'have in fact done.... was to adopt *en bloc* the traditional law of nations as it has developed throughout the course of Western European history .... It would seem very unlikely that any revolutionary ideas will appear as a result of the entrance of these new members which will have power to challenge or supersede the general principles and customary rules of law which have shown their vitality by standing the test of time and circumstance.'[25]

---

[24] Lissitzyn, recognizing the contradiction, has proposed to change the wording of art. 38 para. 1b of the Statute of the International Court of Justice. In stead of the source of law as it is described there, 'International custom, as evidence of a general practice accepted as law,' he proposes the wording 'the practice of states as evidence of general consensus or expectations accepted as law.' Thus the Court would have to take into account any substantial disagreement as to existing rules; see Q. Wright – 'Custom as a basis for international law in the postwar World,' VII Ind. J.I.L. ('67) p. 1.
[25] J. H. W. Verzijl – 'Western European Influence on the Foundation of International Law,' I Intern. Rel. 4 (Oct. '55) pp. 145-146.

These words of an eminent lawyer show a great lack of understanding of the enormous changes that took place in international society, or at least show a lack of insight into its unavoidable legal consequences, if international law is to be kept alive as an effective worldwide system. Verzijl considers the present existing rules as 'one of the outstanding proofs of the ultimate unity of the human race,' whereas they contribute to increasing inequality and whereas 2/3 of the human race is fighting to change them....

If we consider the de-colonization process – of the total of 45% of the entire world's population living in colonies in 1945, only 3% is left –, if we consider the developments in the field of universal Human Rights, in the field of aid, in the field of protection of the poor countries (see the next section), it is hard to understand how that body of traditional international law – as far as it opposes the interests of the newcomers – can be deemed to have 'stood the test of time and circumstance.'

If international law should be a proof of and contribute to human unity, it is inevitable that some of its foundations be rebuilt, accepting the present needs of the new international society and the consent of its various important segments as its starting point. At this moment, international law lags far behind the development of international society.

3. *Towards a strategy of peace through an international law of global welfare*

3.1. *Historical preamble: developments on the national scene*

The search for a sociologically more justified body of international law as part of a system of positive peace does not imply a complete break with existing rules. As a matter of fact, strong arguments can be put forward supporting the proposition that this kind of law has its roots in legal history. These arguments will be discussed in sections 3.2.1.-3.2.3.

Before turning to them, however, it might be illuminating to go back for a moment to the end of the 19th century, and see what happened on the *national* scene in the industrializing states of Europe.

The basic concept of economic liberalism as the pivot of both national and international economic thinking was to be called into question by the end of the 19th century. On the international scene, liberalism conflicted with a system of sovereign, independent states, which soon realized the necessity of protecting their national economy by measures restricting the mechanisms of a free international market system. Wherever international economic acts were allowed, the principle of equality and liberal treatment remained obligatory; but in general the states turned to a decentralized system of state protection of national economies.

On the national scene, the same was bound to occur: classic economic liberalism led to the impoverishment and the alienation of the workers in the towns and countryside. As a result, the industrial revolution contributed to their solidarity. On the one hand, it was gradually realized that an entirely free market system could certainly not guarantee increasing and continuous prosperity; on the other hand, the organization and growing power of the industrial proletariat threatened to break out into violence. Thus, in the first place, it was gradually accepted that the interests of continuous national prosperity demanded economic planning and state control, while in the second place, it was accepted that both the principles of humanitarianism and the interests of economic prosperity demanded that the entire population should share the fruits of progress. In order to keep the system going, the private entrepreneurs had to accept the Trade Union, which was to become one of the most positive factors contributing to the gradual recognition of minimum social rights and protection. Such protection was given by the national authorities, which in due course came to control national economic life to an ever higher degree.

Once it had come to this, the way towards the recognition of social rights and securities on larger scale was open. Particularly after 1919 social rights became broader in scope and more specific, and the tragic consequences of the 1929-economic depression have in many countries given rise to a demand for active state intervention in order to solve and prevent socio-economic problems. Working hours, children's labour, women's labour, minimum wages, employment, and various social securities became accepted as fundamental civil rights. Today, everywhere in the industrialized world states accept the primary responsibility for the implementation and preservation of these rights by means of a national socio-economic strategy, and all their Constitutions have incorporated as a general principle the duty of the state to take care of its citizens.[26] Thus economic liberalism as a national principle was restricted to a high degree. It is of great importance to note here that this policy of intervention in national economic life and protection of social rights of all citizens explains much of the present prosperity in the industrialized countries.

---

[26] see ECOSOC's 'Preliminary Study of Issues Relating to the Realization of Economic and Social Rights Contained in the Universal Declaration of Human Rights and in the International Covenant on Economic, Social and Cultural Rights,' E/CN 4/988 (Jan. 20, '69) pp. 9-12.

Prosperity of the lower classes contributed to the prosperity of the entrepreneurs, while state intervention prevented depressions from occurring too often and guaranteed the steady increase of prosperity for *all* sections of the population. The rich countries which at home have been most successful in national consolidations and economic progress have been those which have carried out the egalitarian reforms most ardently.[27]

These internal policies can now be seen to have been in the long run of interest not only to the backward but also to the most prosperous geographical regions and sections of the population in rich countries. There undoubtedly exists to a considerable degree a

> 'harmony of interests. But it has been a 'created harmony,' reached by not letting the play of the market forces unfold themselves unhampered, but by regulating them and harnessing them to serve the common interests, to which belongs protecting and advancing the lagging regions and groups of people...... The developed countries are now developed and politically consolidated partly because, throughout their recent history, they have interfered in the play of the market forces and framed policies that counteracted and corrected the adverse effects of those forces.'[28]

Today, we have on the international level a situation comparable to the situation on the national level at the end of the 19th century. Again, the economic picture is characterized by extreme inequalities, lack of overall planning, and the need of protection of the poor.

At the time, on the national scene, the idea of a community and a law protecting the interests of that entire community, was accepted. Today, a similar acceptance is needed on the international level.

Such acceptance, however, is only very slowly beginning to develop. Two World Wars and a violent decolonization period were apparently necessary before the old nations accepted the idea of the world-wide expansion of the human race. They refused to accept merely the idea of racial equality at the end of the First World War, but the Second World War initiated enormous changes. Both the emerging Cold War and the decolonization process demanded the organization of world peace and the acceptance of the idea of a global community consisting of equal subjects under international law. The steadily enlarging circle of 'Peace-loving Nations,' however, proved to be merely united in its endeavour to be 'Negative Peace-loving Nations.' The development of international law was not allowed to follow political developments, the older nations fearing that their interests were going to be harmed. International law remained largely what

[27] G. Myrdal, p. 296.
[28] idem pp. 297, 294.

Bluntschli described in 1867 as 'Das Moderne Völkerrecht der Zivilisierten Staaten,' and it was not without reason that Nehru begged the U.N. General Assembly in 1948 to realize that the enlarged circle of nations entailed a new world picture and new international problems:

'May I say, as a representative from Asia, that the world is something bigger than Europe, and you will not solve your problems by thinking that the problems of the world are mainly European problems.'

Like the industrial proletariat in the European countries at the time, the poor countries now claim that they have been exploited long enough, and that the rich are under an obligation to let them share the general prosperity. Then, the idea of the national community was put into practice; but now, the idea of the transnational community is still little more than a dream. International economic law has lost its connection with national law. It is still mainly measured in terms of *restraint*, providing rules intended to restrict political and economic action. *Like national law at the time, international law has reached the point where it must become a law of co-operation, which implies the development of a law of assistance to and protection of the weak, if it is to survive as a common value.*

Such development is in the first place – as has been concluded in the preceding Chapters of this book – in the interest of peace. If peace is wanted, a world community is needed; if a world community is needed, a body of law suited to build that community should be realized. At this moment, however, the welfare state is nationalistic, and this holds not only for the 'capitalists,' but also – perhaps even more – for the lower echelons of the population in the rich countries. But, as Barbara Ward observes

'it is time for the rich to realize that in an interdependent world – and Heaven knows our interdependence cannot be denied when we all stand under the shadow of atomic destruction – the principles of the general welfare cannot stop at the limits of our national frontiers. It has to go forward, it has to include the whole family of man.'[29]

And again, it may be stressed that *this is also in the ultimate economic interests of the rich nations.*
Until recently the arguments put forward to sustain this thesis were based on the belief that the development of the Third World would require no major sacrifices from the rich countries, that on the contrary, such development would further their own economic growth, and that such growth might even be virtually limitless.

[29] Barbara Ward – 'The Rich Nations and the Poor Nations' ('62) pp. 152-153.

Against this background the argument could run as follows:
People in developed countries can draw the conclusion from a national experience, which has shown that the long-term interests of the rich have been served by providing for the welfare of the poor. What they are used to seeing as mere generosity, is a very rational and profitable generosity. Such is explained by Gunnar Myrdal, when he says, in relation to international trade:

> 'As a general rule, cutting down the restrictions of developed countries against imports from underdeveloped countries should actually be in the long-term interest of the developed countries. The industries where the latter countries could compete – resource-based and labor-intensive – are usually not the industries which it is in the developed countries' interest to promote or even to preserve at home. In the developed countries they are often low-wage industries. Rational planning in developed productivity countries should regularly result in moving their scarce labor resources to high-productivity industries, not in tying them to low-wage industries.'[30]

Moreover, prosperity in the Third World entails enormous new markets for the increasing level of production in the industrialized countries. This is of great future importance if large-scale future unemployment is to be prevented (to this we will come back in section 3.3.). It has been calculated, furthermore, that it is not only in the long-term economic interest of the rich states to promote world-wide prosperity, but that this can be done with little or no sacrifice. For the Netherlands, for instance, it has been calculated than an annual contribution of 2% of its Gross National Product to development aid would result in nothing more than a unique stop merely on the *growth* of the national product for three months, after which period the old growth rate of 4% would be re-established. Apart from fear of a decrease of national income, and trouble in specific economic sectors – which should be expected merely in case of fail-planning – another worry put forward regularly is the supposed negative effect on the balance of payments (this worry should also explain the phenomenon of 'tied' aid agreements). This is not the place to go into this problem in any detail, but objective analysis reveals that the payment difficulties of developed countries are self-inflicted and have little to do with their possible liberation, of imports from developing countries. They are mainly the result of internal and external policies on quite other levels, like inflatory fail-planning and extravagant military expenditures.[31] Whatever be the causes of present exchange difficulties, or the perceived danger of such difficulties for the future, it is a very strange situation indeed when the rich nations refuse to take

[30] G. Myrdal, p. 299.
[31] see idem, pp. 300-307.

even very restricted measures of help to the poor countries, whereas they allow at the same time monstruous expenditures on armaments which upset their entire economy'....

Recently, data have become widely available suggesting that the background against which such optimistic future growth-projections were developed may no longer be realistic. Basically, these data suggest that we are approaching the limits of growth, and that the welfare gap could not be bridged unless substantial sacrifices are made by the rich countries. The merits of these data and their consequences are discussed below in section 3.3. and its sub-sections. Anticipating what is discussed there, it can be said here that if these data are essentially correct, i.e. if the world's reserves of natural resources and energy and the level of environmental pollution do not allow the industrial development of the Third World to continue unless the rich part of the world would restrict production in the industrial field, *it can still be maintained that the bridging of the welfare gap is to the ultimate economic interest of the rich countries.* In this case another kind of self-interest becomes involved, namely that of conservation of natural resources and prevention of environmental pollution, which – for reasons explained also in section 3.3. – can be achieved only within the framework of a global development strategy.

A change of principles as proposed here, being both in the interest of world peace, and in the interest of long-term prosperity, for all nations alike, demands that part of the principle of absolute national sovereignty is reduced. But theories, which in this era state that security and prosperity depend on the strength of national walls, can hardly be taken serious. National security today depends in the first place on acceptance of the idea of interdependence and co-operation. This implies to some extent the abolition of the priciple of the national state as the ultimate social goal; this means acceptance in the international sphere of the idea of protection of the weak against unrestricted freedom of the strong. 'The correct attitude,' Kunz wrote in 1950, 'must be equidistant from utopia and from cynical minimising; neither over-estimation, nor underestimation.'[32]
This, I think, is practical realism.

The question, then, is to what extent this kind of international law is developing at the present time. This will be the topic of the next three sections.

[32] J. L. Kunz – 'The Swing of the Pendulum,' 22 AJIL ('50) p. 140; as to this approach see also W. D. Coplin – 'International Law and Assumptions about the State System,' XVII World Politics (July '65) pp. 615-634.

3.2. *The legal roots of the strategy*

To what extent is a socio-economic international law emerging (or has emerged), fulfilling those polemological conditions which serve the aims of positive peace, i.e. which aims notably at the achievement of global prosperity and more equality, protection of the poor, substantial and continuous growth in the less developed part of the world, exclusion of political (above all Cold War) manoeuvring through aid, and – in view of the restricted resources – maximum possible co-operation?
Notwithstanding the general negative picture that has been described above, it can be said that some general positive developments in this respect can be observed. Since the second World War, some legal developments have been initiated, mainly by the United Nations, indicating that a kind of 'soft' law is emerging in the field discussed here. In particular three developments can be observed:
1. the erosion of exclusive national competence on social and economic affairs through the recognition of transnational human rights and duties in the socio-economic field;
2. the recognition of the group of 'developing countries' as special subjects of international law, having specific privileges in the economic field;
3. the emergence of 'mankind' as a supreme social and legal value, and the duty of all states to co-operate for common welfare.

3.2.1. *The emergence of transnational social and economic human rights*

It can certainly be said that one of the most notable developments in the realm of modern international law is the emergence of the individual as one of its subjects. Until far into the present century the only important subject of international law was the state. Gradually, international and supra-national organizations, and the individual joined the national state, thereby breaking through the exclusively inter-national character of traditional rules and priciples.
Nineteenth century international law had almost entirely lost sight of the individual human being and confined itself to rules limiting the exercise of state power for reasons unconnected with standards of justice and morality, unless such values might affect the maintenance of the international system.[33] Gradually, international problems like the protection of minorities and aid to refugees received more attention, and eventually new rules and principles began to develop

---

[33] M. Kaplan & N. de B. Katzenbach, pp. 63-64.

in the socio-economic field as well, as it happened in the case of national Constitutions. This process, putting the individual into the center of international legal attention, and decreasing the absolute competence of the national state in social and economic affairs, was developed mainly after the second World War, but it can be traced in former periods.

1º. As a point of departure the Covenant of the League of Nations can be mentioned, whose article 23a obliged the Members of the League to

'endeavour to secure and maintain fair and human conditions of labour for men, women and children, both in their own countries and in all countries to which their commercial and industrial relations extend, and for that purpose will establish and maintain the necessary international organisations.'

These careful words, although not being worth more than an intention-declaration, meant something new in the international environment of the time: states accepted the duty of trying to bring about welfare measured by some international standard. Though originally intended to serve as a safeguard against Japan's industrial expansion, this provision can be considered a starting point. (It is an example of a rule of law, intended originally to function to the specific benefit of its protagonists against the interests of others, but gradually evolving into a general rule of law).

2º. A related development was the foundation of the International Labour Organization. This step, by the envisaged participation of representatives of employers' and workers' organizations and by legal, technical and political control over the heads of national governments, meant a real break-through: the state as a hitherto supreme authority was to become responsible to an international forum.

3º. The Charter of the United Nations, however, incorporates new ideas on a larger scale. Racial equality and fundamental Human Rights (though put in very vague terms, particularly since they were incompatible with the still existing colonial system) were declared to be new principles of international law, and by the introduction of such principles the exclusive competence of the national state in the socio-economic field was to be called in question. Individual rights were recognized irrespective of concessions by the state, without any reference to nationality or state authority. This endeavour to make the individual a more important point of reference than the state, represented a clear challenge to the old assumption about the state-system, in particular now that in practice these vague norms are being given concrete forms.

The Charter, moreover, linked these fundamental rights with peace.

'During the time of the 'Christian nations,' as Röling puts it, 'there were religious values, during the time of the 'Civilized nations' cultural values, during the time of the 'Peace-loving nations the issue became man himself, man as such.'[34]
Illustrative in this respect is article 55, which reads:

'With a view to the creation of conditions of stability and well-being which are necessary for peaceful and friendly relations among nations based on respect for the principle of equal rights and self-determination of peoples, the United Nations shall promote:
a. higher standards of living, full employment and conditions of economic and social progress and development;
b. solutions of international economic, social, health and related problems; and international cultural and educational co-operation; and
c. universal respect for, and observance of, human rights and fundamental freedoms for all without distinction as to race, sex, language, or religion.'

Similar rights were extended to the peoples of trust-territories in article 76 and, in art. 73, to peoples in colonies. The articles of the Charter, however, were also drafted in a very careful manner. Nowhere these rights as such were *guaranteed*; it was only determined that the purpose of the United Nations and the duty of its Members is to 'encourage' them, to 'further' their realization, to 'promote' respect for them. The Charter therefore, although initiating a fundamental change of thought, is by itself little more than a solemn declaration of intentions.

4°. The Universal Declaration of Human Rights (adopted by the UN General Assembly on 10 Dec. 1948) was different. This document no longer spoke of 'promoting' or 'furthering,' but *rights and such were declared to exist*. A few important examples are mentioned:

art. 1 – 'All human beings are born free and equal in dignity and rights. They, endowed with reason and conscience, should act toward one another in a spirit of brotherhood.'
art. 2 – 'Everyone is entitled to all the rights and freedoms set forth in this Declaration, without distinction of any kind, such as race, colour, sex, language, religion, political or other opinion, national, or social origin, property, birth, or other status.'[35]
art. 23 – 'Everyone has the right to work, to the free choice of employment, to just and favourable conditions of work and to protection against unemployment. Everyone, without any discrimination, has the right to equal pay for equal work.'

---

[34] B. V. A. Röling – 'Human Rights and the War Problem,' XV Ned. T.I.P. ('68) p. 348.
[35] note that here, in contrast to the UN Charter, national origin is expressly mentioned. This could be considered as a further step, if the opinion is correct that the Charter did not yet recognize fundamental rights to people living in a country where nobody would enjoy them. The Charter is ambiguous here by its careful wording.

art. 25 : 1 'Everyone has the right to a standard of living adequate for the health and well-being of himself and his family, including food, clothing, housing and medical care and necessary social services and rights to security in the event of unemployment, sickness, disability, widowhood, old age or other lack of livelihood in circumstances beyond his control.'

art. 28 – 'Everyone is entitled to a social and international order in which the rights and freedoms set forth in this Declaration can be fully realized.'

But even though in the Declaration these rights were proclaimed as existing, yet their value was diminished, since the Preamble states that one should regard 'this Universal Declaration of Human Rights *as a common standard of achievement* for all peoples and nations.'

Yet, the difference remains that the Charter always speaks of endeavours in a certain direction, whereas the Declaration mentions the rights themselves. In order to qualify the Declaration as more advanced than the Charter, however, its legal significance should be beyond doubt. Therefore some attention must be payed to the question of the legal power of this UN-Declaration.

A Declaration is a solemn Resolution of the General Assembly, which has only the power to make recommendations but not decisions (except on some matters like the UN-household). Several arguments, however, can be raised suggesting a stronger degree of legal validity in particular in the case of this Declaration.

In the first place, many authors are inclined to consider Declarations as the expression of the opinion of the world community on a certain matter of law: particularly if they are adopted unanimously. They are inclined, therefore, to attach great value to such documents as the Universal Declaration.[36] One might view Mrs. Roosevelt's remark in this light when she said that the Universal Declaration 'might well become the Magna Charta of all Mankind.'

The term 'Declaration' – in contrast to 'Constitution' – tries to pretend that the General Assembly reaffirms existing law in such a Resolution; one can say 'pretend,' since several important examples (for instance the Declaration on De-colonization of 1960 and the Declaration on Natural Resources of 1962) clearly incorporate new rules, the legally binding character of which had to be established yet. This is not to say that Declarations would have no legal meaning in such cases:

---

[36] see for instance M. Virally – 'La Valeur Juridique des Recommendations des Organisations Internationales,' II Ann. Fr. D.I. ('56) p. 66; A. J. P. Tammes – 'Decisions of International Organs as a Source of International Law,' 94 Rec. Cours ('58) p. 261; Johnson – 'The effect of Resolutions of the General Assembly of the United Nations,' 32 B.Y.I.L. ('55-'56) p. 97; R. A. Falk – 'On the quasi-legislative competence of the G.A.,' 60 A.J.I.L. ('66) pp. 782-791.

they can – the term 'soft law' is often used – strongly contribute to the creation of new customary law.

In the second place, the argument has been put forward, that the Universal Declaration constitutes an authoritative interpretation of the Charter. This opinion was expressed by Cassin during the debates on the Declaration, where he said: 'its legal value derives from the fact that it may be considered an authorized interpretation of the Charter.'[37] Similarly the Montral Conference (March '68) reached the conclusion that 'the Universal Declaration of Human Rights constitutes an authoritative interpretation of the Charter of the highest order, and has over the years become a part of customary international law.'[38] Castañeda calls this way of thinking 'a possible interpretation.'[39]

It may seem rather extreme to speak of 'a part of customary international law' at this moment; it is doubtful whether one can put it in such absolute terms. It seems indisputable, however, that the practice of the United Nations – and this is the third argument – has strengthened the legal validity of the Declaration, because of the fact that it has been used during many discussions *as if it were indeed hard law already*. This has been the case in particular in connection with the discussions on de-colonization and racial discrimination, and, indeed, several important Declarations are based on this view; thus the 'Declaration on the granting of independence to colonial countries and peoples,' Res. 1514 (XV), states categorically:

> '*All states shall observe faithfully and strictly* the provisions of the Charter of the United Nations, *the Universal Declaration of Human Rights* and the present Declaration on the basis of equality, non-interference in the internal affairs of all States, and respect for the sovereign rights of all peoples and their territorial integrity.'

In the same sense the 'United Nations Declaration on the elimination of all forms of racial discrimination,' Res. 1904 (XVIII), states:

> 'Every State shall promote respect for and observance of human rights and fundamental freedoms in accordance with the Charter of the United Nations and *shall fully and faithfully observe* the provisions of the present Declaration, *the Universal Declaration of Human Rights* and the Declaration on the granting of independence to colonial countries and peoples.'

Thus we have two solemn Declarations, both of them *adopted unanimously*, which speak of observing the provisions of the Universal

---

[37] UN Doc. A/C 3/SR ('48) p. 92, and Doc. E/SR. ('48) p. 25.
[38] J. Int. Comm. Jur. 2 ('68) p. 95.
[39] J. Castañeda, p. 47.

Declaration of Human Rights, as one's legal duty. In this connection it may be remembered that on several occasions the non-implementation of Human Rights mentioned in the Universal Declaration (racial discrimination, apartheid, oppression of economic and political rights) has been called by the United Nations 'a crime against humanity' (see e.g. Res. 2022 (XX); 2070 (XX); 2144 (XXI); 2184 (XXI); 2202 (XXI); 2262 (XXII)). In connection with racial discrimination, the situation in S. Africa (Res. 2307 (XXII)), and that in S. Rhodesia (Res. 2022 (XX) have even been characterized by the General Assembly as 'a grave threat to international peace and security.' Thus the legal validity of the Declaration has been increased to such an extent that the non-implementation of Human Rights recognized in it is considered to be a threat to the peace, on the basis of which action has been recommended under Chapter VII of the UN Charter.

In the fourth place, since 1958 a great number of states, beginning with Guinea, have inserted in their constitutions statements expressing their adherence to the Universal Declaration of Human Rights; in some cases (Algeria, 1963; Rwanda, 1962) a direct reference is contained in the body of the Constitution; in others (Senegal, 1963; Dahomey, 1964) the same has been done in the Preamble.[40]

In the fifth place, many Resolutions and treaties, which were adopted after 1948 in this field, contain a reference to the Universal Declaration.

On such grounds it can be argued, that this Declaration has resulted in an international practice which has created at least great expectations concerning the arising of new international law, transcending national frontiers and pushing back state sovereignty.

The Universal Declaration, like the UN Charter, refers to the relation between welfare and peace. In the Preamble it is said to be

'essential, if man is not to be compelled to have recourse as a last resort to rebellion against tyranny and oppression, that human rights should be protected by the rule of law.'

5⁰. Since 1948, innumerable Resolutions have been adopted, and many treaties have been drafted, as such adding to the expectation that a new body of law in this field is emerging. To mention a few treaties:

Conventions on the Prohibition of Discrimination in Employment and Occupation (I.L.O., 1958), and in Education (UNESCO, 1960); the European Convention on the Protection of Human Rights and

---

[40] see the UN-study, note 26 supra p. 46.

Fundamental Freedoms (1950); the Forced Labour Convention (ILO, 1957); the Convention on the Political Rights of Women (1952); the Convention on the Elimination of All Forms of Racial Discrimination (1966).

6°. This development has culminated in the unanimous adoption by the General Assembly of a Resolution embodying the International Convention on Economic, Social and Cultural Rights of 1966.[41] This Convention was intended to be a codification of what had been reached by e.g. the Universal Declaration of Human Rights, as article 5 para. 2 states:

> 'No restriction upon or derogation from any of the fundamental human rights recognized or existing in any country in virtue of law, conventions, regulations or custom shall be admitted on the pretext that the present Covenant does not recognize such rights or that it recognizes them to a lesser extent.'

Thus, the Universal Declaration was certainly not abolished by the adoption of the Treaty, which – as we shall see below when we deal with the duty of co-operation – is very important to note.
The Treaty has derived its formulations largely from the Universal Declaration. Again a few important provisions can be mentioned:

art. 6.1 – 'The States Parties to the present Covenant recognize the right to work, which includes the right of everyone to the opportunity to gain his living by work which he freely chooses or accepts, and will take appropriate steps to safeguard this right.'
art. 7 – 'The States Parties to the present Covenant recognize the right of everyone to the enjoyment of just and favourable conditions of work.'
art. 9.1 – 'The States Parties to the present Covenant recognize the right of everyone to social security, including social insurance.'
art. 11.1 – 'The States Parties to the present Covenant recognize the right of everyone to an adequate standard of living for himself and his family, including adequate food, clothing and housing, and the continuous improvement of living conditions.'
art. 12.1 – 'The States Parties to the present Covenant recognize the right of everyone to the highest attainable standard of physical and mental health.'
art. 13.1 – 'The States Parties to the present Covenant recognize the right of everyone to education.'

In this connection the question should be raised, whether the Covenant can be considered to constitute a real contribution to the *transnational* realization of Human Rights. The argument has been put forward that this Convention directs itself exclusively to the ratifying states independently, obliging them solely to take care of the realization of the respective rights within their respective countries.[42]

---

[41] Annex to GA Res. 2200 (XXI) Dec. 16, '66.
[42] see Harris (US), A/C. 3/Off. Rec., 21st Sess., 1455 para. 31 ('66).

A relevant article in question is article 2, which reads:

> 1. 'Each State Party to the present Covenant undertakes to take steps, individually and through international assistance and co-operation, especially economic and technical, to the maximum of its available resources, with a view to achieving progressively the full realization of the rights recognized in the present Covenant by all appropriate means, including particularly the adoption of legislative measures.
> 2. The States Parties to the Covenant undertake to guarantee that the rights enunciated in the present Covenant will be exercised without discrimination of any kind as to race, colour, sex, language, religion, political or other opinion, national or social origin, property or other status.'

The same problem arises more specifically in relation to article 6, dealing with the right to work.

The wording of these articles can indeed be understood as being directed at the national, internal scene of the contracting party. In particular the last part of paragraph 1, 'including particularly the adoption of legislative measures' seems to support the argument. On the other hand, taking the purpose of the Treaty into consideration, the possibility cannot be excluded that these provisions should also be understood as being directed at the supra-national scene:

In the first place, one could consider the history of the Treaty, which strongly suggests the endeavour to create Human Rights independently of the national state. Such was the purpose of the provisions in the Charter, in the Universal Declaration and in many subsequent Resolutions. In this light one could argue that the ultimate purpose of the Treaty is to achieve the consent from as many states as possible, so that one could in due course speak of the existence of a new general customary law which equally binds non-signatories.

One could add, moreover, that most countries are in a position which renders their endeavours useless, *unless* they are assisted by supporting measures taken by and in the rich countries. Thus, one could interpret the sentence mentioned before ('the adoption of legislative measures') as being *also* intended to mean: those national measures which are adopted by the rich countries – for instance the restriction of certain economic sectors of specific interest to the developing states – as a means to enable the poor countries to realize better conditions for their nationals (although it seems probable that the authors did not have this interpretation in mind, when they drafted the article).

Finally, one should remember the Preamble in which it is recognized that 'the ideal of free human beings enjoying freedom from fear and want can only be achieved if conditions are created whereby *everyone* may enjoy his economic, social and cultural rights.' These words are indicative of the interdependence of well-being in the various countries of the world today. There seems to be no undisputable proof that the 'supra-national' interpretation was *not* the principal intention of the Treaty, and therefore its provisions, recognized by means of *unanimous adoption* by the Members of the United Nations, may be thought to contribute to the expectation that the recognition of these fundamental Human Rights is no longer exclusively dependent on national efforts.

7⁰. In order to finish the present list of examples, it should be noted that the adoption of the draft Treaty in 1966 has been followed by many Resolutions, intended to encourage states to ratify this Treaty. These Resolutions also influence and put pressure upon all UN-Members to act according to the provisions in this and other documents. One example will be mentioned here, the 'Declaration on Social Progress and Development' (Res. 2542 (XXIV), Dec. 11, 1969).
This Declaration is a remarkable document in three ways:
In the first place, this Resolution seems to be a step back (in comparison with preceding documents), in that it places the individual rights in a more relative framework. Whereas former documents speak of the recognition of this and that right, this Declaration merely demands, that

> 'All peoples and all human beings without distinction as to race, colour, sex, language, religion, nationality, ethnic origin, family or social status, or political or other conviction, *shall have* the right to live in freedom and dignity and to enjoy the fruits of social progress....'

This careful wording could – in view of recent legal history – indeed be considered a 'testimonium paupertatis'; to consider it as a step back, however, would seem to be conditioned by a provision in the Preamble, which 'recalls' the rights as recognized in the Universal Declaration of Human Rights and its subsequent documents.
This Declaration is also remarkable in that it urges explicitly that care should be taken 'particularly (of) persons in low-income groups'; a provision recalling the recognition of the specific status of 'low-income countries.' This will be discussed in the next section.
In the third place, this Declaration is noteworthy in that it speaks – be it in a rather indirect way – of *duties* of the individual by international law; thus it is said in art. 1 that all human beings 'should, on their part, contribute to it' – 'it' meaning the right for all 'to live in dignity and freedom and to enjoy the fruits of social progress,' as quoted above. This leads us to the question of the emergence of horizontal rights and duties, rights and duties of individuals vis-à-vis each other, extended to them directly by international law.
This development began – as far as international duties are concerned

– in the field of the international law of war. The Tribunals of Nueremberg and Tokyo established the rule that individuals are under legal duty to refrain from war activities forbidden by international law, irrespective of their national laws and orders. In the field of socio-economic international law it can be said that a similar development is emerging, even though it is only in an embryonic stage.

The Universal Declaration of Human Rights contains several provisions in this respect. First, the Preamble contains a sentence in which the General Assembly proclaims this document 'to the end that every individual and every organ of society keeping this declaration constantly in mind shall strive by teaching and education to promote respect for these rights and freedoms.' Article 1 is clearly directed at the individual, when stating:

> 'All human beings are born free and equal in dignity and rights. *They*, endowed with reason and conscience, should act toward one another in a spirit of brotherhood.'

Article 30 also seems to be directed partly to the individual:

> 'Nothing in this declaration may be interpreted as implying for any state, group, *or person* any right to engage in any activity or to perform any act aimed at the destruction of any of the rights and freedoms set forth herein.'

A similar direct approach can be found in some provisions of the 1966-Convention, the Preamble of which states among other things:

> 'Realizing that the individual, having duties to other individuals and to the community to which he belongs, is under a responsibility to strive for the promotion and observance of the rights recognized in the present Covenant.....';

and article 5 repeats the Declaration:

> 'Nothing in the present Covenant may be interpreted as implying for any State, group or person any right to engage in any activity or to perform any act aimed at the destruction of any of the rights or freedoms recognized herein.'

Although such provisions are of dubious value and character at the present stage of development of international law, they add to that new body of law concerned with fundamental social and economic rights and duties, transcending national borders and independent of governmental action, which is emerging.

The present author is inclined to take a middle position between two opposing opinions in this connection. On the one hand, some authors minimize or even negate the significance of recent developments. Lauterpacht is a good example of this group. He says:

> 'As a result of the Charter of the U.N. – as well as other changes in International Law – the individual has acquired a status and a statue which have transformed him from an object of international compassion into a subject of international right. For in so far as International Law as embodied in the Charter and elsewhere recognizes fundamental rights of the individual independent of the law of state, to that extent it constitutes the individual a subject of the law of nations.' [43]

On the other side we have Schwarzenberger who wrote in the same year:

> 'It does not appear that the international protection of human rights and fundamental freedom as envisaged by the Charter of the U.N., is likely to affect the basic position of the individual as an object of International Law. Such a fundamental change as the transformation of the individual into a subject of supra-national law presupposes the transformation of the existing world society into a federal state.' [44]

The first opinion would seem to be too optimistic, the second one too pessimistic. With regard to Schwarzenberger's point of view it might be argued that without having attained the federal world State, the continuous effort to realize fundamental Human Rights and Duties can very well accelerate and promote supra-national elements in international law; in particular in a non-political field. That his opinion is too negative and pessimistic, is suggested by legal practices in Europe based on the European Convention of Human Rights. Without claiming the existence of new universal customary hard law, it seems justified to conclude that we have reached a stage in which governments no longer have a free competence to decide on the rights and the duties of their nationals in the socio-economic field – we can speak here of 'erosion of domestic jurisdiction' – and in which the international society has recognized in principle the right of all human beings to a life free from fear and want, endowed with human dignity and well-being.

3.2.2. *The recognition of the 'developing countries' as special subjects of international law*

A second legal development of importance is the gradual recognition of the 'developing countries' as a specific group of subjects of international economic law which have the right to enjoy special privileges vis-à-vis the 'developed countries.'

---

[43] H. Lauterpacht – 'International Law and the Human Rights' ('55) p. 4.
[44] G. Schwarzenberger – 'A Manual of International Law' ('50) p. 35.

This legal process was prepared by the legal disputes which arose because of the new claims made by the newly independent states concerning their sovereign rights, and by the extensive effort of the United Nations to achieve some realization of socio-economic Human Rights for the Third World (by its campaign for development assistance). In relation to the first point, the legal conflict on the right to nationalize foreign property should be remembered. One of the few guarantees which the rich countries were able to agree upon with the developing countries, was the provision, embodied in the Declaration on Permanent Sovereignty over Natural Resources of 1962, to the effect that 'the right of peoples and nations to permanent sovereignty over their natural wealth and resources must be exercised in the interest of their national development and of the well-being of the people of the State concerned' (art. 1). By accepting the right of expropriation on the condition that such measures contribute to economic development – the question of compensation not having been solved yet – the rich nations accepted in fact a new legal situation based on the needs of the developing countries.

In relation to the second point, innumerable Resolutions could eb presented in which 'the developing countries' are mentioned as the object of a specific policy or measure recommended by the General Assembly. The work of the G.A. in the field of development assistance has been so complex and so wide, that books could be filled with such examples. Only a few very important Resolutions will be mentioned here, in which the rich countries were urged to assist 'the developing countries' in the socio-economic field:

1⁰. Res. 304 (IV) of 16 Nov. 1949, on the establishment of 'The Expanded Programme of Technical Assistance,' and the many Resolutions adopted within the framework of this programme.

2⁰. Res. 1240 (XIII) of 14 Oct. 1958, on 'The United Nations Special Fund' (the two components of the UN-aid programme were merged through Res. 2029 (XX) of 22 Nov. 1965).

3⁰. Res. 1710 (XVI) of 19 Dec. 1961, on the 'United Nations Development Decade,' art. 1 of which states that the G.A.:

> 'Designates the current decade as the United Nations Development Decade, in which Member States and their peoples will intensify their efforts to mobilize and sustain support for measures required on the part of both developed and developing countries to accelerate progress towards self-sustaining growth of the economy of the individual nations and their social advancement so as to attain in each under-developed country a substantial increase in the rate of growth...'

4⁰. Res. 1714 (XVI) of 19 Dec. 1961, establishing 'The World Food Programme';

5⁰. Res. 1995 (XIX) of 30 Dec. 1964, establishing the 'United Nations Conference on Trade and Development' (UNCTAD), art. 3 of which describes as one of its aims:

'(a) to promote international trade, especially with a view to accelerating economic development, particularly trade between countries at different stages of development....'
and
'(b) to formulate principles and policies on international trade and related problems of economic development';

6⁰. Res. 2186 (XXI) of 13 Dec. 1966, establishing 'The United Nations Capital Development Fund,' in which it is recalled that

'the terms on which the developing countries currently obtain assistance tend, in most cases, to offset the advantages derived therefrom';

whereas it is urged that

'external resources should be made available to the developing countries on terms and conditions which would help to accelerate their economic and social progress';

7⁰. Res. 2218 (XXI) of 19 Dec. 1966, on a 'Projected Charter for International Development';
8⁰. Res. 2542 (XXIV) of 11 Dec. 1969, the 'Declaration on Social Progress and Development', art. 12a of which mentions as one of its objectives

'the creation of conditions for rapid and sustained social and economic development, particularly in the developing countries';

and art. 27a of which relates world peace to economic development by demanding

'The achievement of general and complete disarmament and the channeling of the progressively released resources to be used for economic and social progress for the welfare of the people everywhere and, in particular, for the benefit of developing countries.....';

9⁰. Res. 2571 (XXIV) of 13 Dec. 1969, on an 'International Development Strategy,' whose Preamble recalls the Charter of Algiers, and whose art. 2 (b) states that

'The main objective for the Second United Nations Development Decade should be to promote sustained economic growth, especially in developing countries, to ensure a higher standard of living consistent with human dignity, to bring about sustained improvements in the well-being of the individual, and to facilitate the process of narrowing the gap between the developed and the developing countries';

10⁰. Res. 2626 (XXV) of 24 Oct. 1970, on the 'International Development Strategy for the Second United Nations Development Decade,' art. 19 of which calls for

> 'a continuing effort by all peoples and governments to promote economic and social progress in developing countries by the formulation and implementation of a coherent set of policy measures.'

This list may be enough to indicate to what extent the group of 'developing countries' has become accepted as a particular object of interest.
Such development, however, might be considered by some to be of mainly political interest without entailing direct legal consequences. This point of view, however, would negate the strong influence the General Assembly has proved to bear upon the development of international law. It seems more appropriate to speak of 'soft law,' which indicates the process of legitimization that finally – through practice – results in new rules of 'hard' international law. Indeed, in this case also the 'quasi-legislative' activities of the General Assembly have resulted in a new legal development and have contributed to the legal recognition of the 'developing countries' as particular subjects of law:

1⁰. In the first place the UNCTAD might be reiterated, whose Council is composed by the representatives of states selected according to their level of development. As such this implies a clear recognition of various groups of developing countries.

2⁰. One of the outstanding examples to be mentioned is the General Agreement on Tariffs and Trade (GATT), whose original text (being put into operation in 1948) was amended several times. The amendment most important to the present context is that of 1965. A new Part IV was added and was put into operation in June, 1966. Apart from this Part IV, art. XVIII is illustrative to the present argument, stating:

> '1. The contracting parties recognize that the attainment of the objectives of this Agreement will be facilitated by the progressive development of their economies, *particularly of those contracting parties the economies of which can only support low standards of living and are in the early stages of development.*
> 2. The contracting parties recognize further that it may be necessary for those contracting parties, in order to implement programmes and policies of economic development *designed to raise the general standard of living of their people, to take protective or other measures affecting imports, and that such measures are justified in sofar as they facilitate the attainment of the objectives of this Agreement. They agree, therefore, that those contracting parties should enjoy additional facilities...*'

These provisions are followed by a description of the facilities in articles 2, 3, and 4.
Part IV of the Treaty, entitled 'Trade and Development,' begins with

the observation that 'the basic objectives of this Agreement include the raising of the standards of living and the progressive development of the economies of all contracting parties, ... considering that the attainment of these objectives is *particularly urgent for the less-developed contracting parties...*' (art. XXXVI. 1 (a)). The following articles stress the specific needs of the developing countries (points 2-7), followed by point 8, in which it is declared that

> '*The developed contracting parties do not expect reciprocity* for commitments made by them in trade negotiations to reduce or remove tariffs and other barriers to the trade of less-developed contracting parties.'

Art. XXXVII contains a number of obligations undertaken by the developed vis-à-vis the developing countries, among which is the obligation that

> 'The developed contracting parties shall to the fullest extent possible.... give effect to the following provisions:
> (a) accord high priority to the reduction and elimination of barriers to products currently or potentially of particular export interest to the less-developed contracting parties, including customs duties and other restrictions which differentiate unreasonably between such products in their primary and in their processed forms;
> (b) refrain from introducing, or increasing the incidence of, customs duties or non-tariff import barriers on products currently or potentially of particular export interest to the less-developed contracting parties...' etc.

It is clear that the 'developing countries' have been recognized in this multilateral Treaty as a particular group with specific privileges under international law.

3°. Also in more specialized fields, for example the protection of copyright, the developing countries have been given a specific place. This is the case in the 'protocole relatif aux Pays en voie de developpement,' added to the Bern-Convention in 1967.[45]

4°. A similar development can be observed in the field of the international law of the sea.

In particular, there have been developments in the law on exploration and exploitation of the sea-bed and the ocean floor. On 21 December, 1968, the UN General Assembly established a Commission for the peaceful use of the sea-bed and the ocean floor (Res. 2467 A (XXIII)), whose task was to make proposals on the subject of the prohibition of the use of the sea-bed for military purposes. In due course, the

---

[45] see D. Vignes – 'Droit d'auteur et aide au développement: le protocole a l'acte de Stockholm pour la protection des œuvres littéraires et artistiques,' XIII Annuaire Français de Droit International ('67) pp. 717 ff.

discussions on this topic were broadened by a proposal to establish an international régime for the sea-bed (see the next section) which then gave rise to the endeavours of the developing countries to make the others accept specific provisions aimed at the protection of their interests. They succeeded in this effort, and in Res. 2467 A (XXIII) of 21 Dec., 1968, the General Assembly urges that

> 'the exploitation of the resources of the sea-bed and the ocean floor, and the subsoil thereof, beyond the limits of national jurisdiction, should be carried out for the benefit of mankind as a whole, irrespecttive of the geographical location of States, *taking into account the special interests and needs of the developing countries*.....'

This provision is reiterated in Res. 2574 D (XXIV) of 15 Dec. 1969, and was set down in several articles of the '*Declaration* of Principles Governing the Sea-Bed and the Ocean Floor, and the Subsoil Thereof, Beyond the Limits of National Jurisdiction,' Res. 2749 (XXV) of 17 Dec. 1970. Its art. 7 states:

> 'The exploration of the area and the exploitation of its resources shall be carried out for the benefit of mankind as a whole, irrespective of the geographical location of States, whether land-locked or coastal, and *taking into particular consideration the interests and needs of the developing countries*';

and art. 9 declares:

> '... The régime, inter alia, provide for the orderly and safe development and rational management of the area and its resources and for expanding opportunities in the use thereof and ensure the equitable sharing by States the benefits derived therefrom, *taking into particular consideration the interests and needs of the developing countries, whether landlocked or coastal*.'

Although this is still a provision of 'soft' law, the fact that it is part of a solemn Declaration, which, moreover, was adopted *unanimously* (108 votes against 0, with 14 abstentions), is of great legal importance.

Similar provisions can be found in Resolutions 2750 (XXV) A, B, and C, of 17 Dec. 1970 on the same topic. Resolution D is of specific importance, since it incorporates a proposal of the developing countries which advocates a moratorium on the exploitation of the sea-bed until an equitable international régime has been established. The fear expressed by representatives of developed countries, that such a provision would run counter to Res. A and that it would make present exploitation impossible, seems unfounded since a geographical definition of the sea-bed beyond national jurisdiction (and its demarcation against the continental shelf) does not exist at present. Anyhow, the proposal was adopted with 62 votes against 28 with 28 abstentions, and the G.A., while 'recalling its Res. 2467 A (XXIII) 'in which 'the special interests and needs of the developing countries' were stressed, declares that 'pending the establishment of the forementioned international régime: (a) States and persons, physical or juridical, are bound to refrain from all activities of exploitation of the resources of the area of the sea-bed and ocean floor, and the subsoil thereof, beyond the limits of national jurisdiction; (b) No claim to any part of that area or its resources shall be recognized.'

Resolution 2750 C is of even greater importance to the present discussion: it contains a provision which states that the entire body of the law of the sea might be revised in due course. During the discussions in Dec. 1969 on Malta's Draft Resolution in Commission I on the question of definition of the sea-bed beyond the limits of national jurisdiction, 17 developing countries introduced an amendment in which the Secretary-General was requested 'to ascertain the views of Member States on the desirability of convening at an early date a conference on the law of the sea to review the régimes of the high seas, the continental shelf, the territorial sea and contiguous zone, fishing and conservation of the living resources of the high seas.....'. Against the votes of many developed countries, the amendment was adopted and incorporated in Res. 2574 A. During the next year this endeavour was pushed further by the developing countries, and resulted in the adoption of provisions in Res. 2750 C to the effect that the entire law of the sea be revised so that the needs of the developing countries are taken into particular consideration. After the Preamble has noted 'the fact that many of the present States Members of the United Nations did not take part in the previous United Nations Conferences on the law of the sea,' and that agreements should 'take into account the special interests and needs of the developing countries,' the Resolution – after having proceeded with several provisions on the question of the sea-bed and an international régime for its exploration and exploitation – states in art. 2 that the G.A.

'Decides to convene in 1973, ... a conference on the law of the sea which would deal with the establishment of an equitable international régime – including an international machinery – for the area and the resources of the sea-bed and the ocean floor, and the subsoil thereof, beyond the limits of national jurisdiction, a precise definition of the area, *and a broad range of related issues* including those concerning the régimes of the high seas, the continental shelf, the territorial sea (including the question of its breadth and the question of international straits) and contiguous zone, fishing and conservation of the living resources of the high seas (including the preferential rights of coastal States), the preservation of the marine environment (including, inter alia, the prevention of pollution) and scientific research.'

Indeed, the Geneva Conventions of 1958 and 1960 make no special reference to any country in need of special protection. The 'Convention on Fishing and Conservation of the Living Resources of the

High Seas,' signed at Geneva on 29 April 1958, merely points out 'the need of the world's expanding population for food,' and the danger of resources being overexploited. The developing countries have started their campaign to become recognized as a group which needs special rights and protection in the entire realm of the law of the sea, so important to them in view of their present and future problems of nutrition, industrialization, and employment.[46] To some degree this recognition is forthcoming, but at this moment it may seem a bit premature to say, as Douance does, that 'le droit de la mer est mis en service d'une politique de développement économique.'[47]
But even so, the new notion of the 'developing countries' has grown strong enough as a legal concept to challenge the centuries-old principle of the freedom of the high seas. It is a clear example of the limitation of the traditional concept of liberty in favour of the new principles of assistance and protection.

Even within the group of 'developing countries' a new specification has been announced. In support of Resolution 24 (II) of the second UNCTAD of 26 March, 1968, in which the Conference 'invited international bodies responsible for particular measures to benefit developing countries, generally to design the form of, and elaborate on, the special measures which might be taken in favour of the least developed countries, and to identify such countries,' the UN General Assembly unanimously adopted Res. 2564 (XXIV) on 13 Dec. 1969, and Res. 2724 (XXV) on 15 Dec. 1970. The Resolution first mentioned affirmed the need to alleviate the problems of the least developed among the developing countries by enabling them to benefit fully from the Second United Nations Development Decade; and Resolution 2724 (1) 'affirms the urgency of identifying the least developed among the developing countries in order to enable the countries so identified to benefit as early as possible from the special measures in their favour adopted in the various forums, particularly these incorporated in the International Development Strategy for the Second United Nations Development Decade'; and (3) 'requests the Secretary-General to report to the General Assembly at its twenty-sixth session on the progress made towards the identification of the least developed among developing countries.'

---

[46] on the general necessity and endeavour to conserve the resources of the high seas see Ch. Boasson – 'Resources of the Sea and International Law,' 6 Israel Law Review 3 ('71) pp. 291-308.
[47] U. Cl. Douence – 'Droit de la mer et développement économique sur la côte occidentale d'Afrique,' 71 Rev. Gen. D.I.P. ('67) pp. 110ff., 132.

The Resolution on 'International Development Strategy for the Second United Nations Development Decade' contains three articles in this connection, 56-58, art. 56 of which reads:

'While it is the objective of the Decade to achieve the rapid economic and social progress of all developing countries, special measures will be taken to enable the least developed among them to overcome their particular disabilities. Every possible effort will be made to ensure the sustained economic and social progress of these countries and to enhance their capacity to benefit fully and equitable from the policy measures for the Decade. Wherever necessary, supplementary measures will be devised and implemented at the national, sub-regional, regional and international levels. Organizations and bodies of the United Nations system will consider initiating early in the Decade special programmes to alleviate the critical development problems of the least developed among developing countries; developed countries will assist in the implementation of these programmes.'

At the beginning of this Chapter, under heading 2, the three historical phases of International Law were shortly discussed. It was said there that one of the functions of the basic ideas underlying these periods – Christendom, Civilization, and Peace – has been and is the legitimization of inequalities among states and peoples. Traditionally, such inequalities in position and rights used to be in favour of the strongest subjects of law; in the time of the 'Peace-loving Nations,' in the interest of positive peace, a new kind of inequality has been introduced with the recognition of the developing countries as particular protégé's of an emerging part of international law: inequality in favour of the *weak* members of the family of nations.

3.2.3. *The recognition of 'mankind' as a supreme legal value, and the duty to co-operate for global welfare*

The third legal development to be mentioned in particular is the dual phenomenon of the legal recognition of 'mankind' as a supreme value to be served by economic international law, and the duty of states to co-operate for a supra-national welfare system. Both aspects are closely interrelated and are for that reason discussed under one heading.

3.2.3.1. The notion of *'mankind'* in international law was in fact introduced by the recognition of transnational individual Human Rights. The UN Charter, like many legal documents on Human Rights derived from it, speaks of equal rights for all, without distinction; the welfare of 'mankind' was thus introduced, above the nation, as an ultimate criterion of political and legal efforts in the socio-economic field. The many later legal documents which speak of the bridging of the welfare gap and the achievement of a more equal position for the developing countries also agree with this value. While the Universal Declaration and the International Covenants on Human Rights speak of 'the human family,' the term 'mankind' as such was first used in the Preamble of the UN Charter and was later introduced into several UN documents in the realm of economic development. One of the outstanding examples is Res. 2571 (XXVI) of 13 Dec. 1969, on the 'International Development Strategy,' which was adopted unanimously, and which reaffirms 'the common responsibility and resolve of the international community to work continuously to bring about a substantial improvement *in the lot of mankind....*'

The term has become of particular importance, however, in connection with the recent developments in the realm of the law of the sea. In 1958, the 'Convention on Fishing and Conservation of the Living Resources of the High Seas' resulted partly from the wish to restrict free national activities on the high seas in order 'to meet the need of the world's expanding population for food.'[48] In 1967, the question of the legal regulation of an international régime for the sea-bed was put on the agenda of the UN General Assembly by a proposal of Malta, which provided for 'examination of the question of the reservation exclusively for peaceful purposes of the sea-bed and the ocean floor, and the subsoil thereof, underlying the high seas beyond the limits of present national jurisdiction *and the use of their resources in the interests of mankind.*'

This proposal resulted from the unsatisfactory manner in which the Geneva Convention on the Continental Shelf of 1958 defines the extent of the continental shelf; 'the area adjacent to the coast,' on the resources of which the coastal State has exclusive rights 'to a depth of 200 meters or, beyond that limit, to where the depth of the superjacent waters admits of the exploitation of natural resources' (art. 1).[49] There is, therefore, no clear limit to the rights of coastal States, other than that provided by technology and an ill-defined concept of 'adjacency.'

The industrially non-developed countries and the land-locked states feared that the rapid development of technology would in due course lead to unlimited claims of a few coastal, developed countries. For this reason they supported therefore not only the proposal of discussing the demilitarization of the sea-bed, but also the proposal of discussing the exclusion of national claims in that area. The succeeding discussions in the General Assembly revealed, moreover,

---

[48] see the Preamble to this Treaty, UN Doc. A/Conf. 13/L. 54.
[49] U.N. Doc. A/Conf. 13/L. 55.

that also the highly developed coastal States favoured both proposals. A notable example is the United States, whose President Johnson said already in 1966:

'Under no circumstances, we believe, must we ever allow the prospects of rich harvest and mineral wealth create a new form of colonial competition among the maritime nations. We must be careful to avoid a race to grab and to hold the lands under the high seas. We must ensure that the deep seas and the ocean bottoms are, and remain, *the legacy of all human beings*.'[50]

Consequently, Resolution 2574 (XXIV) of 15 Dec. 1969, was adopted, of which parts of A and D contain references to utilization of the resources of the sea-bed 'for the benefit of all mankind.' Once this principle was accepted, the unanimously adopted 'Declaration of Principles Governing the Sea-Bed and the Ocean Floor, and the Subsoil thereof, Beyond the Limits of National Jurisdiction' (Res. 2749 (XXV) of 17 Dec. 1970), 'solemny declares that:

1. The sea-bed and ocean floor, and the subsoil thereof, beyond the limits of national jurisdiction (hereinafter referred to as the area), as well as the resources of the area, *are the common heritage of mankind;*
7. The exploration of the area and the exploitation of its resources shall be carried out for the benefit of mankind as a whole.....'

Similar references are made in subsequent Resolutions 2750 A and B (XXV) of the same date.
The importance of 'the entire human family,' 'mankind,' or whatever terminology has been used in this connection, as a supreme subject to be served by the rules and principles of international economic law, is strengthened by the gradual recognition of a legal duty to co-operate for more than only national welfare.

3.2.3.2. To what extent has this duty been developed at present?
It should be repeated here, that the necessity of multilateral co-operation for the welfare of humanity has been expressed in innumerable Resolutions of the General Assembly and its subsidiary organs. The eventual legal duty to co-operate for that purpose has been prepared by political activity such as the adoption of Resolutions. The sequence of a large number of Resolutions, in particular if unanimously adopted Declarations are among them, *creates a certain expectation with regard to a legal development*. Partly because of the 'quasi-control' exercised by the UN General Assembly during its

---

[50] quoted in 'The United Nations and the Bed of the Sea,' 19th Rep. of the Commission to Study the Organization of Peace' ('69) p. 12.

annual discussions, states tend to follow such Resolutions through subsequent practice, which may eventually lead to customary international law.

Res. 1710 (XVI) of 19 Dec. 1961, the Declaration in which the First UN Development Decade was announced, is full of 'calls upon' the Members of the United Nations to co-operate for the welfare of all, of reminders of 'the need for concerted action' and 'international economic co-operation.' The same holds for 'The World Food Programme' (Res. 1714 (XVI) of 19 Dec. 1961), Res. 2029 (XX) of 1965 on Development Assistance, the UN Capital Development Fund (Res. 2186 (XXI) of 13 Dec. 1966), Res. 2218 (XXI) of 19 Dec. 1966 on the 'Projected Charter for International Development', and many others. Such Resolutions and Declarations have certainly furthered the expectation that States would have to co-operate in the economic field for the well-being of all, which has been strengthened in subsequent legal documents. Before turning to these, however, it should be noted that the duty to co-operate in this field has a long legal history that goes back as far as the Covenant of the League of Nations. Some examples of relevant documents may be mentioned:

1^0. In Art. 23 (a) of the Covenant of the League of Nations, the Members of that Organization pledged 'to secure and maintain fair and human conditions of labour for men, women and children, both in their own countries and in all countries to which their commercial and industrial relations extend, and for that purpose will establish and maintain the necessary organizations.'

Although this provision is put in very careful words, it might still be considered a first sign of the acceptance of a legal duty to try to promote welfare outside national borders as well.

2^0. This promise was related more specifically to the Constitution of the International Labour Organization, the Preamble of which states that 'the failure of any nation to adopt human conditions of labour is an obstacle in the way of other nations which desire to improve the conditions in their own countries.'

Thus, the idea of interdependence was introduced, necessitating the foundation of a framework of inter-state co-operation, which was considered to be useful only within a broader field of inter-organizational co-operation, as article 12 (1) makes clear:

'The ILO shall' (= must) 'cooperate within the terms of this Constitution with any general international organization entrusted with the co-ordination of the activities of public international organizations having specialized responsibilities in related fields.'

Paragraphs (2) and (3) of this article make arrangements for representatives of public international organizations to participate in ILO-deliberations and make arrangements for consultations with non-governmental international organizations. It may be reiterated in this connection that the Preamble of the ILO-constitution connects international economic co-operation with a reference to world peace; stating

> 'Whereas universal and lasting peace can be established only if it is based upon social justice; and whereas conditions of labour exist involving such unjustice, hardship and deprivation to large numbers of people as to produce unrest so great that the peace and harmony of the world are imperilled; ....'

3⁰. The Charter of the United Nations introduced the idea of the necessity of global co-operation in several interrelated fields. To begin with the Preamble, the peoples of the UN declare themselves:

> 'Determined..... to establish conditions under which justice and respect for the obligations arising from treaties and other sources of international law can be maintained, ... And for these ends... to employ international machinery for the promotion of the economic and social advancement of all peoples.'

Article 1 (3) strengthens the obligation of the Members by stating that the purposes of the UN are:

> 'To achieve international co-operation in solving international problems of an economic, social, cultural, or humanitarian character, and in promoting and encouraging respect for human rights and for fundamental freedoms for all without distinction as to race, sex, language, or religion; and
> (4) –To be a center for harmonizing the actions of nations in the attainment of these common ends.'

By this article the Members of the United Nations accepted in principle the duty *to achieve* international co-operation in these fields and to use the U.N. as the center for solving social and economic problems. The importance of this obligation was underlined by the incorporation into the Charter of an entire Chapter (IX) dealing with international economic and social co-operation (the articles 55-60). Herein the Members of the U.N. *pledge to co-operate with and within the Organization* and to co-ordinate the work of other relevant organizations in order to achieve the solution of social and economic problems, 'with a view to the creation of conditions of stability and well-being which are necessary for peaceful and friendly relations among nations.' Kelsen has denied the existence of a legal obligation in this respect on the ground that the wording of the Charter is so vague and abstract, that no direct legal obligation could be derived from it.[51] It seems hard,

---

[51] H. Kelsen – 'The Law of the United Nations' ('51) p. 100.

however, to accept such an absolute negation of any obligation. Despite the vague terminology of the Charter, a basic general obligation to co-operate and to co-ordinate activities for the realization of welfare for all human beings was accepted, and it was left to the Members of the UN to make it concrete. This might not have occurred in other circumstances, but the emergence of the 'young countries' changed the character of the UN-family fundamentally, thus furthering the legitimization of what was originally, as Röling has put it, 'avant-garde thinking' and making this acceptable as 'establishment principles.'[52] As such it seems beyond doubt that the practice of the UN has strengthened the legal character of these UN Charter provisions.

4⁰. The Universal Declaration of Human Rights refers indirectly to the duty to co-operate in terms of *the right* of those who are striving for a better life; Article 22 states:

> 'Everyone, as a member of society, *has the right* to social security and is entitled to the realization through national effort *and international co-operation* and in accordance with the organization and resources of each state, of the economic, social and cultural rights indispensable for his dignity and the free development of his personality.'

If it were argued that article 22, speaking of 'everyone as a member of society' is meant to refer to the 'national society,' and thus merely obliges each national government to use international co-operation for the benefit of its own population, then article 28 is beyond doubt:

> '*Everyone is entitled to a social and international order* in which the rights and freedoms set forth in this Declaration can be fully realized.'

5⁰. Art. XXXVIII of the G.A.T.T. should also be mentioned in this context, stating that 'the Contracting Parties shall collaborate jointly, within the framework of this Agreement and elsewhere, as appropriate, to further the objectives set forth in Art. XXXVI,' (which deals with the special privileges enjoyed by the developing countries).

6⁰. Further there is the International Covenant on Economic, Social and Cultural Rights, which is disappointing in this particular respect. The provision of a 'right to an international order,' the innovation of the Universal Declaration, was not strengthened by a similar provision in this Treaty. Article 23 merely says:

---

[52] B. V. A. Röling – 'De VN in een wereld in steigers' (The UN in a world in scaffolding), published in a book edited by the Dutch Association for International Legal Order (VIRO) in commemoration of the 25th anniversary of the UN ('71) p. 217.

'The States Parties to the present Covenant agree that international action for the achievement of the rights recognized in the Present Covenant includes such methods as the conclusion of conventions, the adoption of recommendations, the furnishing of technical assistance and the holding of regional meetings and technical meetings for the purpose of consultation and study organized in conjunction within the Government concerned.'

This is a rather meager provision. The question whether the duty to furnish development assistance can perhaps be derived from the ambiguous article 2, has been discussed before. Some articles mention international co-operation as an important means to reach a specific goal; like article 11, which says that 'the States Parties will take appropriate steps to ensure the realization of this right, recognizing to this effect the essential importance of international co-operation on free consent.'

It is clear that the provisions of the Treaty are more dubious and probably less progressive than its preceding documents. Nevertheless, it could hardly diminish the obligation to co-operate for the realization of the most favourable international order, this Treaty being only one among many instruments.

It is most important to observe that this duty has been promoted by many instruments of 'soft' international law, to which we now come.

7⁰. Many Resolutions in the field of development assistance have prepared the way for Declarations which not only speak of 'the necessity of co-operation' or 'the duty to achieve co-operation,' but concern themselves directly with 'the duty to co-operate.' A very important example of this is the Declaration on 'The International Development Strategy for the Second United Nations Development Decade,' which incorporates the outlines for the strategy to be implemented. Having elaborated on the goals and objectives of D.D. II, article 19 of this *unanimously adopted Resolution* states:

'.... Animated by a spirit of constructive partnership and co-operation, based on the interdependence of their interests and designed to promote a rational system of international division of labour, and reflecting their political will and collective determination to achieve these goals and objectives, *Governments, individually and jointly, solemnly resolve to adopt and implement the policy measures set out below.*'

This wording is entirely clear in itself.

The same can be said, again, in relation to the law of the sea. The Convention on Fishing of 1958 states, with reference to 'the need of the world's expanding population for food,' that

'All States have their duty to adopt, or to co-operate with other States in adopting, such measures for their respective nationals as may be necessary for the conservation of the living resources of the high seas' (art. 1); and

'...... Conservation programmes should be formulated with a view to securing in the first place a supply of food for human consumption' (art. 2).

Although the wording of art. 2 is somewhat indirect, and although these provisions are obligatory only for States Parties – notwithstanding the rather courageous formulation of art. 1, which bears witness to the hope that this Treaty might become accepted by so many States that it would constitute general customary law in due course – we have here a clear endeavour to put the interests of humanity before the interests of specific states. This effort has been reflected in the discussions on the continental shelf and the ocean floor. In particular the discussions on global co-operation in the field of exploration and exploitation, as part of the new international régime to be established, are worth mentioning. A clear consensus has been reached, as witnessed among other things by the Declaration on this topic. The Preamble bears in mind that

'the development and use of the area and its resources shall be undertaken in such a manner as to foster healthy development of the world economy and balanced growth of international trade, and to minimize any adverse economic effects caused by fluctuation of prices of raw materials resulting from such activities';

and article 4 declares:

'All activities regarding the exploration and exploitation of the resources of the area and other related activities shall be governed by the international regime to be established';

while articles 10, 11 and 12 declare among other things:

'.... The régime, inter alia, provide for the orderly and safe development and rational management of the area and its resources and for expanding opportunities in the use thereof and ensure the equitable sharing by States the benefits derived therefrom....;

and

'States shall promote international co-operation in scientific research exclusively for peaceful purposes:
(a) By participation in international programmes.....;
(c) By co-operation in measures to strengthen research capabilities of developing countries including the participation of their nationals in research programmes';

and

'With respect to activities in the area and acting in conformity with the international régime to be established, States shall take appropriate measures for and shall co-operate in the adoption and implementation of international rules, standards and procedures for, inter alia:
(b) Protection and conservation of the natural resources of the area and prevention of damage to the flora and fauna of the marine environment'.

As a central point of reference, art. 7 may be reiterated:

'The exploration of the area and exploitation of its resources shall be carried out for the benefit of mankind as a whole....'

The attempt – through global co-operation – to subordinate the economic activities of states to the benifit of all mankind may be expected to continue. In the present day firm roots of this co-operation are established.

3.2.4. *The relevance of these legal roots in their polemological context*

The legal developments that have been discussed above certainly fulfill the conditions set for achieving a polemologically justified development strategy:
The recognition of individual Human Rights and the value of 'mankind' in the socio-economic sphere serve the purpose of reaching a human level of welfare for all human beings, and a more equitable distribution of prosperity; the recognition of 'developing countries' as a privileged group in the economic field also serves the purpose of diminishing international inequalities; the same holds for the duty to co-operate for more than only national welfare, which also serves the purpose of creating unity and a supra-national community; all of these developments can contribute, moreover, to the achievement of substantial progress.

It is of particular importance that as much as possible be done to achieve both substantial, and continuous growth in the developing countries. Apart from the indirect way in which the developments discussed above contribute to this aim, the more direct references to this purpose found in many legal and semi-legal documents are worth mentioning. Part IV of the GATT contains many references to the need of 'rapid and sustained expansion of the export earnings of developing countries' (like the quotation from Art. XXXVI. 2). Resolution 2571 (XXIV) of 13 Dec. 1969, on the 'International Development Strategy' urges '*to work continuously* to bring about a *substantial improvement* in the lot of all members of society'; notably by the attainment of among other things 'the assurance of a *steady improvement* in levels of living and of a just and equitable distribution of income' (art. 19 (c)); and of 'the creation of conditions for *rapid and sustained* social and economic development, particularly in the developing countries.....' The Declaration on the Second UN Development Decade is in fact one great plea for substantial and continuous improvement, rapid decrease of international inequalities, and the prevention of waste.

It should be added that another polemological condition has also been answered to some extent by some UN-Declarations, the condition namely of preventing political manoeuvring through economic assistance.

One could interpret art. 6 of the Declaration on Permanent Sovereignty over Natural Resources in this way, which reads: 'International co-operation for the economic development of developing countries, whether in the form of public or private capital investments, exchange of goods and services, technical assistance, or exchange of scientific information, *shall be such as to further their independent national development....*'

The 'Declaration on the Inadmissibility of Intervention in the Domestic Affairs of States and the Protection of Their Independence and Sovereignty,' Res. 2131 (XX) of 21 Dec. 1965, is quite clear in this respect. Its Preamble having made clear that 'direct intervention, subversion, as well as all forms of indirect intervention are... *a violation of the Charter of the United Nations*', and that one is 'fully aware of the imperative need to create appropriate conditions which would enable all States, *and in particular the developing countries*, to choose without duress or coercion their own political, economic and social institutions,' the General Assembly solemnly declares:

'*2. No State may use or encourage the use of economic, political or any type of measures to coerce another State in order to obtain from it the subordination of the exercise if its sovereign rights or to secure from it advantages of any kind....*'

This Declaration, it would seem, is clear in its prohibition of using development assistance for any other aim than purely extending economic aid. The same holds for art. 46 of the Strategy Resolution:

'Financial and technical assistance should be aimed *exclusively* at promoting the economic and social progress of developing countries and should not in any way be used by the developed countries to the detriment of the national sovereignty of recipient countries.'

Such provisions can be considered – the argument has been discussed – mainly as political provisions; yet, for the reasons outlined above, they constitute the roots of emerging international law, and as such they are important enough to be mentioned here.

Generalizing, it can be concluded that rules and priciples of international law are developing and have emerged to such an extent, that on their basis a sensible, peace preserving development strategy can be outlined.

With this conclusion in mind, and in view of all that has been said in this and the preceding Chapters, art. 1 para 1. of the UN Charter can be considered the most fundamental legal root in the present context:

> 'The purposes of the United Nations are:
> 1. To maintain international peace and security, and to that end: to take effective collective measures for the prevention and removal of threats to the peace...'

Although this article has usually been quoted in connection with threats provoked by armed force, it follows from UN-practice as developed through the years that a threat to the peace is considered to exist in the mass violation of Human Rights. Since 'structural violence,' like 'apartheid,' has been brandished as 'a threat to the peace,' the provision of art. 1 para. 1 has obtained a new and more extensive meaning: *It can now be considered to contain not only the obligation to repel the use of armed force in war, but also the more basic obligation of all UN-Members to co-operate for the realization of universal Human Rights, both in the political and in the socio-economic field, since this realization would remove a major threat to the peace today.*

3.3. *A strategy for global welfare*

Resolution XXIII of the Teheran Conference on Human Rights begins with the statement that 'peace is the underlying condition for the full observance of human rights and war is their negation......' Today the reverse of this statement could be true as well: the full observance of human rights is an underlying condition of peace and their negation leads to war.

International law has been a stimulating factor in making the poor peoples of the world conscious of their rights, in creating new expectations and in making them rebellious against present inequalities existing between them and the rich countries. International law would thus contribute to national and international turbulence, if it would not also become a stimulating and a creative factor in bridging the gap between the poor and rich.

It is clear that the implementation of socio-economic Human Rights for all depends upon the realization of an effective development strategy. Innumerable programs have been proposed and worked out, but most of them either were put in terms of vague aims and contained merely the description of general needs, or were specific programs developed for some detailed field of activity without being adapted to a general framework.

On Dec. 19, 1966, halfway through the First UN Development Decade, the General Assembly adopted Res. 2219 (XXI), in which it called upon 'all concerned to make the utmost effort possible

towards the realization of the modest targets of the present UN Development Decade'; and in which it observed that 'one of the reasons for the slow progress in achieving the modest targets set for the UN Development Decade has been the absence of a framework of international development strategy.' The necessity of this Resolution by itself is proof of the failure of the First Development Decade, as proclaimed by the UN. The sixties have correctly been called 'a development decade without a development policy.'
Resolution XVII of the Teheran Conference notices the same, and 'calls urgently for the preparation of a global strategy of development by the UN,' and 'calls upon all members of the international community to assume their full responsibility in the field of economic and social development and to take immediate effective action with a view to establishing economic and social justice,' after it has been warned that the widening of the gap 'is not conducive to international peace and understanding.'[53]
Only recently some plans for a development strategy on a comprehensive scale have been worked out on the initiative of international organizations; notably the Reports of the so-called 'Pearson-Committee' and the 'Commission-Tinbergen,' prepared on the initiative of the World Bank and the United Nations respectively (see Ch. II, note 293), and (most importantly) the 'International Development Strategy for the Second United Nations Decade,' Res. 2626 (XXV), *adopted unanimously* by the General Assembly on 24 October, 1970. This crucial Resolution does not only incorporate the usual list of general objectives and needs, but incorporates 84 articles, in which a detailed development strategy is outlined.
Apart from their economic merits, these provisions together answer many of the qualifications of a polemologically sound strategy. They answer the conditions of substantial growth, continuous improvement and prevention of sudden stagnation, decreasing international and internal inequalities, co-operation and co-ordination, prevention of waste, integration of national and regional schemes into global planning, prevention of political manoeuvring through aid, preexisting studies on the national level so as to take specific needs and possibilities and specific social problems in developing countries into account, etc. Relevant provisions will be discussed in their respective contexts below.

It seems, however, that such strategies and plans have, without exception, been based on the assumption that economic growth is a

[53] U.N. Publ. A/Conf. 32/41 ('68) p. 14.

rather limitless phenomenon in this world, and that the purpose of equalizing the economies of the developing countries to the present level of prosperity of the rich countries could be achieved without any virtual sacrifice to be made by the group last mentioned.

Recent calculations on the state of the world's resources, such as found in the report of the Club of Rome, have caused, however, serious doubt in this respect. The major areas of concern, which will be discussed below, are the reserves of natural resources and energy, environmental pollution, food, and above all population growth. Very pessimistic projections hold that our resources have been exhausted to such an extent and that pollution is so serious already, that humanity is approaching an inevitable calamity. Less pessimistic projections still refer to serious problems which demand early solutions if they are to be overwon. All predictions in this respect can not take radical technological innovations into account, which might throw a new light on the world's situation – reason for some to consider such predictions as unnecessary gloomy views. In view of the relatively short period that remains to find appropriate solutions, however, the possibility of inventing such radical technological innovations and putting them into practice seems not very promising. At this moment, in any case, many have come to the conclusion that we might have to put an end to our economic growth, and that the bridging of the welfare gap can not be achieved without great sacrifices being made by the rich countries.

The merits of such a view will be discussed in the next sections, where the substance of the envisaged global welfare strategy is outlined. The various problems mentioned before will be discussed there separately for analytical reasons; one should always remember, however, that these problems form in practice one complex of closely interdependent variables: as the rate of population growth will influence the food problem, food production will influence industrial capacity and pollution, and industrial capacity will vice versa influence pollution and food production, etc.

In view of what follows under these headings there is reason to suppose that *under present social and technological conditions* the welfare gap can not be narrowed without substantial sacrifices from the side of the rich countries. The kind of sacrifices that will have to be made depends on the accuracy of the data presently available, and on the time schedule one chooses to reach the goals set. One might expect, however, that at least the rate of economic growth in the rich countries will have to be decreased and perhaps even stopped for some time. If the welfare gap is to be bridged, this might even demand some loss of prosperity in the rich part of the world. If this will indeed have to occur, the rich countries are confronted with a choice: they can either allow the poor countries to starve, or allow the poor countries to sustain privileged economic growth. There seems to be no middle-road anymore; the time when very slow and gradual adaptations were still possible has past, and the rich countries did not use that opportunity.

If they choose the first way (or take half-hearted measures leading to the same consequences) they will not prevent themselves from being confronted with the limits of growth – they will only postpone this by perhaps some decennia: On the one hand, the concurrence among the various economic blocks of rich countries will coerce them to make early conservation regulations if they do not want to exhaust the world's reserves within a relatively short period. On the other hand, the developing countries have now reached a point where they may be expected to try everything in order to get their industrialization started, even without foreign assistance; thus an uncontrolled 'wild' race for resources might be expected, excluding any possibility of conservation of reserves and control of pollution, and harming the interests of poor and rich countries alike.

The poor countries – being rich of many important minerals and fossil energy – would refuse the rich countries the natural resources that they need, unless perhaps they would pay exorbitantly high prices. The rich countries, pressed by scarcity – note, for instance, that already today imports supply over 75% of American needs for 20 different mineral commodities[54] – might eventually feel compelled to use armed force, but then they would meet each other militarily, and a world war might be the end result.

Even if such developments would not take place, the rich countries would have to face the polemological consequences of the lasting welfare gap. Large-scale violence throughout the Third World might be expected, both internally and internationally, and in view of present worldwide political relationships, miracles would have to occur if the rich countries could stay out of this and not become involved sooner or later.

If the rich countries choose the second way, they will probably have to cope earlier with economic growth problems, and they might even have to make relatively substantial sacrifices. They might become confronted with new economic and conflictological problems, which are not discussed here. The only thing to be said is, that such problems might otherwise not have been prevented but merely postponed. Concerning the internal conflicts provoked by stagnation or de-

---

[54] W. Hibbard – 'Mineral Resources: Challenge or Threat?,' 160 Science ('68) p. 144.

terioration, one remark to be added is that such conflicts may be expected to emerge primarily in those large circles of society which perceive their present position as being on the margin of existence, and that it would be sensible therefore if measures were taken to prevent that primarily the less-to-do would become the victims of the welfare strategy. Indeed, the realization of more equality in many rich countries might be a pre-condition for the realization of more worldwide equality.

In any case, accepting a common responsibility for the development of the Third World would open the doors to new ways of co-operation and co-ordination, creating new possibilities of control and conservation. Only within the framework of a global development strategy could the waste of scarce resources and uncontrolled environmental pollution be prevented. This represents a clear *long-term economic interest* not only for the poor countries, but also – and no less – for the rich countries.

Moreover, the emergence of uncontrollable large-scale violence in the Third World resulting from socio-economic conditions would be prevented; a huge difference with the violence and conflicts to be expected during a development process, which may be controllable to a large extent by sensible planning. This represents an *enormous security interest*, also of the poor and the rich countries alike. Finally, the gain in terms of social justice in the world is beyond description. It might well be, that the realization of more social and economic justice would open the doors to new forms of co-operation in the political field, and would contribute to the ultimate establishment of a new form of civilization in which armament would stop being a heavy burden in terms of waste of financial and natural resources.

In view of these considerations, it may be considered utopian, but perhaps not unjustified to pass on to the principles of a global welfare strategy.

3.3.1. *Measures to be taken by developing countries*

Before the implementation of a comprehensive strategy is started, the developing countries should work out national development programmes, which (1) provide detailed information on the internal socio-economic situation and indicate (potential) conflicts which may be provoked by a process of economic of development; (2) describe present and future capacities in terms of resources, employment, population, nutrition, education, etc.; and (3) describe their needs and problems in similar terms. National development planning should in principle be integrated into a global development scheme, in order to achieve the optimal combination of national and universal prosperity. This is important both from a polemological and an economic point of view.

1⁰. As for its polemological importance, the success of such development planning aimed at creating viable national entities depends to a large extent on its capacity to minimize the risk of internal social conflicts; e.g. by promoting social justness and a more equitable distribution of income, and by activating all sectors of the population to participate in and profit from the development process. Several important documents show such considerations also:
The Declaration on Social Progress and Development urges the assurance of equitable distribution of income (art. 10 c) and the realization of specific measures to benefit the low-income groups (art. 10 f), and advises more in particular

'the promotion of democratically-based *social and institutional reforms* and motivation for change *basic to the elimination of all forms of discrimination and exploitation* conducive to high rates of economic and social progress, *to include land reform, in which the ownership and use of land will be made to serve best the objectives of social justice and economic development*' (art. 18b).

Similarly, the Resolution on 'Unified Approach to Economic and Social Planning in National Development' (Res. 2681 (XXV) of 11 Dec. 1970) urges in particular

'(a) *To leave no sector of the population outside the scope of change and development*;
(b) *To effect structural change which favours national development* and to activate *all sectors of the population* to participate in the development process;
(c) To aim at *social equity, including the achievement of an equitable distribution of income and wealth in the nation*.

The Resolution on the Second Development Strategy contains several provisions to this effect; in particular art. 71, which speaks of special attention to 'low-income groups,' and art. 75, which demands that the developing countries 'will undertake, as appropriate, reform of land tenure systems for promoting both social justice and farm efficiency,' should be mentioned. Art. 78 is worth quoting at length here. It reads:

'Developing countries will, as appropriate, *establish or strengthen their planning mechanisms, including statistical services*, for formulating and implementing their national development plans during the Decade. They will ensure that their development plans are both realistic and ambitious enough to have an impact on the imagination of the people, internally consistent, and *widely understood and accepted. Every effort will be made to secure the active support and participation of all segments of the population in the development process*.....'

Each developing country has its own capacities, its own needs, and its own social problems. Relevant to any development strategy is, therefore, what Lasswell has called 'the contextual principle,' by which he means that no single prescription can serve for all times or places.[55] With the necessary international assistance, a unified scheme can be worked out on the basis of which the developing countries develop their respective national programs.

After the analysis presented in Chapter I it needs little comment to add that the developing countries bear primary responsibility for realizing the sometimes fundamental internal changes in the social and economic fields. Many internal relationships as they presently prevail in most Third World countries – a small section of the population exploiting the majority – constitute heavy (if not prohibiting) obstacles to economic progress. Notwithstanding this national responsibility, however, it seems justified to assume that such efforts would yield more success if they become supported by international measures. It may be hoped, moreover, that effective international cooperation will make it easier for such changes to take place peacefully, which might otherwise prove to be impossible.

2⁰. As for its economic importance, the 'nation' will for the foreseeable future remain a principal socio-economic entity, and it is important and expedient, therefore, to take effective measures on the national level and to create economically viable national entities as much as possible and necessary. This is the underlying deliberation of art. 1 of ECOSOC Res. 222 A (IX), Annex 1, on the guiding principles of the Expanded Programme of Technical Assistance, which states, that its primary objective is:

> 'to help those countries to strengthen their national economies through the development of their industries and agriculture, with a view to promoting their economic and political independence......'

The same deliberation resulted in the 'United Nations Development Programme Country Programming' (Res. 2688 (XXV) of 11 Dec. 1970), which is intended to

> 'achieve the most rational and efficient utilization of resources at the disposal of the Programme for its activities in order to have the maximum impact on the economic and social development of the developing countries concerned.'

Also in this respect the Strategy Resolution is very clear, and this principle has been recognized and layed down by the developing countries themselves in the Charters of Algiers and Lima. Without

---

[55] H. D. Lasswell – 'The Policy Sciences of Development,' XVII World Politics ('65) p. 301.

basic efforts of the developing countries themselves on the national level, development is impossible. This doesn't mean, of course, that the developing countries should focus on the national level so much that they neglect mutual co-operation and interdependence; this only implies that within the framework of a general development strategy the respective developing countries can take many measures most expediently by assuming authority in a national setting.

A major example in question is the finding of a solution to the *population problem*. Stopping the present population explosion is considered by many experts as the most important aim to be achieved in as little time as possible. The measures to be taken demand large-scale action on the national level primarily, and for this reason the problem and prospects of exponential population growth will be discussed here.

This growth indeed shows remarkable aspects. By the year 1650 the world's population was about 0.5 billion, this figure increasing at a rate of 0.3% per year. If this rate of growth had continued – the doubling time then being almost 250 years – the amount of 1 billion would have been reached around 1900, and only around the year 2150 2 billion people would have existed. Things have changed rapidly, however. The rate of growth did not remain constant, but increased gradually and permanently, so that already by the year 1810 the figure of 1 billion was reached. Just before 1920 – instead of a figure of slightly over 1 billion – the two billion mark was passed, the world's population by then growing at a rate of 0.6% with a doubling time of 115 years. By the end of 1960, in less than forty years, the third billion had been added.

Assuming that the present growth rate of 2.1% would stay constant, this implies that by the year 2000 there will be about 7,4 billion people, and already by the year 2030 over 14 billion people might be expected to live. This calculation does not count with any slackening of growth, of course. It seems questionable whether it would have to, however, in view of the fact that past decreases in population growth (Great Britain in the 1930's, Japan in the 1960's) have only been temporary ones, the over-all trend showing an exponential rate of growth. For various reasons several experts doubt that such a high growth rate will be sustained, more conservative projections indicating on an average that by the year 2000 about 6 billion people are expected to live. This figure is in accordance with the 'medium' estimate of the United Nations of 1966 to the amount of 6.129 billion. On the basis of this medium projection, only the population of Southern and

Eastern Asia would increase from its present level of some 2 billion to some 3.4 billion by the end of this century.[56]
The reasons behind this exponential growth rate are obvious. Most important are the development of modern medicine and better knowledge and distribution of food, resulting in a constant decline of death rates, whereas the birth rates remain high.
For reasons which are discussed in the next sections of part 3.3., it seems highly questionable at present whether the world could afford to feed and provide jobs for this projected number of people. Anticipating what is analyzed later, it seems justified to state here that the 'population explosion' as projected would confront humanity with large-scale scarcity problems, implying that the future levels of population growth constitute a crucial factor influencing strongly all other deliberations about economic planning. At this moment at least 1 billion people live at the very margin of existence, having to live on less than $ 100 a year, and if the projections given above would come true to some substantial extent, nearly insurmountable problems might result. Such problems are indicated by present developments and short-term expectations in the fields of employment (see below 3.3.3.), nutrition (see 3.3.6.), environmental pollution (3.3.3. and 3.3.6.), availability of resources and energy (3.3.3.), the possibilities of economic growth (3.3.7.) and the availability of financial resources (3.3.8.).
An illustrating example in question is the problem of future *employment*; although it might belong under section 3.3.3., it can be discussed here, since it has an immediate connection with the population growth.
Already today the low economic capacity of most developing countries can not cope with the ever increasing need for jobs. In most parts of the Third World a situation of endemic unemployment and surplus-population prevails already, and it is inevitable that this situation will become worse in the very near future.
In the case of India, for example, one may acknowledge the fact that this country can claim some major economic and agricultural achieve-

---

[56] A. M. Carr-Saunders – 'World Population: Past Growth and Present Trends' ('36) p. 42;
J. D. Durand – 'World Population Estimates 1750-2000,' UN World Population Conference, 1965, vol. II ('66) pp. 17ff.;
Irene B. Taeuber – 'Future Population Trends and Prospects,' idem, vol. I, pp. 191 ff.;
United Nations – 'World population prospects as assessed in 1963,' ST/SOA/Series A/41 ('66) p. 134;
N. Keyfitz – 'US and World Populations,' in 'Resources and Man,' ed. by the Committee on Resources and Man, US National Academy of Sciences ('69) pp. 43 ff.;
US Agency for International Development – 'Population Program Assistance' ('70) p. 172.

ments after having gained independence in 1947. Foremost among these are a 150 per cent increase in industrial productivity, a 400 per cent increase in steel production and in electrical power capacity, and a 62 per cent increase in agricultural production. Unfortunately, most of these aggregate advances have not resulted in comparable per capita gains. On the contrary, India's rate of population growth has virtually nullified almost all the economic progress of the last 20 years. In 1961, there were 8 million unemployed; in 1966, approximately 12 million; and this year there will probably be over 15 million unemployed – all this in spite of the fact that the Indian government created 13 million new jobs between 1961 and 1966, and approximately 20 million new jobs between 1966 and 1971.[57]

It is evident that India's development prospects are inextricably bound to its population growth. Against the background of the unsuccessful endeavours to reduce the rate of growth, many people are hard pressed to imagine how even the present standard of living is to be sustained. It is an alarming and symptomatic fact to note that during the years 1966-1967 the standard of living was found to be 5% *below* the level of the early sixties.

Likewise, to take another example on the other side of the globe, the Ministry of labour of Peru has recently estimated that for every ten new jobs available in the next decade, there will be 55 new workers waiting for employment.[58]

This tendency becomes intensified if a government tries to rationalize and modernize its agricultural sector (which is a pressing task). It is not unusual in such circumstances for the labour force employed in agriculture to be reduced by 50 or more per cent. This development, if not accompanied by an equivalent increase of industrial jobs, is what worries the FAO most, to such an extent that it has predicted that the employment problem might become even more difficult to solve than the food problem.

Some would perhaps doubt such 'cataclysmic' predictions, but probably nobody would harbour the idea that an ever continuing population growth does not eventually constitute an insurmountable problem for the world. Even if an amount of 6 billion would not constitute a serious problem by the end of this century, and even if 12 or 15 billion could be employed and fed by 2030, could the world afford to have 50 billion people by the end of the 21st century? Unless unforeseen technical and social developments take place which open entirely new prospects for humanity, it is clear that the number

---

[57] Th. E. Dow – 'The Population of India,' 54 Curr. Hist. (April '68) pp. 220-221.
[58] W. C. Thiesenhusen – 'Latin America's Employment Problem,' 171 Science ('71) p. 868.

of people has to be restricted, if an over-all chaos is to be prevented. The Committee on Resources and Man of the US Academy of Sciences has urgently recommended that efforts be made to decrease drastically the rate of population growth in order to reach the zero rate by the end of this century. Even this probably unachievable goal, however, would be, according to some, no more than a small first step.[59]

However optimistic one thinks about future developments in the world, the conclusion seems hardly inevitable that serious endeavours must be made to stop the population explosion, primarily in the developing countries. Here lies an urgent task for every government, since measures in the realm of birth control can most effectively be taken on the national level.

Yet, an important observation seems to be – as the failure of the program in India reveals – that any program for birth control is doomed to fail, unless people understand its need and profits. If people in the Third World should be induced to change their long-standing attitudes in this question, such change should first be recognized by them as useful. At this moment many experience their living conditions as so hopeless and poor, that they are hardly susceptible to propaganda in the field of birth control; after all, from ten born children perhaps two will survive, and if these two become three or five, the difference remains small. They must be made to understand that there is a difference, and this can only be realized through substantial improvement of their living conditions; i.e. the only chance for birth control to be realized by the national governments in the Third World would lie in a preceding or at least simultaneous improvement of people's conditions of living, and thus *part of this effort depends on the aid and offers of the rich nations*, whose own future eventually becomes determined by what happens in the Southern part of the globe.

3.3.2. *Employment, agricultural rationalization, and industrial development*

The present rate of growth of the population in many developing countries results in a dramatic cumulation of the basic problems they already have. Overpopulated rural areas, industrial underdevelopment, and endemic unemployment are three images of the same problem: if development should occur, the agricultural sector in many countries must be rationalized and modernized; if agriculture should be modernized, many people must leave the countryside (for

[59] S. R. Eyre – 'Man the Pest,' N.Y.R. Books (Nov. 18, '71) p. 25.

the reasons why there is only a limited capacity to open new areas for agriculture, see below, section 3.3.6.); if the overcrowded countryside were to be rationalized, people have to find a living in towns and cities; if cities were to become more than only centers of transigients living at the very brink of survival, jobs have to be provided; if jobs were to be provided, industrialization must be realized.

Urban civilization is the historical, economic and demographic expression of advanced industrial production. Before 1800, only 8 per cent of the population of the United States and 20 per cent of the population of England lived in towns, in contrast to 90 per cent and 80 per cent respectively in 1950-1960. Thanks to the mechanization of agriculture, 5 per cent of the North American labour force remained in the countryside, as opposed to the 70 per cent engaged in farming in 1870; but at the same time, the United States today produces more wheat, meat, milk, fruit, corn and cotton than a century ago, when just 30 per cent of its total population lived in towns. At present the North American rural population in the strict sense of the word does not exceed 11 per cent; it has been reduced by 59 per cent. Nevertheless, this 11 per cent – with the aid of 4 million tractors and 1 million harvesters – produces a great deal more than the output of the 70 per cent rural population in 1870.

The level of economic and technological development of a country is in inverse proportion to its rural population. England, with only 6 per cent of its population in the countryside, has the greatest mechanization of agriculture: 53 tractors for every 1,000 hectares, in contrast to 2,8 in Argentina, 0,9 in Brazil, 5,9 in Chile, 3 in Columbia, 2.3 in Mexico, and 11 in Urugay. The above figures for Latin America pertain to the period 1960-1964. That Urugay is the country with the highest level of mechanization of agriculture among the Latin American countries can be explained by the fact that it is also the country with the highest percentage of city dwellers: over 80 per cent lives in towns, the figure for Argentina being 73.7 per cent, in Brazil 39.5 per cent, in Paraguay and Bolivia 35 per cent, in Columbia 52 per cent, in Chile 68.2 per cent, in Mexico 50.7 per cent, in Peru 47.4 per cent, in Venezuela 62.5 per cent, in Cuba 60 per cent, in the Dominican Republic 30.3 per cent, and least of all in Haiti only 12.2 per cent – a population composition similar to that in Equatorial Africa, Borneo, Guinea, India, and China, where the rural population exceeds 70 per cent of the total population because of the absence of mechanized agriculture. In general, those countries known for being industrially undeveloped all have a high percentage of rural population: the tropical and subtropical zones of the underdeveloped world still have 65 to 80 per cent of their population living in the

countryside; there is a constant shortage of food; the rate of illiteracy is high (over 50 per cent); the use of chemical fertilizers is virtually unknown; tractors and harvesters are not used – in short, these people have become paralyzed at living conditions being comparable to our middle ages.[60]
At present, people tend to leave the countryside, without as such contributing to modernization of agriculture and even without having any chance of finding a job in the cities, but nevertheless retaining the slight hope that they will be able to overcome the miserable life of a slum-dweller. They simply go, since they have no choice and have nothing to lose at home.

In order to escape from this dilemma, the developing countries need two things primarily:
1. diversification of their production process – to be achieved mainly by exploitation of their natural resources, and by industrialization;
2. money – to be earned mainly by increased export earnings, supplemented by aid as an intermediate measure.
Whereas the first measure provides jobs, the second provides the financial media enabling developing societies to import badly needed products from the industrialized world. For the development process to succeed in the Third World, these two measures are a crucial pivot. On the basis of such deliberations the United Nations have created the UN Capital Development Fund, and the UN Industrial Development Organization. *But what kind of industrialization, and what kind of export increase should be pursued?*
Since time urges, and the magnitude of the problems threatens to reach almost insurmountable levels, it is necessary to base planning on the circumstances as they presently prevail, or may prevail in the near future.
This means that – from the point of view of economic growth – industrial development must:
1. be based on employment criteria;
2. be based on present or short-term potentials, as determined by natural resources, financial resources, levels of education, transport facilities, etc.
It is of tremendous importance, that such industrial development remains not entirely dependent on the (at least in the near future) small internal markets. Industrialization can only contribute to

---

[60] A. Guillen – 'Rural Population and Urban Civilization,' XXI Rev. Int. Aff. 479 ('70) pp. 21 ff.

general development, if it is supported by the rich countries, along two interrelated ways. The rich countries should
1. refrain from extension of and – if possible – strive to abolish those sectors of their production, which are not of great importance to them and which can be substituted by equivalent products from and are of great export importance to the Third World countries;
2. enforce measures in the field of international trade, which enable the developing countries to export products to the industrialized world.

Such a system of mutually interdependent and supplementing economies can at best – if not only – be achieved through a set of interdependent measures, to be discussed separately below.

3.3.3. *International division of labour, endorsed by new patterns of international trade*

The developing countries need diversification of their production, and are dependent for successful endeavours in this direction on the industrialized countries. A feasible system is needed, which would turn out to be in the ultimate interests of all, developing and developed countries alike. Such a system can be worked out if it is based on the *optimal division of labour in a worldwide setting*. It is remarkable and encouraging to see how much the UN Resolution on the Strategy for D.D. II is based on this very thought!
The basic deliberation is as follows:
Industrialization and development should occur in each country in those branches which (1) meet their respective problems and stage of development, and (2) offer the best opportunities to compete on the world market. Employment, natural resources, transportation costs, and capital intensity are among the main factors which decide the quality and quantity of development in a specific direction. In general it can be said that the developing countries are 'labour-intensive' countries; this means that the input of human resources is bound to be many times greater than the input of (almost absent) financial resources. The industrialized countries, on the other hand, are the 'capital-intensive countries,' indicating that the input of financial resources is more crucial than that of human resources. At present it would be most profitable for *all*, if the developing countries would start their development process by concentrating on 'labour-intensive' sectors of industry, whereas the rich countries would more and more concentrate on the 'capital-intensive' sectors.

1^0. In the case of the *developing countries*, this means that, by concentrating on those sectors of industry *which are connected with their specific natural resources, which demand relatively simply technology, and which are dependent on human resources*, they would begin where it is most easy and most appropriate for them to begin. The entire idea has been advocated largely by Prof. Tinbergen, whose thoughts on this point are reflected in the Report of the so-called 'Tinbergen-Commission,' which states that 'there exists a need for further research in the field of the optimal division of labour' (p. 19), it being recommended that 'encouragement should be given to the selection of industries and technologies which are likely to have eventual competitive strength in the export markets'; it also states that 'it is necessary to examine all opportunities for raising the level of employment by bringing about a more labour-intensive product-mix.....' (pp. 17-18).

The UN Strategy Resolution contains many provisions of this nature, which are directed at the developing countries. Two of them are mentioned here, art. 66, and art. 67:

(66) 'Developing countries will make vigorous efforts to improve labour statistics in order to be able to formulate realistic quantitive targets for employment.... Moreover... they will expand their investment through a fuller mobilization of domestic resources and in increased flow of assistance from abroad. *Wherever a choice of technology is available, developing countries will seek to raise the level of employment by ensuring that capital-intensive technology is confined to uses in which it is clearly cheaper in real terms and more efficient..*';

(67) 'Developing countries will formulate and implement educational programmes taking into account their development needs. *Educational and training programmes will be so designed as to increase productivity substantially in the short run and to reduce waste.....*'

It is of importance that the developing countries choose those branches in which they are relatively most competitive vis-à-vis the industrialized countries. This means that they should not only take into consideration their internal human and natural resources, but also the resources and levels of production in developed countries, in order to devise optimal productivity on a worldwide scale. This is necessary for making the strategy also attractive to the rich countries, and to achieve success. This realistic consideration is reflected in the Strategy-Resolution, in articles 73 and 76, which read:

(73) '... *production policies will be carried out in a global context designed to achieve optimal utilization of world resources, benefiting both developed and developing coubtries*. Further research will be undertaken, by the international organizations concerned, in the field of optimal international division of labour to assist individual countries or groups of countries in their choice of production and trading structures...';

(76) 'Developing countries will take parallel steps to promote industry in order to achieve rapid expansion, modernization and diversification of their economies. They will devise measures to ensure adequate expansion of the industries that utilize domestic raw materials, that supply essential inputs to both agriculture and other industries, and that help to increase export earnings.....'

2⁰. The introduction by the Resolution of a 'global context' brings us to the measures to be taken by the *developed countries*.
It is important that they pave the way for increased imports from the developing countries of those products which are of particular importance to the development of the Third World, and in which the developing countries are relatively most competitive. This can be achieved only if the developed nations, on the one hand, refrain in general from extending their own production of these products, and – whenever possible – gradually strive at abolishing them; and if they, on the other hand, open their doors for such products from the Third World by allowing preferential treatment.

2⁰.1. This means – to elaborate on the first point – that the industrialized countries should more and more concentrate on the production of capital-intensive sectors of industry, and leave specific labour-intensive sectors to the developing part of the world. As has been indicated above,[61] this is also in the long-term interest of the developed countries themselves. Since the rich countries are capital-intensive and short of cheap labour, the industries where the developing countries could compete are usually not the industries of which it is in the developed countries' interest that they be promoted or even be preserved. Rational planning in developed countries 'should regularly result in moving their scarce labour resources to high-productivity industries, not in tying them to low-wage industries.'[62] An additional argument, which has often been given to show that an international labour division would bring large profits to the rich countries also, is based on the prediction that potential unemployment resulting from the adaptation process will be met by a large expansion of sophisticated industries, since a developing and wage-earning Third World population becomes increasingly able to buy such products from the industrialized world. The validity of this argumentation, however, becomes at present considered somewhat doubtful in view of the problems connected with future economic growth (see below, pp. 303-315 and section 3.3.6., where these problems are discussed). Whether or not large profits for the rich world may be expected, an international production division seems to offer the only chance for the developing countries to overcome their present difficulties within a relatively short period.

---

[61] see G. Myrdal, note 30 supra.
[62] idem.

The Strategy-Resolution states rather carefully in art. 35:

'The developed countries, having in mind the importance of facilitating the expansion of their imports from developing countries, will consider adopting measures and where possible *evolving a programme early in the Decade* for assisting the adaption and adjustment of industries and workers in situations where they are adversely affected or may be threatened to be adversely affected by increased imports of manufactures and semi-manifactures from developing countries.'

In connection to those fields where the import of crucial products from the developing countries is hindered by the production of substitutes, the Resolution states:

(29) '.... In their financial and technical assistance programmes, developed countries and the international organizations concerned will give sympathetic consideration to requests for assistance for developing countries producing natural products which suffer serious competition from synthetics and substitutes, in order to help them diversify in other areas of production including processing of primary products. *Where natural products are able to satisfy present and anticipated world market requirements, in the context of national policies no special encouragement will be given to the creation and utilization of new production, particularly in the developed countries, of directly competing synthetics.*'

2⁰.2. Concerning those products which are of special importance to the development of the Third World – to elaborate on the second kind of measures to be taken by the developed countries –, the Strategy Resolution contains many clear provisions. Article 31 states that special attention will be given to the expansion and diversification of the export trade of developing countries in manufactures and semi-manufactures; article 33 forbids 'ordinarily' to raise existing or to establish new tariff barriers on exports from developing countries, as far as manufactured and semi-manufactured products are concerned; art. 26 treats the same subject, but adding that trade barriers should be reduced or eliminated 'for products in which they (the developing countries) are *presently or potentially competitive*. Art. 32 should be quoted:

'Arrangements concerning the establishment of generalized, non-discriminatory, non-reciprocal preferential treatment to exports of developing countries in the markets of developed countries have been drawn up in the UNCTAD and considered mutually acceptable to developed and developing countries. *Preference-giving countries are determined to seek as rapidly as possible the necessary legislative or other sanction with the aim of implementing the preferential arrangements as early as possible in 1971.* Efforts for further improvements of these preferential arrangements will be pursued in a dynamic context in the light of the objectives of resolution 21 (II) of 26 March 1968, adopted by the UNCTAD at its second session.'

A recent step taken by some donor countries should be mentioned here. This is the decision made by the EEC to offer non-discriminatlry and non-reciprocal preferential treatment for products originating from developing countries.

This decision was the result of prior proposals and recommendations made within the framework of GATT in May '63, UNCTAD I in '64, UNCTAD II in '68, and the UN General Assembly in December '70. Resolution 21 (II) of UNCTAD II recommended a system of mutually acceptable, general, non-discriminatory, and non-reciprocal preferential treatment concerning imports of products originating from developing countries.

In order to carry out this recommendation, the European Commission made a proposal to the Council of Ministers of the EEC on March 17, '71, resulting in a decision of the Council on March 30, in which such preferential treatment was announced, and in which other rich countries were urged to co-operate in the same way. On June 21 and 22 the Council made a number of decisions which reinforced its general decision of March.

In general, the substance of these decisions is that a system of preferential treatment be adopted for a period of 10 years, whereas the application of it as layed down in the specific decisions of June would be restricted for the time being to a period of 6 months, after which an evaluation would take place.[63] According to the decisions, preferential treatment will be given to all semi-manufactured and finished industrial products, and to 'worked-up' agricultural products, originating from all developing countries belonging to the 'group of 77' within UNCTAD without further condition; and from dependent countries and territories on the condition that other donor countries allow similar preferential treatment.

As far as industrial products are concerned, the system is based on three principles: freedom of taxes, for certain quantities of the various products, and for all products without distinction mentioned in Chapters 25-99 of the nomenclature of Brussels. Special arrangements apply to textile products.

Concerning agricultural processed products, the system provides for reduction of tariffs.

Notwithstanding the promising image of these regulations on first sight, the question should be answered: to what extent do they really bring about a substantial improvement of the developing countries' position on the world market? The regulation concerning industrial products seems most promising; it has been calculated that the offer

---

[63] for the text of these decisions see 14 Journal officielles des Communautés Européennes no. L. 142 (June 28, '71).

by the EEC in this field might amount to some $ 1 billion. At this stage of development, however, the regulations concerning agricultural products seem to be of much higher importance to the developing countries, but exactly these regulations are disappointing; the offer in this respect might amount to some $ 30 million only, no offer having been made, moreover, in the field of primary agricultural products, and several escape clauses decrease its worth.
In connection to industrial products it has often been pointed out that only the few more advanced among the poor countries would profit from preferential treatment. The system as envisaged by the EEC tries to restrict this effect to some extent by means of regulations which forbid one country from holding more than 50% of the total quota for each product, while in some cases the ceiling is even 20%.
It is doubtful whether any real assets exist in the new provisions offered by the European Community. The import of these products from developing countries in general is of minor importance – only 6.6% in 1968, when tariffs were already relatively low. Moreover, the special preferential treatment allowed to the associated African countries is not changed by this system (and as such, its value in terms of global orientation and co-operation is limited).[64] Nevertheless, for the first time in history a major economic Power has extended non-discriminatory and non-reciprocal preferential treatment, a step which might encourage the acceptance of new patterns in the field of international trade for the benefit of the poor countries.

It has been argued that the usefulness of preferential treatment would be of a very restricted value in general, for three reasons:
(1) Preferential treatment would only encourage the development and production of synthetics and substitutes;
(2) Exports from the developing to the developed countries would only be increased by some $ 6 billion annually (the absolute ceiling being some $ 10 billion);
(3) Only the most developed among the developing nations would profit, as the less and least developed among them cannot compete with these few – Taiwan, Hongkong, Mexico, Brazil, India, and Pakistan.
As to the first point, if this result were to occur, it would be incompatible with art. 29 of the Strategy Resolution, which has been quoted in length above.

---

[64] see 'Europa van Morgen' (in Dutch) 6 ('71) pp. 34-35; and L. Metzemaekers in 24 'Nieuw Europa' (also in Dutch) (May, '71) p. 99.

As to the second point, it would seem that such calculations are based on present circumstances, and do not take into account the possibilities created by a system of international division of production as outlined here.

As to the third point, it would seem that also this would loose part of its relevance against the background of this new system, since several measures are feasible to involve the lesser and least developed among the developing nations into the development process (see e.g. the EEC-provision above). The Strategy-Resolution contains three articles in this respect (56-58), art. 56 of which reads:

> 'While it is the objective of the Decade to achieve the rapid economic and social progress of all developing countries, special measures will be taken to enable the least developed among them to overcome their particular disabilities. Every possible effort will be made to ensure the sustained economic and social progress of these countries and to enhance their capacity to benefit fully and equitable from the policy measures for the Decade. Wherever necessary, supplementary measures will be devised and implemented at the national, sub-regional, regional and international levels. Organizations and bodies of the United Nations system will consider initiating early in the Decade special programmes to alleviate the critical development problems of the least developed among developing countries; developed countries will assist in the implementation of these programmes.'

Art. 58 declares more in particular in connection to the field of exports:

> 'Special measures will be taken early in the Decade by national and international organizations to improve the capacity of the least developed among the developing nations to expand and diversify their production structure so as to enable them to participate fully in international trade... In the field of manufactures and semi-manufactures, measures in favour of developing countries will be so devised as to allow the least developed among developing countries to be in a position to derive equitable benefits from such measures...'

This, in short, is what Tinbergen has called the plan for 'the best division of labour' among the countries of the world; 'more precisely,' he says, 'it is the problem of minimizing costs of production of all the goods under a number of restrictions'. The most important restriction he mentions is obvious: 'the developing countries may have to produce a number of goods in which they are not yet competitive but in which they are as competitive as possible.' One should not try to find the *absolute minimum* of joint production costs, since this would mean that the situation remains largely as it is; instead, one should search for a *relative minimum*, taking both the fundamental needs of the developing countries and the optimal division of labour into account.

A second qualification is that a reasonable ratio should be established between the prices of sophisticated products on the one hand, and the prices of less-sophisticated products and primary products on the other hand. At this moment, the difference is most frustrating to the developing countries, a situation characterized by Tinbergen as the 'anti-processing structure'.[65]

(We come back to the problem of the decreasing prices of primary products on the world market in section 3.3.5. separately, because this is a problem by itself and stands partly apart from that of the international division of labour).

In the third place, it has often been argued that such division of labour would lead to a new polarization of inequality, fixing the poor countries for ever into an industrially inferior position. That result, however, would follow only if the measures taken were considered as a one-time process. It is clear that a proposal as outlined here is done under the pressure of the circumstances, and is intended to realize more equality and worldwide prosperity on the basis of the present situation. It is of particular importance, therefore, *that the process envisaged be considered a continuous process, resulting in continuing transformation, to be realized by permanent deliberation and adaption.* One should not overlook in this connection that, as for products which are not severely restricted because of their limited availability, the growing population of wage-earning people in the Third World provides a steadily increasing market for products of all kinds, thus enabling developed and the developing countries alike to increase their production gradually both in a vertical and in a horizontal direction (but see below, at the end of this section). The Strategy Resolution provides for a steady review and appraisal of both objectives and policies (Part D).

The fourth qualification is of a different kind and concerns the public shock provoked by the report of the Club of Rome: the profits hitherto believed to result from an international division of labour are now feared by many not to be forthcoming, because the world could not afford any further expansion of production, and because economic growth would have to stop.

Indeed, although various data presented in this report were known in scientific circles, their combined effect and the projected developments based on them have come to many as a doomsday bell.

---

[65] see J. Tinbergen – 'Wanted: a World Development Plan,' XXII Int. Org. I ('68) pp. 417-431.

Hitherto, the starting point of the projections presented by development economists and politicians alike was generally, that the rich world could only benefit from an international labour division, since – as has been indicated above – they would invest more rationally in capital-intensive sophisticated industries (leaving low-wage industries to the developing nations) and since a wage-earning Third World population would increasingly become a tremendous market for exports expansion.

E.g. MacNamara, the President of the World Bank, has presented such considerations in his addresses to its Board of Governors. In 1969, he pointed out the contradictory character of present development efforts:

> 'It is wholly absurd for the rich countries to invest billions in developing the poor countries, and then to refuse to be repaid in those goods which are the first fruits of development.'

Elaborating on the re-structuring of industry on a global scale he said:

> 'There is no genuine economic reason for the developed nations to fear the industrial growth of the less advanced countries and the establishment of new patterns of international trade in manufactured goods. On the contrary, the wealthier nations should target their own growth in the direction where their greatest comparative advantage already lies; the production of goods and services requiring sophisticated levels of technology. It would be to the benefit of the world economy as a whole for the technically advanced societies to concentrate more in these fields, and gradually to relinquish the simpler and less complicated manufacturing to those developing nations which can efficiently do the job.'[66]

Presupposing for a moment that basic problems are not involved indeed, adaptive measures, of course, could create temporary problems for specific sectors of the production-apparatus. The emergence of these minor problems, however, could be largely prevented by rational planning on basis of the global strategy suggested. Wherever transitional difficulties might may arise nevertheless, they could be solved, for instance, by creating an international fund for temporary assistance in serious cases. As a general rule, however, this would not be come necessary, there being no absolute need for the industrialized nations to preserve the branches discussed here. The developed countries, being sourceful and wealthy enough to handle such problems without great difficulties, could in some cases even

---

[66] Address to the Board of Governors of the World Bank Group by R. S. MacNamara (Wash., Sept. 29, '69) pp. 15, 21-22.

preserve existing branches by directing their production in such branches to higher-grade goods. Myrdal mentions the example of Sweden in this connection, as a country with a tradition of an enlightened trade-union movement, where this policy line has become accepted even by the union representing the workers in the low-wage industries. A notable example is the much debated textile industry, which has rationalized radically and directed its production to those high-grade goods, with which the developing countries are not yet in the market and will not be for the near future. Meanwhile, the number of workers in the textile industry decreased between 1950 and 1968 by around 50 per cent, indicating a rational and timely planning. Why could not other countries provide for a similar planning, instead of merely complaining about the bad situation in their textile sector, which at this moment, indeed, has very little to do with imports from the developing countries? Such adjustment problems are constantly created by economic and technological changes, or by efforts to lower tariffs (as witnessed recently by the Kennedy-round – indeed, the rich countries might profit in the long run from a division of labour among themselves! –) and they are handled as a part of normal policy routine, when the developed countries 'inter se' are concerned. Why should there be insurmountable problems when the developing countries are involved? In short, these considerations are based on the view that an international development strategy is *not a matter of economic possibility, but a matter of political will.*

Traditional schemes for the improvement of welfare conditions in the Third World presuppose, however, a rather unlimited potential for industrial and agricultural expansion in the world. In particular the industrialization of the developing countries was not considered to entail serious reserve- and environmental problems, and it was even doubted whether the rich part of the world would have to bring any sacrifice at all. Such rosy predictions seem by now doubtful to many, since data on the possibilities of future economic growth would seem to forbid their realization. The most desparate predictions hold that world economic prosperity is impossible, since the remaining reserves are so small, that neither the rich countries can afford any further economic growth, nor the poor countries can afford to develop industrially. Before passing a judgement over any such negation of a welfare strategy, the merits of the basic arguments should be discussed. One of the major problems in this connection, exponential population growth, has been discussed in section 3.3.1., and will not be reiterated here, although it lies like a shadow over all considerations that follow in the present and next sections. Another closely related problem, food production, will be discussed separately in section 3.3.6., but it should be stressed again that these problems and the other major areas of concern dealt with here – natural resources, energy, and environmental pollution – are highly interdependent and constitute in fact an integrated block of problems. The only reason for dealing with them separately is clearness.

Any process of increasing industrial output in the world demands higher levels of resource depletion and use of energy, which in their turn would produce a higher level of pollution. The question, then, is to what extent the world's natural reserves and the after-effects of various levels of industrial production are prohibitive to increased levels of industrialization or even demand a decrease.

To begin with *natural resources*, a first observation to be made concerns the huge difference in consumption of these resources between the industrialized and the developing part of the world.

Taking metallic copper as a first example, the industries of Europe, the US and the USSR (about 850 million people) consumed well over 75% of the world smelter production of six million tons in the year 1965. The industries in the whole of Asia, Africa and Latin America (about 2.5 billion people) have consumed far less than 25%, and if the very considerable copper consumption of Japan and South Africa is deducted, an insignificant amount is left. Taking tin as a second example, in 1967 the industries of Western Europe and North America consumed 75% of the total of 166.000 short tons consumed by the non-communist world (including Yugoslavia); Southern Asia, Africa, and Latin America consuming less than 10%. Taking aluminium as a third example, Europe, North America, the USSR and Japan consumed in 1965 about 7.300.000 tons out of a total of 7.415.000 tons.

Another illustrating figure mentioned by Eyre is that the Netherlands (with 13 million people) consumed more tin in 1967 than the whole of the Indian sub-continent (with 600 million people) and nearly twice as much as the whole of Africa (with 280 million people). Steeman Nielsen has calculated that the US in 1965 consumed between 30 and 40 per cent of the total non-communist mineral supply; other, more specific, calculations indicating that the industries of the US alone today consume 50% of the world's annual production of aluminium, 25% of smelted copper, 40% of lead, over 36% of nickel and zinc, about 30% of chromium, etc. Simple projections based on growth of the population and the national product suggest that by 1980 consumption of minerals by the United States will in general increase by 50% and in many cases even double.[67]

[67] S. R. Eyre, note 59 supra; he derived his statistics from the Minerals Yearbook of the US Bureau of Mines, and from the UN Statistical Yearbook; W. Hibbard, p. 144.

This background can clearly illustrate the problems we are confronted with while thinking of world development, and pondering the question: is our globe so rich of minerals that it could afford to supply the quantities required for the Third World's industrial development?

Precise data are not available, a major problem being that the magnitude of reserves is determined not only by the absolute quantity of resources prevailing in rocks, but also by the relative possibility of exploiting them. Many independent calculations have been made on various kinds of minerals, however, and these suggest generally, that without conservatory measures we are rapidly approaching exhaustion of many crucial minerals.

World reserves of mercury, for instance, at a price of $ 200 per flask were estimated by the US Bureau of Mines to be 3.160.000 flasks, the current production being 275.000 flasks per year. If total world production were to increase at only half the rate at which the demand is increasing in the United States, all mercury would be exhausted within 20 years from now; a price as high as $ 1000 per flask – enabling investors to produce mercury from very low-grade ore – might maintain world production for some 50 years.

In the case of copper, estimates suggest that if India alone were to consume this metal at the same rate per capita as the United States, without any increase of rate, India would need 450 million tons during the coming century, which is certainly more than the world can still supply! This makes any comment superfluous if one would assume that all developing countries would begin to consume copper at the US level, which would demand 1.25 billion tons...[68]

Such figures, even if their reliability would be only partial, are indeed shocking, and have led to statements negating any chance for global welfare at a level presently achieved by the rich nations:

> '... before any area can reach the per capita energy and mineral consumption rate of the United States, it must first build up its industry to that level. Were the whole world to have done this... the presently estimated world supply of ores of most industrial metals, producible by present technology, would have been exhausted well before such a level of industrialization could have been reached...'[69]

Of course, the condition introduced by the words 'by present technology' is a very important one. The total quantities of reserves expected to become available by present technology could be increased

[68] Th. S. Lovering – 'Mineral Resources from the Land,' in 'Resources and Man' op. cit., p. 128; S. R. Eyre, p. 23.
[69] M. King Hubbert – 'Energy Resources,' a report to the Committee on Natural Resources of the National Academy of Sciences ('62).

in the following five ways: (1) pursuing new exploration and discovery; (2) inventing improved technologies of mining, production and processing; (3) inventing entirely new technologies and substitutes; (4) recycling of scrap and waste; (5) increasing the quality and durability of consumer goods.

As for the first way, new discoveries, an important type of unknown ore body includes those that do not come to the surface, the so-called 'blind' ores. New methods of exploring effectively at large depths could indicate the availability of resources additional to the resources still to be discovered from outcrops.

There is a misleading notion, however, that a great variety of resources are available in large volumes in the ocean-bed. At present about 5 per cent of the world's known production of geological wealth comes from the shelves and seawater, and the trend is upward. Oil and gas are by far the most important products, but geological knowledge suggests as Cloud points out, that

> 'the ocean basins beyond the continental margin are not promising places to seek mineral resources.... if present conceptions of earth structure and of sea-floor composition and history are even approximately correct, minerals from the seabed are not likely to compare in volume or in value with those yet to be taken from the emerged lands. As for seawater itself, despite its large volume and the huge quantities of dissolved salts it contains, it can supply few of the substances considered essentially to modern industry.'[70]

As for the second way, new technologies in the field of exploitation and processing, more efficient methods for mining ores and for upgrading them before smelting and refining could make the use of leaner ores feasible. Nearly all elements are present in nearly all rocks, but usually in such small proportions as to make them hitherto economically unexploitable. New processes might be found to make the exploitation of such low-grade ores economically feasible, although this is widely doubted. On the other hand, new techniques could perhaps be found and put into practice which might make it possible to exploit some of the resource bodies hidden in the depths of the earth, if they are discovered.

As for the third way, substitution, it is very difficult to predict what innovations will be found by physical metallurgy and polymer chemistry. In view of the results achieved hitherto in the field of substitutes for the most crucial commodities, however, many doubt that major categories of the scarcity problem could be solved on relatively short notice.

As for the fourth way, recycling of scrap and waste, it is noteworthy

---

[70] P. Cloud – 'Resources from the Sea,' in 'Resources and Man' op. cit., pp. 153-154.

that already today large quantities of the production of several commodities come not from primary ores, but from reclaimed scrap; e.g. in 1968, 40% of the production of lead and 25% of copper in the United States were derived from such secondary sources.[71] It is questionable whether improved collection and processing techniques could provide substantially more quantities.

As for the fifth way, it can merely be said that present production schemes are based upon the principle of increasing production by supplying consumer goods of lower quality and shorter durability. It would require large-scale transformations to change this basis.

One crucial and general observation, however, concerns the time factor; time urges to such an extent, that it seems doubtful at present whether we are in a position to wait for such enormous technological innovations and their introduction into practice which would enable us to acquire resources in the quantities needed for an increased or even a sustained industrial production. And even if such innovations would be made and would prove to be practically feasible, the question remains whether the world can afford the probably tremendous expenses required for massive new investments and large-scale transformations. It seems not without reason, therefore, that some experts consider that 'the time scale with which the crisis is concerned is to be measured in decades rather than in centuries.' Lovering thinks that this is particularly true with regard to the cost factor, even as far as the technically most sophisticated nation is concerned. He says that

> 'all postponements allowed for, however, it is clear that exhaustion of deposits of currently commercial grade is inevitable. Yet it is equally true that the increased costs of capital, labor, energy, and transportation for mining deposits of lower grade have in the past been largely offset by improved technology. The question is, can this continue? The answer remains to be given, but there are many signs that technology is *not* keeping pace with increasing costs of extraction in the United States.'[72]

In view of the magnitude of the problems, the period of time that remains, and the probably tremendous amount of funds required to solve these problems, the conclusion seems justified that from the point of view of resources alone an industrialization process in the Third World of the same order as it has occurred in the rich countries, is presently beyond the world's capacity, and that industrial development in 'the South' can not take place without substantial shrinking of industrial production in 'the North.'

---

[71] W. Hibbard, p. 145.
[72] S. R. Eyre, p. 23; Th. S. Lovering, p. 130.

This is underlined by an investigation into the future capacity of *energy*.

Present technology is very dependent on fossil fuels, particularly coal and oil, and natural gas. About 96 per cent of the energy used in the industrialized countries is supplied by these substances. Also these reserves are fastly diminishing, however. Taking the example of petroleum, estimates of world resources show that they may be expected to be exhausted for about 90% between the years 2020 and 2030 (depending on the growth rate of its use). On the basis of the estimates considered most accurate, calculated by Ryman, King Hubbert points out that the peak of production of the world's crude oil, amounting to about 37 billion barrels, will occur by the year 2000, while the middle 80 per cent of the ultimate cumulative production of 2.090 billion barrels in total would be produced during the 64-year period since 1968.[73] These figures, however, do not take an increased demand into account as would result from substantial industrial development in the Third World. In that case, reserves might last for perhaps only a few decennia.

Total resources of coal are expected to be larger – resources determined by mapping and exploration amounting to 9.500 billion short tons, unexplored resources amounting to 7.330 billion short tons, in total amounting to 16.830 billion short tons – and they might supply energy for some centuries. Even without a sharp increase of demand the time span for exploitation might be shortened, however, since the gradually increasing costs of exploitation, transport, and transformation might become unbearable.

Some figures concerning the needs of a modern industrial infrastructure clearly illustrate the problems we are confronted with while thinking about future industrialization of the Third World: although coal has been mined for 800 years, half of the coal produced hitherto has been mined during the last 31 years; half of the world's cumulative production of petroleum has occurred during the twelve-year period between 1956 and 1968; in general, most of the world's consumption of energy from the fossil fuels during its entire history has occurred during the last 25 years.[74]

Such figures suggest that the steady rates of growth sustained during a period of several decades in each instance cannot be maintained for much longer periods, and the rate of growth required if the Third World were to develop industrially along with the rich countries would perhaps result in the total exhaustion of presently producible

---

[73] M. King Hubbert – 'Energy Resources' in 'Resources and Man' op. cit., pp. 194 ff.
[74] idem, pp. 166 ff.

fossil resources within some decades. The relative shortness of time that remains and the relatively time-consuming process of introducing new technologies on a large scale, moreover, explains the rather pessimistic point of view several experts have expressed.

Many hope, therefore, for sensational developments in other fields, notably those of water power, tidal power, geothermal power, solar energy, and nuclear power. Concerning the potential water power capacities, American geological survey data give a total world capacity of 2.857.000 megawatts, of which by 1964 210.000 megawatts (or about 7.5%) were used. If fully developed, this would be of a magnitude comparable to the world's present rate of energy consumption. Three considerations seriously qualify the logical conclusion that by water power alone the world could maintain its present industrial level. In the first place, enormous investments would have to be made on relatively short notice; in the second place, people would have to sacrifice several of their most beautiful natural sceneries (of which the world becomes even poorer); in the third place, the dammed streams filling the reservoirs continuously deposit their loads of sediments, so that in the period of a century or two most reservoirs are due to become completely filled by such sediments. This problem has not been satisfactorily solved, and may never be. By that time, such water power resources will stop their activity.

Concerning tidal power, it appears that world capacities in this field are very restricted, calculations showing that total potential tidal power amounts to less than 1 per cent of potential water power.

The same holds true for potential geothermal power, which is estimated to be in the tens of thousands of megawatts, and which, although being capable of sustaining a large number of small power plants, represents only a small fraction of the world's energy requirements.

An inspiring source of future energy supply is solar radiation, and in theory its power would be of adequate magnitude. To put it in practice poses enormous, and at present insurmountable problems, however; it has been calculated, for instance, that the area of the earth's surface required to collect 10^{10} watts of solar power would be 42 km². Although there is no question of its being physically possible to cover such an area with energy-collecting devices, and to transmit, store, and transform the energy so collected into electric power, the complexity of such a process and its costs in terms of metals and equipment required might prove to be prohibitive.

As for nuclear energy, neither this source seems to be regarded at present as the widely believed cheap, limitless alternative. Increased consumption of the rare uranium-235 in non-breeder reactors would result in its complete exhaustion within a short period of time. Fast breeder reactors will be available before the end of this century. Since these reactors also need uranium-235 as an initial fuel, this transformation program should be achieved before the economically exploitable quantities of this source become exhausted. Once operating, they are capable of producing their own fuel while consuming low-concentration uranium or thorium, and could thus provide an adequate source of long-range industrial power. The transition program of switching to nuclear energy supplied by full-breeder reactors, however, demands enormous investments. Fusion reactors, whose fuel is a component of seawater, are a promising alternative and may become available eventually, but this is considered a rather remote solution.[75]

In view of the tremendous capital to be invested if present systems of energy consumption have to be transformed, it seems highly questionable whether the world could afford to invest those amounts which are required to generate enough nuclear energy to supply the whole future world. But this is perhaps not even the most problematic obstacle envisaged at present in this connection: many fear that the vastly increased radioactive and thermal pollution resulting from worldwide use of nuclear fission-energy might become prohibitive to such transformation.

This brings us to the third category of concern, *environmental pollution*.

If metallic and fossil energy resources would not be so limited as they appear to be, the question still remains whether the envisaged industrialization process in the developing countries – without sacrifices in this field being made by the rich countries – could take place without destroying the world's biological environment.

In the industrialized part of the world – the Netherlands being a good example – we hear more and more about the fatal effects of industrial pollution. Several animal species have become extinct, fish in the internal waters is dying, flora and fauna are destroyed in many areas, and people's health becomes increasingly endangered. This already unbearable situation could as such constitute a strong additional argument pleading for an international division of labour, based on the idea that only a spread of industry over the globe could save us from further pollution, without having to harm the developing countries seriously. Now it appears, however, that it is not true that the world is big enough to have all industries mankind needs to

[75] idem, pp. 208-209, 211, 218, 226ff. resp.

achieve a high level of over-all prosperity. It seems not only justified to say that any higher level of pollution would endanger the whole world, but that even present levels of pollution are beginning to be fatal. Calculations have been made showing that if we go on poisoning the oceans merely at the present level, life within this biggest food reservoir in the world may become extinct within decades.

How then could the world afford any higher level of industrialization and mechanization without life being destroyed?

Fossil fuels, on which present technology depends so much, release, if burned, the highly toxic carbon dioxide into the atmosphere. Automobiles, several industrial processes, and agricultural pesticides release toxic metals in huge quantities; mercury and lead being among the most worrying examples. Atmospheric dusts are increasing, endangering people's health severely and contributing to climatic disturbances. The most quoted agricultural poisoning species appearing everywhere on earth is DDT, which is released into the environment at a rate of 100.000 tons annually. It has been found even in the fat tissue of the penguins on the Antarctic, several fish species have been declared unsafe for consumption, animals and human beings are being poisoned by it.

Unfortunately we do not know the limits of our and nature's ability to sustain atmospheric poisoning and ecological disturbances. What is known at this moment, however, can hardly lead to the conclusion that higher levels of environmental pollution would not confront the world with serious consequences.

To transform at least our energy systems so as to generate vastly increased amounts of nuclear fission-energy, would bring no solution either. In the first place, such nuclear power is always accompanied by the production of radioactive waste – even such plans as the disposal of this waste in underground salt mines cannot prevent some waste to be released in the neighbourhood of every plant. In the second place, nuclear power is accompanied by thermal pollution (energy being dissipated as heat into the atmosphere) and if nuclear power would become our primary source of energy this thermal pollution might reach such levels as to change atmospheric and climatic conditions, the ecological consequences of which cannot be foreseen. Taking such effects into consideration, it would appear that a mere spread of industries does not easily solve the problem of pollution, and that a spread of industries accompanied by increased industrialization would confront humanity with enormous problems.

Again it should be repeated that such considerations do not take technical innovations into account. Several anti-pollution devices have been developed for various sources of pollution, new ones may be invented, and new sources or production processes might be discovered. It may be true that most forms of pollution are fleeting compared to other adverse variables, and it may be true – as is alleged – that even solid wastes present no unsolvable problems, and that they are the accompaniment of a technology that is more than adequate to handle them, provided there is a will or a demand expressed by laws. Then, these laws are badly needed. In view of the level of pollution reached already, and the short period of time which might remain to do something about it, early and effective preventive measures on a large scale are a *sine-qua-non* for sustained prosperity.

This is the background against which plans for a global development strategy have to be constructed today. Even if the data, of which a few have been mentioned here, would appear to be unnecessary pessimistic, even if they would prove to be only partially reliable, they show that under conditions of continuous population growth the time is approaching – if not soon, than later – when any further industrial expansion places the world for insurmountable problems. Sooner or later the rich countries are compelled to make protecting regulations, even if they would forget about the fate of the poor nations. But if that other great danger, large-scale violence in the Third World, is to be prevented, the poor countries will have to be involved in the state of welfare, and thus in the process of industrialization.
One may expect, moreover, that even if the rich nations would prefer to keep wealth and prosperity within their own circles, the poor nations will increasingly become able to build up an industrial infrastructure themselves. Apart from the polemological consequences of the slackening of development in such circumstances, this might eventually lead to unco-ordinated exploitation and 'wild industrialization', excluding practical schemes for conservatory measures and ending up in exhaustion and unlimited pollution. *This is another reason why the rich nations can not afford to neglect the development of the Third World.* We are all involved alike, and we can only profit from the early realization of a general strategy aimed at global welfare and global conservation. Whatever the prospects and whatever sacrifices the rich countries might have to make to realize this, the necessity of an international division of labour remains beyond doubt. It will certainly demand today, however, a much larger extent of worldwide and regional co-ordination and co-operation than would have been the case if the world were not confronted with scarcity and pollution problems.

The system of international division of labour needs the support

and supplement of specific measures and regulations in various fields of activity, like financial and technical assistance, acquisition of raw materials, price-regulation and price-stabilization, the building of modern infra-structures in the developing countries, education, health, etc.
Because such measures, however, are needed by themselves and are related to problems which present themselves independently of any scheme of division of labour, they will be treated separately below. All of them constitute, however, parts of this scheme in one way or another.

3.3.4. *The acquirement by the developing countries of specific natural resources*

The developing countries are in need of many natural resources for the benefit of their industrial development. Several of them are rich in various resources, and they can be helped to exploit these with the assistance of foreign governments, firms, and international organizations. Others lack most of the resources they need, and for them the envisaged multilateral regulations would create the possibility of acquiring the resources they need. In view of the relative scarcity of various species it becomes the more important that a general plan for the optimal division of labour be accepted as the basis for industrial development in the Third World. This plan should decide on the fundamental question concerning the ways countries or regions are going to develop in the various fields of industrial production. On the basis of this, the plan would decide on the modality of exploitation, exports and imports of specific natural resources of each country. The level of freedom of choice is perhaps an enormous problem which depends on the level of acceptance of such a general plan. In any case improved regional co-operation among the developing countries inter se is recommendable; co-ordination of production, mutual aid in transport questions, common use of natural harbours or power-stations located at the border, etc., could greatly help to prevent waste.

An important legal development on the question of the acquirement of natural resources is taking place – as has been described above – in the realm of the law of the ocean-floor.
A Resolution on a temporary moratorium has been adopted (at present, halas, without effect), an international régime will be worked out, and all steps envisaged must take the special interests of the developing countries into account. An interesting report on these questions, called 'The United Nations and the Bed of the Sea,' has been worked out by the 'Commission to Study the Organization of

[76] see note 50 supra.

Peace' under the chairmanship of Louis Sohn.[76] The proposals as embodied in this report are most remarkable on the point of the exploitation of the resources of the sea-bed:

Some have proposed that the technologically less developed states directly share the wealth of the sea-bed through acquiring preferential treatment in the allocation of exclusive rights; that is, they should receive such rights on the basis of needs rather than on the basis of full payment of royalties or bids. Such a system, however, was rejected by the Commission which feels that it would neither benefit the world community at large, nor would it benefit the developing countries. It would lead to waste and an economically inefficient use of natural resources, and as a result the developing countries would be encouraged to make inefficient use of their scarce technical skills and capital.

This opinion would seem to be in line with the theory of international division of labor, since we are confronted here with a quite sophisticated activity that demands a high level of technological skill and capital investment. The Commission seeks the solution to this problem by suggesting that the holders of exploitation rights pay royalties to the world community, to be used for reducing the welfare gap between developed and developing nations, like research-projects on ways to overcome protein malnutrition. The funds raised would become an independent source of income for the United Nations.

It is questionable, however, whether the hope of the Commission that this solution would make this kind of 'free-market-system' for the exploitation of the sea-bed acceptable to the developing countries, is justified. They are not so much interested in the revenues of royalties, as they are in acquiring their share of natural resources they need for their industrial development. Such is indicated by the wording of the UN Declaration on the Sea-Bed, which demands in several articles that the exploration and exploitation of the natural resources there shall be carried out for the benefit of mankind as a whole, 'taking the specific needs of the developing countries into particular consideration,' while ensuring 'the equitable sharing by States the benefits derived therefrom.' The Resolution recommending a moratorium until an international régime has been established, reflects the same demand (see sections 3.2.2. and 3.2.3.).

Perhaps a feasible system can be worked out which combines efficiency with equality; for instance, a system based on the establishment of a regulating authority acting on behalf of the world community (this has already been accepted), exploration and exploitation by nations and firms best equiped for the task, and obligatory transfers of certain quanta of specific natural resources to the international authority which distributes them among non-exploiting states according to criteria of needs and performance.

The United Kingdom has recently introduced a proposal according to which an international organization would divide the ocean-floors into sections, of which all countries – including the land-locked states – would acquire a part proportional to their area. Every country could then either exploit its part by itself or extend concessions to foreign firms. If such concessions would not deprive those countries who cannot exploit the resources themselves of all the natural resources they need (for instance through a clause demanding that certain quantities be transferred to the country in question), such a partition might be acceptable in principle also to the developing countries. The problem, however, of determining who gets which part – given the fact that the finding-places of several important materials are virtually known – might become an insurmountable one. The English object to schemes, such as proposed by France, to create an international organization which would exploit the ocean-floors by itself. They feel that such an organization would develop into a money-swallowing bureaucracy. But this might be not as serious an obstacle as the problem of partition.

The Commission has also made valuable proposals on the question of the definition of the continental shelf.

In this respect it has concluded that 'the Convention on the Continental Shelf should be revised so as to provide that national exploitation rights over sea-bed resources end at the 200-meter depth line or 50 nautical miles from shore, whichever occurs further out'; in the meantime it recommends that 'the United Nations appeal to all States to refrain from granting leases to mineral resources beyond the 200-meter depth limit until the revision of the Convention on the Continental Shelf comes into force.'[77] This might be a valuable supplement to the moratorium Resolution, because this has shown little effect hitherto. Since 1969 over 100 concessions have been extended to some 30 countries, involving over 2 million km² of the sea-bed at depths greater than 200 meters.

In the meantime a special United Nations Commission, established in 1968 (res. 2467A (XXIII) and re-instructed in 1970 (Res. 2750 (XXV)) tries to find solutions to the various problems involved keeping in mind the scheduled Conference in 1973.

[77] idem, pp. 24, 25.

3.3.5. Trade in and prices of primary commodities

Despite future developments of industrialization the developing countries will remain important exporters of many raw materials and primary products. It is important, therefore, that recent efforts to create a more reasonable price ratio between industrial products and primary products be encouraged much more then has been the case. The situation for many products still is highly unreasonable for the developing countries. Also in this respect the rules of a free market system should be adapted to the needs of planned development. Some figures may illustrate this point:[78]

Between 1960 and 1967 the share in world trade of
'Western' industrial countries increased from: 67 to 70%
'Socialist' industrial countries remained: 12%
Developing countries decreased from: 21 to 18%
Between 1959 and 1965 annual exports of
'Western' industrial countries increased with: 8,8%
'Socialist' industrial countries with: 8,3%
Developing countries with: 6,0%

The developing countries' exports, amounting to some $ 35 billion a year – of which $ 15 billion worth of oil (exported by only 5 countries, S. Arabia, Lybia, Koewait, Venezuela, and Nigeria), and only $ 5 billion worth of non-primary products, thus existing for 85% of primary commodities – increased with only 77%. During the same period world trade in industrial commodities increased with 203%.

At the same time the developing countries as suppliers of primary products suffered from another trend: whereas the prices of industrial products (their imports) increased up to 200%, the prices of primary products (their exports) decreased between 1950 and 1964 with 17% on average, and between 1960 and 1966 with 4%. The developing countries have suffered from price drops for products such as rubber, oils and oilseeds, jute, hard fibrins and iron ore.

The efforts to stop these trends have been made most ardently. First success was achieved in the field of oil through OPEC. In general, the rich countries are reluctant to discuss such matters directly with the poor countries – as in UNCTAD – and prefer to use organizations of their own choice, where they do not feel such strong pressure upon them; notably GATT has been used for the purpose to offer the developing countries more favourable treatment.

Four important steps were taken in the framework of this forum, with correspondingly unimportant results:

[78] figures derived from the Statistical Yearbooks from the UN, and the Annual Reports on International Trade from the GATT.

1⁰. In December 1961, the GATT Parties adopted a solemn 'Declaration on Promotion of the 'Trade of Less-Developed Countries';
2⁰. In May 1963, in this connection an 'Action Program' was set up together with an 'Action Committee';
3⁰. In February 1965, a new Chapter IV was added to the GATT of 1948. All these activities added no virtual improvement to the position of the poor countries.
4⁰. The 'Kennedy-Round,' since 1964, is seen by the poor as a manoeuvre of the 'rich men's club' and has indeed resulted in more wealth for the rich and relatively more poverty for the poor.

In view of the refusal of the rich countries to meet the demands of the poor countries, the last mentioned have tried everything to reach better results through UNCTAD, but they were also disappointed on that count. At UNCTAD I (Geneva, 1964) the rich countries refused to accept new obligations, and they did the same at UNCTAD II (New Delhi, 1968). Adebanjo of Nigeria consequently translated UNCTAD into 'Under No Circumstances Take Any Decision.' Even the recommendations adopted were meager. 132 governments, 600 UN-servants and 300 experts in the field struggled for weeks without any notable results for the developing countries. The unwillingness of the rich countries was expressed clearly in Commission II; although all said to be convinced of the necessity of industrialization in the developing countries, the rich countries – instead of outlining a general strategy to make that possible – drew up a list of industrial products for preferential treatment *which could only help themselves*. In stead of crucial products such as textile or fruit preserves, radar equipment was put on the list..... It seems only naturally that the poor countries feel cheated and betrayed. After the Conference Nossiter wrote:

> 'the performance staged here, a kind of international Theater of the Absurd, has surpassed even the most pessimistic projections.'[79]

In New Delhi, the story went around that two types of telegrams had been sent to the various home ministers; one reading 'Conference success. We gave away nothing'; the other stating 'Conference Failure. We got nothing.'[80]

It is very important that the negative trends described above be stopped, and that trends in the opposite direction be advanced. An

[79] B. D. Nossiter in Int. Her. Trib. (March 30, '68) p. 4.
[80] B. Gosovic – 'UNCTAD: Noth-South Encounter,' Int. Conc. no. 568 (May '68) p. 76.
In general see the General Report on UNCTAD II by J. A. Encinas del Pando in UNCTAD, 2nd. Sess., Report and Annexes, UN Publ. Sales no. E. 68. II D. 14 (68).

endeavour of this kind constitutes an essential precondition to the realization of an international division of labour.

The problem of scarcity of resources adds another dimension to the context of price stability. Now that various resources are in danger of becoming exhausted, it appears not only necessary to prevent 'wild industrialization,' but also to prevent the uncontrolled export of exploited quantities. Regulation concerning the use of resources demands regulation concerning the trade in them, which might be achieved on one level by establishing more equal prices for primary commodities vis-a-vis industrial products. If the use and export of scarce resources were to continue uncontrolled, the present inferior prices might suddenly be substituted by exorbitantly high prices, once the resources approach exhaustion. Such events would certainly benefit noone.

The realization of a global development plan can not be achieved without new price regulations for primary products.

3.3.6. *Nutrition*

Between 1958 and medio 1967, the world's population increased by 518 million. Up to this moment the developing countries have in no way been able to manage the problem of their increasing need of food. Two thirds of the entire world population is undernourished; of these people 60% is younger than 20 years, 40% being younger than 14 years. The problem is, that lack of important foodstuffs during the early years is bound to have a negative impact on physical well-being for the rest of people's life. The diet-deficit areas include all of Asia except Japan (and probably China), the Middle East except Israel, all but the Southern tip of Africa, and almost all of Latin America and the Caribbean. The diet of people in these areas averaged 900 calories per day below the level of the other third of mankind living in countries with adequate diets during the early sixties. The deficit consisted of an average of 300 calories per person per day below the minimum nutritional level of 2.300 calories required for normal activity and health. The daily consumption of proteins was less than two-thirds and the consumption of fat was less than one-third that of the diet-adequate countries.[81] Within this picture it must be realized, moreover, that in most of the poor countries lives a rich minority, which accounts for the fact that for innumerable people the situation must be much worse than would appear from these figures.

[81] US Dept. of Agriculture, For. Regional Analysis Division, Economic Research Service – 'world Food Needs' ('66);
FAO – 'The State of Food and Agriculture' ('66).

The situation becomes even more clear if we estimate, for example, that prevailing food supplies in India during the early sixties had been distributed at this minimum rate of 2.300 calories per person per day; in that case 48 million people would have been left without any food. If the same food supply would have been distributed at the United States' consumption rate of 3.190 calories per person per day, 153 million of India's people would have been without food.[82]

This situation now tends to deteriorate even further because of the population explosion. In spite of sometimes energetically planned agricultural projects, the less developed regions as a whole have registered no gains, and sometimes have even registered losses in food production per capita. In Latin America, food production per person exceeded the pre-war level only in the particularly favourable season of 1958-1959, and has fallen below that level since; the pre-war level was regained in the Far East (excluding China) in 1959-1960, but some years later the figure fell below that of the pre-war years; Africa, too, exceeded the pre-war level briefly for a few years after the war, but fell below that level later; in the Near East, the figures remain steady.

While food production during the 1960's in Latin America, and the Far and Near East increased just as much as the population (thus keeping food production per capita fairly constant), the increase of food production in Africa was not even enough to prevent a decrease of per capita production.[83]

The developing countries are confronted with an enormous problem here, the solution of which is energetically searched for in several directions.

1°. In the first place, substantial efforts by the developing countries in the field of agriculture are often considered possible and promising rapid results.

The question is, however, to what extent such efforts are indeed promising. Usually two ways are mentioned as being appropriate ones to achieve the results wanted: in the first place the opening of new land for agriculture; in the second place the increase of output from land presently cultivated.

In relation to the first way, it can be said that the possibilities are perhaps more limited than is often believed.

A large percentage of the vast, sparsely populated areas on earth, in

---

[82] US Dept. of Agriculture, Economic Research Service – 'Changes in Agriculture in 26 Developing Nations, 1948-1963' ('65).
[83] C. Taeuber – 'Population and Food Supply,' 369 Annals ('67) p. 78; FAO – 'The State of Food and Agriculture' ('70) p. 3.

which new areas for cultivation must be sought, consist of arid deserts, rocky mountains, and cold tundras which could only be made productive in part and then only with a capital input which would be prohibitive even for rich, technologically advanced nations. Even the possibilities in such well-watered tropical areas as the Amazon and Congo basins, or Borneo are very restricted. These areas have a soil consisting mainly of old sedimentary rocks, in which the clay-humus complex is often less than 5 per cent base-saturated as compared to the 70 per cent required for a moderately productive soil.[84]

The US President's Science Advisory Panel on the World Food Supply has calculated that there are about 3.2 billion hectares of land suitable for agriculture, approximately half of which is under cultivation today, the other half of which will require immense capital costs to make it productive. Likewise, the FAO has recognized the fact that it will be extremely difficult to open much more land for agricultural purposes. It is of great importance to note, however, that much of the world's vacant land is in South America and Africa. If financial and social (migration) problems are overcome, these continents provide possibilities.[85]

As to the second way, similar problems may be expected. On the one hand, the amounts of capital needed to convert low-level agriculture into mechanized high-level output agriculture, will be enormous. On the other hand, the amounts of mineral fertilizers needed might even become prohibitive. In order to achieve a 34% increase in world food production between 1960 and 1966, investments in nitrate fertilizers had to be increased by 146%. The problem in this respect is illustrated by the pattern of phosphate consumption, the most important one among all mineral fertilizers. During the year 1968-1969, out of a world consumption of 17.3 million metric tons, North America, the USSR, and Europe accounted for 13.1 million metric tons, whereas the whole of Latin America, Africa, and Asia (less Japan and China) used less than 2.2. million metric tons. The agriculture of West Germany (population 60 million) consumed twice as much as the combined agricultural complex of India, Pakistan, and Indonesia (population over 700 million). World reserves of mineral phosphates, however, are of a very limited extent, and were the developing countries to use them at the same rate as the developed countries, supplies would soon be exhausted.[86]

---

[84] S. B. Hendricks – 'Food form the Land,' in 'Resources and Man' op. cit., pp. 70ff.
[85] idem, pp. 66-68.
[86] FAO – 'Provisional Indicative World Plan for Agricultural Development' ('70) p. 41.

Apart from this problem, one of another category might pose an even larger obstacle, i.e. pollution. The consequences stemming from the use of DDT, of which 100.000 tons are released into the environment annually, have been indicated already. Between 1950 and 1966 the use of all kinds of insecticides has increased by 300%, and if one recognizes the serious consequences of any further increase of the use of these substances, the endeavour to achieve great increases in agricultural output from existing cultivated areas might seem a doubtful one. In view of the present state of affairs the fear seems justified that improvement of food production on land through the use of such poisonous substances might kill all life in the oceans and destroy the possibility of food production in the seas. More attention must be given to methods of biological control of pests, and to problems of making pesticides biodegradable, more pest-specific, and less toxic to man and animals. This is considered not an insurmountable problem, but it demands early action and constant vigilance.

2^0. This brings us to the second category of potential solution of the food problem: food from the oceans.

Contrary to wide belief, the oceans are not a practically limitless source of food. Although precise data are not prevailing, it is noteworthy that various experts, basing their calculations on independent approaches, have reached similar estimates. Meseck, Kask, Schaefer, and Ryther have calculated that the maximum sustainable yield of ocean fish per year is about 100 million tons.[87] Ricker estimates that eventually a total of about 150 million tons of food from all marine life might be harvestable at a sustained yield. In view of the figure showing that already by 1966 half of this amount (60 million tons) was caught, the problematic character of relying on the seas for the world's future protein need becomes clear. If the world's population would have increased to the expected 6 billion people, and the estimated attainable production of 100 million tons could be achieved by the year 2000, this would be only sufficient to supply about 30 per cent of the world's minimal protein requirement, and only a little over 3 per cent of its biological energy requirements. This would demand, moreover, investments in ships and equipment of about three times that of the present, while investments of five to six times might be re-

---

[87] G. Meseck in 'Fish in Nutrition' ('62) pp. 23 ff.;
J. L. Kask – 'Fisheries in the Year 2000,' Canadian Fisherman (June '63) pp. 42 ff;
M. B. Schaefer – 'The Potential Harvest of the Sea,' 94 Am. Fish. Soc. Trans. 2 ('65) pp. 123 ff.;
J. H. Ryther – 'Photosynthesis and Fish Production in the Sea,' 166 Science ('69) p. 76.

quired to reach 150 million tons which constitutes an enormous problem.[88] Then there is the inherent danger of over-exploitation of various species. In 1970 the total catch of fish in the world decreased for the first time since 1950. Several proposals have been made to increase the productivity of the oceans by raising its nutrient status, but this realization seems to be considered a rather long-term possibility. As has been indicated before, the future capacity of the seas depends, moreover, on the level of poisoning resulting from efforts to raise food production on land. This consideration seems to add to the present food problem the dimension of a vicious circle.

3°. *Innovation* appears to offer a faint glimmer of hope by the production of protein and fats. One possible advance might be bacterial conversion of petroleum products for human consumption. This would imply, however, the use of a wasting nonrenewable resource, which is for the foreseeable future indispensable for the supply of energy.

4°. The over-production of food achieved in many rich countries seems to be the most promising prospect.

In the rich regions of the world agricultural production has far outgrown their needs, leading to over-consumption and non-use. During the decennium from 1958 to 1967 food production per capita increased in North America, Eastern Europe, and Western Europe by 15.5%, 15.5%, and 18.9% respectively. Estimates for the year 2000 indicate that on the basis of the present annual rate of growth of food production in these regions (1.9% in the US and 2.7% in Europe) production by then might be sufficient for 6 billion people, if this rate of growth can be sustained.

These considerations lead to the following tentative conclusions: In the first place, the developing countries themselves have a responsibility in this field. Indeed, many UN-documents speak of a primary responsibility in the sense of Resolution 2682 (XXV) of 11 Dec. 1970 on 'Multilateral Food Aid,' which reads

'the ultimate solution of the food problem of the developing countries lies in increased production in the developing countries with a food deficit, in the context of their general economic development...'

In view of the capacity of many of them it seems doubtful, however, whether the main responsibility can be theirs. One might think here of a social rather than of an economic responsibility: on the one hand the most promising solution of all lies in birth control; on the other

[88] W. E. Ricker – 'Food from the Sea,' in 'Resources and Man' op. cit., pp. 105-106.

hand a major source of present lack in many of these countries is the prevailing system of land tenure. Food production and consumption could certainly be increased if social structures were changed. The Strategy Resolution is remarkably direct on this point, where it demands that

> 'developing countries will formulate, early in the Decade, appropriate strategies for agriculture (including animal husbandry, fisheries and forestry) designed to secure a more adequate food supply from both the quantitative and qualitative viewpoints, to meet their nutritional and industrial requirements, to expand rural employment and to increase export earnings. *They will undertake, as appropriate, reform of land tenure systems for promoting both social justice and farm efficiency.....*'

In the second place, the rich countries have, at least in the near future, a major responsibility. In view of their surplus-production they can supplement the needed food supplies of the developing countries as long as this remains necessary. If one thinks of aid in the proper sense of the word, it would seem that here lies an important field for assistance. Regulations are needed for the transfer of food-supplies in excess of domestic demands to the developing countries. Although transport facilities might pose a problem at present, the major obstacle to be overwon is a political one: the readiness of the tax-payers in the rich countries to make a sacrifice, probably lasting for some decennia. The Resolution on Multilateral Food Aid recommends the developed countries urgently to use their food supplies in excess of domestic needs in this sense, and to adopt the UN World Food Program for this purpose (art. 3c).

In the third place, the primary responsibility is a common one.

Developed and developing nations together should increase investments in scientific research in the field of nutrition. The possibility of deriving protein from fossil resources has been reported, and other new techniques and methods should be searched for. Most important, however, is co-operation and co-ordination in the field of conservation of the living resources of the sea and of agricultural production in the developing countries.

As for the first point it is clear that the fisheries convention of 1958 does not provide adequate regulations. The complex of problems in connection with fishing, freedom of the high seas, and width of territorial waters demands an early solution and it may be hoped that the envisaged conference of 1973 will use the need of conservation through co-operation as an important point of departure.

As for the second point, a number of developing countries have the capacity to become important producers of fruit and meat, if their export capability is enhanced. It would be an important part of the general scheme for international labour division, if such countries would be given the chance to develop here, at the expense – in this field – of other countries, including the developed ones. In particular such development might appropriately be combined with an industrialization process in the field of preserves, leather commodities, etc. Part of the fertilizers, insecticides, etc. used presently in rich countries would alternatively – not additionally – be employed by developing countries, preventing early exhaustion and increased pollution. If policies are based on such a worldwide co-ordination, there is not only the possibility that developing countries become self-supporting in the field of food, but also that part of the world's food requirements is produced where it can most economically be produced, while minimizing the danger of environmental pollution.

It may be repeated here that the ultimate solution of the food problem, i.e. population control, is considered largely dependent on improvement of people's conditions of living, implying that a process of substantial development might eventually contribute to taking away this major problem of mankind's future.

3.3.7. *Economic growth*

From 1958 to 1967 the growth of GNP amounted annually in:
'Western' industrial countries to: 5%
'Socialist' industrial countries to: 7%
Developing countries to: 4.5%

At a first glance this is not so bad. If one takes into account, however, population increases – 1.2% in Western industrial countries; 1.6% in socialist countries; 2.5% in developing countries – a quite different picture presents itself.

The total growth per capita during this period was in:
'Western' industrial countries: 39%
'Socialist' industrial countries: 65%
Developing countries: 21%

The annual growth per capita during the period 1960-1965 was in:
'Western' industrial countries: 3.8%
'Socialist' industrial countries: 5.4%
Developing countries: 2.0%

In addition to this, those of the developing countries which are most densely populated have not even reached the meager 2%. During the period 1955-1960 33% of the world's population lived in countries with an annual growth below 1.5%; during the period 1960-1965 this percentage has even doubled to 66%.

At this moment 1/3 of the world's population earns 85% of the world's income. Of the remaining 2/3, the half (about 1 billion people) must do with only 5% of the world's income.[78] Measured in terms of income per capita, the gap between rich and poor at it's widest amounts at this moment to over $ 3000 a year. Projections for the year 2000 show an even more serious picture if nothing is done about it: by then – according to MacNamara in 1969 – per capita income in the United States is expected to be approximately $ 10.000; in contrast to Brazil where it will be $ 500 and India where it will not exceed $ 200!

Propositions to prevent these prospects to become realities have been made by various instances.

In this respect the recommendations of the 'Tinbergen-Committee' and those of the 'Pearson-Commission' reflect their different background. Both are in favour of sustained growth in the developing countries, but whereas the 'Pearson-Commission' recommends 'self-sustaining growth' in the developing countries, the 'Tinbergen-Committee' bases its recommendation on the deliberation that the prosperity gap between rich and poor countries should be narrowed, and that therefore a more rapid growth should be realized in the developing countries than in the developed countries (6-7% in the first case). The Strategy Resolution reflects the ideas of the Tinbergen Committee. Its articles on economic growth are based on the deliberation

'at least to make a modest beginning towards narrowing the gap in living standards between developed and developing countries';

while

'in countries with very low incomes per head, efforts should be made to double (such) incomes within a shorter period.....' (art. 14).

According to this Resolution the average annual rate of growth of the gross product of the developing countries during the Second Development Decade should be *at least 6 per cent, with the possibility of attaining a higher rate in the second half of the Decade,* to be specified on the basis of a comprehensive mid-term review. The recommended average annual rate of growth per capita in the developing countries as a whole during the Decade is 3.5 per cent, with the possibility of accelerating it during the second half of the Decade. This would amount to a doubling of average income per head in the course of two decades. Such figures imply among others an average annual expansion of 4 per cent in agricultural output, and 8 per cent in manufacturing output (see articles 13-17).

Again, the calculations in the reports and Resolution mentioned have been based on the idea of unlimited economic growth. The problematic character of future world economic growth has been indicated in the foregoing sections, and, indeed, here the various observations meet and could be reiterated as one complex. Since it seems unnecessary to repeat the considerations presented above, a few general remarks may be sufficient at this place.

Until recently, plans for economic development of the Third World were based on the belief that this goal could only be achieved if the rich countries would not have to make substantial sacrifices, and, indeed, sacrifices were considered not necessary. In order to bridge the welfare gap, the major consequence was thought to be a difference in rate of growth between developing and developed nations. Much of the data available today suggest, however, that world economic growth has its limits, and may be approaching these limits, even if nothing would be done to help the poor countries develop. For the developing countries this implies that it might perhaps not be possible to reach a sustained level of welfare measured in terms of the conditions presently prevailing in the industrialized countries.

If the data and projections discussed above are essentially correct, we are all confronted with a situation in which optimal alternatives must be chosen rather than schemes providing everything for everybody without limits. If food production in the oceans must be increased, less funds will be available for industrialization, and there will have to be less environmental pollution; if industrialization has to increase, large-scale investment in new sources of energy is required, and there may be less funds available and fewer possibilities for food production; if developing countries have to industrialize, rich countries may have to restrict in certain fields if conservation and pollution are to be kept under control; etc.

The question to what extent disarmament could influence the world's scarcity-complex, lies beyond the present discussion. Too little is known, moreover, about the military part of the waste cycle, but a survey would show it to be substantial.

At present in many circles in the rich countries it is not allowed or it is even considered a scandal to talk of a restriction of economic growth. Yet, in view of present and future conditions, it seems inevitable that certain freedoms – like the number of children people can have, or the unrestricted use of energy and consumption of resources, and thus the unrestricted pursuit of economic growth –

be subordinated to the demands of survival. Peace, economic self-interest, and justice demand that certain freedoms which serve only a few be restricted for the interest of many. Fighting the restriction of such freedoms today – as many in the rich countries do, even in the name of democracy against totalitarianism – might appear in due course to be nothing more than a 'lemming-policy': it would result eventually in a calamity for all.

Apart from the economic consequences – it may be repeated – the polemological consequences of refusing to bridge the welfare gap if this demands certain sacrifices from the people in the rich part of the world, may with reason be considered so serious, that the choice should not be too difficult.

3.3.8. *Financial assistance*

To achieve the aims as put forward in the preceding pages, substantial and effective financial assistance is of high importance.

1°. Although official figures on the present flow of financial resources to the developing countries are far from encouraging, Gunnar Myrdal has warned that even these are usually presented as much more positive than they really are. This is explained in part by the circumstance that many observers have introduced the figures of the DAC-Secretariat on 'the flows of financial resources' (as presented in its 'Development Assistance Reviews') as if they were merely figures on aid. Myrdal accuses the Development Assistance Committee of the OECD of having done little or nothing to prevent this opportunistic misuse of its figures and, indeed, of having occasionally supported this misconception. When the DAC reported on July 10 1969, that during 1968 the 'flows of financial resources' to developing countries had increased to almost $ 13 billion, this was commonly understood and commented upon as encouraging, and indicating that 'aid was increasing again – although this implied in fact a decrease in 'official flows' and a somewhat bigger increase in 'private flows.'[89]

Concerning 'private flows,' the DAC-statistics are defined as 'net values,' in which interest payments, payments for licencies, and profits taken out from the developing countries are not included in the backflows, while reinvestments are counted as inflows. $ 2.2-$ 2.3 billion annually flow back to the United States alone as payments on and earnings of its private capital investments in the Third World.[90]

In Latin America in particular, such 'private outflows,' not accounted for in the DAC-statistics, amount to huge sums; it has been calculated

[89] G. Myrdal, note 9 supra, pp. 316ff.
[90] see 'Survey of Current Business' (Sept. 1965, 1966, 1967).

that the total of outflows from Latin America to the United States is five times as large as is often contended. Myrdal quotes Ch. Mc. C. Mathias Jr., a US Senator, who has recently explained:

> 'Capital flows from Latin America and into the United States are now over four times as great as the flow south. The countries of Latin America, in a way, are actually giving foreign aid to the United States, the wealthiest country in the world.'

All this implies, according to Myrdal,

> 'that the DAC statistics, quoted everywhere as authoritative, leave entirely open the problem of what the total net private flow of resources from developed to underdeveloped countries amounts to and, indeed, whether there is such a net flow at all to many of the underdeveloped countries or, instead, an outflow.....'[91]

Both for 'private flows' and 'official flows' the conclusion holds, moreover, that the practice of extending aid in the form of loans results in heavy financial burdens for the recipient countries. The more so, when loans – and this applies also to both forms of flows – are tied to donor exports. Export credits – particularly if they are double-tied, that is if the recipient becomes obligated not only to buy products in the donor country but even to buy specific products – often imply a heavy burden for the recipient, since he cannot buy what he needs at the most favourable prices in the most favourable country. The negative effects of this kind of 'aid' have been negated, but it has been variously estimated, that they result in additional costs up to 40 per cent! The dilemma is that the amount of aid, if it were not tied, would probably be even less than it is now. The practice of extending loans without their being adapted to a general development plan and the practice of tying such loans to export provisions has resulted today in huge debts to be paid by the poor countries.

According to the UN, the total debt in 1967 was estimated to be $ 28 billion,[92] other sources even speaking of $ 40 billion. The amount of foreign debts keeps increasing while the flow of official resources is decreasing (between 1960 and 1968 from 0.52% to 0.38% of the rich countries' BNP) which makes experts expect that by the year 1975 the developing countries have to pay back as much to the developed countries as will be extended to them. The DAC figure on 'net flow' of resources (both private and official) amounted to $ 11.4 billion. This figure sharply contrasted with that of the UN Secretary-General who based his data on the statistics of the IMF. The net inflow of resources to the developing countries had in fact only been $ 3 billion.

[91] G. Myrdal, note 9 supra, pp. 322-323, 319.
[92] UN Doc. TD-35, supp. I (Nov. 17, '67) p. 34.

The UN General Assembly has expressed its concern over 'the increasing rate of outflow of capital from the developing countries which substantially reduces the net volume of external resources available to the developing countries.' At this moment the situation might well be that these total outflows, including those of profits of capital, from the developing countries at large are approximately of the same dimension as the total private and official 'net inflows' found in the DAC statistics.[93] In view of this alarming situation the Strategy Resolution demands (not without reason) that '.... financial assistance will, in principle, be untied. While it may not be possible to untie assistance in all cases, developed countries will rapidly and progressively take what measures they can in this respect both to reduce the extent of tying assistance and to mitigate any harmful effects. Where loans are tied to particular resources, developed countries will make to the greatest extent possible such loans available for utilization by the recipient countries for the purchase of goods and services from other developing countries' (art. 45).

2º. The present system of financial 'aid' hardly deserves that name. It is of great importance, that the entire flow of foreign financial resources be brought into harmony with the effort to achieve global welfare.
  1. This demands primarily that financial assistance function within national development programs, if possible, based on the general strategy of international division of labour. In particular, as far as loans are concerned, equal profit to donors and recipients can be expected only if these loans function within a general development scheme. In the case of private flows, the following considerations seem relevant:
From what has been said on the question of nationalization and expropriation it is obvious that at this moment there is little incentive for investors from industrialized countries to make new investments in the developing countries.[94] Yet, such investments can be very profitable to the developing countries *under specific conditions*, and new rules could guarantee an increased flow of private capital to the Third World (OECD's investment code still serves mainly the interests of the rich countries). The danger of adverse reactions and the prospect of fruitful co-operation depend largely on the creation of *a common basis*

---

[93] G. Myrdal, p. 322.
[94] on the negative opinion of potential investors see US Dept. of Commerce, Office of International Trade – 'Study of Factors Limiting American Private Foreign Investment. Summary of Findings and Conclusions' (July '53).

of interest in this respect. Such common basis could be established if the following deliberations are taken into account:

a. Private investments should function within the framework of a planned international division of labour, in order to contribute to the development of the recipient country in question and the prosperity of all. It should not – as is often the case at present – run counter to the interests of the developing countries, but it should be subservient to their specific development programs.

b. Foreign investors should to the highest possible degree provide for employment and training to local labour, and should provide an increasing share of local personnel in positions at the managerial, administrative, and higher technical levels. They should aim not only at financial profit, but also at the transfer of know-how in order to contribute to a broader local basis of skilled labour.

c. Rules should be worked out providing for a reasonable ratio between profits which can be transferred to the investor's country and profits which have to be reinvested in the recipient country. Wherever possible and appropriate, an increasing share of local capital should be allowed to participate in joint ventures.

d. A valuable idea is the 'management contract.'[95] This means that a foreign concern contracts with the government of a developing country to set up and manage, either alone or in co-operation with the government, a new plant for a limited period. The foreign concern could either make a direct investment for the period agreed upon, or provide a loan for the duration of the management contract. The foreign concern would be assured of a management fee and the return at fixed dates of the capital provided including a normal profit, while the government of the developing country would be assured of acquiring technology and management skills through appropriately trained local personnel.

Such measures could create new common interests and mutual benefits, and could provide the basis upon which to construct new rules on foreign investment and nationalization, acceptable to developed and developing countries alike. This hope has been expressed in the Strategy Resolution, which contains an article on private foreign investment in this sense, urging efforts 'to foster better understanding of the rights and obligations of both host and capital-exporting countries, as well as of individual investors' (art. 50).

2. In the second place, loans could in principle be reserved for those projects which may be expected to bear profits on a relatively short

---

[95] G. Myrdal – 'An International Economy: Problems and Prospects' ('56) p. 117.

term. Gifts should be used for typical long-term projects, like the building-up of social and health infrastructures, basic education, etc. Loans and gifts could thus become supplementary and adapted to each other, so their effectivity is increased.

3. The allocation of funds needs to be based not only on the criterium of *'performance* in making productive use of such assistance,' as recommended by the 'Pearson-Report,' but also on the criterium of the *needs* of respective developing countries, as recommended by the 'Tinbergen-Report' and the 'Jackson-Report.' The latter Report states in connection to the UN Development Programme that 'the co-operation offered through these channels cannot be donor-centered: it must accept the interests of the recipient as of prime importance.'

4. It is important that financial resources be extended during the early phases of development to balance the import expenditures of the developing countries. Even if the developing countries would be able to extend their exports to the developed countries by, let us say, $ 10 billion (the maximum amount estimated feasible for the near future) and their balance of payments would be positive, much of the increased export-earnings would have to be used for payments of foreign debts, etc. Moreover, the developing countries need to be helped with increasing their imports as well without having to suffer from too negative figures on their balances of payment. Until their export capacity and production apparatus are such as to enable them to pay themselves for the imports they need, the deficits on their balances can only be filled up by aid.[96] The amount needed for this purpose for the coming 20 years has been estimated at $ 30 billion annually for the whole Third World. *This is equal to about 1% of the BNP of the developed countries, which they have for years promised to provide.*
The 'Pearson-Report' recommends to reach the level of 1% by 1975, of which amount 70% should be transferred in the form of public aid. The 'Tinbergen-Report' is more ambitious on this point too, recommending to reach 1% by 1972, of which in that year 0.75% should be transferred in the form of public funds. The Strategy Declaration is rather disappointing in this connection:

'Each economically advanced country *should endeavour to* provide by 1972 annually to developing countries financial resource transfers of a minimum net amount of 1 per cent of its gross national product at market prices in terms of actual disbursements, having regard to the special position of those countries which are net importers of capital.....';

---

[96] L. Stepanov – 'One Percent: The Problem of Economic Aid,' 386 The Annals (Nov. '69) pp. 41 ff.

while

> 'Each economically advanced country will progressively increase its official development assistance to the developing countries and will exert its best efforts to reach a minimum net amount of 0.7 per cent of its gross national product at market prices by the middle of the Decade' (articles 42 and 43).

3.3.9. *The necessity of a global center of co-operation*

A Strategy as outlined above could not be realized without effective global co-operation. A decision-making authority, in which all states are represented, is needed. Whatever national development programs, bilateral aid programmes, or regional co-operation systems are tried out, under present international economic conditions they are in most cases bound to fail in the objective of achieving more equality and substantial development, unless they are fit into a general welfare strategy. If all states co-operate, the widening of the gap can be stopped and gradually narrowed; if they do not, efforts will be patchy and doomed to end up in failure.

1. Much attention has been given during the last years to *regional co-operation*. So much so, that one outstanding lawyer, Friedmann, expects that new rules of co-operation and welfare will develop as the law of regional systems.[97] Regional co-operation can be a very positive development, since it often means co-operation among neighbours who understand (and can profit by) their interdependence. Power stations located at a border, enabling more than one state to profit from it, common use of harbors, supplementary activities in industrial fields etc., are often measures very appropriate in advancing national development.

Regional co-operation is of particular importance in the case of 'mini-states,' which never might become economically viable entities by themselves, and in the case of the 'least-developed' among the developing countries.

The developing countries understand such advantages, as becomes clear from several articles in the Strategy Resolution (see articles 56-58, dealing with the 'least developed' countries, and articles 39, 40 and 77). They realize also, however, that regional co-operation is only useful to them, if it is accompanied and in fact dominated by global co-operation. In the Charter of Algiers they have stressed this

---

[97] W. Friedmann – 'The Changing Dimensions of International Law,' 62 Columbia Law Review ('62) pp. 1154-1155.

point and have pleaded for a worldwide dynamic system of international division of labour.

At this moment there is a tendency – perhaps an expression of desperation – *to replace global co-operation with regional co-operation*, mainly on the side of the rich countries, but to some extent also on the side of the developing countries. This is not a sound development, neither economically, nor politically.

As far as the political argument is concerned, the developing countries may regard regionalism as offering them possibilities for the enhancement of political and economic power without losing their national identity in the framework of a global context. That is exactly why regionalism, though very profitable and positive under certain circumstances, may provoke adverse effects and may even constitute a peace-endangering factor. 'The makers of several snowballs,' as Claude puts it, 'are as likely to throw them at each other as to use them for creating a single snowman.'[98] Economic and military regional co-operation may further transnational thinking, but it may as easily block global thinking.[99]

The aid-giving nations may also further regionalism for political reasons. Latin America is a clear example of this with the United States in the background. Also the present Association of African states with the European Community has (or had) at least a very pleasant political side-effect as far as the EEC-countries are concerned – although it must be said, that the second Yaounde-Treaty furthers not only co-operation among the associated states, but also with the 'English' African countries and even with developing countries in other continents; a break-through which is reflected in EEC's offer of non-discriminatory preferential treatment of imports from developing countries in general (see above p. 300). On the other hand, regional bloc-formation among the donors can have positive economic effects, since in the field of foreign aid at least more co-operation and co-ordination would be the result. Such efforts, however, as the endeavour to co-ordinate the bilateral assistance programmes of the OECD-countries through its Development Assistance Committee, contributes to accusations of neo-colonialism and adverse reactions from the side of the socialist countries. Proposals, therefore, as the one by the Dutch general and economist Broekmeyer, to extend aid by NATO-countries selectively for the interest of NATO and at the expense of the Warschau-Pact, runs counter to evidence of economic and political

[98] I. L. Claude – 'Swords Into Plowshares' ('59) p. 118.
[99] see R. J. Yalem – 'Regionalism and World Order,' in R. A. Falk & S. Mendlovitz (eds.) – 'The Strategy of World Order' I ('66) pp. 215-229.

common sense.[100] The realization of such proposals would not only impede a real chance for development of the poor countries, but also constitute a threat to the peace.

Regional co-operation can function very effectively and positively by itself, but in the long run it can optimally bring prosperity to the poor and optimally protect the prosperity of the rich, if it functions within a global setting. This is the kind of integrated European policy Dr. Mansholt pleads for in connection to the EEC.

2°. Another important topic in this connection is that of *control and appraisal*. It seems obvious that both donors and recipients would be prepared to have their economic development activities supervised to some extent only if this would occur within a multi-lateral framework in which they all take part. The United Nations system is evidence of this in many fields: the Expanded Program, the Development Fund, the UN Development Programme Country Programming, the International Labour Organization, the work of the UN in the field of Human Rights, and the envisaged authority for the sea-bed – to mention a few – prove that states are prepared to accept some degree of supra-national control if this is exercised in a global setting. The most important proof of this for the present context is Part D of the Strategy Resolution, in which the UN Members have accepted the recommendation of making

'appropriate arrangements..... to keep under systematic scrutiny the progress towards achieving the goals and objectives of the Decade – to identify shortfalls in their achievement and the factors which amount for them.... Such reviews and appraisals will be carried out at various levels, involving both developed and developing countries, keeping in view the need for streamlining the existing machinery and avoiding unnecessary duplication or proliferation of review activities' (art. 79).

Articles 80, 81 and 82 provide for appraisals on the national and regional levels and by specialized international organizations. All these activities, moreover, are co-ordinated, not in the least through an over-all appraisal by the General Assembly to be made *biennially* (art. 83). Apart from appraisal and control, a multilateral organism is the best medium in the present world of sovereign states to realize some degree of sanction, at least if all states are interested in the success of the efforts made. The political pressure exercised by a forum in which the entire world is represented, can today be an important factor in preventing states from failing to live up to their promises, as has often been shown.

[100] M. W. J. M. Broekmeyer – 'Developing Countries and NATO' ('63).

3⁰. The most crucial observation remains, however, that the level of co-ordination and co-operation required for a successful effort can be achieved best by integrating all measures on the national, bilateral, and regional levels into a global co-operation system. In view of all that has been discussed hitherto, it seems that the organization recommended for this task by the 'Pearson-Commission,' i.e. the World Bank, is not the appropriate one. Not only has the World Bank the image of a 'money-making rich men's club' – notwithstanding the recent trend to extend the role of IDA and IFC, and to spend more funds on programme-financing –, for which it is at present unacceptable to the developing countries as the highest authority; but the political background of this organization makes it unacceptable also to the socialist countries. We are confronted here with another dilemma. The organization which is most effective and which could easily be transformed into the best functioning center for the transfer of capital, is politically unacceptable. Pearson's Report, moreover, makes it clear that even the Western countries are unwilling to accept the Bank as a supreme authority because they don't want this Organization to supervise their economic activities.

The most fundamental objection to the proposal of the Pearson group, however, is that the Bank's activities are restricted and are only part of the entire development structure. It is hard to see how this institution should be adapted to the comprehensive task of co-ordinating all those economic measures which together constitute the global development strategy.

Only one organization would seem potentially equipped and apt to implement this strategy of global welfare, and that is the United Nations.

In the United Nations we have a center embracing nearly all States of the world – including the divided countries in the near future, as may be hoped;

In the United Nations we have an organization in which the recipients are secured of an equal voice vis-à-vis the donors, preventing fear on the side of the former of 'neo-colonialism,' dependence and inferiority;

In the United Nations we have a center of co-ordination of the activities of specialized agencies, regional commissions, etc. in all the various fields of economic planning.

In the United Nations we have an organization whose authority has been established throughout the world, and whose supervisory capacity is unique.

In the United Nations we have a center with an outstanding experience in the field of economic assistance;

In the United Nations, in short, we have an organization where co-ordination and co-operation can be optimally realized.[101]

If States become prepared to accept the necessity of global development, there is no reason why they would not make use of all these existing facilities.

The complaint is often heard that the present UN-system is inadequate for its present tasks already, and would be the more so for a more comprehensive task. This is a relevant complaint, and the Jackson-commission has been appointed to study the question of improvements of that system. Yet, it must be said that the real problem is not so much a technical one, as it is one of political will: the present system is inadequate primarily *because governments want it to be that way*. Mr. Jackson has expressed himself rather optimistically about the readiness of governments to improve the UN-machinery:

'Personal discussions with representatives of many of the main donor countries have confirmed that further substantial funds would be channeled through the UN-Development Programme if its ability to handle increased resources effectively could be established.'

It would certainly be an advantage if they would do this, but it would be in vain if governments do not change their fundamental attitude towards the entire question of economic inequality in the world. The crux of the problem is indicated by the Jackson-report itself in its conclusion that

'in short, the UN system should not simply constitute one more channel for giving aid, but universal and mutual co-operation in the true sense.'

Global co-operation on the economic level could have the positive effect of opening doors to a closer political co-operation as well. This applies both to East-West relations and to North-South relations. It is of enormous importance *that the countries of the world get used to the idea of the possibility of co-operation* in a not primarily political field, and it can only be beneficial to mankind if states get accustomed to the idea of a worldwide structure of decisionmaking.

I think we have reached a point in history where it becomes of vital necessity to do what Coste expressed as:

'Non pas planer dans le possible, mais saisir avec courage le réel.'

---

[101] Fawcett has written: 'It is only through the UN and its agencies as world organizations that the new nations can realize their full development and that the 'one world' we all need is likely to be reached';
J. E. S. Fawcett - 'The New States and the United Nations,' in W. V. O'Brien (Ed.) - 'The New Nations in International Law and Diplomacy' ('65) p. 252.

3.3.10. *The emerging law of the world community*

1⁰. The realization of a global welfare strategy needs a legal structure based upon some new rules and principles. One of these principles is the acceptance of a certain extension of the supra-national idea, as far as this is necessary to adapt national economic planning to the larger framework of global welfare. Many States may be expected to refuse this kind of legal development in particular because they are anxious to maintain their sovereignty to a maximum degree.

Yet, the welfare strategy constitutes a fundamental contribution to world peace and its neglect may contribute to large-scale violence, if not to a new World War. This book may have provided enough evidence to sustain that conclusion. It is this insight which makes ILO's Philadelphia-Declaration so relevant in stating that 'poverty anywhere is a danger to prosperity everywhere.' Such a prominent expert as E. Rostow has written: 'We know that prosperous democracies cannot subsist infinitely as islands of affluence in a sea of poverty, and that on grounds both of conscience and of self-interest we must seek to end the polarization of the world into rich and poor nations.'[102]

It is important also that the rich nations think more in terms of long-term economic planning (which tends to be overshadowed by short-term deliberations) and realize that this global strategy is to their own economic interest as well. This has been stressed above, but it might be repeated here since little else seems to compel the rich countries to adopt new economic policies *except their very own benefit*.[103]

Both interests, that of lasting peace and that of long-term prosperity, merge in this welfare strategy, benefiting the rich and the developing countries alike.

The realization of important self-interests might make new patterns of international co-operation acceptable, even if it implies a partial restriction of national sovereignty. Forty years ago, Cordell Hull said: 'We cannot have a peaceful world, we cannot have a prosperous world, until we rebuild the international economic structure.' This advice still holds true for today, probably more so than ever. This is also what international law must stand for today.

---

[102] E. V. Rostow – 'Law, Power and the Pursuit of Peace' ('68) p. 110.
[103] The final report of a student Conference, organized by the US Military Academy concludes:
'it is in the long-term interests of the United States that Latin America become more highly developed for at least one basic reason: Latin America will not be a good market for our highly specialized and technically sophisticated products unless it is economically more developed';
Proc. 21st Ann. Stud. Conf. on US-Affairs (Dec. '69), Ed. US Mil. Acad. ('70).

2⁰. There is nothing new, moreover, in accepting new structures in international society. Similar developments have taken place in the past in the realm of *ius ad bellum*:
In the 19th century it was entirely up to the sovereign states to decide why and when to go to war. The League of Nations succeeded in restricting this absolute freedom to some degree by way of the Covenant's provision that 'any war or threat of war, whether immediately affecting any of the Members of the League or not, is hereby declared *a matter of concern to the whole League.....*' (art. 11). This provision was supplemented by others which made it legally not impossible, but nevertheless more difficult for states to resort to war. After the Briand-Kellogg Pact had provided the first absolute prohibition to use armed force as a means of national policy – be it, that the decision whether to take up arms in the right of self-defense was left entirely up to the individual states –, the Charter of the United Nations provided an absolute prohibition of warfare as a means of national policy within a framework which should prevent any abuse of the right of self-defence: 'All Members shall refrain in their international relations from the threat or use of force.....' (art. 2 para. 4).
Urged by technical developments, the development of nuclear technology in particular, states have accepted a gradual restriction of the right to go to war from absolute freedom to theoretical extinction, implying *a legal restriction of a major sovereign right to the interest of the entire community of mankind.*

3⁰. A similar development is needed now in the realm of international economic relations.
In 1954 Scheuner could still state: 'Mit der inneren Wirtschaftsordnung der Staaten, die zum Bereich ihrer souveränen Entscheidung gehört, und mit den Rechten und Interessen der Individuen im wirtschaftlichen Verkehr befasst sich das Völkerrecht grundsätzlich nicht.'[104] This opinion could not be upheld today anymore. Manifold are the inroads and impacts of the international environment which restrict the domestic jurisdiction of national governments in the realm of national economies. States have accepted such restrictions, because they realize the dependence of their respective prosperity on what happens elsewhere in the world. Nevertheless, despite the existence of many legal regulations to this effect, states often behave as if their full sovereign independence in this field still prevails. They often tend to follow short-term national deliberations rather

---

[104] U. Scheuner – 'Die Völkerrechtlichen Grundlagen der Weltwirtschaft in der Gegenwart' ('54), Sonderdruck aus 'Verhandlungen des 40. Deutschen Juristentages B. II, p. a 21.

than long-term global planning, which eventually should be to the disadvantage of all.

It is time to venture a real breakthrough on the global scene, furthered and supported by international law.

Many prominent international lawyers have in some way or another pleaded for this. Those who tend to consider such ideas as suggested here with great scepticism, might be answered with a quotation from Jenks who said that there is now 'need of a full measure of practical idealism.'

This is what characterizes the views of the foremeant prominent authors who all present their own terminology for an emerging law of global development:

Jenks has called it *'the common law of mankind,'* and says it presupposes

'the acceptance by us all, irrespective of differences of ideology or interest, of a common responsibility for the common peace, a common respect for the freedom and dignity of the common man.'[105]

Röling has written about *'the international law of welfare'* and he explains:

'Here, as on the national plane, the emphasis no longer falls on the concept of liberty or equality, but on that of fraternity, the idea of humanity, which implies responsibility for and the duty of caring for the welfare of the whole....... Traditional international law, taking as starting point the individual States, was a law of liberty. The thought of mutual assistance as a legal duty was foreign to it. The new international law, now coming to the fore, necessarily will have as its starting point the community of states, the world.'[106]

Fenwick calls it *'the international law of cooperation'* and he says:

'A new world has now been opened up in which the old international law of rights and duties is being supplemented by an international law of cooperation.'[107]

Friedmann speaks likewise of 'co-operative international law,' to describe

'the growing number of fields in which all or part of the family of nations co-operate for purposes of international welfare.'[108]

McWhinney speaks of *'the international law of positive cooperation'* and says:

'The prime task of the international lawyer today in a world Community undergoing continuing revolution, becomes, therefore, one of building a new system of World Public

---

[105] C. W. Jenks – 'Law in the World Community' ('67) p. 2.
[106] B. V. A. Röling – 'International Law in an Expanded World' ('60) pp. 85-86.
[107] Ch. S. Fenwick – 'International Law: The Old and the New,' 60 A.J.I.L. ('66) p. 482.
[108] W. Friedmann – 'The Changing Dimensions of International Law,' 62 Colombia Law Rev. ('62) p. 1162.

Order with an ideological base broad enough to derive support from, and to compass, all the main competing, social and economic systems of the present day.'[109]

From the socialist countries we have *Bartoš*, the proponent of *'active coexistence,'* of which he says it should

'limiter la liberté d'action des Etats à la réalisation des buts et principes des Nations Unies, à savoir au respect des règles essentielles sur lesquelles repose la communauté internationale.'[110]

From the developing countries we have Anand, who in a recent excellent article pleads for a new approach towards international law based on 'universal values,' which he prefers to call, like Jenks, 'a common law of mankind.'[111]

Further there is *Prakash Sinha*, who writes about *'the emerging law of world society,'* and states:

'there seems to be no doubt that the rules of law created by instruments, institutions and practices of contemporary international economic development are different from the rules based on the principle of reciprocity of traditional international law. They mark a significant stage in the evolution of law governing international action.'[112]

Since we already have such a long list of descriptions – which could include many other prominent names –, the present author might as well add another one, reflecting the idea of the necessity of pursuing some degree of supra-national economic interest: what lawyers should advocate today, is *'the emerging law of the world community.'*

---

[109] E. Mc. Whinney – 'International Law and World Revolution' ('67) p. 11.
[110] M. Bartoš in his report to ILA, Proc. ILA ('58).
[111] R. P. Anand – 'The Development of a Universal International Law,' Festschrift for Quincy Wright (eds. Lepawski, Buehrig, and Lasswell, '71), p. 179.
[112] S. Prakesh Sinha – 'New Nations and the Law of Nations' ('67) p. 52.

Appendix

Non-Intervention

It might perhaps be possible to find a new approach for the complex problem of intervention within the framework of the strategy outlined above.

On December 21, 1965, the UN General Assembly, worried by the increasing practice of intervention into the internal affairs particularly of the young countries, adopted the general Declaration on the Inadmissibility of Intervention (Res. 2131 (XX)). Herein, the Members of the United Nations expressed themselves,

> '*deeply concerned* at the gravity of the international situation and the increasing threat soaring over universal peace due to armed intervention and other direct and indirect forms of interference threatening the sovereign personality and the political independence of States.'

1^0. Because intervention – whether upon request or not – in its manifold manifestations has become, as has been discussed in Ch. II, the main method of power politics in relation to the Third World, and because through interventionary practices on different levels the Super Powers are plunged into an increasing number of direct and indirect confrontations, intervention has become – together with the nuclear arms race – the most dangerous phenomenon of post-War politics. That explains the manifold efforts made by international lawyers to find a legal construction contributing to its restriction.

The complexity of this problem and the variety of approaches have resulted in a great deal of confusion among international lawyers today. Generalizing somewhat, it can be said that legal thinking has been concentrated primarily on intervention in civil wars, and that three main legal theories have been developed in this respect, all of which have their proponents among present-day authors.

1. First, there is the theory according to which international law must protect international order and thus cannot allow for assistance to

anti-status quo forces. In case of civil war, only the 'legal' government may be the object of foreign assistance. This theory, adopted by the Institut de Droit International in 1900 in its 'Réglement concernant l'intervention,'[1] was propagated in 1937 by Garner in relation to the Spanish civil war. He wrote:

> 'There is no rule of international law which forbids the government of a state from rendering assistance to the established legitimate government of another state with a view of enabling it to suppress on insurrection against its authority'; (whereas) 'the assistance furnished (the Spanish) rebels.... is an act of unjustified intervention in the internal affairs.'

The same theory has been adopted in general by – among others – Verdross, Schwarzenberger, Briggs, Ross, Scelle and Rousseau.[2] Recently, Moore has expressed the same point of view in relation to the Vietnam war. He links – as all pupils of Mc. Dougal do – the right to intervene to a 'minimum world public order, that is, the avoidance of unilateral coercion as a modality of major change'; and concludes that

> 'it is not surprising, then, that prevailing international law seems to permit assistance to the recognized government but not to the insurgents.'[3]

2. Another theory which refers to the dangers of any kind of intervention and/or the unjustness of the first theory; by allowing assistance to an existing government and withholding assistance from the anti-status quo factions, one could impede the right of self-determination in cases where the existing government is little more than a ruling dictatorship and the 'rebels' have the support of the population of the country. This theory, therefore, forbids any interference with an ongoing civil struggle, in case – as Falk puts it – the 'control of a national society' is at stake. As Brownlie writes:

---

[1] Annuaire de l'Institut de Droit International (1900) p. 227; its article 2 forbids to supply weapons, munitions and other military assistance to rebels. Only if rebels satisfy the classical conditions concerning the status of belligerents, the rules of neutrality should be applied.

[2] J. W. Garner – 'Questions of International Law in the Spanish Civil War,' 31 AJIL ('37) p. 68; A. Verdross – 'Völkerrecht' ('64) p. 205; G. Schwarzenberger – 'A Manual of International Law' ('60) I pp. 200-202; H. W. Briggs – 'The Law of Nations' ('52) pp. 999-1000; A. Ross – 'A Textbook of International Law' ('47) p. 122; G. Scelle in Rev. Gen. D. Int. P. ('39) p. 197; C. Rousseau in Rev. D.I. Lég. Comp. ('38) p. 2.

[3] N. J. Moore – 'The Lawfulness of Military Assistance to the Republic of Vietnam,' 61 AJIL ('67) p. 31.

'foreign intervention would increase chaos and create an even more serious threat to the peace as a result of the introduction of foreign forces and resulting suspicions on the part of third states.'[4]

In this sense Wright denounces the assistance given by the United States to Chamoun in Lebanon in 1958, this government being not 'in firm possession of the territory.'[5] This theory is advocated further by Murti, Hyde, Lawrence, Hall, Starke, Fischer, Stowell, Wehberg and Lauterpacht.[6]

3.1. A third theory exists which is based on political practice and which revives to some extent the thinking of de Vattel who taught:

'foreign nations may assist that one of the two parties which seems to have justice on its side.'[7]

His theory equated the right to intervene with the just war doctrine. Perhaps in those days (18th century) a certain *communis opinio* concerning the merits of a 'just' war still existed. Today, however, opinions concerning a 'just cause' are so divergent, that little has been left of that common opinion.

The young countries claim that they have the right to use force against colonial Powers and white minority régimes, since colonialism and apartheid are considered to be a permanent form of aggression against which they would have the right of collective defence.

The communist countries claim the right to assist 'wars of national liberation,' since Western imperialism impedes the right of self-determination.

The Western countries claim the right to assist 'legal' governments against any communist threat.

Today we have what Julius Stone has called 'the national version of truth and justice.'[8] When one uses a 'iusta causa' as a basis for uni-

---

[4] R. A. Falk – 'International Law and the US role in the VietNam war,' 75 Yale L.J. ('66) pp. 1122ff; J. Brownlie – 'International Law and the Use of Force by States' ('63) p. 323.
[5] Q. Wright – 'US Intervention in the Lebanon,' 53 AJIL ('59) p. 119.
[6] B. S. N. Murti – 'The Vietnam Conflict; A legal perspective,' 7 Ind. J.I.L. ('67) pp. 369ff; C. Hyde – 'Intervention in Theory and Practice' ('11) pp. 9-10; G. Lawrence – 'Principles of International Law' ('30) pp. 131-132; W. E. Hall – 'International Law' ('24) pp. 346-347; J. J. Starke – 'An Introduction to International Law' ('63) pp. 97-98; R. Fischer – 'Intervention: Three problems of Policy and Law,' in R. J. Stanger (Ed.) – 'Essays on Intervention' ('64) p. 7; E. C. Stowell – 'Intervention in International Law' ('21) p. 329; H. Wehberg – 'La guerre civile et le droit international,' 63 Rec. Cours ('38) p. 57; E. Lauterpacht – 'Intervention by Invitation,' VII Int. Comp. L.Q. ('58) p. 103.
[7] E. de Vattel – 'The Law of Nations' (1758) II par. 56, p. 151 (in 'Classics of International Law' ('16) vol. III).
[8] J. Stone – 'Aggression and World Order' ('58) p. 148.

lateral intervention today, the risk of provoking counter-intervention and of escalation of an internal into an international conflict is inherent.

3.2. This third theory has culminated in the post-War period into a fourth one, embodied in the so-called 'Johnson-doctrine' for Latin America on the American, and in the so-called 'Breznhev-doctrine' for Eastern Europe on the Russian side. These doctrines based on the defence of democracy and communism respectively as an overriding 'just cause,' have added an important element to the third theory: the Super Powers claim the right to decide for themselves if they will intervene in the internal affairs of a 'state under their protection,' a preceding invitation by the local government being no longer considered as a necessary precondition for a legal intervention. In legal literature today, the reasoning of the Johnson-doctrine has been defended among others by Alford. He states that the United States would not even be obliged to leave Vietnam if the Vietnamese population wished them to go:

> 'an official request for withdrawal, even if backed by unverified claims of widespread South Vietnamese support, should not necessarily result in cessation of US military action, and we would probably have to strengthen US forces in South Vietnam to prop up a wavering government and achieve whatever policies *US officials* now have in view.'[9]

This seems also to be Mc.Dougal's way of thinking in connection to his famous 'international law of human dignities.' He writes, for instance:

> 'it is not the particular physical modality of destruction that is relevant to law and policy, but rather the purposes and effects to the value of a free world society.'[10]

Chayes states that the legal system is an entity 'which must provide satisfying legal support for the proposed action,' which cannot be unlawful, according to his opinion, as long as the action defends accepted (American) values.[11]

This opinion explains the confusion over the difference between intervention and collective self-defense today. Since any endeavour to achieve a leftist government in Latin America is considered to be the beginning of an imposed communist take-over, the United States and the Latin American governments have declared that the OAS has the

---

[9] N. Alford – 'The Legality of American Military Involvement in Vietnam: A Broader Perspective,' 75 Yale Law Journal 7 ('66) p. 50.
[10] M. S. McDougall c.s. – 'Studies in World Public Order' ('60) p. 817.
[11] A. Chayes in Proc. Am. Soc. I.L. ('63) p. 11.

right to use armed force against any such movement. Since democracy is considered as the ultimate desire of all peoples, and communism per definition is perceived as the result of dictatorial aggression or subversion, interventions as in Guatemala and the Dominican Republic – although communists were hardly involved here – are said to constitute not 'interventions' but 'collective self-defense': thus, any intervention is legalized as an act of self-defense. Thomas, Fenwick and Murdock are among the lawyers who accept this reasoning as legally correct.[12]

ad 1. The first theory has been deprived of all sense in practice, because of the impossibility of solving the problem of determining who the 'legal' government is. The dilemma today has dramatically been illustrated by the fact that the Soviet Union and China accept the NLF as the legal representative of the South Vietnamese people, whereas the Western countries denounce the NLF as a group of rebels and instead accept the Saigon régime as the legal representative. Accepting this theory in the present era of ideological confrontation would open the doors to unrestricted interventionist policies – the more so, as the policy of the intervening Powers is not consistent. The United States, for instance, has proclaimed its right and duty to assist legal governments against rebels; but in Iran in 1951, and in Indonesia in 1965, it supported the rebels against the existing régime, when *that* course of action was in the American interest.
In fact, this theory would result today in returning to the times of the Holy Alliance; with the difference that now several 'Holy' Alliances confront each other.

ad 3. The third theory entails likewise the inherent danger of counter-intervention. Its acceptation bears the risk of internationalizing every internal conflict. Indeed, this theory, being based on subjectively and differently interpreted Human Rights and ideological values, threatens to throw the world back into the era of the religious wars. This is true of the fourth theory to an even larger degree.

ad 2. The second theory seems to be the only one serving the cause of national self-determination and world peace. But, alas, present day policy has deprived it of its practical value. Innovations like the 'demarcation line' have clouded the distinction between internal strife and international war, and accusations of external assistance – serving

---

[12] A. J. Thomas jr. – 'The OAS and Subversive Intervention,' Proc. Am. Soc. I.L. ('61) pp. 19-24; C. G. Fenwick – 'Intervention and the Inter-American Rule of Law,' 53 A.J.I.L. ('59) pp. 873-876; J. O. Murdock – 'Collective Security Distinguished from Intervention,' 56 A.J.I.L. ('62) pp. 503-505.

as a justification for intervention – is easily made and difficult to refute. The fear that the opponent might profit in case of non-activity has made intervention a daily tool of power politics.

2⁰. What is the practical value in the prevailing circumstances of general UN Declarations such as the one on the illegality of intervention? In the 'Declaration on the granting of Independence to Colonial Countries and Peoples' the General Assembly states that

'All peoples have the right to self-determination; by virtue of that right they freely determine their political status and freely pursue their economic, social and cultural development;'

and in the Declaration on the Inadmissibility of Intervention it is said:

'No State may use or encourage the use of economic, political or any other type of measures to coerce another State in order to obtain from it the subordination of the exercise of its sovereign rights or to secure from it advantages of any kind.'

What ever could be reached by such general statements *if not circumstances are created preventing those situations to arise which sooner or later provoke intervention?*
Moreover, there is the problem to determine what exactly constitutes 'unlawful intervention,' as contrasted to lawful practices – like economic boycot – which may severely interfere with the internal affairs of other states. It can even be said – thinking of President Nixon's 10% as an extreme case – that the countries of the world have become interdependent to such an extent that every important national economic measure is bound to have effects abroad. Even deliberate omittance of action may have so serious results that they are considered interference in the affairs of other states. Where is the line of demarcation, where is the point where interventionary activities become unlawful?

Hitherto, the discussion on the problem of intervention has taken place largely within a political context and in connection to civil war. Economic forms of interference (inside as well as outside the scope of internal war) have, however, become as important as military or political interference. The mere concentration on military and political intervention – probably both the result of fear of war, and of the defense of economic liberalism – has led to the intolerable situation that, as Friedmann puts it, 'any national measures that effect another nation's economic life are legitimate, even though they may starve it to death. The slightest act of physical violation of sovereignty is not.'[13]

[13] W. Friedmann – 'Intervention, Civil War and the Role of International Law,' Proc. Am. Soc. I.L. ('65) p. 69.

In view of the daily practices of economic and political life and their often hidden interdependence, it seems a useless endeavour to try to draw a theoretical line between legal interference and illegal intervention. It seems more useful to take *practical steps* appropriate to improve the chances of restricting intervention and Cold War confrontation.

A strategy of global welfare, realized through global co-operation, would decrease the opportunity of exploiting economic assistance as a political medium in the Cold War. It has proved to be little helpful to try to prevent interventionary practices by means of solemn Declarations forbidding political and military intervention; it might be much more effective to take first practical measures impeding *economic* intervention. When social and economic conditions in the developing countries have become such that they contribute to stability and peace and thus remove a major opportunity for *interventionary practices in general*, the legal discussion on political and military intervention might become more relevant and useful.

Selected Bibliography

The following list of books and articles contains some selected sources in the field of four different topics:
(1) Relations between poverty, economic development, and internal conflict in the Third World (Chapter I).
(2) Relations between poverty, economic development, and international conflict (Chapter II).
(3) Legal and economic aspects of a global welfare strategy (Chapter III).
(4) Legal aspects of intervention (Annex).

(1) Relations between poverty, economic development, and internal conflict in the Third World.

ALMOND, G. & COLEMAN, J. S. – 'The Politics of Developing Areas' ('60).
ALTHOFF, PH. – 'The Latin American Common Man: Political Integration or Civil War,' XXIV Int. J. 3 ('69).
ANBER, P. – 'Modernisation and Political Disintegration: Nigeria and the Ibos,' 5 J. Mod. Afr. St. 2 ('67).
ARRIGHI, G. & SAUL, J. S. – 'Socialism and Economic Development in Tropical Africa,' 6 J. Mod. Afr. St. 2 ('68).
BAILY, F. G. – 'Politics and Social Change; Orissa in 1959' ('63).
BEHRENDT, R. F. – 'Soziale Strategie für Entwicklungsländer' ('65).
BENHAM, F. – 'Economic Aid to Underdeveloped Countries' ('62).
BERKOWICZ, L. – 'Aggression' ('62).
BERLINER, J. S. – 'Soviet Economic Aid' ('58).
BERREMAN, G. D. – 'Caste and Community Development,' XXII Human Organisation (Spring '63).
BHALERAO, C. N. – 'Some Social, Political and Administrative Consequences of Panchayati Ray,' IV Asian Survey ('64).
BLOOMFIELD, L. P. & WEISS, AMELIA C. – 'Arms Control and the Developing Countries,' XVIII World Politics ('65-'66).
BOULDING, K. E. – 'The Economics of Human Conflict,' in E. B. McNeil (ed.) – 'The Nature of Human Conflict' ('65).
BOUTHOUL, G. – 'La Surpopulation. L'inflation démographique' ('64).
BRINTON, C. – 'The Anatomy of Revolution' (Vintage Books, '56).
CAREY, J. C. – 'Peru and the U.S., 1900-1962' ('64).
CARROLL, TH. F. – 'Latin American Issues' ('61) in A. O. Hirschman (ed.) – 'Changes in Agriculture in 26 Developing Nations, 1948-1963,' For. Agric. Econ. Rep. no. 27 ('65).
COLEMAN, J. S. – 'Political Aspects of Modernization,' Int. Enc. Soc. Sc. 10 ('68).

COLLINS, R. O. – 'The Southern Sudan, 1883-1898' ('62).
O'CONNELL, J. – 'The Inevitability of Instability,' 5 J. Mod. Afr. St. 2 ('67).
DASGUPTA, S. – 'Peacelessness and Maldevelopment,' Proc. IPRA ('68) vol. II.
DAVIES, J. C. – 'Political Stability and Instability: Some manifestations and Causes,' XIII J. Confl. Res. ('68).
DAVIES, J. C. – 'The J-Curve of Rising and Declining Satisfactions as a Cause of Some Great Revolutions and a Contained Rebellion,' in D. Graham & T. R. Gurr – 'The History of Violence in America' ('69).
DAVIES, J. C. – 'Toward a Theory of Revolution,' 27 Am. Soc. Rev. 1 ('62).
DEUTSCH, K. – 'Social Mobilization and Political Development,' IV Am. Pol. Sc. Rev. ('61).
DOLLARD, J. et al. – 'Frustration and Aggression' ('39).
DUFF, E. A. & MCCAMANT, J. F. – 'Measuring Social and Political Requirements for System Stability in Latin America,' LXII Am. Pol. Sc. Rev. ('68).
EISENSTADT, S. N. – 'Transformation of Social, Political, and Cultural Orders in Modernisation,' XXX Am. Soc. Rev. 5 ('65).
ELKAN, W. – 'Urban Unemployment in East Africa,' 46 Int. Aff. (London) 3 ('70).
FAIRBAIRN, J. – 'Crisis in Uganda,' New Statesman (May 27, '66).
FEIERABEND, I. K. & FEIERABEND, ROSALIND L. – 'Aggressive Behaviors within Polities, 1948-1962: a cross-national study,' J. Confl. Res. ('66).
FELDMAN, H. – 'The Communal Problem in the Indo-Pakistan Subcontinent: Some Current Implications,' XLIII Pac. Aff. 2 ('69).
FITZGERALD, S. – 'China and the Overseas Chinese: Perceptions and Policies,' The China Q. 44 (Oct-Dec. '70).
FOSSUM, E. – 'Factors Influencing the Occurrence of Military Coups d'état in Latin America,' J. Peace Res. 3 ('67).
FRANKEL, FRANCINE R. – 'Ideology and Politics in Economic Planning; the Problem of Indian Agricultural Development Strategy,' XIX World Politics ('66-'67).
GALTUNG, J. – 'A Structural Theory of Aggression,' 1 J. Peace Res. ('64).
GALTUNG, J. – 'Violence, Peace, and Peace Research,' 6 J. Peace Res. ('69).
GERSCHENKRON, A. – 'Reflections on Economic Aspects of Revolution,' in H. Eckstein (ed.) – 'Internal War. Problems and Approaches' ('64).
GHAI, D. P. & GHAI, Y. P. – 'Asians in East-Africa: Problems and Prospects,' 3 J. Mod. Afr. St. ('65).
GOODSELL, J. N. – 'Mexico: Why the Students Rioted,' 56 Curr. Hist. (Jan. '69).
GRAY, R. – 'A History of the Southern Sudan, 1839-1889' ('61).
GRAY COWAN, L. – 'The Military and African Politics,' XXI Int. J. ('66).
GRUNDY, K. W. – 'Nationalism and Separatism in East Africa,' 54 Curr. Hist. (Febr. '68).
GUILLEN, A. – 'Rural Population and Urban Civilization,' XXI Rev. Int. Aff. 479 ('70).
GURR, T. R. – 'A Causal Model of Civic Strife: A Comparative Analysis Using New Indices,' LXII Am. Pol. Sc. Rev. ('68).
GURR, T. R. & RUTTENBERG, CH. – 'The Conditions of Civil Violence: first test of a causal model' ('67).
GURR, T. R. – 'Why Men Rebel' ('70).
HAGEN, E. – 'On the Theory of Social Change' ('62).
HAGEN, E. – 'A framework for Analyzing Change,' in 'Development of the Emerging Countries' ('62).
HARRISON CHURCH, R. J. – 'Urban Problems and Economic Development in West Africa,' 5 J. Mod. Afr. St. 4 ('67).
HEILBRONER, R. L. – 'The Great Ascent' ('63).
HERSKOVITZ, M. – 'Economic Anthropology' ('62).
HIRSCHMAN, A. O. – 'The Strategy of Economic Development' ('62).

HOPKINS, N. S. – 'Socialism and Social Change in Rural Mali,' 7 J. Mod. Afr. St. 3 ('69).
HOROWITZ, J. L. – 'Three Worlds of Development' ('66).
HOSELITZ, B. F. & WEINER, M. – 'Economic Development and Political Stability in India,' VIII Dissent (Spring '61).
HOSELITZ, B. & ANN WILLNER – 'Economic Development, Political Strategies, and American Aid,' in M. A. Kaplan (ed.) – 'The Revolution in World Politics' ('62) p. 363.
HUNTINGTON, S. P. – 'Political Development and Political Decay,' XVII World Politics ('64-'65).
HVEEM, H. – 'Military Coups and the Political Development in Africa,' Syn Og Segn (Oslo) 5 ('66).
JOHNSON, CH. – 'Revolution and the Social System' (Hoover Inst. Studies, '64).
JOHNSON, J. J. – 'The Military and Society in Latin America' ('64).
JOHNSON, L. L. – 'US Business Interests and the Rise of Castro,' XVIII World Politics 17 (April '65).
KENWORTHY, E. – 'Argentina: The Politics of Industrialization,' 45 For. Aff. (Oct. '66).
KIRSCH, A. TH. – 'Development and Mobility among the Phu Thai of Northeast Thailand,' VI Asian Survey ('66).
KLING, M. – 'Toward a Theory of Power and Political Instability in Latin America,' IX W. Pol. Q. ('56).
KORNHAUSER, W. – 'The Politics of Mass Society' ('59).
KRAUS, J. – 'On the Politics of Nationalism and Social Change in Ghana,' 7 J. Mod. Afr. St. ('69).
LAWSON, R. – 'Frustration, the Development of a Scientific Concept' ('65).
LEFEVER, E. W. & YOUNG, C. – 'Politics in the Congo: Decolonization and Independence' ('65).
LERNER, D. – 'The Passing of Traditional Society' ('58).
LERNER, D. – 'Social Aspects of Modernization,' Int. Enc. Soc. Sc. 10 ('68).
LERNER, D. – 'Toward a Communication Theory of Modernization,' in L. Pye (ed.) – 'Communications and Political Development' ('63).
LEVY jr., M. – 'Social Patterns (Structures) and Problems of Modernization,' in Moore and Cook (eds.) – 'Readings in Social Change' ('67).
LEWIS, O. – 'The Culture of Poverty,' Scientific American (Oct. '66).
LEYS, C. – 'What is the Problem about Corruption?,' 3 J. Mod. Afr. St. ('65).
LIEUWEN, E. – 'US Policy in Latin America' ('65).
LIPSET, S. M. – 'Political Man: The Social Basis of Politics' ('63).
MAGDOFF, H. – 'The Impact of US Foreign Policy on Underdeveloped Countries,' XXII Monthly Review 10 ('71).
MAIER, N. R. F. – 'Frustration: The Study of Behavior Without a Goal' ('49) pp. 92 ff.;
MAIER, N. R. F. – 'The Role of Frustration in Social Movements,' LXIX Psychological Review ('42) p. 587.
MALINOWSKY, B. – 'Die Dynamik des Kulturwandels' ('51).
MANGIN, W. T. – 'Mental Health and Migration in Cities: A Peruvian Case,' in Heath and Adams (eds.) – 'Contemporary Cultures and Societies of Latin America' ('65).
MASON, E. – 'Economic Planning in Underdeveloped Areas' ('58).
MASON, PH. – 'Race Relations' ('70).
MAUNG, MYA – 'Cultural Value and Economic Change in Burma,' IV Asian Survey ('64).
MACNAMARA, R. S. – 'Montreal speech', Survival (July '66).
MIDLARSKY, M. & TANTER, R. – 'Toward a Theory of Political Instability in Latin America,' J. Peace Res. ('67) 3.
MILLER, N. E. et al. – 'The Frustration-Aggression Hypothesis,' XLVIII Psychological Review (July, '41).

MILLER, N. N. – 'The Political Survival of Traditional Leadership,' 6 J. Mod. Afr. St. ('68).
MILLIKAN, M. F. & ROSTOW, W. W. – 'A Proposal; Key to an Effective Foreign Policy' ('57).
MILLINGTON, TH. M. – 'Bolivia Under Barrientos,' 56 Curr. Hist. (Jan. '69).
MORGENTHAU, H. – 'A Political Theory of Foreign Aid,' LVI Am. Pol. Sc. Rev. ('62).
MUDDATHIR 'ABD AL-RAHIM – 'Self-Identification in the Sudan,' 8 J. Mod. Afr. St. 2 ('70).
MYRDAL, G. – 'An American Dilemma' ('44).
MYRDAL, G. – 'Challenge to Affluence' ('65).
NAIR, KUSSUM – 'Blossoms in the Dust: The Human Factor in Indian Development' ('62).
NARAIN, J. – 'Democratic Decentralization and Rural Leadership in India: The Rayasthan Experiment,' IV Asian Survey ('64).
NASH, M. – 'Party Building in Upper Burma,' IV Asian Survey ('64).
NAZEER, M. M. – 'Urban Growth in Pakistan,' VI Asian Survey ('66).
NEEDLER, M. C. – 'Political Development and Military Intervention in Latin America,' LX Am. Pol. Sc. Rev. ('66).
NEEDLER, M. C. – 'Political Development in Latin America: Instability, Violence and Evolutionary Change' ('68).
ODUHO, J. & DENG, W. – 'The Problems of the Southern Sudan' ('63).
OLSON, M. – 'Rapid Growth as a Destabilizing Force,' XXIII J. Econ. Hist. (Dec. '63).
ORENSTEIN, H. – 'Gaon: Conflict and Cohesion in a Maharashtrian Village' ('64).
OSBORNE, H. – 'Indians of the Andes: Aymaras and Quechuas' ('52).
PACKENHAM, R. A. – 'Political Development Doctrines in the American Foreign Aid Program,' XVIII World Politics ('65-'66).
PARK, R. L. – 'India's Foreign Policy: 1964-1968,' 54 Curr. Hist. (April '68).
PETRAS, J. – 'Klassenstruktuur en Politiek' (Class Structure and Politics), 16 Te Elfder Ure no. 3/4 ('69).
ROTHCHILD, D. – 'Ethnic Inequalities in Kenya,' 7 J. Mod. Afr. St. 4 ('69).
RUDEBECK, L. – 'Developmental Pressure and Political Limits: A Tunesian Example,' 8 J. Mod. Afr. St. 2 ('70).
RUSSETT. B. M. – 'Inequality and Instability: the Relation of Land Tenure to Politics,' XVI World Politics ('63-'64).
RUSSETT, B. M. – 'World Handbook of political and social indicators' ('64).
SCHILDKROUT, E. – 'Strangers and Local Government in Kumasi,' 8 J. Mod. Afr. St. 2 ('70).
SCHWEINITZ, K. DE – 'Industrialization and Democracy' ('64).
SENDUT, H. – 'Contemporary Urbanization in Malaysia,' VI Asian Survey ('66).
SHEPHERD jr., G. W. – 'National Integration and the Southern Sudan,' 4 J. Mod. Afr. St. 2 ('66).
SHILLS, E. – 'Political Development in the New States' ('62).
SILVERMAN – 'The Precipitants and Underlying Conditions of Race Riots,' 30 Am. Soc. Rev. (Dec. '65).
SILVERT, K. H. – 'Parties and the Masses,' 357 The Annals (March '65).
SKINNER, G. W. – 'The Nature of Loyalties in Rural Indonesia' in idem (ed.) – 'Local, Ethnic and National Loyalties in Village Indonesia; a Symposium' ('59).
SPILERMAN, S. – 'The Causes of Racial Disturbances: a comparison of alternative explanations,' 35 Am. Soc. Rev. 4 (Aug. '70).
STALEY, E. – 'The Future of Underdeveloped Countries' ('54).
STONE, L. – 'Theories of Revolution,' XVIII World Politics ('65-'66).
TAEUBER, C. – 'Population and Food Supply,' 369 Annals ('67).
TOCQUEVILLE, A. DE – 'De la Démocratie en Amérique' II (éditions M-Th. Génin, '51).

TOCQUEVILLE, A. DE – 'L'Ancien Régime et la Revolution,' oeuvres complètes (ed. J. P. Mayer) II, Gallimard, 7e ed. vol. I ('52).
UPPAL, J. S. – 'Implementation of Land Reform Legislation in India: A Study of Two Villages in Punjab,' IX Asian Survey ('69).
VERBA, S. & ALMOND, G. A. – 'National Revolution and Political Commitment,' in H. Eckstein (ed.) – 'Internal War. Problems and Approaches ('64).
WARD, BARBARA – 'The Rich Nations and the Poor Nations' ('62).
WEINERT, R. S. – 'Violence in Pre-Modern Societies: Rural Colombia,' LX Am. Pol. Sc. Rev. ('66).
WERTHEIM, W. F. – 'Agrarian Problems and Communism in Southeast Asia' in 'Nationalism in the Third World' (Polemological Studies no. 11, in Dutch) ('70).
WEST, Q. M. – 'World Food Needs,' US Dept. of Agriculture, Foreign Regional Analysis Division, Economic Research Service ('66).
WILLIAMSON, R. C. – 'Toward a Theory of Political Violence: the case of rural Colombia,' XVIII W. Pol. Q. (March '65).
WILLMOTT, W. E. – 'The Overseas Chinese Today and Tomorrow,' LXIII Pac. Aff. 2 ('69).
WOETZEL, R. K. – 'Political Rights in Developing Countries,' Proc. Am. Soc. Int. L. ('66).
WORSLEY, P. – 'The Third World' ('64).
WRAITH, R. & SIMPKINS, E. – 'Corruption in Developing Countries' ('64).
YOUNG, K. – 'Thailand's Role in Southeast Asia,' 56 Curr. Hist. ('69).

(2) *Relations between poverty, economic development, and international conflict.*

Accounts of the USSR Communist Party Congresses – edited in English by Novosti Press Agency House.
ADIE, W. A. C. – 'The Communist Powers in Africa,' Conflict Studies, no. 10 (Dec.-Jan. 70/71).
AGUILAR, A. – 'Latin America and the Alliance for Progress,' Monthly Review Pamphlet Series no. 24 ('63).
ALEXANDRE, P. – 'Note on the Activities of the Communist Powers in French Speaking Africa,' in 'East-West Confrontation in Africa' ('60).
ALLEN, R. L. – 'Soviet Economic Warfare' ('60).
ANDREWS POOLE, P. – 'Communist China's Aid Diplomacy,' VI Asian Survey ('66).
ASHFORD, D. – 'The Irredentist Appeal in Morocco and Mauretania,' XV W. Pol. Q. ('62).
BARBER, W. F. – 'Can the Alliance for Progress Succeed?,' 351 The Annals ('64).
BARNET, R. J. – 'Intervention and Revolution' ('68).
'Batchers of the People's Revolution in Southeast Asia,' Peking Review (May 16, '69).
BEIM, D. – 'The Communist Bloc and the Foreign Aid Game,' XVII W. Pol. Q. ('64).
BENHAM, F. – 'Economic Aid to Underdeveloped Countries' ('62).
BIGGS-DAVIDSON, J. – 'Portugese Guinea, a lesser Vietnam,' 13 Nato's Fifteen Nations ('68).
BILLERBECK, K. – 'Die Auslandshilfe des Ostblocks für die Entwicklungsländer' ('60).
BILLERBECK, K. – 'Soviet Bloc Foreign Aid to the Developing Countries' ('60).
BLOOMFIELD, L. P. – 'Future Small Wars: Must the US Intervene?,' XII Orbis 3 (Fall '68).
BLOOMFIELD, L. P. & WEISS, AMELIA C. – 'Arms Control and the Developing Countries,' XVIII World Politics ('65-'66).
BOOG, P. – 'People's War in Burma,' Far Eastern Economic Review (Nov. 16, '67).
BORCHGRAVE, A. DE – 'Scandal of the Century: Rich and Poor,' Newsweek (Oct. 30, '67).
BOULDING, K. E. – 'The Economics of Human Conflict,' in E. B. McNeil (ed.) – 'The Nature of Human Conflict' ('65).
BOYD, R. G. in G. Modelski (ed.) – 'SEATO: Six Studies' ('62).

BRANDT, C., SCHWARTZ, B. & FAIRBANKS, J. K. – 'A Documentary History of Chinese Communism' ('52).
BRIGHTMAN, C. & KLARE, M. – 'Campus Counterinsurgency. Focus: Latin America,' Viet Report (April-May '68).
BROWN, N. & GUTTERIDGE, W. F. – 'The African Military Balance,' Adelphi Papers, no. 12 ('64).
BRZEZINSKI, Z. – 'The Politics of Underdevelopment,' World Politics (Oct. '56).
BULL, H. – 'The Control of the Arms Race' ('61).
CASTAGNO, A. A. – 'Somalia Republic,' in J. S. Coleman & C. S. Rosberg (eds.) – 'Political Parties and National Integration in Tropical Africa' ('66).
CHAUDHRI, M. A. – 'Pakistan's Relations with the Soviet Union', VI Asian Survey ('66).
CHARKSON, S. – 'The Soviet View of Aid to India,' XXVI Int. Journal ('66-'67).
CHOUET, J., in Problèmes africaines, no. 204 (24 Oct. '63).
CLEMENS, W. C. – 'The 1970's,' XIII Orbis 2 ('69).
COLE, A. B. (ed.) – 'Conflict in Indo-China and International Repercussions: A Documentary History 1945-1955' ('56).
Committee to Strengthen the Security of the Free World (Clay-Comittee) – 'The Scope and Distribution of the US Military and Economic Assistance Programs' ('63).
COSER, L. A. – 'The Functions of Social Conflict' ('56).
COUNTS, R. – 'Chinese Footprints in Somalia,' The Reporter (Febr. 2 '61).
CRABB JR., C. V. – 'The US and the Neutralists: A Decade in Perspective,' 362 The Annals (Nov. '65).
DEAS, M. – 'Columbian Prospects,' XXIV Int. J. (Summer '69).
DECREANE, PH., in Problèmes africaines no. 181 (May 6, '63).
DOAK BARNETT, A. – 'Communist Economic Strategy: the Rise of Mainland China' ('59).
DULLES, A. W. – 'The Craft of Intelligence' ('65).
EHRLICH, A. & SONNE, CH. R. – 'The Soviet Union: Economic Activity,' in Z. Brzezinski (ed.) – 'Africa and the Communist World' ('63).
ESAKI, M. – 'China's Military Preparations,' IX Survival (Jan. '67).
FEINSTEIN, O. – 'Which Way Security? How we can counter growing instability in the Underdeveloped Countries,' in – 'A Strategy for American Security; an Alternative to the 1964 Military Budget' ('63).
FENWICK, CH. G. – 'The Dominican Republic: Intervention or Collective Selfdefence?,' 60 A.J.I.L. ('66).
FISTIÉ, P. – 'Communisme et indépendence nationale: le cas thailandais (1928-1968),' XVIII Rev. Franc. Sc. Pol. ('68).
FITZGERALD, C. P. – 'The Sino-Soviet Balance Sheet in the Underdeveloped Areas,' 351 The Annals (Jan. '64).
FRANK, L. A. – 'The Arms Trade in International Relations' ('69).
FREEMAN, O. L. – 'Food – America's Secret Weapon,' US N.W. Rep. (July '67).
FRIEDMANN, W. – 'Interventionism, Liberalism and Power Politics; the Unfinished Revolution in International Thinking,' LXXIII Pol. Sc. Q. ('68).
GABELIC, A. – 'New Accent in Soviet Strategy,' Survival (Febr. '68).
GARVEY, E. – 'The CIA bungles on,' LXXXVII Commonweal (Febr. 9 '63).
GHAI, D. P. – 'Asians in East-Africa: Problems and Prospects,' 3 J. Mod. Afr. St. ('65).
GILBERT, S. P. – 'Soviet-American Military Aid Competition in the Third World,' XIII Orbis ('70).
GILBERT, S. P. – 'Wars of Liberation and Soviet Military Aid Policy,' IX Orbis ('66).
GITTINGS, J. – 'Survey of the Soviet-Sino Dispute 1963-1967' ('68).
HAAS, E. R. & WHITING, A. S. – 'Dynamics of International Relations' ('56).
HAFTENDORN, HELGA – 'Stabilität und Unsicherheit im Horn von Afrika,' XXII Eur. Arch. ('67).

HANNING, H. – 'Insurgency and World Order,' XIII Disarmament (March '67).
HARRIS, R. – 'A New 30 Years War?,' The Times (Febr. '68).
HARRISON, S. S. – 'Troubled India and her Neighbours,' 44 For. Aff. (Jan. '65).
HASKINS, H. L. – 'Aid and Diplomacy in the Middle East,' 53 Curr. Hist. (July '66).
HENKIN, L. – 'Force, Intervention, and Neutrality in Contemporary International Law,' Proc. Am. Soc. I.L. ('63).
HINDLEY, D. – 'Indonesia's Confrontation with Malaysia: a Search for Motives,' IV Asian Survey ('64).
HINTON, H. C. – 'Communist China in World Politics' ('66).
HOFFMAN, S. – 'The American Style: Our Past and Our Principles,' 46 For. Aff. 2 ('67).
HOOGLAND, J. H. – 'Arms in the developing world,' XII Orbis (Spring '68).
HOROWITZ, J. L. – 'Three Worlds of Development' ('66).
HOVEY, H. A. – 'United States Military Assistance' ('65).
HOWARD, P. – 'Soviet Politics in Southeast Asia,' XXIII Int. J. ('68).
JOHNSTONE, W. C. – 'Political Commitment in Southeast Asia,' 54 Curr. Hist. (Jan. '68).
KATZENBACH, Under-Secretary – 'US Arms for the Developing World: Dilemmas of Foreign Policy,' Dept. of State Bull. (Dec. 11, '67).
KAZEMBE, MUSOA 'Why Should I Die?,' Atlas (June '68).
KEMP, G. – 'Arms Sale and Arms Control in the Developing Countries,' XXII The World Today ('66).
KEMP, G. – 'Arms Transfers to Developing Countries,' Proc. IPRA II ('68).
KHALILI, J. E. – 'Sino-Arab Relations,' VIII Asian Survey ('68).
KOVNER, M. – 'The Challenge of Coexistence' ('61).
KRETZSCHMAR, W. W. – 'Auslandshilfe als Mittel der Aussenwirtschafts- und Aussenpolitik' ('64).
KRIPPENDORFF, E. – 'Waffenhandel,' Atomzeitalter ('67).
LAGOS, G. – 'International Stratification and Underdeveloped Countries' ('63).
LARY, H. B. – 'Import of Manufactures from Less Developed Countries' ('68).
LEE, J. M. – 'African Armies and Civil Order' ('69).
LEIFER, M. – 'Cambodia and Her Neighbours,' XXXIV Pac. Aff. 4 ('61-'62).
LENCZOWSKI, G. – 'Soviet Policy in the Middle East,' 55 Curr. Hist. (Nov. '68).
LERSKI, G. J. – 'The Pakistan-American Alliance: A reevaluation of the present decade,' VIII Asian Survey ('68).
LIEUWEN, E. – 'US Military Assistance of Doubtful Value in Latin America,' in – 'A Strategy for American Security' ('63).
LIEUWEN, E. – 'US Policy in Latin America' ('65).
LIN PIAO – 'Long Live the Victory of the People's War,' 8 Peking Review, 36 (Sept. 3, '65).
LOEWENTHAL, R. – 'China,' in Brzezinski (ed.) – 'Africa and the Communist World' ('63).
MAGDOFF, H. – 'The Age of Imperialism' ('69).
MAGDOFF, H. – 'The Impact of US Foreign Policy on Underdeveloped Countries,' XXII Monthly Rev. 10 ('71).
MARSOT, A. G. – 'China's Aid to Cambodia,' XLIII Pac. Aff. 2 ('69).
MASON, E. E. – 'Foreign Aid and Foreign Policy.'
MATTHEWS, R. O. – 'Domestic and Inter-State Conflict in Africa,' XXV Int. J. 3 ('70).
MCLANE, CH. B. – 'Soviet Doctrine and the Military Coups in Africa,' XXI Int. J. ('66).
MCLAREN, J. P. S. – 'The Dominican Crisis: An Inter-American Dilemma,' IV Can. Y.J.L. ('66).
Military Balance (The) – edited by The Institute for Strategic Studies, London.
MOHIDDIN, A. M. – 'Report on Tanzania,' VIII Kron. Afr. 2 ('68).
MONTGOMERY, J. D. – 'Foreign Aid in International Politics' ('67).
MORGENTHAU, H. – 'A Political Theory of Foreign Aid,' LVI Am. Pol. Sc. Rev. ('62).

MORISON, D. – 'The USSR and Africa' ('64).
MOSELY, PH. E. – 'The Kremlin and the Third World,' 46 For. Aff. (Oct. '67).
MOZINGO, D. P. – 'Containment in Asia,' VII Survival (July '67).
MYRDAL, G. – 'The Challenge of World Poverty' ('70).
NELSON, J. M. – 'Aid, Influence, and Foreign Policy' ('68).
NIELSEN, W. A. & HODJERA, Z. S. – 'Sino-Soviet Bilateral Approach,' CCCXXIII The Annals (May '59).
NOLLAU, G. & WIEHE, H. J. – 'Russia's South Flank' ('63).
NOURRY, PH. – 'Camping Tonight,' Atlas (May '68).
NUECHTERLEIN, O. E. – 'Thailand: A Year of Danger and Hope,' VI Asian Survey ('66).
OHLIN, G. – 'Foreign Aid Policies Reconsidered' ('66).
OSGOOD, CH. E. – 'Escalation as a Strategy,' W.P. Report (Sept. '65).
PACKENHAM, R. A. – 'Political Development Doctrines in the American Foreign Aid Program,' XVIII World Politics ('65-'66).
'Peiping and Ghana Set Up Closer Ties' – N.Y.T. (August 19, '61).
PHIBBS, PH. M. – 'India's Economic Aid Programs,' 54 Curr. Hist. (April '68).
RA'ANAN, U. – 'The USSR Arms the Third World' ('69).
Randall-Commission – 'Report to the President and the Congress' ('54).
'Relationship (On the) between Political and Economic Independence' – Renmin Rihbao (Dec. 17, '65).
RESHETAR, J. S. – 'The Soviet Union and the Neutralist World,' 362 The Annals ('65).
ROBINSON, TH. W. – 'Peking's Revolutionary Strategy in the Developing World: the Failure of Success,' 368 The Annals (Nov. '69).
ROSECRANCE, R. N. – 'Action and Reaction in World Politics' ('63).
ROSENAU, A. – 'US Economic Commitment in Southeast Asia,' 54 Curr. Hist. (Jan. '68).
ROSTOW, E. – 'Law, Power and the Pursuit of Peace' ('68).
ROTHERMUND, D. – 'India and the Soviet Union,' 368 The Annals ('69).
ROTHSTEIN, R. L. – 'Alignment, Nonalignment and Small Powers: 1945-1965,' XX Int. Org. ('66).
RUBINSTEIN, A. Z. – 'Soviet Policy Toward Underdeveloped Areas in the Economic and Social Council,' IX Int. Org. 2 (May '55).
RYMALOW, W. W. – 'Die UdSSR und die wirtschaftlich schwach entwickelten Länder' ('64).
SCALAPINO, R. A. – 'The Sino-Soviet Conflict in Perspective,' 351 The Annals ('64).
SCOTT, M. M. – 'Internal Violence as an Instrument of Cold Warfare,' in J. N. Rosenau (ed.) – 'International Aspects of Civil Strife' ('64).
SETH, S. P. – 'Russia's Role in Indo-Pak Policies,' IX Asian Survey (Aug. '69).
SHASTRI, S. K. – 'A Possible Strategy,' Seminar No. 83 (July '66).
SHOUP, D. M. & DONOVAN, J. – 'The New American Militarism,' The Atlantic Monthly (April '69).
SIMMEL, G. – 'Conflict and the Webb of Inter Group Applications' ('55).
SINGH, L. P. – 'Die Ausstrahlung des Vietnam Krieges auf Laos, Kambodscha und Thailand,' XX Eur. Arch. ('68).
SINGH, L. P. – 'National Defense in Nuclear Age: Dilemma of India,' Political Scientist (Jan/June '66).
SIPRI (Stockholm) – 'the Arms Trade With the Third World' ('71).
SMITH, R. F. – 'Social Revolution in Latin America; the role of US policy,' 41 Int. Aff. (London, Oct. '65).
STARUSCHENKO, G. – 'Peaceful Coexistence and Revolution,' Kommunist 2 ('62).
STEEL, R. – 'Pax Americana' ('67).
SUBBA-RAO, M. V. – 'Neo Colonialism: The Invisible Government,' IV Afro-Asian World Affairs I ('67).

SUTTON, J. L. & KEMP, G. – 'Arms to Developing Countries, 1945-1965' Adelphi Papers, no. 28 ('66).
TANG TSON & HALPERIN, M. – 'Mao Tse-tung's Revolutionary Strategy and Peking's International Behavior,' LIX Am. Pol. Sc. Rev. ('65).
THAYER, G. – 'The War Business: the international trade in armaments' ('69).
TRISKA, J. F. & FINLAY, D. D. – 'Soviet Foreign Policy' ('68).
US Congress, Gen. Committee on For. Relations – 'American Private Enterprise, Foreign Economic Development, and the Aid Program' ('57).
US Congress, Joint Econ. Committee – 'Current Economic Indicators for the USSR' ('65).
US Congress, 85th Cong., 1st Sess. – 'Foreign Aid Program, Compilation of Studies and Surveys' ('57).
US Dept. of State – 'Communist Economic Policy in the Less Developed Areas' ('60).
US Dept. of State – 'Communist Governments and Developing Nations: Aid and Trade in 1965', Res. Mem. RSB-50 ('66).
US Dept. of State – 'idem..... in 1967,' Res. Mem. RSB – 120 ('68).
VALKENIER, E. K. – 'Sino-Soviet Rivalry in the Third World,' 56 Curr. Hist. (Oct. '69).
VERSHININ, V. & DEMIDOV, V. – 'Disinterested Aid,' Int. Aff. (Moscow, Jan. '60).
VINACKE, H. M. – 'Communist China and the Uncommitted Zone,' The Annals (Nov. '65).
WALLERSTEIN, J. – 'Implicit Geology in Africa. A Review of Books by Kwame Nkrumah,' XI J. Confl. Res. ('67).
WILD, D. – 'The Organisation of African Unity and the Algerian-Moroccan Dispute,' XX Int. Org. ('66).
WILLMOTT, W. E. – 'The Overseas Chinese Today and Tomorrow,' LXIII Pac. Aff. 2 ('69).
WILLNER, ANN RUTH – 'The Underdeveloped Study of Political Development,' XVI World Politics ('63).
WISE, D. & ROSS, TH. B. – 'The Invisible Government' ('60).
WOLDE MARIAN, M. – 'The Background of the Ethio-Somalia Boundary Dispute,' I. J. Mod. Afr. St. ('63).
WOOD, D. – 'Armed Forces in Central and South America,' Adelphi Papers no. 34 ('67).
WRIGHT, Q. – 'A Study of War' II ('42).
WRIGHT, Q. – 'Subversive Intervention,' 54 A.J.I.L. ('60).
WRIGHT, Q. – 'US Intervention in the Lebanon,' 53 A.J.I.L. ('59).
YU, G. T. – 'China's Failure in Africa,' VI Asian Survey ('66).
YU, G. T. – 'Sino-African Relations: A Survey' ('65).
ZAGORIA, D. S. – 'The Sino-Soviet Conflict 1956-1961' ('62).
ZARTMAN, I. W. – 'International Relations in West-Africa' ('66).

(3) *Legal and economic aspects of a global welfare strategy.*

ABI-SAAB, G. M. – 'The Newly Independent States and the Rules of International Law: An Outline,' 8 Howard Law Journal (Spring '62).
ANAND, R. P. – 'The Development of a Universal International Law,' Festschrift for Q. Wright (eds. Lepawski, Buehrig, and Lasswell, '71).
BARTOS, M. – report to the ILA, Proc. ILA ('58).
BROEKMEYER, M. W. J. M. – 'Developing Countries and NATO' ('63).
CARR-SAUNDERS, A. M. – 'World Population: Past Growth and Present Trends' ('36).
CASTANEDA, J. – 'The Underdeveloped Nations and the Development of International Law,' XV Int. Org. 1 ('61).
CLAUDE, I. L. – 'Swords Into Plowshares' ('59).
CLOUD, P. – 'Resources from the Sea,' in 'Resources and Man,' National Academy of Sciences, Nat. Res. Council ('69).
Commission to Study the Organization of Peace – 'The United Nations and the Bed of the Sea' ('69).

DOUENCE, U. CL. – 'Droit de la mer et développement économique sur la côte occidentale d'Afrique,' 71 Rev. Gen. D.I.P. ('67).
DOW, TH. E. – 'The Population of India,' 54 Curr. Hist. (April '68).
DURAND, J. D. – 'World Population Estimates 1750-2000,' UN World Population Conference 1965, vol. II ('66).
ECOSOC – 'Preliminary Study of Issues Relating to the Realization of Economic and Social Rights Contained in the Universal Declaration of Human Rights and in the International Covenant on Economic, Social and Cultural Rights' E/CN 4/988 (Jan. 20, '69).
ENCINAS DEL PANDO, J. A. – The General Report on UNCTAD II. in UNCTAD, 2nd. Sess. (New Delhi), Report and Annexes, UN Publ. Sales no. E. 68. II D. 14 ('68).
EYRE, S. R. – 'Man the Pest,' N.Y.R. Books (Nov. 18, '71).
FALK, R. A. – 'The New States and International Legal Order,' Hague Rec. Cours II ('66).
FALK, R. A. – 'On the quasi-legislative competence of the G.A.,' 60 A.J.I.L. ('66).
FAO – 'Provisional Indicative World Plan for Agricultural Development' ('70).
FAO – 'The State of Food and Agriculture' (annually).
Commission on International Co-operation (Pearson-Commission) – 'Partners in Development' ('69).
FAWCETT, J. E. S. – 'The New States and the United Nations' in W. V. O'Brien (ed.) – 'The New Nations in International Law and Diplomacy' ('65).
FENWICK, CH. S. – 'International Law: The Old and the New,' 60 A.J.I.L. ('66).
Flow (The) of Financial Resources to Less-Developed Countries, 1956-1963,' OECD ('64).
FRIEDMANN, W. – 'The Changing Dimensions of International Law,' 62 Columbia Law Review ('62).
GOSOVIC, B. – 'UNCTAD: North-South Encounter,' Int. Conc. no. 568 (May '68).
HACKWORTH, G. H. – 'Responsibility of States for Damages Caused in Their Territory to the Person or Property of Foreigners,' 24 A.J.I.L. ('30).
HAMBRO, B. – Address at the opening of the 25th Session of the UN Gen. Ass., A/PV 1839 (sept. 15, '70).
HENDRICKS, S. B. – 'Food form the Land,' in 'Resources and Man' op. cit.,
HIBBARD, W. – 'Mineral Resources: Challenge or Threat?,' 160 Science ('68).
HIGGINS, ROSALYN – 'Conflict of Interests; International Law in a Divided World' ('65).
HYDE, J. N. – 'Permanent Sovereignty Over Natural Wealth and Resources,' 50 A.J.I.L. ('56).
Indicative World Plan for Agricultural Development, a synthesis and analysis of factors relevant to world, regional and national agricultural development – 3 vols., FAO ('69).
JENKS, C. W. – 'Law in the World Community' ('67).
JOHNSON, – 'The Effect of Resolutions of the General Assembly of the United Nations,' 32 B.Y.I.L. ('55-'56).
KAPLAN, M. A. & KATZENBACH, N. – 'Political Foundations of International Law' ('61).
KEYFITZ, N. – 'US and World Populations,' in 'Resources and Man.' op. cit.
KING HUBBERT, M. – 'Energy Resources' in 'Resources and Man' op. cit.
LASSWELL, H. D. – 'The Policy Sciences of Development,' XVII World Politics ('65).
LAUTERPACHT, H. – 'International Law and the Human Rights' ('55).
LISSITZYN, O. J. – 'International Law in a Divided World,' 542 Int. Conc. ('63)
LOVERING, TH. S. – 'Mineral Resources from the Land,' in 'Resources and Man' op. cit.
MACNAMARA, R. S. – Address to the Board of Governors of the World Bank Group (Wash., Sept. 29, '69).
MACNAMARA, R. S. – 'Security in the Contemporary World,' 54 Dept. State Bull. (June 6, '66).
MYRDAL, G. – 'The Challenge of World Poverty' ('70).
MYRDAL, G. – 'An International Economy: Problems and Prospects' ('56).
OECD – 'The Flow of Financial Resources to Less-Developed Countries, 1956-1963' ('64).
PRAKESH SINHA, S. – 'New Nations and the Law of Nations' ('67).

PREUSS, L. – 'Article 2, paragraph 7, of the Charter of the UN and matters of domestic jurisdiction,' 74 Rec. Cours ('49).
Proceedings of the International Law Association – Committee on Peaceful Coexistence.
RICKER, W. E. – 'Food from the Sea,' in 'Resources and Man' op. cit.
ROBOS, J. – 'The Sea, Development and Latin-America' XXI Rev. Int. Aff. 493 ('70).
RÖLING, B. V. A. – 'Human Rights and the War Problem,' XV Ned. T.I.R. ('68).
RÖLING, B. V. A. – 'International Law in an Expanded World' ('60).
RÖLING, B. V. A. – 'Peace Research, the Science of Survival,' XVIII Impact of Science on Society ('68).
RÖLING, B. V. A. – 'De VN in een wereld in steigers' ('The UN in a world in scaffolding,' published in a book edited by the Dutch Association for international Legal Order (VIRO) in commemoration of the 25th anniversary of the UN ('71).
ROSTOW, E. V. – 'Law, Power and the Pursuit of Peace' ('68).
RYTHER, J. H. – 'Photosynthesis and Fish Production in the Sea,' 166 Science ('69).
SCHEUNER, U. – 'Die Völkerrechtlichen Grundlagen der Weltwirtschaft in der Gegenwart' ('54), Sonderdruck aus 'Verhandlungen des 40. Deutschen Juristentages.'
SCHWARZENBERGER, G. – 'The Standard of Civilization in International Law,' VIII Curr. Legal Problems ('55).
SCHWARZENBERGER, G. – 'A Manual of International Law' ('50).
State (The) of Food and Agriculture,' FAO.
STEPANOV, L. – 'One Percent: The Problem of Economic Aid,' 386 The Annals (Nov. '69).
SYATAUW, J. J. G. – 'Some Newly Established Asian States and the Development of International Law' ('61).
TAEUBER, C. – 'Population and Food Supply,' 369 Annals ('67).
TAMMES, A. J. P. – 'Decisions of International Organs as a Source of International Law,' 94 Rec. Cours ('58).
THIESENHUSEN, W. C. – 'Latin America's Employment Problem,' 171 Science ('71).
TINBERGEN, J. – 'Wanted: A World Development Plan,' XXII Int. Org. I ('68).
'United (The) Nations and the Bed of the Sea,' 19th Rep. of the Commission to study the Organization of Peace ('69).
United Nations, Committee on Development Planning (Committee-Tinbergen) – Reports of the 4th, 5th, and 6th Sessions, E/4682 ('69), E/4776 ('70).
United Nations, Jackson-Commission – 'A Study of the Capacity of the UN Development System' 2 vols. ('69).
United Nations – 'World population prospects as assessed in 1963,' ST/SOA/Series A/41 ('66).
US Agency for International Development – 'Population Program Assistance' ('70).
US Dept. of Agriculture, Eco. Res. Serv. – 'Changes in Agriculture in 26 Developing Nations, 1948-1963,' For. Agric. Econ. Rep. no. 27 ('65).
US Dept. of Agriculture, For. Regional Analysis Division, Economic Research Service – 'World Food Needs' ('66).
US Dept. of Commerce, Off. of Int. Trade – Study of Factors Limiting American Private Foreign Investment. Summary of Findings and Recommendations. (July '53).
US Task Force on International Development (Petterson-Commission) – 'US Foreign Assistance in the 1970's: a new approach' ('70).
VERZIJL, J. H. W. – 'Western European Influence on the Foundation of International Law,' I Int. Rel. 4 (Oct. '55).
VIRALLY, M. – 'La valeur juridique des Recommendations des Organisations Internationales,' II Ann. Fr. D.I. ('56).
WARD, BARBARA – 'The Rich Nations and the Poor Nations' ('62).
WHINNEY, E. MC. – 'International Law and World Revolution' ('67).
WITHE, G. – 'Nationalisation of Foreign Property' ('61).

WEST, Q. M. – 'World Food Needs,' US Dept. of Agriculture, Foreign Regional Analysis Division, Economic Research Service ('66).
WRIGHT, Q. – 'Custom as a basis for international law in the postwar World,' VII Ind. J.I.L. ('67).
YALEM, R. J. – 'Regionalism and World Order,' in R. A. Falk & S. Mendlovitz (eds.) – 'The Strategy of World Order' I ('66).

(4) *Legal aspects of intervention*

ALFORD, N. – 'The Legality of American Military Involvement in Vietnam: a broader perspective.' 75 Yale Law J. ('66).
BOHAN, R. T. – 'The Dominican Case: Unilateral Intervention,' 60 A.J.I.L. ('66).
BROWNLIE, J. – 'International Law and the Use of Force by States' ('63).
CHAYES, A., in Proc. Am. Soc. I.L. ('63).
COSTE, R. – 'Réflexion Philosophique sur le problème de l'intervention' 71 RGDIP ('67).
Declaration on the Inadmissibility of Intervention in the Domestic Affairs of States and the Protection of their Independence and Sovereignty – A/Res/2131 (XX) ('65).
DOMMEN, A. J. – 'Conflict in Laos, the politics of neutralization' ('64).
FALK, R. A. – 'International Law and the US role in the Vietnam war,' 75 Yale LJ ('66).
FALK, R. A. – 'The international regulation of internal violence in the developing countries,' Proc. A.S.I.L. ('66).
FALK, R. A. – 'Janus tormented: The International Law of Internal War,' in J. N. Rosenau (ed.) – 'International Aspects of Civil Strife' ('64).
FALK, R. A. – 'World Law and Human Conflict,' in E. B. McNeill (ed.) – 'The Nature of Human Conflict' ('65).
FENWICK, C. G. – 'The Dominican Republic: Intervention or Collective Self-Defense?,' 60 A.J.I.L. ('66).
FENWICK, C. G. – 'The Issues at Punta del Este: Non-Intervention v. Collective Security,' 56 A.J.I.L. ('62).
FENWICK, C. G. – 'Intervention and the Inter-American Rule of Law,' 53 A.J.I.L. ('59).
FISCHER, R. – 'Intervention: Three Problems of Policy and Law,' in R. J. Stanger (ed.) – 'Essays on Intervention' ('64).
FRIEDMANN, W. – 'Intervention, Civil War and the Role of International Law,' Proc. Am. Soc. I.L. ('65).
FRIEDMANN. W. – 'Law and Politics in the Vietnamese War: A Comment,' 61 A.J.I.L. ('67).
GARNER, J. W. – 'Questions of International Law in the Spanish Civil War,' 31 A.J.I.L. ('37).
GERARD, A. – 'L'opération Stanleyville-Paulis devant le Parlement belge et les Nations Unies,' R.B.D.I. ('67).
GILMOUR, D. R. – 'The meaning of 'Intervene' within art. 2 (7) of the UN Charter – A historical perspective,' 16 I.C.L.Q. ('67).
HALPERIN, M. – 'The morality and politics of intervention,' in J. N. Rosenau (ed.) – 'International Aspects of Civil Strife' ('64).
HYDE, C. – 'Intervention in Theory and Practice' ('11).
KAPLAN, M. A. – 'Intervention in Internal War: some systemic sources,' in J. N. Rosenau (ed.) – 'International Aspects of Civil Strife' ('64).
LAUTERPACHT, E. – 'Intervention by Invitation,' VII Int. Comp. L.Q. ('58).
LERCHE, C. O. – 'Development of rules relating to peacekeeping by the Organisation of American States,' 59 Proc. A.S.I.L. ('65).
LIEUWEN, E. – 'US Policy in Latin-America' ('65).

MARCUM, L. A. – 'Unilateral intervention in the Congo and its political consequences,' Proc. A.S.I.L. ('61).
MCDOUGALL, M. S. – 'Studies in World Public Order' ('60).
MCLAREN, J. P. S. – 'The Dominican Crisis: An Inter-American Dilemma,' 4 C.Y.I.L. ('66).
MEEKER, L. C. – 'The Legality of the United States Participation in the Defense of Vietnam', 60 A.J.I.L. ('66).
MODELSKI, G. – 'The International Relations of Internal War,' in J. N. Rosenau (ed.) – 'International Aspects of Civil Strife' ('64).
MOORE, J. N. – 'Law and Politics in the Vietnamese War,' 61 A.J.I.L. ('67).
MOORE, J. N. – 'The Lawfulness of Military Assistance to the Republic of Vietnam,' 61 A.J.I.L. ('67).
MOZINGO, D. P. – 'Containment in Asia,' IX Survival 7 (July '67).
MURDOCK, J. O. – 'Collective Security Distinguished from Intervention,' 56 A.J.I.L. ('62).
MURTI, B. S. N. – 'The Vietnam Conflict; A legal perspective,' 7 Ind. J. of Int. Law ('67).
NIXON, R. M. – 'Asia after Vietnam,' 46 For. Aff. ('67).
OAS-Resol. 'Communist Offense in America,' 13 Jan. '62 (Punta del Este).
PUSTAY, J. S. – 'Counterinsurgency Warfare' ('65).
ROSENAU, J. N. – 'Internal War as an International Event,' in idem (ed.) – 'Internal Aspects of Civil Strife' ('64).
ROUSSEAU, C. in Rev. D.I. Lég. Comp. ('38).
SCELLE, G. in Rev. Gen. D.I.P. ('39).
SCHACHTER, O. – 'Preventing the internationalization of internal conflict: a legal analysis of the UN Congo experience,' Proc. A.S.I.L. ('63).
SCHEER, R. – 'How the US get involved in Vietnam,' A Report to the Center for the Study of Democratic Institutions ('65).
SCOTT, A. M. – 'Internal violence as an instrument of cold warfare,' in J. N. Rosenau (ed.) – 'International Aspects of Civil Strife' ('64).
SCHLESINGER, A. M. – 'The bitter heritage, Vietnam and American democracy 1941-1966' ('67).
SMITH, R. F. – 'Social revolution in Latin America, the role of US policy,' 41 Int. Aff. (Oct. '65).
STONE, J. – 'Aggression and World Order' ('58).
STOWELL, E. C. – 'Intervention in International Law' ('21).
TEMPTSOU & HALPERIN, M. H. – 'Maoism at home and abroad,' XVI Problems of Communism (July/Aug. '65).
THOMAS, A. J. JR. & THOMAS, ANN VAN WYNEN – 'Non-Intervention' ('56).
THOMAS, A. J. JR. – 'The OAS and Subversive Intervention,' Proc. Am. Soc. I.L. ('61).
TRAVIS, M. B. JR. – 'The political and social basis for the Latin American doctrine of non-intervention,' Proc. A.S.I.L. ('59).
VERWEY, W. D. – 'Economic Development, Peace and International Law: A New Approach to the Problem of Intervention,' 2 Bull. Peace Proposals ('71).
VINACKE, H. M. – 'Communist China and the uncommitted zone,' The Annals (nov. '65).
WEHBERG, H. – 'La guerre civile et le droit international,' 63 Rec. Cours ('38).
WRIGHT, Q. – 'The Goa Incident,' 56 A.J.I.L. ('62).
WRIGHT, Q. – 'Intervention,' 51 A.J.I.L. ('57).
WRIGHT, Q. – 'Legal Aspects of the Vietnam Situation,' 60 A.J.I.L. ('66).
WRIGHT, Q. – 'US Intervention in the Lebanon,' 53 A.J.I.L. ('59).